Practical
Gardening
Illustrated

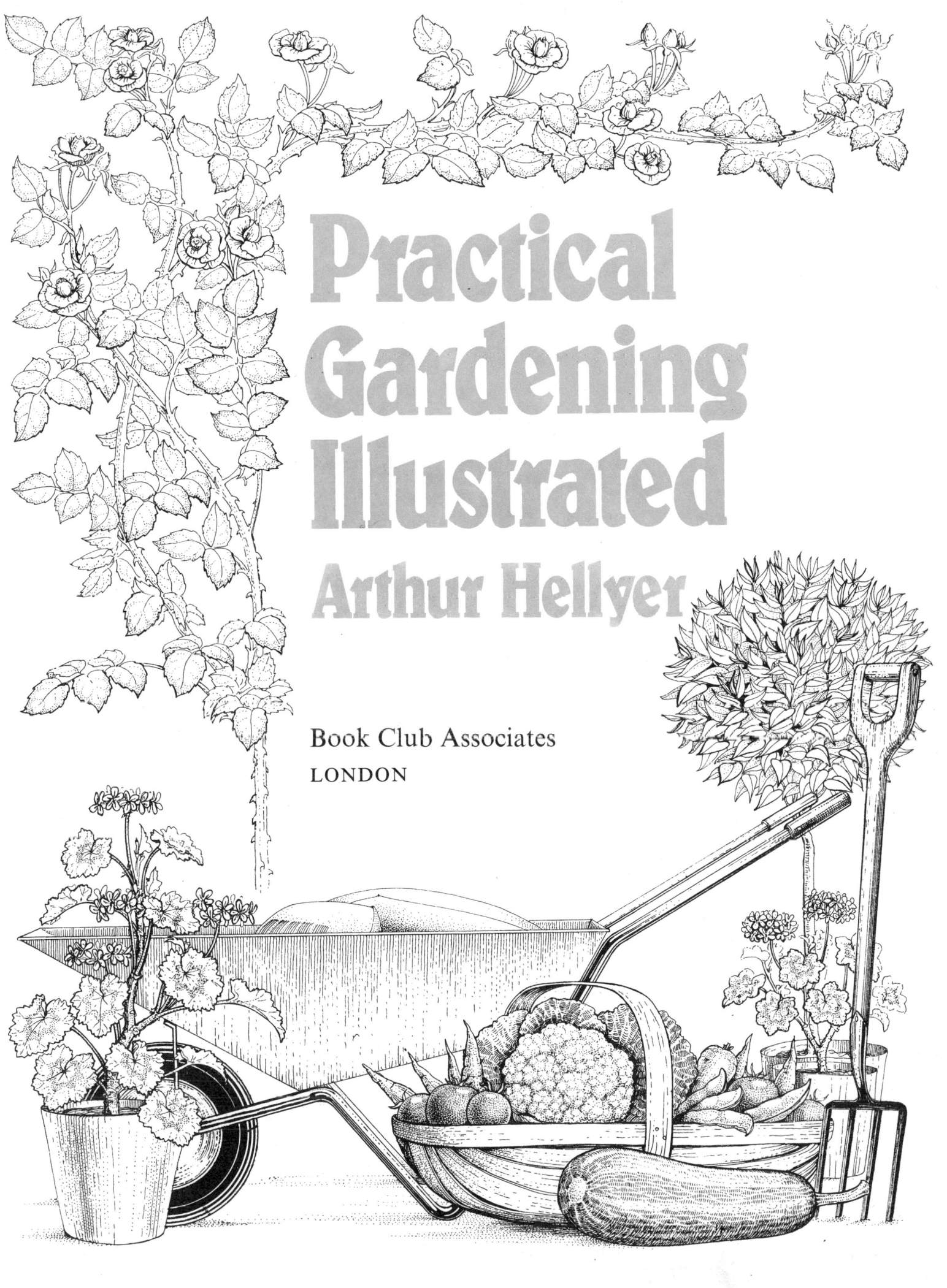

Practical Gardening Illustrated

Arthur Hellyer

Book Club Associates

LONDON

Contents

First published in 1967 as *Find Out About Gardening*
Second, fully revised edition published as
Practical Gardening Illustrated in 1976 by Book
Club Associates by arrangement with The Hamlyn
Publishing Group Ltd.,
London · New York · Sydney · Toronto
Astronaut House, Feltham, Middlesex, England
Copyright © The Hamlyn Group Ltd., 1976

Filmset, printed and bound in England by
Jarrold and Sons Ltd., Whitefriars, Norwich, Norfolk
Set in 9 on 10½ pt. Times New Roman

ACKNOWLEDGEMENTS
The publishers would like to thank the following
for the illustrations used in this book:
Amateur Gardening, Pat Brindley, Robert Corbin,
Country Life, John Cowley, Ernest Crowson,
The Harry Smith Horticultural Photographic Collection,
Humex Ltd., Anthony Huxley, Elsa Megson, Robert Pearson,
Plant Protection Ltd., Kenneth Scowen and Dennis Woodland.

Line drawings by Meg Rutherford
(Drawings on pages 113 and 128 by Norman Barber)

Foreword

Much of this book first appeared a few years ago as *Find Out About Gardening*, a name intended to indicate that it had been written primarily for newcomers to gardening who would probably be unfamiliar with even the simplest technical terms used by gardeners and would know little, if anything, about plants. In preparing it I therefore took nothing for granted and tried to explain all the basic facts about gardening in everyday language and to give as wide a coverage as possible, including ornamental plants, vegetables and fruits. Unfortunately though many readers found the book helpful some apparently found the title confusing, and so when it was decided to enlarge and re-illustrate the book and give it a new format it seemed a good opportunity to provide it with a new and completely unambiguous title.

Practical Gardening Illustrated is just that, a book which sets out to tell you how to make a garden, how to choose the best plants for it, where to buy them, and how to look after them intelligently and well.

I have borne in mind that readers may not know the difference between a hardy and a half-hardy plant, may be puzzled as to how a perennial differs from an annual, a bulb from a corm or tuber, or a deciduous shrub from an evergreen. I have also remembered that many facts about gardening are more readily explained by illustrations than by words so diagrams and photographs have been used to clarify many operations.

Of course gardening is such a vast subject that it is impossible to compress all of it into a single volume. But I have tried to include all that a new gardener would need to know, in the certainty that as experience grows so will the ability to decide which of the many aspects of gardening is most attractive and to search out the specialist books which deal with those particular subjects in greater depth.

The Different Kinds of Plants

Almost before spade is put to ground, certainly before any attempt is made to plan a garden in detail, one must have some idea of the plants with which one is going to work. There are tens of thousands of different kinds and one can spend a lifetime studying them in detail if one feels so inclined, but a much simpler, broader view will be quite sufficient to enable an attractive and satisfying garden to be made.

First one must learn to distinguish between hardy, half-hardy and tender plants. Hardy plants are those that can be grown outdoors throughout the year in the locality in which the garden is to be made. Naturally enough the list will vary with the climate. The extreme south-west of England and the south of Ireland are almost as mild in winter as the French Riviera, and it is possible there to grow plants that would die of cold in the north or east of Britain. But the great majority of plants that are sold as being hardy can really be planted outdoors and left outdoors without protection in most parts of the British Isles.

Tender plants are those which, in the locality under discussion, need protection all, or at least most of, the time. They are plants for greenhouses and conservatories, or to be grown in rooms that are adequately heated in winter.

Between these two major groups are half-hardy plants, which need protection in winter but can be grown outdoors in summer. They include some very popular plants, such as the dahlia and the geranium, but in general they involve the gardener in more work and require a greater degree of understanding than hardy plants.

The next big division is into annuals, biennials and perennials.

Annuals Annuals must be grown afresh from seed every year. They develop very quickly, start to flower within a few months (some within a few weeks) of being sown, but rapidly complete their life cycle and die. Many of them can be produced very cheaply and they are admirable for a quick display and for filling in gaps, but a garden that relies too heavily on annuals is likely to fluctuate greatly in its degree of interest and beauty. For a few weeks in summer it may be a blaze of colour and yet have little to offer at other seasons.

Hardy annuals are those that can be sown outdoors where they are to grow and flower. Half-hardy annuals must be raised under glass, either in a greenhouse or frame, but later on, as the weather gets warmer, they can be planted outdoors to flower. In some fairly mild places it is possible to sow half-hardy annuals outdoors in late spring. Tender annuals are raised and grown under glass.

Biennials Biennials resemble annuals in needing to be raised anew from seed each year, but they differ in taking more than one year to complete their growth cycle. Seed sown one year will give flowering plants the following year, after which the plants produce seed and die.

Perennials Perennials are plants that go on living for many years. Some will live longer than others, an oak tree for hundreds of years, a lupin probably only for four or five years, but both, in gardening terms, are perennials. They are the plants that give permanence to the garden and, if wisely chosen, they are the plants that involve the gardener in least labour.

Perennials are of two major kinds, herbaceous and woody. Herbaceous perennials have comparatively soft growth and many, though by no means all, die back to ground level each autumn and then grow up again in the spring. Woody plants, by contrast, make a permanent framework of growth. They are the plants we know as trees and shrubs, and because their stems and branches, and sometimes their leaves, are there in the winter just as much as in the summer, they play a particularly important part in the garden.

Herbaceous perennials, like all the other groups, may be divided into hardy, half hardy and tender, with all the differences which these distinctions make to cultivation. Hardy herbaceous perennials are amongst the easiest plants to grow, and it is almost certain that some will be used in every garden.

Bulbs, Corms and Tubers Bulbs, corms and tubers are really herbaceous plants in that they are perennials and have soft growth. But gardeners tend to think of them separately, partly because many of them do need different treatment, partly because they tend to be commercially grown and sold by different people. Bulb growing is a big industry on its own and since many bulbs can be left out of the ground for long periods, they fit in very well with shop trade and are sold in great quantities by many shopkeepers who would hesitate to handle plants that had to be kept moist and in soil.

Rock Plants Rock plants, too, are very largely herbaceous plants, though some are small shrubs. But again gardeners tend to think of them separately because of their different use in the garden and the fact that they are usually offered in separate trade catalogues, often prepared by firms which grow nothing but rock plants. Their peculiar characteristic is that they are small and suitable for growing in rock gardens or on walls, but many of them have other uses as well.

Aquatic Plants Aquatics, or water plants, are also herbaceous plants, but they are invariably kept in a separate category because of their very special requirements. There are nurseries that specialize in them and issue catalogues devoted to them. These are the plants to be grown in ponds and in slow moving water. Few of them will survive in swift flowing streams.

Shrubs Shrubs are an immensely important group to the gardener, for they provide much of the best material for giving permanence and solidity to the garden scene. They are divided into deciduous and evergreen categories, the former losing their leaves in autumn and growing a fresh lot the following spring, whereas the evergreens retain their leaves throughout the winter.

Trees Trees, too, can be either deciduous or evergreen, and are distinguished from shrubs mainly by their greater size. It is, in fact, often impossible to determine precisely whether a given woody plant should be considered as a shrub or a tree. A cypress, for example, clipped as a hedge, would reasonably be called a shrub, whereas precisely the same plant allowed to grow naturally to its full size, which might be 50 or 60 ft (15 to 18 m) high, would certainly be a tree. A tree need not necessarily have a bare main trunk with branches on top. Such trees are referred to as standards and when a tree branches right from ground level it is sometimes referred to as 'skirted'.

Trees, like shrubs, give the permanent framework to a garden. Even more than shrubs they can provide the dramatic points of interest but they must be used with discretion because of their ultimate size. Too many trees, or badly chosen trees, may eventually completely obscure a garden and make it difficult to grow anything else.

Roses Roses are shrubs but they have been so highly developed by gardeners that they tend to be grown by specialist nurserymen and to appear in separate catalogues. Certainly in the garden they are often used in a different manner from most other shrubs.

How, When and Where Plants Are Bought

In describing the different categories of plants I have already mentioned several times that there are firms specializing in this or that class. This is important because it is useless to look for plants in the wrong catalogues or expect to find them in the wrong nurseries.

Annuals and Biennials Annuals and biennials are grown commercially by seedsmen who issue special catalogues devoted to their products. One way to start a garden is with annuals or biennials and if one has the facilities to raise them from seed it can be the cheapest way, but it is not the only way to start, nor necessarily the best way for the beginner.

Many nurserymen specialize in raising plants from seed and these they either offer for sale themselves or sell through retail shops and garden centres. Many such plants are grown in shallow wooden boxes containing 40 or 50 small plants which can be sold at a very reasonable price. The peak of this trade is in the late spring, but it continues into early summer and resumes again in the autumn, when seed-raised plants to flower the following spring are offered.

Hardy Herbaceous Perennials Hardy herbaceous perennials, often loosely referred to simply as hardy plants, though this term is rather misleading as it really covers a much wider range of plants, also tend to be grown by specialist nurseries and to be offered in separate lists and catalogues. Many of them can be raised from seed, but as a rule it is a couple of years before sizeable, flowering plants are obtained.

Container-grown plants should be planted with the root ball intact

To save time and to be certain of obtaining precisely the varieties one requires it is best to purchase hardy herbaceous perennials as plants. If these are grown by the nurseryman in the open ground, the most favourable periods for transplanting them are spring and autumn. However, a great many nurseries now grow these plants in containers of some kind, usually plastic pots, or even strong polythene bags. It is easy to plant from these with practically no disturbance of the roots or of the soil around them, and this makes it possible to plant at practically any time of the year, the only limiting factor being the state of the soil. If it is very wet or frozen it becomes physically almost impossible to plant – certainly impossible to plant successfully.

Rock Plants Rock plants are nearly always container grown, usually in small pots, and

so, like container-grown herbaceous plants, can be planted whenever soil conditions permit. They can be obtained from specialist nurseries, and also from garden centres. In spring many shops and stores offer a limited range of rock plants.

Bulbs, Corms and Tubers Bulbs, corms and tubers, as I have already said, tend to be produced by specialist nurseries. Vast quantities of daffodils, tulips and hyacinths are grown in quite a small area in Holland, and there are similar bulb fields in Lincolnshire and Cambridgeshire and in other parts of Britain. Many lily bulbs are imported from America and Japan, and gladioli also come in from America and Europe.

The fully hardy bulbs, such as daffodils (a term that includes narcissi), tulips, hyacinths, crocuses and snowdrops, are offered for sale as dry bulbs from late summer to early winter, but the peak planting season is in early and mid-autumn. Half-hardy corms such as the gladiolus (a corm is a specialized type of bulb) are kept in a frost-proof store most of the winter and are offered for sale throughout the spring. Lilies would ideally be offered in autumn, but imported supplies do not always arrive in time for this and sales continue into the spring.

Aquatic Plants Aquatics have a rather brief planting season, roughly in the latter half of spring and early summer, and are almost all bought direct from specialist nurseries; the bigger general nurseries and garden centres usually stock a few.

Shrubs Shrubs are grown in vast quantities by nurserymen, many of whom are specialists who issue lengthy and highly informative catalogues. If they are grown in the open ground the lifting and dispatching season is from mid-autumn to early spring, but increasing numbers of shrubs are being grown in containers so that they can be purchased and planted at any time of the year.

Roses All that I have said about shrubs applies equally to roses and many of the best specialist rose nurseries issue catalogues well illustrated in colour, which makes the task of selection easier.

Trees Trees are usually grown by the nurserymen who specialize in shrubs and the same planting times apply. Some are grown in containers for all-year-round planting, but because of the greater size of trees, even when quite young, this is not as easy as with shrubs. Special techniques have been developed for moving large trees with powerful earth-shifting machinery, and for spraying their leaves with a plastic substance to check loss of water while they are becoming established, but this is work for experts and is quite costly. It is only under special circumstances that it is likely to be required in the garden.

How Plants Are Named

A great many plants are easily and accurately identified by simple English names and some are called by botanical names which have become so familiar that they have become a part of everyday language. Rose, wallflower, carnation and marigold are examples of the first kind, dahlia, chrysanthemum, gladiolus and delphinium of the second kind. Such names give no one any trouble.

Unfortunately simple names of this kind are not adequate to describe all the many thousands of plants that may be grown in gardens. Some are not sufficiently familiar to have acquired popular names and some have popular names which are not sufficiently precise for the gardener's needs. There are, for example, around 450 species of shrub commonly known as barberry and no adequate means of distinguishing one from another by popular names.

To meet this situation gardeners have had to make use of the names devised by botanists. These have the advantage of being precise and internationally recognized but they have the drawback of being in a kind of dog Latin or Greek which is often awkward to pronounce and hard to remember. Moreover botanists change names as their knowledge of plants increases and this can cause confusion. In fact there is no need for gardeners to follow every such change, and they rarely do. As a rule they base their botanical nomenclature on some comprehensive and authoritative horticultural dictionary, such as the Royal Horticultural Society's *Dictionary of Gardening* and only change as this changes with successive editions. Even so it can be disconcerting when a plant one has known for a lifetime as veronica turns up one day as hebe.

Formation of Botanical Names A botanical name consists basically of two parts, first a generic name and secondly a specific epithet. These may be likened to christian and surnames in reverse. Just as Mr David Buddle would be a particular member of the Buddle family adequately identified by those two names, so *Buddleia davidii* is a particular species named *davidii*, of a genus of shrubs named *Buddleia*. Occasionally a third name is added to indicate some small variation in the species. For example, *Buddleia davidii* normally has purple flowers but it also has a white-flowered variety called *Buddleia davidii alba*, *'alba'* being the Latin for white.

The botanical name for barberry is *Berberis* and every one of those 450 or more species is called *Berberis* plus a second distinguishing name, e.g. *Berberis darwinii*, an evergreen with orange flowers and blue-black berries; *Berberis wilsonae*, a deciduous shrub with yellow flowers and red berries, and so on.

Botanists are not, as a rule, interested in varieties raised in gardens, and so they leave it to gardeners to give them names if they wish to do so. These varieties are known as 'cultivars' (i.e. cultivated varieties) to distinguish them from varieties that occur in the wild. Occasionally cultivar names are of a botanical form, but nowadays they are usually fancy names. For example, there are numerous garden varieties of *Buddleia davidii* supposedly finer than the wild white form named *alba*. One of these is called White Profusion, and since the rules of plant nomenclature forbid the use of the same fancy name for more than one plant in any one genus, *Buddleia* White Profusion

is a perfectly accurate mode of designation which can only apply to that particular plant. For the sake of simplicity garden nomenclature is tending towards this use of a generic with a fancy name, e.g. *Berberis* Buccaneer, *Sedum* Autumn Joy, *Iberis* Snowflake, etc., and this is to be encouraged.

Pronunciation Botanical names can be interesting and helpful if one cares to study

them, for they indicate some of the relationships between one plant and another. There is no need to worry about pronunciation for, since most are made-up names, there is no such thing as a correct and incorrect way of pronouncing them. One can state what is common or sophisticated practice, but no more, and no one has a right to laugh if your pronunciation is different from his.

Making a Start

When a new plot is taken over from the builder it is generally in a very rough condition. Foundations and drains have been dug, soil may have been bulldozed to level the site for the house, cement mixers and other machines have stood on it, workmen have walked over it, pieces of brick, cement and wood are left lying about.

Under these conditions the best policy is usually to have the whole plot dug irrespective of what one is going to plant. If it is a large plot it may be worth employing a garden contractor with a power-driven cultivator to carry out this initial work. All burnable refuse can be burned and the ash spread over the ground. Brick ends and other hard rubble can be set aside to form the foundations of paths. When it has been determined where those paths shall be, they can be marked out with pegs and twine, and the soil from them excavated to a depth of 6 to 8 in (15 to 20 cm) and spread over the rest of the ground. In this way some semblance of order will be achieved and it will be possible to consider the site more realistically.

When an old garden is taken over the problems are different. If the garden has been well made and maintained, it may be acceptable as it stands, or with minor alterations. If it is badly neglected and overgrown, it will be wise to clean it up first before making any decision about altering it. Long grass should be cut with a scythe,

Before construction work is undertaken, undesirable contours are levelled out

hook, or rotary grass cutter, herbaceous plants cut down if it is autumn or winter, or thinned and tidied if it is spring or summer. Overgrown trees and shrubs can be cut back sufficiently to make it possible to work around them and at least see the main outlines of the existing plan. Grass, leaves and other soft rubbish can be built into a heap in some convenient corner to rot down into compost for soil dressing, and prunings

can be burnt. If the garden is taken over in winter, when everything is dormant, it may be wise to wait at least until the spring before digging anything up, to see what really is there.

Making a Plan

Only when the new plot has been straightened out or the old one cleaned,

should one decide upon a plan. What it shall be must be determined by many considerations: one's own personal preferences regarding plants, the amount of work one is prepared to put into the maintenance of the garden, the architecture of the house and the character of soil and situation. It is fortunate that most ornamental plants have a very wide tolerance of soils and will grow in almost anything that could be termed 'reasonable', which roughly means that it is not pure clay, nor pure sand or shingle, nor yet pure chalk, but a mixture of ingredients recognizable as soil.

Soil Testing But there are exceptions to this tolerance, and, in particular, one large group of shrubs, including rhododendrons, azaleas and many heathers, which dislike free lime in the soil. It is quite easy to find out whether soil does contain free lime, for if it does it will be alkaline, whereas if it does not it will, almost certainly in Britain, be acid. These are conditions that can be measured by simple tests. Chemical testing outfits can be purchased from many chemists and garden shops. These simple tests rely on chemical reagents which change colour according to the degree of acidity or alkalinity of the soil. A colour chart containing eight or ten colours for matching is provided with the kit, and against each colour is a figure which represents what is termed the pH of the soil. This is the scale by which acidity/alkalinity is measured. A reading of pH 7 indicates neutrality, i.e. an exact balance between acidity on the one hand and alkalinity on the other. Such a soil would grow almost anything, but would not be so good for the lime-hating plants as one that is more acid, say pH 5·5 to 6·5. This is the ideal range for many ornamental plants. A soil of pH 7·5 to 8·0 is markedly alkaline, and excellent for those plants that like lime.

It is possible to overcome alkalinity by

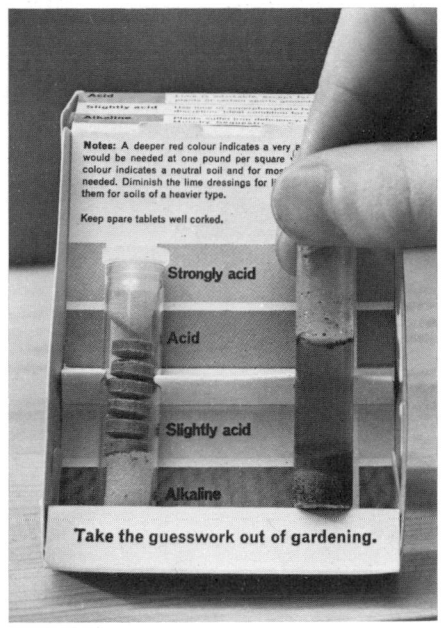

A simple soil test kit will give an indication of soil acidity; lime can be added to adjust the pH of acid soils

making special beds for lime-hating plants, or by feeding them with special fertilizers, but this is adding to the burdens and hazards of gardening. It is better to garden with one's soil rather than against it.

Site and Aspect As with soil, it is also better to garden with one's site and aspect. Most plants will grow where they get the full benefit of sunlight or in partial shade. A smaller number will grow in quite dense shade. But there are plants that prefer full sun and others that prefer some shade, and it is wise to bear these preferences in mind when planning. I have referred to them in greater detail in the descriptive lists of plants which appear later.

Some people are so keen on plants that they want to devote every possible square

yard of ground to their cultivation. Others see plants only as embellishments to a design which is mainly architectural in conception. More frequently the garden owner will require some combination of both elements, maybe a patio or terrace near the house and a less formally planned area for plants beyond.

Comparative Costs When considering expense in construction and maintenance, it is worth noting that the formal or architectural garden is usually more economical in upkeep than the informal or plant garden but is more costly to make.

Growing Plants on Walls Decision must be made as to whether the walls of the house are to be used as supports for climbing plants, and also any outside walls or fences if they exist. Some people dislike plants on the house, believing that they make walls damp, loosen cement work and encourage the entry of insects to the living rooms. Personally I believe all these objections to be considerably exaggerated and anyway would put up with them for the satisfaction of clothing my house with beautiful climbers.

But if it is decided to have plants growing up the walls, the question of aspect must be considered. A wall facing south may get very hot in summer, and some plants will not like this. By contrast a plant on a wall facing north will get little or no direct sunlight, and this will not suit all climbers.

It may be considered wise to make beds on the north side of a house or wall narrower than those on the south side, since there will be fewer plants that will appreciate such a situation.

Garden Boundaries Boundaries can cause a lot of trouble. If an apple tree is planted so close to the boundary of a garden that many of its branches in time overhang the neighbouring garden the owner of this will have a perfect right to retain any fruits that fall into his garden or even to cut the

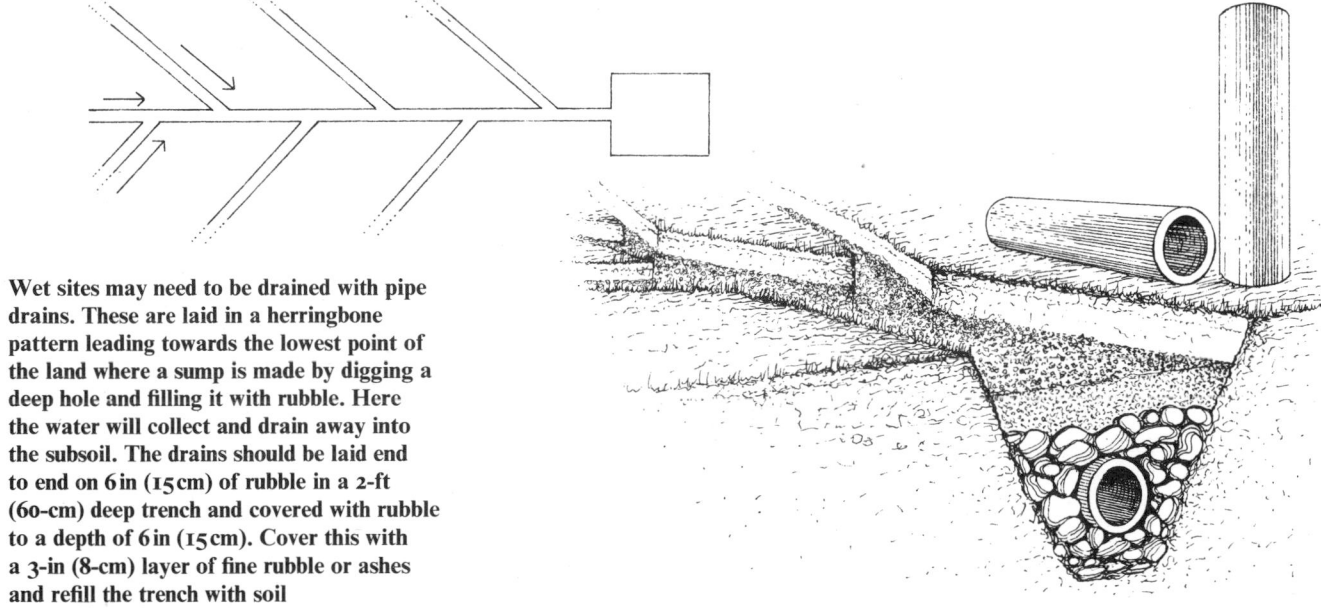

Wet sites may need to be drained with pipe drains. These are laid in a herringbone pattern leading towards the lowest point of the land where a sump is made by digging a deep hole and filling it with rubble. Here the water will collect and drain away into the subsoil. The drains should be laid end to end on 6 in (15 cm) of rubble in a 2-ft (60-cm) deep trench and covered with rubble to a depth of 6 in (15 cm). Cover this with a 3-in (8-cm) layer of fine rubble or ashes and refill the trench with soil

branches off although this may spoil the look of the tree. Hedges can present problems of maintenance if they are planted too close to the boundary and a good deal of dispute between neighbours is due to lack of common sense in these matters.

Aspects of Design In garden planning too much emphasis can easily be placed on 'features' included for their own sake. A garden may become so cluttered up with sundials, statues, pools, rock gardens and so on that it ceases to have any coherent design at all. Too many plants can equally destroy design though some gardeners may actually prefer it that way if their main interest is in plants.

It is difficult to define 'good' design but it is certainly compounded of balance, coherence and suitability for the site. Simplicity is usually to be preferred to elaboration and is certainly easier to handle. Formality is usually more acceptable near a house and informality away from it, but even this rule can be broken as witness any of the splendid 'landscape' gardens of the eighteenth century, where parkland was brought right up to the walls.

It is possible to get whole books of garden plans, and plans are often published in garden and home magazines. A study of these can be most useful, but mainly in suggesting ideas for one's own garden. It is seldom that a plan prepared for one site can be transferred unchanged to another.

The Use of Grass

Unless a garden is to be entirely formal and architectural, grass is almost certain to enter into it. As it will eventually form the carpet upon which the rest of the planting is displayed, it will be wise to give very careful consideration to its extent and character.

In Britain there is a strong tendency to think of grass in the garden exclusively in terms of the close-mown lawn. On the Continent and in America this is not so, and grass is permitted greater freedom of growth. There is something to be said for both conceptions and a good deal for using them in combination to give a contrast of textures.

A lawn that is to be close mown must be made with dwarf, fine-leaved grasses such as the fescues and bents. Lawns that are to be allowed to grow an inch or so of grass, and maybe more at times, can be made with stronger growing, broader leaved grasses, such as the best forms of rye grass and meadow grass. Seed of these is often cheaper than that of fine grasses, and such a lawn is almost always easier to establish.

In late spring and early summer, when grass is growing most rapidly, a close-

A rotary lawn mower is used where coarse or longer-growing grass predominates

A cylinder lawn mower is ideal for fine or close-cropped lawns

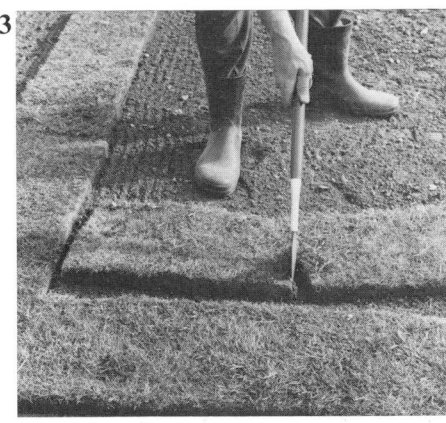

1. **Turfing a lawn:**
The turves should be of equal thickness.

2. Each turf is laid in the box and the
excess soil cut off with an old scythe blade.

3. After preparing the soil the turves are
laid as close together as possible.

4. Turves are bonded like bricks but here
they are too far apart.

5. Finally the crevices are filled with a
mixture of sifted soil and peat

mown lawn may need to be cut every third or fourth day. A Continental-type lawn need only be cut once a week. For the very best close finish a cylinder lawn mower is required. It will not work well or cleanly if the grass is wet, nor will it cope with the grass easily if it gets long while the owner is away.

A Continental-type lawn can be cut with a power-driven rotary machine, and this can be used even when the grass is wet or very overgrown.

In a very small garden, if grass is considered appropriate at all, it will probably be best to have it as a fairly close-trimmed lawn. In larger gardens the ideal may well be to have some area, or areas, probably those nearest to the house or formal features, close mown, and some kept cut at a height between 1 and 2 in (2·5 and 5 cm). The contrast will be similar to that seen between putting green and fairway on a golf course. Time in cutting will be reduced and, if desired, some bulbs, such as crocuses, snowdrops and daffodils, can be planted in the longer grass to give a delightful display in spring. But then one must be prepared to let the grass around the bulbs go on growing uncut at least until late spring. To cut earlier would be to remove the bulb foliage before it had finished its work of supplying the bulbs with food so that they can flower another year.

Making a Lawn

Seed or Turf? Grass of any kind, whether for close or long mowing, can be established either from seed or turf. Seed is cheaper and permits the choice of particular kinds of grass to suit the purpose in mind. Turf is quicker and makes it less necessary to clean the land of weeds before the turves are put down.

Preparing the Site Whichever method is decided upon, the ground should first be dug. Surface stones should be removed, also roots of perennial weeds such as docks, dandelions, nettles, couch grass and bindweed. Then, a week or so before the turf is to be laid or the grass seed sown, a compound fertilizer should be scattered over the surface and the lumps of soil left by the spade or cultivator broken down. Most seed merchants, garden shops and garden centres stock ready-mixed fertilizer specially formulated for lawns. These are to be preferred and must be used strictly in accordance with the manufacturer's instructions on the bag or container. Failing this a general garden fertilizer can be used, and again the manufacturer's instructions should be followed.

The final preparation for either seeding or turfing is to rake the surface so that there are no sudden humps or depressions, and to remove stones and other hard objects.

Laying Turf Turf can be laid at practically any time of year, but by far the best time is autumn. The next best is early spring. In winter the soil is too wet and cold for the grass to grow down quickly into the soil below. In summer it is too hot and dry and, unless the newly laid turf is watered very freely, it may die.

Turves should be cut about 1½ in (4 cm) thick. Usually commercial turves are cut in strips 3 ft (1 m) long and 1 ft (30 cm) wide, and are rolled for delivery. They are rather heavy and difficult to handle without breakage. Turves cut in 1-ft (30-cm) squares are really better, but are likely to cost more.

The turves are laid in straight rows on the levelled soil, and in alternate rows the turves are staggered so that, though in one direction the joins between them make continuous lines, in the other direction they do not. It is exactly the same principle as bonding bricks in a wall, and is done for the same reason, to give greater stability to the newly laid turves. After a few weeks they should have grown into one another and no joins should be visible.

Great care should be taken to keep the turves level and to butt them together as closely as possible. They can be lightly beaten down with the back of a spade as they are laid. Then, when all are in place, a mixture of sifted soil and peat can be scattered lightly over the surface and brushed about so that it fills up any small crevices left.

After a week or so the newly laid lawn can be rolled and as soon as it starts to grow freely it should be mown.

Seed Sowing The best periods for making a lawn from seed are spring and early autumn. Seedsmen offer various mixtures of seeds for particular purposes: fine grass mixtures for bowling and putting greens and other lawns that are to be close mown; mixtures of stronger grasses for cricket

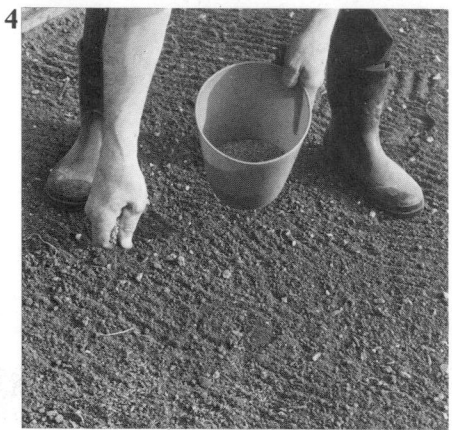

1. Sowing a lawn:
First, clear the land of all debris.

2. After digging break the soil down to a reasonably fine tilth with the rake.

3. Firm the soil by treading and then lightly rake to give a level surface.

4. The seed is sown broadcast working backwards across the plot.

5. Lightly rake in the seed so that the majority of it is covered

pitches, football fields and the Continental type of lawn; even mixtures for shady places or wet ground. Most seed is pretreated to repel birds, and this is highly desirable.

The appropriate mixture should be purchased, sufficient being obtained to permit seeding at 1 oz (25 g) per square yard or square metre. This should be scattered as evenly as possible over the surface. If it is done by hand it is wise to divide the seed into two halves and to sow one half moving backwards and forwards across the plot in one direction, and then to sow the other half moving backwards and forwards at right angles to the first direction. In this way an even peppering is far more likely to be obtained than if all the seed is sown in one operation. Better still is to make use of one of the small seed and fertilizer distributors stocked by most horticultural dealers. All that is then necessary is to get the right setting, fill the hopper with seed and push the distributor up and down the plot, taking care not to overlap nor to leave gaps.

The seed needs to be covered, and this can be done either by scattering sifted soil over the surface or by raking the soil lightly, so stirring the seed in. If the seed has been treated against birds and is properly covered, no further protection will be necessary.

Germination may take anything from a fortnight to a month. As soon as the young grass is 2 in (5 cm) high it should be cut, but not closer than 1 in (2·5 cm). Mowing can then continue at regular intervals and can gradually become closer. The lawn can be lightly rolled if it is not too wet.

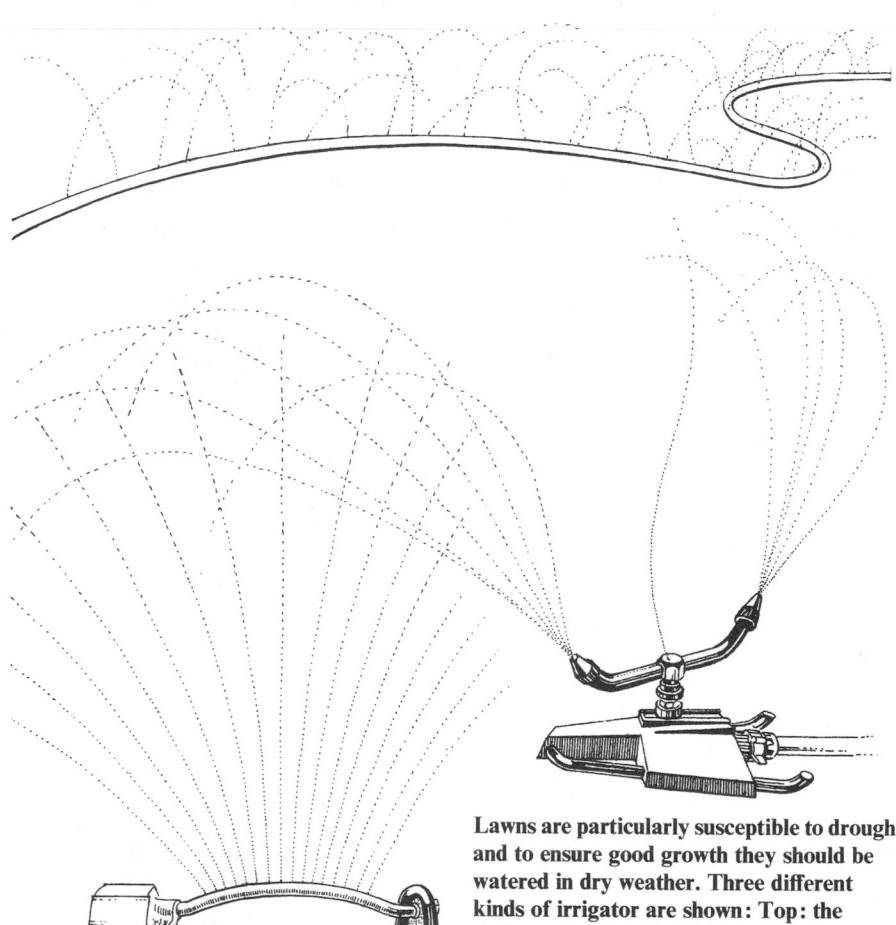

Lawns are particularly susceptible to drought and to ensure good growth they should be watered in dry weather. Three different kinds of irrigator are shown: Top: the perforated hose; Centre: the revolving sprinkler; Bottom: the oscillating type which sprinkles back and forth over a roughly rectangular area

Lawn Maintenance

Weed Control Subsequent maintenance of lawns has been greatly simplified by chemical aids. If weeds are troublesome the turf can be dressed with a selective weedkiller such as 2,4-D or MCPA. Spring is the most effective time for this but these weedkillers can be used at any time while grass is growing. Some fertilizer manufacturers mix them with lawn fertilizer, so that in feeding the lawn one is also weeding it. Selective lawn weedkillers can also be purchased as concentrated fluid to be diluted with water and applied from a watering-can, either fitted with a very fine spray rose or, preferably, with a straight dribble bar specially made for the purpose. A few weeds are resistant to these weedkillers and, if they persist, may have to be removed by hand. Clover, though resistant to 2,4-D and MCPA, can be killed with mecoprop, and moss can be killed by sprinkling mercurized lawnsand over the turf in spring or early summer.

The Mowing Season Cutting should be continued while grass is growing, approximately from mid-spring to mid-autumn, but should be discontinued in winter.

Worm Control Fallen leaves and worm casts should be removed by brushing, and if worms become very troublesome they can be reduced in numbers by treating the turf with one of the advertized worm killers.

Feeding Grass To maintain it in tip-top condition, grass should be fed two or three times a year, in spring with a compound fertilizer, preferably a specially compounded lawn fertilizer, in early summer with a similar mixture and in autumn with bonemeal or a specially compounded autumn lawn dressing, which should contain little nitrogen. The analysis will be on the bag or container, so look for this important difference. The spring and early summer mixtures will have quite a high nitrogen content, plus some phosphorus and potash. The autumn dressing will have the phosphorus and potash but much less nitrogen.

1. Lawn herbicides may be applied using a rose (as shown) or a dribble bar.

2. A fertilizer spreader makes feeding and topdressing easier and more accurate.

3. In March and September clear the lawn of moss and dead grass with a springbok rake.

4. For routine lawn edging, edging shears give a neat finish.

5. A half moon iron is useful both for edging lawns and cutting turves to size

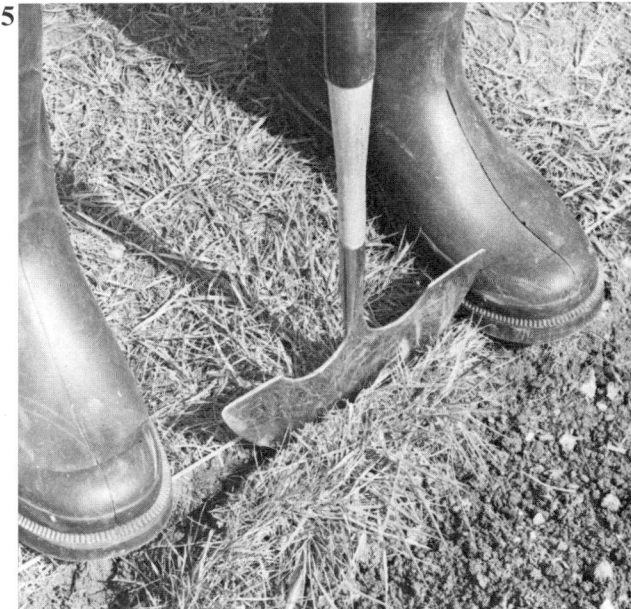

The Rules of Planting

Many very different kinds of plants may have to be planted in the garden, some large, some small, some with masses of fine roots, others with thick, thongy or tuberous roots. But whatever the character of the plant, the basic techniques of planting, the rules to be observed and the pitfalls to be avoided are much the same and so, to avoid constant repetition, I will deal with the whole matter of planting here, leaving for mention under individual plants only those points where for some reason they depart from the normal.

First, there is the state of the ground. Ideally this should be neither very wet nor very dry, certainly not frozen and preferably not very hot. A pleasant mean of all these things is best, and these conditions are most likely to be met in spring and autumn, so these are the peak planting seasons.

Even so it is quite possible that plants will arrive at an inconvenient moment, when

Shrubs which cannot be planted on arrival can be heeled in until a site is ready

one is too busy to attend to them properly, or there has been a downpour which has made the soil impossibly sticky, or a sudden frost that has crusted the surface. Under these circumstances it is better to wait a while. If the plants have plenty of soil around their roots and this is kept moist, and some straw or sacking or other protective material is wrapped around the roots (but not over the shoots) to keep out wind and frost, they will take no harm for days. If they are likely to remain longer, a hole or short trench can be dug, the plants lined out in this as close together as possible, soil thrown back over the roots and trodden firmly. This is known as heeling in, a temporary form of planting, and if properly done the plants may be left for weeks.

When the time for permanent planting comes, be sure to prepare a hole of adequate size for each plant. This may vary from a hole no more than 2 in (5 cm) wide and deep for a small rock plant, to one several feet across and as much as 18 in (45 cm) deep for a large tree or shrub. What governs this is the spread of the roots, so, if in doubt, stand the plant on the ground for a moment where it is to go and spread out the roots evenly around it. Note just how far they go, and then dig a hole a little larger than this, but while you are digging do not leave the plant lying around with its roots exposed. Throw a sack or something of the kind over them as protection from sun and wind, so that they keep moist and fresh.

For big plants holes are best dug with a spade; for little ones a trowel is more convenient. When you have a hole you think large enough, stand the plant in it. Spread out the roots and make certain that there is room for all of them. If it is a tree or a shrub, look for the soil mark low down on the stem (or stems) which will indicate where the soil came to in the nursery bed. The hole should be sufficiently deep to allow this soil mark to be just slightly below the natural level of the soil. If in doubt, lay a stick across the hole from side to side and measure the soil mark against this. If the hole is not big enough, remove the plant and enlarge the hole. Do not try to crowd or press roots into too small a hole to save

Opposite: The autumn tints of _Acer palmatum_

time. It is a bad way to establish plants.

The Planting Operation When you have a hole the right shape, size and depth, put the plant into it, spread out the roots and throw some of the most finely broken soil around them. If the natural soil of the garden is lumpy, prepare a heap of sifted soil mixed with peat and even some sand, if this is needed to make it crumbly. Such a heap, kept dry under a sheet of polythene, is a most useful aid to planting. A little bonemeal stirred into it will help the plant to make new roots quickly and strongly.

Tree planting:
On arrival inspect the tree and cut off any damaged roots and shoots

Excavate a hole large enough to take all the roots, insert the stake and then the tree, spreading out the roots

Return the soil, firming it in with the foot. The old soil mark should be level with the surface

When all the roots have been covered, firm the soil. For trees and shrubs this is best done with the feet, treading first on one side then on another, until all the soil is evenly firmed. For herbaceous and rock plants, annuals and other small to medium-sized plants, firming with the fingers or knuckles or with the handle of the trowel is usually sufficient.

Finally, return the rest of the soil removed when making the hole, scattering it about so as to fill in all foot or hand marks and leave a loose, level surface.

Staking Trees and Big Shrubs Trees and big shrubs will need support, at least for the first year or so. It is best to drive in stakes as the holes are made and before the plants are put in, as then there is no danger of driving stakes through roots and damaging them. There is another advantage in this. The tree or shrub can be immediately tied to its stake, leaving both hands free to get on with the work of returning the soil and working it between the roots.

Planting Bulbs Bulbs that have been lifted and permitted to become dry, the usual method with daffodils, tulips, crocuses, bulbous iris, lilies, gladioli and many others, will have no roots and no soil mark, and so slightly different rules will have to be followed. Holes must be wide enough to take the bulbs easily and allow them to sit squarely and firmly on the soil at the bottom. Holes made with a pointed stick, or dibber,

are bad, as there is almost certain to be a cavity left beneath the bulb. The depth of the hole will vary according to the type of bulb, and I have referred to this under the various kinds of bulb. When in doubt make a hole three times the depth of the bulb itself, i.e. a hole that enables the bulb to be covered with twice its own depth of soil. It is a rough and ready rule which works quite well.

Planting Depth for Small Subjects Many small plants may have no very clear soil mark. Plant these so that their uppermost roots are just covered with soil. The point at which leaves or stems join the roots is known as the 'crown' and it is a good general rule to keep this just level with the surface.

Container-grown Plants When planting from containers some different considerations must be taken into account. The major object of the container is to avoid disturbance of the roots, so the aim should be to get the whole ball of soil out of the container and into its hole as nearly intact as possible. Tins are slit vertically on opposite sides so that they can be opened outwards, and the ball of soil lifted out. Polythene bags and paper pots are cut and stripped off actually in the hole. Plants in earthenware or plastic pots are removed by being inverted and the edge of the pot rapped on something hard like the handle of a spade. One hand should be held under the pot with fingers spread on each side of the plant to support the ball of soil and roots as it slides out.

In all cases the ball of soil should be left intact, no attempt being made to disen-

Purpose-made tree ties provide a good means of support

tangle or spread out the roots. Simply stand the ball in a hole sufficiently large to contain it with the top of the ball very slightly below the normal surface of the ground. Then replace the soil around it and make thoroughly firm.

Aftercare

Watering When planting in autumn or winter it is unlikely that any watering will be required. In spring water may be needed if the weather becomes dry, and if planting is done in summer watering will almost certainly be necessary, at least for the first few weeks. In late spring and summer it also helps if the leaves are syringed with water towards evening, and this is particularly useful with evergreens but should not be done if frost threatens.

Feeding As a rule plants newly moved should not be fed. Wait for a while until they are established and have started to grow again before giving any fertilizer, either in solid or liquid form. This does not mean that manure or decayed vegetable refuse (compost) cannot be used when preparing ground for planting, but they must be well rotted and thoroughly mixed with the soil. A little bonemeal scattered over the surface or mixed with the soil removed from the planting holes also helps, as it is very slow and mild in action and does help to promote root growth.

When bulbs are to be naturalized in grass a bulb planter is used to remove cores of **soil which are replaced firmly when the bulbs have been inserted**

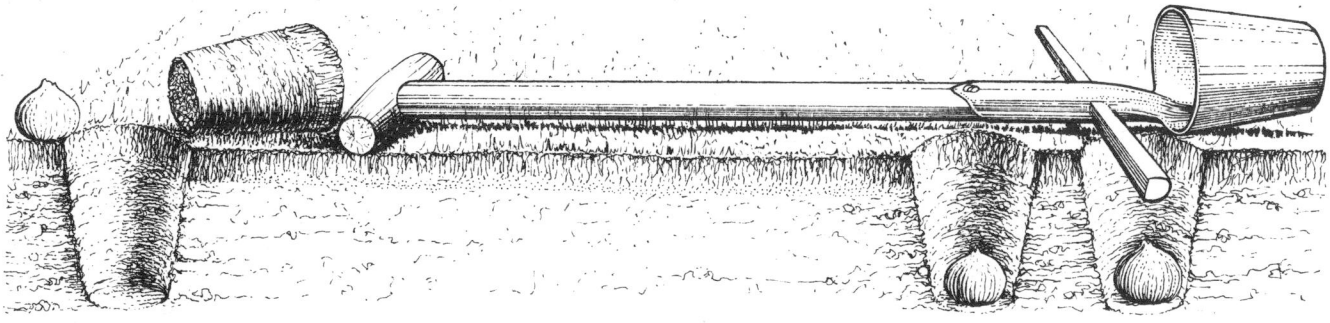

Stepping stones make a pleasing pathway

Success with Seeds

Seeds provide the cheapest way of producing many plants and the only way of producing annuals and biennials. Some seeds are very easy to grow; others are more difficult and there are a few that give trouble even to experienced gardeners.

Three things are necessary for the germination of all seeds: warmth, moisture and air, but they are necessary, particularly the first two, in varying degree according to the nature of the seeds. Those of very hardy plants, such as chickweed and groundsel, two of the commonest annual weeds in the garden, will commence to grow at temperatures around 7°C. (45°F.) whereas seeds of tomato will not start to germinate below 13°C. (55°F.) and those of the Indian shot plant, or canna, may need as much as 21°C. (70°F.) to stir them into growth. Again, seeds of cacti will grow readily in soil that is only just moist, whereas seeds of the common run of non-succulent plants grow faster and more reliably in a moderately moist soil, and aquatics require a very wet soil, maybe one actually submerged in water. However, just as there are basic rules for planting, so there are basic rules for sowing, and to avoid repetition I shall deal with these here, leaving exceptions to be described under the particular plants.

Preparations Outdoors

Seeds of hardy plants, such as hardy annuals, hardy herbaceous perennials and most vegetables, can be sown out of doors. The most favourable times are in spring, late summer and early autumn. During the winter the soil is likely to be too cold and wet for germination, and if the seeds lie around dormant for months, many of them may be eaten by birds, slugs, insects, etc., or may rot. In summer the soil tends to be too hot and dry, but these are faults that can be more readily overcome by watering and shading.

Soil in which seed is to be sown should be crumbly and reasonably fine. Small seedlings cannot push their way past big clods of compacted soil. To get this crumbly condition it is necessary to cultivate the soil well so that surplus water can run away

and air can penetrate to dry the clods. Frost also helps, for the expanding ice pushes the particles of soil apart and when the thaw comes they crumble. This is the reason for the frequently repeated advice to dig seed beds in the autumn and leave them rough throughout the winter so that a considerable surface of soil is exposed to frost.

Final Soil Preparation Whatever the preliminary preparation may be, the final preparation must be done shortly before the seed is to be sown and when the physical condition of the soil is right. This means that it must be moist below and, if possible, dry or drying out, on top. When the clods are struck with a rake or fork they should fall apart into crumbs, and it should be easy with these tools to break the whole surface down to a fine, crumbly, level seed bed. Sometimes it is necessary to watch quite closely for the right moment to do this. It is much easier to prepare good seed beds on sandy soils than on those containing a lot of clay and it may even be necessary to mix sand and peat with the clay to get a seed bed suitable for some of the more difficult seeds.

Under Glass

Under glass things are much more under control. A mixture of soil can be prepared that has exactly the right qualities, or substitutes for soil can be prepared.

John Innes Seed Compost What is known as the John Innes Seed Compost is used by many gardeners and can either be prepared at home or purchased ready mixed. The basic ingredients, by volume, are 2 parts medium loam, 1 part peat and 1 part sand. The loam should be of good quality, without free lime but not too acid (*p*H 6·5 is ideal) and neither too heavy nor too light. Before use it should be sterilized, preferably by steam, at a temperature of 93°C. (200°F.) for 20 minutes. The peat should be fibrous or granular and reasonably free from dust. The sand must be very coarse and sharp, ranging in particle size up to $\frac{1}{8}$ in (0·25 cm). All ingredients must be mixed thoroughly, and to every bushel of this mixture should

be added $1\frac{1}{2}$ oz (40 g) superphosphate of lime and $\frac{3}{4}$ oz (21 g) of finely ground chalk or limestone. These are required to rectify certain chemical changes caused by the sterilization. This mixture, and others containing sterilized loam, can be stored for a time but tends to deteriorate with age.

Soilless Composts An alternative to soil mixtures are those based on peat, either by itself with suitable fertilizers, or with sand, vermiculite etc., but without soil. In a simple mixture of half moss peat and half coarse sand or horticultural grade vermiculite, most seeds will germinate well, but as this contains little plant food the seedlings should be moved fairly quickly to mixtures containing either soil or fertilizers or be fed with liquid fertilizer.

Soil Moisture and Temperature Requirements Under glass the seed compost (as the mixture is called) can be made just as moist as is ideal. Usually this should be sufficiently moist to allow the compost to bind into a ball when squeezed in the palm of the hand, but sufficiently dry to permit this ball to break up into small fragments when tossed lightly back on to the heap.

Under glass, too, the temperature can be adjusted to suit the seeds being sown. A good average to aim for is 16 to 18°C. (60 to 65°F.), in which most seeds will germinate well.

Preparing the Containers Under glass seeds may be sown in pots, pans or shallow boxes usually known as 'trays' or 'flats'. Whatever is used there must be holes or slits in the bottom for drainage, and, except in the case of plastic pots and trays, it is a good plan to cover these with some broken pieces of flowerpot, known as 'crocks', or with specially shaped pieces of perforated zinc to prevent fine soil washing down into the holes and blocking them up. The containers, of whatever nature, should be not quite filled with soil, which should be made firm with the fingers and then made quite level by pressing with a smooth, flat piece of wood, usually referred to as a 'patter'. Little or no firming is needed with peat and sand, peat and vermiculite or pure peat composts which should simply be settled in by rapping the container smartly on a

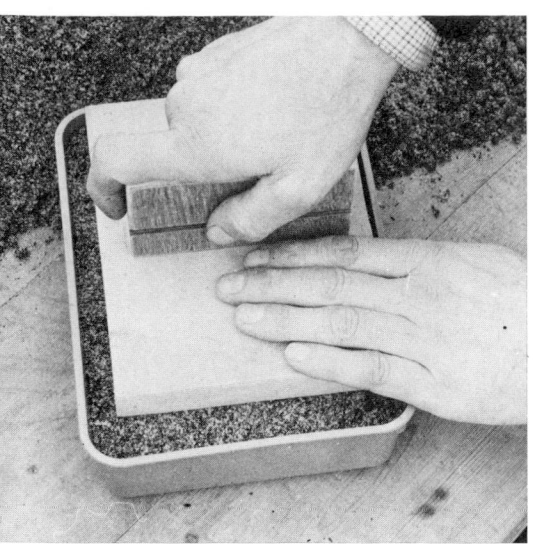

Seed sowing under glass:
The box should be evenly filled and firmed

Most seeds are broadcast thinly over the surface of the soil. If sown too close together they may rot off on germination

The seed is lightly covered with sifted soil. Glass covered with paper is placed over the box until the seed germinates

solid surface such as the potting bench.

Seed Sowing Seeds can be sown broadcast, in drills or singly. Broadcasting is mainly used for hardy annuals sown outdoors where they are to flower and for seeds sown in pots, pans or boxes under glass. The seeds are simply scattered very thinly all over the particular area where they are to grow, and then some sifted soil is scattered over them, or outdoors the soil is gently raked to stir the seeds in, just as I have described when sowing grass seed to make lawns.

Sowing in drills is used for most vegetables and also for seeds of ornamental plants when sown outdoors with the object of transplanting the seedlings later. This is necessary with most biennials and perennials. The method is to stretch a line, or place a rod to serve as a straight edge and then, using this as a guide, to draw a little furrow with a pointed stick or the corner of a hoe. The seeds are then scattered thinly in this furrow, or drill, and the displaced soil is raked or pushed back over them.

The advantage of sowing in drills is that, when the seedlings germinate, it is much easier to see them and to distinguish them from weeds because they are in straight rows, and it is also easier to stir the soil between them with a stick or hoe to kill weeds.

Sowing singly is practised outdoors with big seeds such as peas, beans and sweet corn, which can be dropped one at a time into a drill or into little holes made with a stick. Under glass it is sometimes used for valuable seeds or to save time in pricking out, as the seedlings will be evenly spaced and have room to grow on undisturbed for several weeks. But the time so saved is usually more than lost in the rather fiddling task of spacing out the seeds.

Pelleting seed, i.e. coating each seed with smooth paste which dries to form a little

'pill', makes it much easier to space seeds singly. Pelleted seeds can be purchased but cost more than untreated seeds.

Aftercare

Watering and other Attentions Outdoors there is little to be done until the seeds appear, unless the soil becomes very dry, when it should be watered from a sprinkler, or with a watering-can fitted with a rose. Under glass more watering may be necessary, though if each seed box, pan or pot is covered with a sheet of glass or polythene film, water will not evaporate very rapidly. Some seeds germinate better in the dark

As soon as they are large enough to handle, the seedlings are pricked off into a seedbox

and so, when sown under glass, are covered with newspaper, but if this is done the newspaper must be removed directly the seedlings appear or they will be greatly weakened. Sheets of glass should also be tilted up a little a day or so after the first signs of germination, and removed altogether a day or so later. Most seedlings need plenty of light and air, and become thin and pale and tend to decay if deprived of them.

Thinning out Seedlings Out of doors seedlings are usually thinned where they grow, which simply means that where they come up crowded some are carefully pulled out to leave the rest sensibly spaced.

Pricking out Seedlings Under Glass Under glass the seedlings are 'pricked out', a term used for transplanting a seedling. They are lifted very carefully with a pointed stick or anything else convenient, are separated out

singly and then replanted in other boxes, pans or pots, for which purpose a pointed stick or dibber is generally used. With this holes are made about 1½ to 2 in (4 to 5 cm) apart, the seedling is carefully held by a leaf between finger and thumb, its roots are dropped into the hole and the soil is pressed around them with the stick. Later on it may be necessary to transplant the seedlings again, and then it is usually done singly into small pots. Sometimes pots made of compressed peat or sawdust are used,

and then, if the seedlings are to go outdoors later on, pot and all can be planted as it will gradually rot away in the soil.

For pricking out, the same compost as that used for seed sowing may be used, except that if it is a peat/sand, peat/vermiculite, or pure peat mixture, a little compound fertilizer should be added. Proprietary peat-based seed composts have the right kind and quantity ready mixed in.

Hardening off Seedlings All seedlings raised under glass must be hardened off

before they are placed outdoors. This means that they must be gradually accustomed to the very different conditions they are going to face. First the greenhouse can be allowed to get cooler, or the seedlings can be moved to the coolest part of the house. Then, a week or so later, they can be removed to a frame where they should be given increasing ventilation, or to a very sheltered place outdoors. Only when they have become thoroughly accustomed to full exposure should they be planted out.

Foundation Planting

The idea behind foundation planting is that it is more or less permanent and so provides a framework or foundation around which, if desired, other more temporary schemes can be organized. It consists in the main of trees and shrubs, and it is with these that I shall deal in this chapter.

Foundation planting deserves careful consideration, for it will give character to the garden for many years to come. It involves some effort of imagination for many of the plants that are used will gain steadily in size during the years and will end up looking very different from their appearance when planted. Sometimes growth can be restricted by pruning, though with trees there is a danger that pruning may destroy their natural beauty. Some trees and shrubs should be regarded as expendable, to be removed after 10 or 15 years' growth, either to make more room for their neighbours, or to be replaced by young plants which will repeat the process all over again.

In foundation planting, thought should be given to the appearance of each plant throughout the year. If it is deciduous it will look quite different in winter, when its branches and stems are bare, than in summer, when they are covered with leaves. This can be a positive advantage, giving a

Shrubs and small trees make an effective background for other subjects

Most buddleias are vigorous shrubs which keep their shape better and produce finer flowers if pruned hard back each March

Heaths and heathers benefit from being clipped with shears after flowering. Cut back far enough to remove all the old flower heads

changing appearance to the garden which prevents it from becoming too boring.

Evergreens tend to be more conspicuous in winter than in summer because they then appear as solid objects among the open tracery of bare stems of deciduous trees and shrubs. The clever designer will make use of this, placing evergreens so that they make one pattern in summer in association with the leaves of deciduous plants and quite another pattern in winter when they are practically the only leafy objects in the garden.

Some trees and shrubs are so spectacular when in flower that one is inclined to forget what they look like at other times. Rhododendrons are a striking example of this for many of them are rather uninteresting in shape and leaf, more or less rounded bushes covered with fairly large dark green leaves. A rhododendron border can be the most spectacular thing in May and June and as dull as a Victorian laurel shrubbery for the rest of the year. Shrubs and trees which are only beautiful when in flower must be used with discretion and should be associated with other shrubs and trees that have beauty

of leaf shape and colour of general form.

The Time Scale and Plant Growth Gardeners continually ask 'How big will it grow?' With many shrubs and trees it is difficult to give a helpful answer for two reasons. First, ultimate size may well be determined by the character of the soil and situation. Second, it may be many years before the shrub or tree reaches this ultimate size and quite likely the questioner will not be thinking anything like so far ahead. Often it is what the plant is going to look like in five or ten years' time that really matters and it is information of this order, rather than what it will look like after 40 or 50 years, that I have tried to give in the following notes.

Suckers A good many shrubs and a few trees make new growths direct from the roots and sometimes several feet away from the main plant. These growths are known as 'suckers' and, if left, will grow into full-scale bushes or trees of their own so that, in time, what started as one plant will become a thicket. This may or may not be desirable and if the suckers are likely to be a nuisance or spoil the symmetry of the plant they should be removed. If they are dug up with roots attached they can be planted elsewhere to grow on into new plants.

However, all this applies only when the shrub or tree is on its own roots, i.e. has been

grown from a seed, cutting or division. If it has been grafted or budded on to a different rootstock (and this is a common nursery practice with cherries, apples, lilacs, rhododendrons and some other trees and shrubs) then suckers will reproduce the characters of the rootstock and not of the garden variety joined to it. Such suckers are seldom of any value and should be destroyed.

Recommended Trees and Shrubs

Abutilon Some abutilons are only suitable for greenhouse cultivation in Britain, or for use as temporary fillers in summer beds from which they will be removed to the greenhouse in autumn. But two kinds can be regarded as foundation plants in the milder parts of the country, near the coast, for example, and in the West and South-west. One is a tall shrub with upright branches, soft greenish-grey leaves and pale mauve flowers in late spring and early summer. It is known as *Abutilon vitifolium*, the vine-leaved abutilon, from the shape of its leaves,

Pruning cuts, left to right: too close to the bud; too far away from the bud; sloping the wrong way; correct

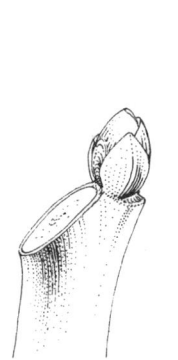
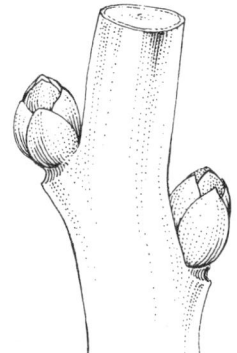
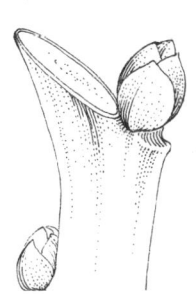
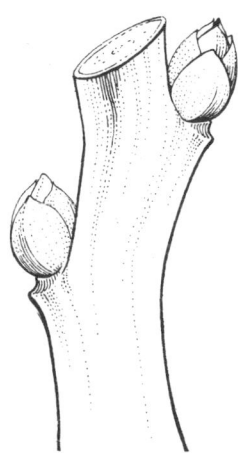

and will quickly reach a height of 10 to 12 ft (3 to 4 m). It is not, as a rule, very long lived. The other, *A. megapotamicum*, the Brazilian abutilon, is a very different plant with thin, rather sprawling stems (it can be trained against a wall or fence if desired) and drooping crimson and yellow flowers in late summer.

Both these shrubs are deciduous and both like sunny places and prefer light, well-drained soils. They can be increased by seed in spring and, in some favourable places, *A. vitifolium* will regenerate itself from seed scattered naturally around the plant in autumn and germinating freely the following spring. Both can also be increased by cuttings of firm young growth in spring, summer or early autumn.

Pruning, to rid the plants of winter-damaged growth, to restrict their size and keep them well balanced, should be done in mid-spring.

Acer (Maple, sycamore) There are maples so small as to be little more than big bushes, and some so large that they are forest trees. All are deciduous and nearly all those that are planted in gardens are grown primarily for the beauty of their leaves, usually deeply lobed and often turning to brilliant shades of crimson, orange and yellow before they fall in the autumn. Best for the small garden are the Japanese maples, varieties of *Acer palmatum* and *A. japonicum*. These are shrubs or small trees, 8 to 12 ft (2·5 to 4 m) high, and in some varieties the leaves are so freely and deeply divided as to be almost fern like. They colour well in autumn.

Acer negundo variegatum is a useful tree of medium size, about 20 ft (6 m) high, with light green leaves heavily variegated with white. It does well in towns.

The sycamore, *A. pseudoplatanus*, and the Norway maple, *A. platanoides*, are large,

Acer griseum

fast-growing trees that will soon reach 30 or 40 ft (9 or 12 m). The sycamore often produces seedlings so freely that it becomes a nuisance, but it has an attractive variety, *brilliantissimum*, with pink and gold young leaves in spring that is slow growing. *A. platanoides* Goldsworth Purple and Crimson King have shining beetroot-purple leaves.

The snake-bark maples, *A. hersii*, *A. capillipes* and *A. davidii*, are trees of medium size grown primarily for their green bark striped with white, and *A. griseum* is grown for its peeling cinnamon-coloured bark.

All will thrive in ordinary soils and sunny or shady places but the Japanese maples require good drainage and may die if the soil remains very wet in winter.

Adam's needle, see Yucca

Almond The common almond is a member of the prunus family, which also includes the peach, nectarine, plum and cherry, and its botanical name is *Prunus amygdalus*. It is one of the loveliest of early spring-flowering trees, making a rounded shapely head of branches, and averaging 15 to 20 ft (4·5 to 6 m) in height. It can be kept smaller by a little thinning and shortening of long branches immediately after flowering.

The almond is deciduous and will grow in practically any soil that is not liable to become waterlogged in winter. It does particularly well on chalky soils and it likes a sunny position. It can be raised from seeds (the stones in the fruits) sown in spring either outdoors or in a frame. Nurserymen usually graft or bud it on to plum stocks to save time. It is a fast-growing tree, soon making its effect in the garden.

Amelanchier (Snowy mespilus) These are spring-flowering trees of moderate size well suited for planting in gardens, yet seldom seen. The flowers are white, small but very numerous, so that when a tree is in flower it is like a white cloud. In autumn the leaves turn orange scarlet before they fall. The best kind is *Amelanchier laevis*, which makes a round-headed tree eventually 20 to 25 ft (6 to 8 m) high, but it may take many years to reach that size. It flowers in spring and will thrive in any ordinary soil and open, sunny position. No pruning is required, but if a tree does get too big its branches can be thinned and shortened in autumn.

If suckers appear from the base of the trunk or direct from the roots they should be removed. Nurserymen usually graft it on to seedlings of mountain ash and suckers from such trees will be of mountain ash, not of snowy mespilus. But if trees have been raised from seed, which germinates readily if sown in spring, the suckers will be of snowy mespilus and can be dug up with roots in autumn or winter and replanted.

American currant, see Ribes

Apple, Crab A number of crab apples are very handsome flowering trees of moderate size. All are botanically known as *Malus*. Some such as the red crab (*M. lemoinei*), with deep carmine flowers, the purple crab (*M. purpurea*), which is an even darker crimson and the Japanese crab (*M. floribunda*), a lovely apple-blossom pink, are grown principally for their flowers; others such as Golden Hornet with small yellow apples, John Downie with small egg-shaped yellow and red crab apples, and Dartmouth with large rounder, redder fruits, are grown mainly for their abundant and highly coloured fruits, but these, too, have attractive white and pink blossom. All flower in spring.

All are hardy, easily grown trees thriving in almost any soil and liking best an open, sunny position. Most will eventually reach a height of 25 ft (8 m) if left to their own devices, though *M. floribunda* rarely exceeds 15 ft (4.5 m) even after many years. All can be kept smaller by a little thinning and shortening of long branches in winter. Some can be raised from seed sown in spring, but this is a slow process and there is likely to be some variation in the seedlings, so the usual method of increase is by budding in summer on to apple stock.

Arbor-vitae, see Thuja

Artemisia (Southernwood, lad's love) These are grey-leaved plants, most of which are more suitable for the border or rock garden than for foundation planting. But one, by reason of its size and character, is truly a foundation plant. This is *Artemisia abrotanum*, a shrub 4 ft (1.25 m) high, with very finely divided grey-green leaves which have an aromatic scent when bruised.

It likes sunny places and light, well-drained soils. It can be pruned every March to keep it neat and bushy; indeed it can be clipped again in July if it is being used to make a little hedge or a shaped specimen.

Artemisia abrotanum is easily increased by cuttings of firm young growth in summer or of more mature growth in autumn.

Azalea Botanists regard azaleas as no more than a particular section of the rhododendron family, and some nurserymen follow this lead and list azaleas as rhododendrons. But most keep them separate and they have such a very distinct decorative value in the garden that this seems entirely sensible.

Like rhododendrons, azaleas dislike lime and thrive in acid soils. They will grow in full sun or partial shade, but if the shade is too dense they may not flower freely.

There are two big divisions in azaleas, the evergreen varieties and the deciduous varieties, and the evergreens are further subdivided into two groups, one of which, usually referred to as Indian azaleas, is only suitable for greenhouse cultivation in Britain, whereas the other group, which includes the popular Kurume, Kaempferi and Glenn Dale azaleas, is sufficiently hardy to be grown outdoors in most parts of Britain. There is, however, a difference in hardiness between varieties, and as there are far too many varieties to describe here, this is a point worth keeping in mind when ordering. Nurserymen should be able to give the necessary information as to the relative hardiness of the varieties they offer.

The Kurume azaleas are evergreen and hardy and they produce great quantities of small flowers in spring. Most do not grow more than 3 ft (1 m) high, though some with age may reach 5 ft (1·5 m), but all are spreading shrubs which may easily become 5 ft (1·5 m) wide in time. They have small leaves and flowers of many colours, white, mauve, lilac, pink, rose, carmine, and scarlet. The Kaempferi and Glenn Dale hybrids in general have larger flowers.

The deciduous azaleas mostly flower in late spring and make bigger, more open bushes, 4 to 8 ft (1·25 to 2·5 m) high, but not usually quite as much through. The flowers are much larger, often in brilliant shades of orange, yellow and coppery red with a wide selection in the pink to crimson range as well. They are among the most brilliant and free-flowering shrubs of their season and some, particularly the yellow *Azalea lutea*, have a rich spicy fragrance as well. Yet another bonus from some varieties (and here again *A. lutea* is outstanding) is yellow and crimson foliage colour in autumn before the leaves drop.

The evergreen azaleas can be raised from cuttings of firm young shoots in summer and so can the deciduous kinds, though they are more difficult. Usually they are raised from seed sown in sand and peat in a frame or greenhouse in spring, but it is three or four years before the seedlings will start to flower and they are certain to vary considerably in colour so it is much better to start with sturdy plants selected for the suitability of their colour for the purpose in mind.

Bachelor's buttons, see Kerria

Bamboo These belong to numerous different genera and, as their names are confused, it is sometimes not easy to identify the different species with accuracy in nursery catalogues. All are elegant plants which will grow in most soils but look particularly well near water. They differ greatly in size and some kinds spread rather rapidly by underground stems. All can be increased by division in spring or by chopping out rooted suckers.

The most frequently planted kind is *Arundinaria japonica* (often called *Bambusa metake*), 10 to 12 ft (3 to 4 m) high with fairly large leaves. *A. nitida* does not spread so much and is more elegant in leaf. *A. fastuosa* is one of the tallest kinds, up to 20 ft (6 m) high and *A. viridistriata* is a semi-dwarf, 3 to 4 ft (1 to 1·25 m) high with

yellow-striped leaves. *Phyllostachys nigra* is known as the black bamboo because its canes become black as they age. It is up to 8 ft (2·5 m) high and it has a fine variety, Henonis, with deep yellow canes.

Barberry, see Berberis

Berberis (Barberry) This is a big family of shrubs including some highly decorative kinds. From a garden standpoint these may be divided into two very distinct groups: evergreens grown for their foliage and flowers, and deciduous kinds grown for their berries and, in some kinds, for their autumn foliage colour.

There are a great many deciduous barberries, almost all with red or crimson berries and some much alike. Typical of them, and an excellent garden plant, is *Berberis wilsonae*, which makes a dense, spiny bush about 3 ft (1 m) high with yellow flowers in summer followed by abundant crops of coral-red fruits. *B. thunbergii* has crimson fruits, not so numerous nor so decorative, but its leaves turn scarlet and crimson before they fall. The variety *atropurpurea* has purple leaves all summer.

The two finest evergreen kinds are *B. darwinii*, which forms a big bush with small, holly-like leaves, and has clusters of small orange flowers in mid-spring, and *B. stenophylla*, an even larger, looser bush with arching branches, narrow leaves and sweetly fragrant yellow flowers a week or so later than *B. darwinii*. There are much smaller varieties of *B. stenophylla* such as *gracilis* and *corallina*. Medium-sized barberries include such species as *B. candidula* and *B. verruculosa*.

All these can be grown in almost any soil and open place. They can be increased by seed, but cuttings of firm young growth in summer in a propagating frame or under mist are to be preferred for specially selected varieties as there may be variation in seedlings. *B. stenophylla* often makes suckers, and these can be dug out with roots in autumn or early spring and used as new plants. *B. darwinii* does not much like root disturbance and nurserymen often grow it in pots so that it can be transplanted with its roots intact.

Pruning is not essential but the evergreen kinds can be trimmed without harm after flowering and are sometimes grown as hedges, for which purpose they are both suitable and beautiful if there is room for a fairly large hedge.

The mahonias are sometimes known as berberis, but are here dealt with as mahonia.

Betula (Birch) The silver birch, *Betula pendula*, is one of the few forest trees that can be planted even in fairly small gardens. In time it will grow 30 ft (9 m) high, but can be replaced long before that as it is cheap and easy to grow. The colour of the bark varies a lot so, when buying, be sure that a

good white-stemmed tree is chosen. There are weeping forms which are even more decorative, the best being known as *youngii*.

All will grow in almost any soil and place, but are particularly good on light soils. They are increased by seed in spring, or selected forms, such as the best weeping varieties, by grafting in spring on seedlings of common birch.

Birch, see Betula

Blue spiraea, see Caryopteris

Bridal wreath, see Spiraea

Broom, see Cytisus and Genista

Buckthorn, Sea, see Hippophaë

Buddleia These are quick-growing deciduous shrubs, the most popular and useful of which is *Buddleia davidii*. This is a loosely branched shrub, 7 to 10 ft (2 to 3 m) high, which carries long, cone-shaped spikes of small, purple, honey-scented flowers in late summer. An additional asset is that its flowers are attractive to butterflies, particularly the beautiful red admiral. It is a shrub that seeds very freely and seedlings often appear all over the place. They tend to be variable in flower colour, from quite a pale lavender to deep purple. Some kinds have been selected and named. Royal Red is a particularly fine purple. There are also several white-flowered varieties. All can be pruned hard each March, and this restricts their size and improves the quality of the flower spikes.

Another species is *B. alternifolia*, a more graceful but less showy shrub of similar height with slender arching stems wreathed in small lavender flowers in early summer. A third species, *B. globosa*, bears little globe-shaped clusters of orange flowers in early summer and is often known as the orange ball tree, but it is not quite so hardy as the others and likes a warm sheltered place. It will soon reach 8 or 10 ft (2·5 to 3 m) in height.

All are quick growing and will succeed in almost any soil, preferring those that are reasonably well drained. *B. davidii* thrives on chalk. All can be raised from seed sown under glass or outdoors in spring, but selected forms must be raised from cuttings because of the variability of seedlings. Cuttings of firm young growth root readily in summer in a propagating frame or under mist, and cuttings of riper growth taken in autumn will root in sandy soil in a sheltered place outdoors.

Calico bush, see Kalmia

Californian lilac, see Ceanothus

Calluna (Ling, Scottish heather) There is only one species, *Calluna vulgaris*, but it has produced numerous garden varieties. Typically the ling is a low-growing but slightly straggly plant, up to 3 ft (1 m) high and quite as much through, with small heather-pink flowers held close to the stem and produced in late summer and early autumn. More decorative for the garden are varieties with double flowers, such as H. E. Beale and Peter Sparkes. Others such as *aurea*, Golden Feather and Gold Haze have yellow leaves; *alba* is the white heather and *foxii* is extremely dwarf. There are many more.

All need exactly the same treatment as the more numerous heathers belonging to the genus *Erica*. They like acid, peaty soils, and the taller kinds are all the better for being trimmed with shears each spring. They are increased by cuttings of firm young shoots in sandy peat in a frame in summer or by layering in spring.

Camellia Most of these beautiful evergreen shrubs are quite hardy but the flowers and flower buds, which come very early in the spring (even in winter in some kinds) are subject to frost injury. For this reason camellias are best planted in rather sheltered places such as in thin woodland or where they are protected by other shrubs or a wall. There are a great many garden varieties of *Camellia japonica*, the most commonly grown kind. The flowers of these vary greatly in form, some being single, some semi-double, some fully double and with petals arranged with such precision as to appear almost artificial. The colour range is from white and palest pink to deep red. There is a fine hybrid between *C. japonica* and *C. saluenensis* named *C. williamsii*, and there are selected garden varieties of this, including Donation with large, double bright pink flowers. One merit of *C.*

williamsii is that the dead flowers usually drop off, whereas those of *C. japonica* tend to hang on, giving the bushes a rather untidy appearance.

All camellias eventually make big bushes 10 or 12 ft (3 or 4 m) high and through but they are rather slow growing and may take many years to reach anything like this, so they are really quite suitable for small gardens. All dislike lime in the soil and thrive in the same sort of slightly acid soils that suit rhododendrons, azaleas and heathers. They need no pruning but if they get too large they can be reduced after flowering or some branches in flower can be cut for home decoration. All can be increased by cuttings either of firm young shoots in summer or of well-developed leaves cut with a small portion of stem and a growth bud. Either type of cutting should be inserted in a mixture of equal parts sand and peat in a propagating frame or under mist, preferably with soil-warming cables to heat the rooting medium. Growing camellias in this way can be fun, but it takes a long time and it is better to start with well-grown bushes.

Caryopteris (Blue spiraea) Small shrubs with clusters of fluffy-looking blue flowers in late summer and early autumn. The kind commonly grown is named *Caryopteris clandonensis*. The stems are rather soft and often get damaged in winter but the plant usually sends up strong new growth from the base. It is, in any case, a good thing to prune all growth hard back each spring to within an inch or so of the woody stems at the base. This keeps the bushes dwarf and compact and improves the quality of the flowers. Treated in this way each bush will be about 3 ft (1 m) high and through by flowering time. Caryopteris likes sunny

places and well-drained soils and can be increased by cuttings of firm young growth inserted in sandy soil in a frame in summer.

Catalpa (Indian bean tree) A fast-growing, rounded deciduous tree with large leaves and, in July and August, candelabra clusters of white flowers spotted with yellow and purple, the effect being rather like that of a horse chestnut. Its full name is *Catalpa bignonioides* and it has a yellow-leaved variety, *aurea*, which is a handsome foliage plant but does not flower so well.

Both kinds like good fertile soil and sunny places and do well in towns. A drawback is that they come into leaf late, usually not until the end of May, so they are bare for a good many months. The golden-leaved variety is often pruned each spring to keep it relatively small but increase the size of its leaves.

Ceanothus (Californian lilac) These lovely shrubs have no connection with the true lilac, despite their popular name which was presumably given because the small, usually blue flowers are produced in clusters which have a very superficial resemblance to those of a lilac, but on a much reduced scale. Some kinds are evergreen and these are all a little tender, benefiting from the shelter of a sunny wall except in very mild districts. One of the most popular of these is *Ceanothus veitchianus*, which has neat, shining green leaves and thimble-like heads of powder-blue flowers in late spring, but it is more tender than either *C. thyrsiflorus*, which is similar in colour, or *C. impressus*, which is a deeper blue. All will in time grow 12 to 15 ft (4 to 4·5 m) high against a wall, but can be kept smaller by pruning as soon as the flowers fade, when stems can be cut back as much as is necessary to keep the plants in shape.

There are also deciduous kinds that flower in late summer, and these are in general hardier and make fine bushes in the open. Good varieties are Gloire de Versailles, blue; Topaz, violet purple, and Perle Rose, pink. All these deciduous varieties benefit from pruning early each spring when all stems made during the previous year can be cut back to within 2 to 3 in (5 to 8 cm) of the older wood. Treated in this way the bushes will make strong new stems bearing flower sprays of greater size. The average height is 6 ft (2 m).

Both evergreen and deciduous kinds can be increased by cuttings of firm young growth in summer in a propagating frame or under mist.

Cedar The botanical name of cedar is *Cedrus* and it is listed under this in many nursery catalogues. There are three principal kinds, the Atlas cedar, *Cedrus atlantica*, a broadly conical tree with branches held

Camellia williamsii Inspiration

out more or less horizontally; the Himalayan deodar, *C. deodara*, more drooping in habit, and the cedar of Lebanon, *C. libani*, a slower-growing tree which becomes flat-topped with age. There is a variety of *C. atlantica*, named *glauca*, which is blue grey instead of green and this is even more popular for garden planting.

All are evergreen, will make big spreading trees and are spoiled by pruning, so are unsuitable as long-term plants for small gardens, but could be replaced after fifteen years or so. They will grow in any reasonable soil and open position. They can be raised from seed or selected garden forms by grafting.

Ceratostigma (Leadwort) The little shrub known as *Ceratostigma willmottianum* is a beauty for the front of a border, but as it often gets killed almost to ground level by frost in winter, many gardeners will regard it more as a herbaceous plant than as a shrub. Yet a shrub it is, as much as 3 ft (1 m) high in favourable places, with a succession of blue flowers from mid-summer until the first frosts of autumn. It must have a sunny place and prefers well-drained soils. It can be increased by cuttings of firm young growth in summer in a frame or under mist.

Chaenomeles (Japanese quince) This is the correct name for the showy, early spring-flowering shrubs that most gardeners call cydonia and some refer to as *japonica*. In the open they make densely branched spiny bushes 3 to 5 ft (1 to 1·5 m) high and usually a good deal more through as they spread slowly by suckers. But more usually they are planted against walls or fences up which they are trained to a height of 6 to 7 ft (2 to 2·5 m), all forward pointing shoots, which cannot conveniently be tied in, being cut back to an inch or so as soon as the flowers have faded. Alternatively, the tips of young shoots can be periodically pinched out throughout the summer to keep them short.

The form most commonly grown has scarlet flowers but there are numerous varieties differing in colour, in size of bloom and in habit. Excellent examples of these are Knap Hill Scarlet, very wide spreading; *moerloesii*, pale pink and spreading, and *nivalis*, white. All will grow in ordinary soil and a sunny or partially shady place.

Chamaecyparis, see Cypress

Cherry The ornamental cherries are all members of the genus *Prunus* and in many nursery catalogues they are listed under that name. They are amongst the most beautiful of spring-flowering trees and one, *Prunus subhirtella autumnalis*, will actually commence flowering in November. It has smaller flowers than most, white or shell pink, but they are produced in great numbers. It is,

however, the large-flowered Japanese cherries flowering in spring that make the greatest display. All produce their flowers in fine clusters, some being fully double, as in rose-pink Pink Perfection or pale pink Fugenzo; some single, as in pure white Tai-Kaku and Yoshino. They also vary greatly in habit, some being of shuttlecock form as in Kanzan, pink; others widely spreading, Shirofugen, light pink; some weeping, Cheal's Weeping, deep pink; some narrowly erect, Amanogawa, light pink; some round headed, Ukon, pale lime yellow. Many cherries give fine autumn colour before the leaves fall and *P. sargentii*, soft pink flowers, is one of the most brilliant of these. One cherry, *P. serrula*, is cultivated exclusively for the beauty of its shining bark which is like highly polished mahogany.

Most of the foregoing are trees of small to moderate size from 12 to 25 ft (4 to 8 m) high, but the bird cherry, *P. padus*, is a much larger tree with numerous slender trails of small white flowers in late spring. It is a very attractive tree, but sometimes suffers severely from attacks by blackfly and is not really suitable for small gardens.

All cherries are deciduous, hardy and easy to grow. They will succeed in any reasonably good soil, but have a special liking for chalk and limestone. They will grow in full sun or partial shade. No regular pruning is required, nor is it desirable, but

Choisya ternata

if trees get too big, branches can be shortened or removed as soon as the flowers have faded. Wounds should be painted with a tree wound dressing.

Cherries are increased by budding in summer on to various stocks, often seedlings of the wild British cherry (*P. avium*).

Chimonanthus (Winter sweet) *Chimonanthus praecox* is not one of the easiest of shrubs to grow, nor are its very pale yellow and maroon flowers, which are almost transparent in texture, at all showy, but they come in late winter and are intensely fragrant so that it is certainly worth planting in warm, sheltered gardens where there is room for a large shrub 8 ft (2·5 m) high.

It likes a good, well-drained soil and can be planted against a wall for protection, in which case it should be pruned each spring sufficiently to keep it tidy. It can be increased by seed sown in a greenhouse in spring or by layering in spring or early summer.

Choisya (Mexican orange blossom) A fine evergreen shrub, *Choisya ternata* is useful for its shining green leaves, well-branched rounded habit and fragrant white flowers, like orange blossom. These are at their best in late spring, though some may be produced more or less all the summer. The

Clematis Nelly Moser

plant is a little tender when young, but becomes hardier with age and can be planted outdoors with safety in all but the coldest parts of Britain.

It will grow well in most soils and likes a warm sunny position. Cuttings of firm young shoots taken in summer will root quite readily either in a frame or under mist.

Cistus (Rock rose) These evergreen shrubs are none too hardy, but in fairly mild places they are certainly worth planting because of the great display they make in early summer. The flowers are rather like single roses, very freely produced, though individually they are fragile and do not last long. One of the hardiest is *Cistus laurifolius*, which grows about 5 ft (1·5 m) high and has pure white flowers. Similar in appearance,

but with a deep purple blotch on each white petal, is *C. cyprius*. A hybrid named Silver Pink has pale pink flowers and *C. purpureus* has rose-coloured flowers with a maroon blotch on each petal. There are many more. All flower in early summer and all produce seed freely by which they can be increased, though Silver Pink, being a hybrid, will not come true to colour from seed. It, and other specially selected varieties, should be raised from cuttings of firm young growth taken in summer and rooted in a frame or under mist.

All kinds like warm, sunny places and well-drained soils. They do not require regular pruning, but if stems are damaged by frost they should be cut back to sound growth in spring.

Clematis These are amongst the most showy and popular of flowering climbers, but not all varieties are easy to grow. They can be

broadly divided into two groups, the small-flowered clematis, most of which are wild species, and the large-flowered clematis, which are mainly garden hybrids. *Clematis montana*, a very vigorous climber with innumerable small white or soft pink flowers in late spring, is one of the best and easiest to grow of the species, and *C. jackmanii* and *C. jackmanii superba* with deep violet-purple, wide-sepalled flowers in summer, are among the most beautiful and easy of the hybrids.

There are many other kinds. *C. armandii* is evergreen and has small white flowers in mid-spring; *C. tangutica* has small yellow flowers, shaped like little hoods, in early autumn, followed by silvery, silky seed heads; *C. macropetala* has nodding lavender-blue flowers in late spring. All these are species.

There are scores of hybrids and it is difficult to make a short selection from them, but *henryi*, white; Comtesse de Bouchard, pink, and Mrs Cholmondeley, light blue; Nelly Moser, mauve and carmine; Hagley Hybrid, rose pink; Barbara Dibley, deep violet purple; Perle d'Azur, lavender blue, and Lasurstern, purplish blue, are good and reliable.

One difficulty experienced with the large-flowered varieties is that they will sometimes mysteriously wilt when they are in full growth. They may never recover, or the following year growth may reappear, apparently unharmed, perhaps to wilt and die a year or so later. This is due to a fungal infection and can be prevented by spraying fortnightly in April and May with a copper fungicide.

Clematis thrive in a wide variety of soils, including those of a chalky nature. They like to be so placed that their roots are in the shade and their stems in the sun. This can often be arranged by planting them behind small shrubs which will shade the soil but permit them to climb up into the light. Clematis climb by tendrils, and their stems are thin and brittle so should be given good support such as trellis-work or wires.

The very vigorous, small-flowered species require little or no pruning, though, if they become too large or crowded, they can be cut back or thinned out after flowering (in early spring for *C. tangutica*). The large-flowered hybrids are better for annual pruning.

For this purpose it is convenient to divide them into two groups, one composed of those that have normally finished flowering by midsummer, the other of those that go on flowering much of the summer. The first can have some of the older stems removed and sidegrowths from the previous year shortened to one or two pairs of buds; the second can be pruned more drastically, all stems being cut back to within 2 or 3 ft (60 to 120 cm) of ground level. Both types of pruning can be done in February or March.

All kinds can be increased by layering in

late spring and the species can usually be raised from seed sown in a frame or greenhouse in spring, though sometimes the seed takes a very long time to germinate.

Clerodendrum There are two shrubby kinds, neither very hardy but suitable for planting in sunny sheltered places and useful because they flower late. One, named *Clerodendrum trichotomum*, makes a big shrub or small tree 10 or 12 ft (3 to 4 m) high, and has clusters of very fragrant small white and red flowers in late summer which, in a favourable season, are followed by little turquoise-blue berries. The other, named *C. bungei*, is shorter, and as it frequently gets cut back to ground level by frost in winter, seldom exceeds 4 ft (1·25 m) in height. It has dome-shaped heads of light purple flowers in late summer. Both kinds have leaves which emit an unpleasant odour when bruised.

Apart from their tenderness they are not difficult to grow, thriving in any reasonably good, well-drained soil and sunny position. They can be pruned in spring as necessary to keep them in shape and get rid of frost-damaged growth. Both produce suckers freely and if more plants are needed suckers can usually be dug up with roots any time between autumn and early spring.

Cornus (Dogwood) From the garden standpoint the dogwoods fall into two groups, those grown primarily for the colour of their stems or leaves, and those grown for their flowers. All are deciduous.

Typical of the first group is *Cornus alba*, which has deep red stems seen to best advantage in winter, particularly if it is cut hard back each spring, so making it produce strong young stems which are the most highly coloured. There is a variety, known as *sibirica*, which has brighter red stems. Another variety, named *elegantissima* has grey-green leaves heavily marked with cream, and another variety, *spaethii*, has yellow-variegated leaves. All these will grow in any soil, but have a particular liking for moist places.

Fine examples of dogwoods grown primarily for their flowers are *C. florida* and *C. kousa*. Both make very large bushes or small, spreading trees with attractive foliage and, in late spring and early summer, they bear flowers which, though inconspicuous themselves, are surrounded by large, white or creamy-white bracts which look like petals. There is a pink form of *C. florida* named *rubra*. All these are trees for good, well-worked, reasonably well-drained soils and sheltered positions. Their young growth is liable to be damaged by spring frost.

All dogwoods can be increased by cuttings of firm young growth in a frame or under mist in July, but *C. alba* also roots readily outdoors in autumn and as it suckers freely it can also be increased by digging up and replanting suckers with roots in autumn or winter.

Cotinus (Venetian sumach, smoke tree, wig tree) The shrub that owns all these popular names is *Cotinus coggygria*. It is a big bush, at least 6 ft (2 m) high and more through, with round leaves that turn crimson in autumn or, in such forms as Notcutt's Variety and *purpureus*, are purple throughout the summer. The flowers are quite extraordinary as they appear like tangled masses of pink silk changing to grey. These are handsome shrubs where there is room to let them spread unrestricted.

They like warm, sunny places and good well-drained soils and, as they sucker freely, can usually be increased by digging up suckers with roots in autumn or winter.

Cotoneaster This very big family provides some of the most decorative shrubs of autumn and winter when carrying their abundant crops of scarlet, crimson, or occasionally black berries. Some are evergreen, some deciduous, and there is also a great range of heights and habits, from completely prostrate creeping kinds such as *Cotoneaster dammeri*, an evergreen, to tall, spreading, tree-like shrubs such as *C. frigidus*, which is deciduous, and *C. cornubia*, semi-evergreen.

One of the most popular is *C. horizontalis*, known as the fishbone cotoneaster because of its close, parallel rows of thin branches like the skeleton of a fish. The leaves are small and round, dark green in summer but turning crimson before they fall in autumn. The small white flowers are followed by abundant scarlet berries. Planted in the open it will spread out horizontally; against a wall it will grow vertically to a height of 6 or 8 ft (2 to 2·5 m) without support. The evergreen *C. microphyllus* somewhat resembles it but has darker evergreen leaves and berries and a more weeping habit which makes it very suitable for planting on top of a bank or terrace wall.

Completely different in character is *C. salicifolius*, with slender arching branches which may reach a height of 10 ft (3 m), long narrow shining evergreen leaves and clusters of scarlet berries. *C. franchetii sternianus* resembles it but has broader leaves and is even more effective in berry.

C. simonsii is stiffly erect and will soon reach 8 ft (2·5 m) if left to its own devices, but can be clipped to form a hedge. It is, however, only partly evergreen and may lose all its leaves in a very cold winter. *C. conspicuus decora* makes a close 4-ft (1·25-m) mound of stiff, arching branches with small evergreen leaves and big crops of bright red berries.

All these cotoneasters are completely hardy and easily grown in almost any soil and situation, but will fruit more freely in light, open places. Pruning is not essential, but if they get too big they can be thinned or cut back in early spring. All can be raised from seed sown in a frame, greenhouse, or outdoors in spring, and self-sown seedlings will often appear from seeds dropped by birds. Cotoneasters can also be increased by cuttings of firm young growth in a propagating frame or under mist in summer.

Crab apple, see Apple, Crab

Crataegus (Thorn, quick) The two common hawthorns, *Crataegus monogyna* and *C. oxyacantha*, are useful dense and spiny hedge plants for outer boundaries, but the second has two beautiful double-flowered forms which are well worth planting as ornamental trees of modest size. One named Paul's Double Scarlet has bright red flowers; the other, Double Pink, has soft pink flowers. Both will take a number of years to reach 15 ft (4·5 m), but will grow still larger in time. The Glastonbury thorn (*C. m. biflora*) is occasionally planted because of its habit of flowering twice, in mid-winter and again in late spring. Better as a garden tree is *C. prunifolia* because of its fine scarlet fruits and the wonderful autumn colours of its rather large leaves.

All thorns are perfectly hardy and will grow practically anywhere. If it is necessary to restrict them, they can be pruned in winter. The single-flowered forms are best increased from seed sown outdoors in spring, but this is rather a slow process. Double-flowered forms are grafted in spring on to seedlings of the common thorn.

Cryptomeria (Japanese cedar) *Cryptomeria japonica elegans* makes a bushy evergreen tree or large shrub, up to 20 ft (6 m) high, with feathery green leaves which turn to a beautiful russet red in the autumn. It is quite hardy and likes a good rich soil. It is raised from summer or autumn cuttings

Cupressocyparis, see Cypress

Cupressus, see Cypress

Currant, American, see Ribes

Cydonia see Chaenomeles

Cypress These are amongst the most useful cone-bearing trees and shrubs for the garden. Botanists split them into several groups, giving these different names such as *Cupressus*, *Chamaecyparis* and *Cupressocyparis*. All are evergreens and most are hardy, quick growing and tolerant of a wide variety of soils.

Chamaecyparis lawsoniana will make a big tree clothed to ground level with good green foliage but it can equally well be planted at 3-ft (1-m) intervals and trimmed to make a hedge or screen. It has a lot of varieties differing in habit and colour. For example, *allumii* is columnar and blue green; *erecta* is similar in habit but bright green; *fletcheri* is smaller, taking years to reach 12 or 15 ft (4 to 4·5 m), and grey green, and *stewartii* has golden leaves. There are many more

Chamaecyparis obtusa nana aurea (foreground)

which make excellent individual specimens in the garden.

Chamaecyparis obtusa is a slow-growing tree which has produced some dwarf varieties useful for the rock garden. *C. pisifera* is particularly valued for the featheryleaved varieties it has produced such as *plumosa* and *squarrosa*. Both these have golden-leaved forms.

Cupressus glabra (in gardens usually called *C. arizonica*) makes a narrow spire of blue-grey leaves but is less hardy than some. *C. macrocarpa* has bright green leaves and is very fast growing but is liable to be damaged by cold wind. Golden-leaved varieties are hardier and Donard Gold and Goldcrest are excellent spire-shaped varieties with yellow leaves. The ordinary greenleaved form was once much planted as a screen or hedge but has been largely superseded by the much hardier and equally

quick-growing *Cupressocyparis leylandii*. This also makes an excellent specimen and will reach a height of 30 ft (9 m) in about 10 years. It is a good rich green.

All are easily grown in any reasonable soil and open or partially shaded position. The species can be raised from seed but garden varieties vary from seed and must be increased by summer or autumn cuttings.

Cytisus (Broom) These are splendid shrubs for light, well-drained, even quite poor and stony soils and there are few places in which they will not grow. All are sun lovers.

The commonest kind is *Cytisus scoparius*, a big, loosely branched shrub 6 or 7 ft (2 to 2·5 m) high and often more through, with thin green stems which give it an evergreen appearance, though in fact the small leaves fall off in autumn. The flowers are yellow and they come in late spring and early summer. There are numerous forms and hybrids with flowers of various colours, yellow and crimson in *andreanus*, crimson

in Dorothy Walpole and *burkwoodii*, rose in *dallimorei*, pale primrose in Cornish Cream and so on. These are tremendously showy shrubs, but not usually very long lived.

Cytisus albus is known as the white Portugal broom. It has more slender branches than *C. scoparius* and smaller but numerous white flowers in late spring. *C. praecox* flowers a little earlier, is pale yellow and rather unpleasantly scented though this is scarcely noticed in the garden. *C. ardoinii*, deep yellow, and *C. kewensis*, light yellow, are dwarf spreading shrubs, the former not much over 6 in (15 cm) high, the latter to 1½ ft (45 cm).

Very different from all these is *C. battandieri*, a big, loosely branched shrub which will soon reach 8 ft (2·5 m) in height and carries its yellow, pineapple-scented flowers in little erect clusters in early summer. The leaves are silvery.

Brooms do not like hard pruning, but they can be lightly trimmed back after flowering, though not into the hard old wood. All can be raised from seed sown in spring, and the common broom will often spread itself naturally by self-sown seedlings. Specially selected forms and hybrids do not come true from seed and must be increased by cuttings of firm young growth in a propagating frame or under mist in July. The cuttings are not at all easy to root.

Daisy bush, see Olearia

Daphne Most kinds have extremely fragrant flowers and some have the additional merit of flowering very early. One of the first to bloom is *Daphne mezereum*, a deciduous shrub which makes a rather stiff bush about 4ft (1·25m) high with purple or white flowers clustered on the bare branches in late winter and early spring. It has a habit of dying suddenly for no obvious reason. Its flowers are followed by scarlet berries and the seeds from these often germinate around the bush. It is wise to retain a few of these seedlings to replace losses.

Flowering at almost the same time is *D. odora*, an evergreen 3ft (1m) high with clusters of purple, intensely fragrant flowers. It is not very hardy, but it has a variety named *aureomarginata*, with a narrow yellow band round each leaf, which will stand greater cold.

The 3-ft (1-m) deciduous hybrid known both as *D. burkwoodii* and as *D. Somerset* is a splendid shrub for any sunny position, producing clusters of soft pink fragrant flowers in late spring.

All daphnes like sunny places and will grow in most reasonably good, well-drained soils. *D. mezereum* is best raised from seed sown under glass or outdoors in spring and all the other kinds by cuttings of firm young growth either in a frame or under mist in summer.

Dawn redwood, see Metasequoia

Deutzia Hardy deciduous shrubs with elegant sprays of small white, pink or purplish flowers in early summer. They are easily grown in any reasonably open place and ordinary soil, and deserve to be far better known. There are a number of varieties such as *elegantissima*, rose pink, scented; Pride of Rochester, double flowered and white, slightly flushed with purple; Mont Rose, single and purplish pink; Magician, single, mauve pink; and Boule de Neige, single white.

All can be pruned after flowering if it is desired to restrict their size, the flowering branches being shortened to non-flowering side growths. Left unpruned, most will eventually make big bushes, 7 or 8ft high (2·25 to 2·5m). All can be increased by cuttings in mid-summer or autumn.

Diervilla, see Weigela

Dogwood, see Cornus

Elaeagnus The most decorative kind is *Elaeagnus pungens maculata*, an evergreen notable for the brilliance of its yellow variegation. In winter it can be one of the most conspicuous shrubs in the garden. It is quite hardy, may eventually grow 10ft (3m) high but will take a long time doing so, and is a fine background plant.

It will grow in any reasonable soil, gets its best colour in a sunny place and can be pruned in spring if it gets too big. It is increased by cuttings in a frame in summer.

Erica (Heather) This is the second genus known popularly as heather, the other being calluna, the Scottish heather or ling. Erica has a number of species, several of which have produced numerous excellent varieties. The special value of the smaller heathers is as ground cover, which can be so dense that practically all weed growth is eliminated. There is great variety in habit and size and time of flowering. *Erica carnea* is low growing and spreading, and flowers in winter and early spring. It has many good varieties including Springwood Pink, heather pink, and Springwood White, white. *E. darleyensis* is another splendid plant, smothered in soft rosy-red flowers right through the winter and on into the spring, and growing to about 18in (45cm). The Cornish heath, *E. vagans*, is similar in height but flowers from mid-summer onwards. Mrs D. F. Maxwell is a fine cerise form of this, and Lyonesse a white form.

Some heathers are much taller. *E. arborea* will reach 10ft (3m) in favourable places, but is more likely to be about 6ft (2m) high. It flowers in spring, as does *E. mediterranea*, a fine heather 3 or 4ft (1 to 1·25m) high. Many more will be found in catalogues.

All thrive best in open places and peaty or sandy soils that are lime free, though *E. carnea* and its varieties, as well as *E. darleyensis* and *E. mediterranea*, will stand a little lime or chalk. They are best planted in spring and should be trimmed with shears immediately after flowering to prevent them becoming untidy. All can be increased by cuttings of firm young shoots in sandy peat in a frame in summer and the low-growing kinds also by layering in spring.

Escallonia The best kinds are all evergreen shrubs with neat shining leaves and small pink or red flowers carried along slender, often arching branches in summer. Not all are fully hardy and some kinds are only seen at their best in the milder places or near the sea. But there are several hardier kinds including *Escallonia langleyensis*, soft carmine; Apple Blossom, pale pink, and C. F. Ball, rosy-crimson. All will grow at least 6ft (2m) high but can be kept smaller by shortening their branches in late summer, immediately after flowering.

All like sunny places and will grow in any reasonably good soil. They can be readily increased by cuttings in summer.

Cytisus kewensis

Elaeagnus pungens maculata

Euonymus (Spindle tree) There are both evergreen and deciduous kinds of euonymus and they look so unalike that to the casual eye they appear quite unrelated. The deciduous kinds, of which *Euonymus europaeus* and *E. latifolius* are the best, make big, rather loosely branched bushes, to 8ft (2·5m) high, which are not particularly decorative until the autumn when they ripen good crops of cerise fruits which split open to reveal orange seeds within. At about the same time the leaves turn yellow and red before they fall and for a few weeks these spindle trees are very decorative.

The evergreens are of two very distinct kinds; the Japanese euonymus, *E. japonicus*, a tall, well-branched shrub with rather thick shining leaves, an excellent plant for hedge making, especially near the sea; and the creeping euonymus, *E. radicans*, a low-growing shrub which will carpet a bed or, if planted against a wall, will ascend it like a climber. Both kinds have varieties with variegated leaves, and this variegation may be either silver or gold. The flowers of all are insignificant.

The evergreen kinds can be grown in sun or shade and in practically any soil. In very cold districts the Japanese euonymus may be damaged by frost. The deciduous spindle trees are all perfectly hardy and equally tolerant of soil, but they prefer sunny places. It is best to plant several bushes

Hedera colchica dentata variegata

close together so that they fertilize one another, otherwise the crops of fruit may be sparse.

The evergreen kinds can be cut back quite hard in spring and can also be trimmed occasionally in summer. They are readily increased by cuttings taken in autumn and inserted in sandy soil in a frame.

The spindle trees need little or no pruning and are readily increased by seed sown in spring.

Fatsia A handsome shrub grown primarily for its large, deeply divided leaves, though it also has distinctive creamy-white flowers. These are borne in autumn and take the form of globular heads produced in stiffly branched sprays. *Fatsia japonica* can reach 10 or 12 ft (3 to 4 m), but can be kept much smaller by pruning in spring.

It will grow in most soils in sun or shade and can be increased by cuttings in a propagator in summer. This is a shrub to add an architectural touch to the garden.

Firethorn, see Pyracantha

Forsythia The abundant yellow flowers of these shrubs are among the most brilliant to be seen in early spring, but in some country districts the expanding flower buds are badly attacked by birds so that it becomes almost impossible to get a display. The finest kind is *Forsythia intermedia* and of this there are several varieties differing in the size and richness of colour of their flowers. The best is probably Lynwood. It soon grows 8 ft (2·5 m) high but can be kept smaller by pruning immediately after flowering, when the branches that have just carried flowers are cut out at a point from which younger branches or shoots that have not yet flowered grow. Another useful kind is *F. suspensa* with longer, more flexible stems that can readily be trained against a wall or fence. The flowers are pale yellow.

All forsythias thrive in any ordinary soil and sunny or partially shaded position. All can be increased by cuttings in autumn or by layering in late spring.

Fuchsia Many varieties of fuchsia are greenhouse or summer bedding plants but there are also some sufficiently hardy to be grown outdoors all the year round, particularly in the milder parts of the country and near the sea; these are useful for they bloom continuously from early summer to the autumn. In Devon and Cornwall and the West of Ireland *Fuchsia magellanica riccartonii* is frequently grown as a hedge and in some parts has actually established itself as a wild plant, spreading by seeds carried by birds. This fuchsia has small sealing-wax flowers but there are other hardy kinds, with larger flowers, such as Mrs Popple, red and violet; Madame Cornelissen, carmine and white, and Margaret, carmine and purple.

In cold winters these fuchsias may be cut down by frost but they usually send up growth from the roots in the spring. They like sunny or partially shaded places and well-drained but not dry soils and they can be pruned hard each spring if desired. All can be readily increased by cuttings at any time in the summer.

Garrya The only species is *Garrya elliptica*, a fine evergreen shrub which makes a rounded bush, 8 or 10 ft (2·5 to 3 m) high and covers itself in winter with long, slender, grey-green catkins. There are male and female plants and it is the male form that has the longest and most attractively coloured catkins.

Garrya will grow in any reasonably good, well-drained soil and it likes a warm, sunny, sheltered position. It can be trained against a sunny wall, in which case badly placed or overcrowded stems can be removed in spring. It is increased by cuttings of firm young shoots in summer in a frame.

Genista (Broom) These shrubs are closely allied to cytisus, which is also popularly known as broom, and they are also much alike in appearance and requirements. Genistas vary greatly in size and some are suitable for the rock garden. All have yellow flowers.

Spanish gorse is the popular name of *Genista hispanica*, a dense, spiny shrub about 3 ft (1 m) high and many feet through, with clusters of yellow flowers in late spring. It is a good shrub to cover a sunny bank. The Madeira broom is *G. virgata*, a loosely branched shrub 3 to 10 ft (1 to 3 m) high, producing its yellow flowers in summer. Largest of all is the Mt. Etna broom, *G. aethnensis*, 15 ft (4·5 m) high, with whiplike, pendulous branchlets carrying small yellow flowers in the middle of the summer.

All these genistas like warm, sunny places and well-drained soils. The larger kinds can be pruned a little immediately after flowering, when the flowering stems can be shortened, but not right back into hard old wood which may refuse to produce new growth.

All can be raised from seed sown in spring, and some also from cuttings in summer.

Ginkgo (Maidenhair tree) There is only one kind, *Ginkgo biloba*, and this is a most beautiful tree with fan-shaped leaves which are green in summer and turn bright yellow before they fall in autumn. There are various forms but the most suitable for small gardens is that known as *fastigiata*, as the branches grow erect like those of a Lombardy poplar and so take up little room even though the tree may reach a height of 40 ft (12 m) or more. It likes good soil and a warm, sunny position.

Gleditsia (Honey locust) Fairly fast-growing deciduous trees with compound leaves composed of small leaflets giving the tree an elegant ferny appearance. The best kind to plant is *Gleditsia triacanthos* Sunburst, in which the young leaves are yellow. Unlike many other kinds which have nasty spines, Sunburst is unarmed.

It grows well in most soils, likes sunny places and is an excellent town tree which will grow large in time but can be kept smaller by pruning in winter. It is increased by grafting on to stocks of the common honey locust.

Gorse, see Ulex

Guelder rose, see Viburnum

Hamamelis (Witch hazel) Winter-flowering shrubs with remarkable flowers, having narrow, twisted, yellow or coppery petals and a pleasant fragrance. Some varieties start to open their flowers in late autumn and others continue until late winter, but the best, *Hamamelis mollis*, is usually in full flower soon after Christmas.

All are quite hardy and will grow well in

rather good, slightly moist, lime-free soils and open or partly shaded places. They make big, open bushes 12 ft or more high, but can be kept smaller by pruning after flowering. Increase may be by layering in spring or detaching rooted suckers in autumn.

Hawthorn, see Crataegus

Heather, see Erica

Heather, Scottish, see Calluna

Hebe (Veronica) This is now the correct name for shrubs formerly known as veronica. All are evergreen but, apart from this similarity, there is great diversity among them. Some are pygmies, more suited to the rock garden than for foundation planting, some are small shrubs with leaves of various kinds. Not all are fully hardy and some, such as the very showy hybrids of *Hebe speciosa*, are most suitable for seaside planting or for mild places. These have good foliage and quite large spikes of flowers from mid-summer onwards, purple in Alicia Amherst; pink in Gloriosa; crimson in La Seduisante.

The hardiest is *H. brachysiphon*, also known as *H. traversii*, a neat 5-ft (1·5-m) bush with abundant small spikes of white flowers from mid-summer. One of the largest is *H. salicifolia*, with narrow leaves and slender spikes of white flowers in summer. It will grow 6 to 8 ft (2 to 2·5 m) high. Midsummer Beauty is intermediate between this and *H. speciosa*, with rather long spikes of lavender-purple flowers from mid-summer till the frosts come. It seldom exceeds 3 ft (1 m) in height and is a very useful and beautiful shrub for a sheltered place.

Among the best of the smaller kinds are *H. armstrongii*, 2 ft (60 cm) high, with golden-bronze leaves, and *H. pinguifolia pagei*, 1 ft (30 cm), with grey leaves and white flowers in early summer, excellent as ground cover. Autumn Glory is 2 ft (60 cm) high with small spikes of violet flowers from mid-summer throughout the autumn.

None of these hebes is at all fussy about soil and all like sunny places. All can be pruned in spring to keep them more compact and all can be readily increased by cuttings taken in summer or early autumn.

Hedera (Ivy) Many people object to ivy on the grounds that it damages buildings and trees. In fact there is little evidence that it does either and it is certainly unlikely to do any harm to modern brickwork or stonework bonded with cement mortar. On the contrary, ivy protects masonry from the weather and in the right place can be very decorative, but like other vigorous climbers it must be kept in check and not permitted to block rainwater gutters, etc.

The common ivy is *Hedera helix* and is

Hamamelis mollis

hardly worth planting as there are so many more decorative garden varieties. These may have smaller or larger leaves or leaves variously coloured with cream, yellow or red. A few of the best are Buttercup, young leaves all yellow; Gold Heart, leaves yellow in the centre; Silver Queen, leaves edged white and pink, and Tricolor, leaves grey green, edged white and pink.

Hedera colchica is another kind of ivy with very large leaves and it also has a splendid variety, *dentata variegata*, with leaves which are heavily margined with pale yellow.

When ivies flower they become bushy and cease to climb and if cuttings are rooted from these parts they, too, will grow into bushy flowering plants. Some nurserymen offer these shrubby forms.

All, climbers or otherwise, are easily grown in any soil and sun or shade. They can be increased by cuttings in summer or autumn and may be pruned as required in spring.

Hibiscus Some kinds of hibiscus are annuals to be raised from seed each year and some are tender shrubs suitable only for greenhouse cultivation in the British Isles. But one is an excellent deciduous shrub, quite hardy and especially valuable because it flowers in early autumn when there are few shrubs still in bloom. Its name is *Hibiscus syriacus* and it makes a rather stiff bush, eventually about 8 ft (2·5 m) high, though it is slow growing and can be kept considerably

smaller by a little pruning each February. Its flowers are like those of a small hollyhock and may be single or double. Varieties include Blue Bird, single blue; Hamabo, single and maroon; Woodbridge, single red; Souvenir de Charles Breton, double lilac; and Ardens, double purple.

All like warm, sunny places and good, well-drained soil. They can be increased by cuttings of firm growth in a frame or outdoors in autumn.

Hippophaë (Sea buckthorn) This is a large deciduous shrub or small tree grown for its narrow silvery leaves and abundant crops of orange berries. Its full name is *Hippophaë rhamnoides* and it thrives in any light, well-drained soil and open position, but does particularly well near the sea. There are two sexes and only the female bushes produce berries and then only if a male bush grows near by to fertilize their flowers with pollen. The sea buckthorn usually grows 10 or 12 ft (3 to 4 m) high. It needs no pruning though lower side growths can be removed each autumn if it is desired to give it a more tree-like form. It is increased by seed sown in spring.

Holly, see Ilex

Honey locust, see Gleditsia

Honeysuckle, see Lonicera

Hydrangea These very handsome summer-flowering deciduous shrubs thrive well in the warmer parts of the country and near the sea, but some kinds are liable to be damaged by frost in cold districts. The hardiest are *Hydrangea paniculata*, up to 6 ft (2 m) high, which carries large cone-shaped clusters of creamy-white flowers in late summer, and *H. arborescens grandiflora*, to 4 ft (1·25 m), with globular heads of white flowers in early summer. Both can be pruned hard back each spring if desired; treatment which improves the size of flowers.

The most popular hydrangeas, with large ball-shaped heads of blue, purple, pink, red or white flowers, are all varieties of *H. macrophylla*. Another race developed from this same species has flat heads of flowers in which all the central flowers are small and bead like and are encircled by a ring of the typical broad, flat flowers. This type is often called lace-cap, and the best known variety is perhaps Blue Wave. In all types the colours are affected by the soil, becoming more pink or red in an alkaline soil and more blue or purple in an acid soil. White flowers are unaffected.

All these hydrangeas succeed in sunny or partially shaded places. They like good rich soils but will also succeed in the light sandy soils so often found near the sea. *H. macrophylla* and its varieties require no pruning beyond the removal of weak stems and of faded flower trusses in early spring. All kinds are readily increased by cuttings of firm young growth at any time during spring and summer in a propagating frame or under mist.

Hypericum (St John's wort, rose of Sharon) This is a big family of plants, many of which are suitable for the rock garden. But there are also some fine shrubs, such as *Hypericum patulum*, a deciduous bush 4 ft (1·25 m) high with saucer-shaped yellow flowers from mid-summer onwards. There are several garden varieties, of which the best is Hidcote with flowers of superior size and semi-evergreen foliage.

Hypericum calycinum, the rose of Sharon, is a creeping evergreen shrub spreading by underground stems and excellent for binding the soil on banks or for covering ground densely. It will thrive in sun or shade and has large yellow flowers throughout the summer.

All will grow in any ordinary soil and *H. calycinum* has a particular liking for chalk soils. It can be increased by division in autumn or winter, and *H. patulum* and its varieties by cuttings in summer in a frame. None requires regular pruning, but if plants get too big they can be cut back in spring.

Ilex (Holly) The botanical name of holly is *Ilex* and it will be found under this in many catalogues. All kinds are evergreen trees but they grow so slowly that in gardens

they are usually thought of as shrubs. If they do get too large they can be cut back in spring but this may stop berry production for a year. However, not all hollies will produce berries since, in most, male and female flowers are produced on separate bushes. Only the females can bear berries and then only if fertilized with pollen from a nearby male. However there are a few varieties which have flowers of both sexes so will fruit in isolation or can be used as pollinators for females. A fine example of this kind is J. C. van Tol, also sometimes listed as *polycarpa*. Some hollies are grown primarily as foliage plants. Golden King and Golden Queen have yellow-edged leaves; *argenteomarginata* has white-edged leaves and there are many more.

All hollies will grow in most soils, in sun or shade and can be pruned or clipped in spring and summer. All can be increased by summer or autumn cuttings and also by seed sown in spring, but seedlings may differ from their parents and leaf variegation is not transmitted by seed.

Indian bean tree, see Catalpa

Ivy, see Hedera

Japanese cedar, see Cryptomeria

Japanese quince, see Chaenomeles

Japonica, see Chaenomeles

Jasmine, see Jasminum

Jasminum (Jasmine, jessamine) The two most popular jasmines are both deciduous climbers. One, named *Jasminum nudiflorum*, is a rather angularly branched plant with thin green stems carrying buttercup-yellow flowers in winter. The other, named *J. officinale*, is a much more rampant climber, making a tangled mass of twining growth and bearing sprays of white, fragrant flowers throughout the summer.

Both will grow in almost any soil. *J. nudiflorum* will succeed in sun or shade and is a useful covering for a north-facing wall. *J. officinale* prefers a sunny position and may be used to cover a fence, trellis or arbour. Neither needs regular pruning, but if they become too big or untidy they can be thinned or cut back in spring. Both are increased by layering in late spring or early summer.

Jerusalem sage, see Phlomis

Jessamine, see Jasminum

Jew's mallow, see Kerria

Juniper The botanical name for the junipers is *Juniperus* and they are usually listed under this in nursery catalogues. They are ever-green cone-bearing trees, some of which

are particularly suitable for the garden because of their comparatively small size and interesting shapes. *J. communis hibernica*, the Irish juniper, makes a dense, narrow column 10 or 12 ft (3 to 4 m) high after some years. *J. c. compressa* is similar but so slow growing that after 10 years it may barely be 1 ft (30 cm) high, which makes it first class for the rock garden. Another kind which will make a slender spire, eventually 15 ft (4·5 m) or so high, is *J. virginiana* Sky Rocket. It is blue grey and very distinctive.

By contrast *J. sabina tamariscifolia* spreads horizontally and is unlikely to exceed 3 ft (1 m) in height even when it has attained a diameter of 8 or 9 ft (2·5 to 3 m). *J. media pfitzeriana* is a bigger shrub which spreads out like a wide shuttlecock. There are many more, all easy to grow in almost any soil and sunny or partially shaded place. Increase by cuttings in summer.

Juniperus, see Juniper

Kalmia (Calico bush) These very beautiful evergreen shrubs carry, in early summer, clusters of pink and white flowers like little Chinese lanterns. They dislike lime and chalk and do best in rather moist peaty soils and sheltered positions. The most showy kind is *Kalmia latifolia*, a big bush to 8 ft (2·5 m) high, a little like a rhododendron in habit. A smaller plant with deeper pink flowers is *K. angustifolia*, sometimes called the sheep laurel. Neither needs any pruning and both can be increased by layering in early summer.

Kerria (Bachelor's buttons, jew's mallow) There are two varieties of *Kerria japonica*, one with single yellow flowers and the other with fully double yellow flowers like little balls, and it is only the latter that is called bachelor's buttons. Though varieties of the same species, they differ considerably in habit, the single-flowered form making a dense thicket of growth 5 ft (1·5 m) high and the double-flowered form making much longer, less dense growth, with some stems up to 10 ft (3 m) tall. It is often trained against a wall or fence where it looks very attractive when in flower in spring, but it is not a true climber and needs some support.

Both kinds will grow in sun or shade and in any reasonable soil. They can be raised from cuttings of firm young growth in autumn, and also by the very simple method of digging up suckers with roots in autumn or winter.

Laburnum These popular early summer-flowering trees can be grown almost anywhere, though they prefer sunny places and reasonably well-drained soils. They make open, branching trees 15 to 20 ft (4·5 to 6 m) high, carrying trails of yellow flowers which are usually very freely produced. As a rule they are not long lived, but they can

Wisteria floribunda

be readily renewed from seed, which often germinates of its own accord around the trees. The finest kind, because of the extra length of the flower trails, is a hybrid named *Laburnum vossii*, but it does not breed true from seed. *L. vulgare* does and flowers a little earlier.

If trees get too big, branches can be shortened or removed in winter.

Lad's love, see Artemisia

Laurustinus, see Viburnum

Lavandula (Lavender) The common lavender makes a rounded bush with narrow grey leaves and spikes of fragrant lavender-blue flowers in summer. It is 3 ft (1 m) high and may grow thin and straggly with age, a tendency that can be checked by clipping it annually with shears as soon as the flowers fade. But it also has several varieties which differ in size and intensity of colour. The variety Hidcote is only 1½ ft (45 cm) tall and has deep purple flowers. Grappenhall Variety is 4 ft (1·25 m) high and its flowers are a rather light lavender-blue. Twickle Purple is intermediate in height and colour and there are several more.

All like well-drained soils and sunny places and all will thrive on chalk and limestone. Lavenders are not, as a rule, long lived, but they can be easily increased by cuttings of firm young growth inserted in a frame in summer or outdoors in autumn.

Lavatera (Tree mallow) The plant which most people think of as lavatera is a very showy annual, but there is also a shrubby kind, *Lavatera olbia*, known as the tree mallow, though it is no more than a shrub, 6 or 7 ft (2 to 2·5 m) high, with rather soft stems, some of which may die back in winter. It flowers all the summer and may be anything from rose to soft pink.

Lavatera olbia does best in light, well-drained soils and is particularly good near the sea. It grows rapidly and can be cut back considerably each spring if it gets too big. Seed sown in a frame or greenhouse in spring germinates readily but seedlings may vary in the colour of their flowers, so especially desirable forms should be raised from cuttings in a frame in summer.

Lavender, see Lavandula

Lavender cotton, see Santolina

Leadwort, see Ceratostigma

Leycesteria Only one kind is grown in gardens, *Leycesteria formosa*, a shrub of very rapid growth that makes long bright green stems bearing, in late summer, small trails of pendent chocolate and white flowers, often followed by deep purple berries. This is not a showy plant but it is distinctive in habit and flower and will grow

practically anywhere in sun or shade. The rather soft stems are often damaged by frost in winter, but this does not much matter as fresh stems are thrown up from the base. It is, in fact, wise to cut some stems nearly to ground level each spring to encourage a good crop of new ones which carry the best flowers. Leycesteria often seeds itself about freely. Seed can be sown outdoors in spring or rooted offsets or suckers can be dug up in autumn or winter and used as new plants.

Lilac Botanically the lilacs are known as *Syringa* and this sometimes causes confusion in gardens as syringa is occasionally used as a common name for philadelphus.

The common lilac is *Syringa vulgaris*, a big bush, often 12 ft (4 m) or more in height, with close sprays of light purplish-blue fragrant flowers in May. Many improved varieties have been raised, some with much deeper coloured flowers, some with larger flowers or double flowers, some pure white, and one that is a pale primrose yellow. In addition there are several other kinds of lilac worth growing, notably the Preston Hybrid lilacs, *S. prestoniae*, and the Rouen lilac, *S. chinensis*, which have smaller flowers in looser, more graceful sprays, though the Preston varieties lack the distinctive lilac perfume. All are equally hardy and can be grown with ease in almost any soil and reasonably open place. Their flowering is improved if the dead flower heads are removed in early summer.

Lilacs can be increased by layering directly after flowering and also by digging up suckers with roots attached in autumn or winter, but, as nurserymen often graft the good garden varieties on to common lilac or privet, it is quite likely that suckers taken from purchased plants will not be of the grafted variety. Suckers from layered plants, however, will reproduce all their desirable characteristics.

Lilac, Californian, see Ceanothus

Ling, see Calluna

Lonicera (Honeysuckle) The familiar climbing honeysuckles are botanically known as *Lonicera*, but this genus also contains evergreen bushy plants which gardeners tend to call lonicera rather than honeysuckle.

The common honeysuckle is *Lonicera periclymenum* and needs no introduction as its fragrant flowers in summer are familiar to all, but there are many other climbing honeysuckles not so well known. The two finest scented varieties are the early Dutch and late Dutch, both very similar varieties of the common honeysuckle with flowers of superior size and colour.

The Japanese honeysuckle is *Lonicera japonica*, a nearly evergreen climber best known in a variety named *aureo-reticulata* which has leaves veined with yellow.

Laburnum vossii

Lonicera japonica aureo-reticulata **trained round a gate post**

These climbing honeysuckles thrive in almost any soil and situation, and all are readily increased by layering at any time in spring or summer.

Of the shrubby kinds, the most popular is *L. nitida*, a densely branched evergreen with little rounded leaves rather like those of a box tree. It stands clipping well and makes an excellent hedge up to about 5 ft (1·5 m) in height. It will grow practically anywhere and can be increased by cuttings of firm young growth in a frame in early autumn.

Magnolia highdownensis

Lupinus (Tree lupin) The plant which most people think of as a lupin is herbaceous but there is also a much bushier species, *Lupinus arboreus*, which is called the tree lupin, though it never makes more than a rather soft-stemmed and short-lived shrub about 5 ft (1·5 m) high. It is, all the same, a showy and useful plant especially for poor, sandy soils and seaside gardens where it succeeds very well. The flower spikes are yellow or white, smaller than those of a herbaceous lupin and appearing in early summer. It is very easily raised from seed sown outdoors in spring and it often renews itself by self-sown seedlings. Seedlings may vary in flower colour, so especially good forms are increased by cuttings of firm young growth in a frame in summer.

Magnolia Some of the loveliest flowering trees are included in this very large genus but some are difficult to grow or slow to bloom so selection should be made with care. Most kinds are deciduous but two are evergreen and of these the better for general garden planting is *Magnolia grandiflora*, sometimes known as the laurel magnolia because of its big shining green leaves. The large white flowers are produced in late summer and autumn. This species is a little tender, for which reason it is often planted against sunny walls and trained like a climber, but where the climate is favourable it will make a big tree in the open.

The deciduous magnolias can be roughly divided into spring-flowering and summer-flowering kinds. The spring-flowering magnolias all have erect flowers shaped a little like tulips, whereas many of the best of the summer-flowering kinds have hanging saucer-shaped flowers, each with a central boss of crimson stamens. Among the best of the spring kinds are *M. stellata*, the first to open its white or pale pink flowers, forming a big bush almost 8 ft (2·5 m) high; *M. denudata*, sometimes known as the yulan, 15 to 20 ft (4·5 to 6 m), with large white flowers in April; *M. soulangiana*, similar in size and a fine hybrid with numerous forms, all with large flowers in April and early May, but varying in colour from white to quite a deep rosy purple, and *M. kobus*, 15 to 20 ft (4·5 to 6 m), with quite small but very numerous white flowers in April and May.

Best of the summer-flowering deciduous magnolias are *M. sinensis* and *M. highdownensis*, both 12 to 15 ft (3·5 to 4·5 m) high, with very fragrant white and crimson flowers.

All magnolias like deep loamy soils and though some, such as *M. highdownensis*, will put up with some lime or chalk in the soil, most are better without it. The spring-flowering kinds and evergreens do best in sun but the summer-flowering deciduous kinds do not object to some shade. None requires any regular pruning. All can be increased by layering in late spring or by seed sown in peat and sand in a frame or greenhouse in spring, but seedlings may take years to flower.

Mahonia Evergreen shrubs, some of which have leaves composed of holly-like leaflets. Mahonias are grown partly for the beauty of their leaves and partly for their small yellow flowers which come very early.

The most familiar kind is *Mahonia aquifolium* which grows up to 4 ft (1·25 m) high, spreads slowly by suckers and has clusters of yellow flowers throughout the spring. A very fine species is *M. japonica*

with pale yellow fragrant flowers produced in late winter and early spring. A hybrid named Charity is stiffer and more upright in habit with deep yellow flowers in autumn and winter, but it is not scented.

All three will grow in any reasonably good soil, *M. aquifolium* in sun or shade, but *M. japonica* and Charity like protection from cold winds. *M. aquifolium* can be pruned or trimmed each spring after flowering and is sometimes used to make a small hedge. All kinds can be increased by cuttings of firm young growth in a frame in summer and *M. aquifolium* by division in autumn.

Maidenhair tree, see Ginkgo

Mallow, Tree, see Lavatera

Malus, see Apple, Crab

Maple, see Acer

Metasequoia (Dawn redwood) *Metasequoia glyptostroboides* is a fast-growing tree which has feathery leaves, bright green in summer but turning russet red before they fall in the autumn. It makes a fairly narrow cone and can be grown in gardens of medium size even though it will make a tall tree in time. It is not fussy about soil but likes an open and fairly moist place. It can be increased by summer cuttings.

Mexican orange blossom, see Choisya

Mezereon, see Daphne

Mock orange, see *Philadelphus*

Olearia (Daisy bush) The popular name is apt as all kinds carry masses of small daisy-like flowers in summer. All are evergreen and the most popular is *Olearia haastii*, a shapely rounded shrub 6 ft (2 m) high with neat leaves and white flowers in summer. It will grow almost anywhere and is a particularly good town shrub.

More exacting are *O. stellulata* and *O. scilloniensis*, both 4 ft (1·25 m) high with greyish leaves and white flowers in spring. Neither is very hardy and they should be given a particularly warm and sheltered spot in well-drained soil. *O. macrodonta* is a larger shrub up to 9 ft (3 m) high with grey-green holly-shaped leaves and fine clusters of white flowers in June. It makes an excellent windbreak near the sea but is not hardy enough for cold places inland. All can be increased by cuttings of firm young growth in summer in a frame.

Orange ball tree, see Buddleia

Osmanthus These are evergreen shrubs of which the best garden kind, *Osmanthus delavayi*, is a densely branched bush with small dark green shining leaves. Small but numerous and intensely fragrant white flowers are borne in spring.

It is not very hardy and should be given a sheltered position but it is not fussy about soil and it will grow in sun and shade. No pruning is necessary and it can be increased by cuttings of firm young growth in a frame in late summer.

Paeonia (Tree peony) Most people think of peonies as herbaceous plants, which some certainly are, but there are also shrubby kinds of which the best for garden planting is *Paeonia suffruticosa*. It is a rather soft-stemmed, open-branched bush up to 5 ft (1·5 m) high and is notable for the opulence of its huge flowers in late spring and early summer. There are single- and double-flowered forms and a considerable range of colours including white, pink, carmine, crimson and purple. The young growth may be cut by frost so plants should be given a sunny and fairly sheltered place.

They like good, well-manured soil and require no pruning. They are not easy to propagate and nurserymen often graft them on to roots of the herbaceous peony. This does not make a very happy partnership and when such plants are purchased it is wise to replant them a little more deeply than before so that the tree peony can make roots of its own. In the garden tree peonies can be increased slowly by layering in spring or early summer.

Parthenocissus (Ampelopsis, Boston ivy, Virginia creeper) These are all quick-growing and vigorous climbers grown solely for their leaves which colour up in autumn before they are shed. The most popular is the Boston ivy or ampelopsis, *Parthenocissus tricuspidata*. It has vine-shaped leaves and will cling to a wall or other support by means of little adhesive discs on its tendrils. It colours brilliantly and is often known as Virginia creeper, a name that really belongs to another species, *P. quinquefolia*. This also climbs by adhesive discs, but its leaves are much larger and the habit is not so neat. *P. vitacea* is much like the last in appearance but it climbs by tendrils and must have the support of trellis, wires or a tree.

All will grow in any reasonable soil. They will survive in shade but prefer and colour better in sun. If they get too big, they can be cut back as required in spring. All can be increased by layering in late spring or early summer or by ripe cuttings in autumn.

Passiflora (Passion flower) These are very quick-growing climbers with exceptionally distinctive flowers, but they are all rather tender. The only one that is at all reliable outdoors, and then only in a sheltered sunny place, is *Passiflora caerulea*, a very vigorous plant which will attach itself to any available support by tendrils. It can be grown against a south wall and will flower in late summer, the flowers in the common

Paeonia suffruticosa

form being blue and white, or pure white in the variety Constance Elliott.

It likes a good soil and needs no pruning beyond the removal of frost-damaged growth each spring. It can be increased by seed sown in a warm greenhouse in spring or by cuttings of young growth in a frame in summer and it is advisable to keep a few young plants in reserve in a frame or greenhouse in case the established plant should be lost in winter.

Passion flower, see Passiflora

Peach The peaches belong to the genus *Prunus* and the ornamental kinds are all varieties of *Prunus persica*, under which name they will be found in many nursery catalogues. They are small trees, 10 to 15 ft (3 to 4·5 m) high, bearing profuse crops of double pink, red or white flowers in spring. The most popular is Clara Meyer with rose-pink flowers; Iceberg is white, and Russell's Red is deep carmine.

All like fairly rich soils and warm, sunny places, as they are liable to be damaged by winds and are not as robust as the nearly related plums and cherries. They need no regular pruning but diseased or damaged stems or branches should be removed in winter or immediately after flowering. They are increased by budding in summer, usually on to plum stocks.

Peony, see Paeonia

Periwinkle, see Vinca

Pernettya An evergreen shrub, no more than 3 ft (1 m) high, with neat dark green foliage, *Pernettya mucronata* has small white flowers in summer followed by most remarkable berries in a variety of colours including pink, lilac, purple, near black, red, crimson and white. There are male and female bushes and with these only the females bear berries and then only if a male plant grows nearby. But there are also varieties which combine both sexes, such as Bell's Seedling and Davies' Hybrids, and those are to be preferred in a small garden.

Pernettya does best on rather moist, peaty soils, though there are few lime-free soils in which it cannot be grown. It will grow in full sun or partial shade and requires no regular pruning. As it spreads by suckers it can be increased very readily by digging these up with roots attached in autumn. It can also be increased by seed sown in sand and peat in spring and in favourable places will often produce many self-sown seedlings.

Perovskia This is a shrub that looks a little like a rather leggy lavender. The kind most commonly grown, *Perovskia atriplicifolia*, has grey leaves and long thin spikes of lavender-blue flowers in late summer.

It likes a warm, sunny place and well-drained soil. As the plants resent root disturbance they should be purchased in pots or other containers and be planted from these with the soil still around their roots. Oddly enough the best method of increase is by root cuttings, i.e. short lengths of root inserted in sandy soil, but these should be put singly in small pots so that they can be grown on without further disturbance.

Philadelphus (Mock orange, syringa) Hardy deciduous shrubs mostly with white, very fragrant flowers in mid-summer. In *Philadelphus coronarius* the flowers are creamy white and almost too heavily perfumed. Among the best are Belle Etoile, Beauclerk and Sybille, all with single white flowers flushed with purple or cerise, and Virginal which has double white flowers. Most will soon reach a height of 7 ft (2·5 m) if left to their own devices, though they can be kept smaller by cutting out the old flowering stems as soon as the flowers fade. Sybille, however, seldom exceeds 4 ft (1·25 m) and is particularly suitable for small gardens and *P. microphyllus*, white, is another useful small kind.

All are very easily grown in almost any soil and position though they flower most freely in a sunny place. They can be increased by cuttings of firm growth in autumn inserted in sandy soil outdoors.

Phlomis (Jerusalem sage) *Phlomis fruticosa* is a rather soft-stemmed shrubby plant about 3 ft (1 m) high with grey, sage-like leaves and clusters of yellow, hooded flowers in mid-summer. It is a plant which loves sun, warmth and good drainage. It may be damaged by frost in winter, but usually grows from the base the following spring and is all the better for being trimmed back a little each spring to keep it from becoming straggly. It is easily raised from cuttings in summer.

Picea, see Spruce

Pieris Evergreen shrubs with clusters or sprays of white flowers in spring which resemble those of lily of the valley. Associating well with rhododendrons, pieris also require lime-free soils. They will grow in sun or semi-shade but the young growth of *Pieris formosa forrestii*, which is bright red, is a little tender so this kind should be given a sheltered place. *P. japonica* is much hardier but lacks the highly coloured young growth. However, there is a hybrid between the two kinds known as Forest Flame which combines the best qualities of both; like them it will grow to a height of about 8 ft (2·5 m). *P. floribunda* seldom exceeds 5 ft (1·5 m) and is slow growing. All can be increased by summer cuttings in a propagator or by layering in spring.

Plum All plums are members of the genus *Prunus* and the most popular ornamental kinds are varieties of *Prunus cerasifera*, under which name they will be found in many catalogues. *P. c. pissardii* (syn. *P. c. atropurpurea*) is the purple-leaved plum, one of the first trees to flower in spring, sometimes opening its small pale pink flowers in late winter. The leaves are a rich purple. The hybrid *P. blireana* has lighter coloured, more coppery leaves and larger, deeper pink, double flowers. Neither requires regular pruning but if they become too large they can be thinned or cut back after flowering. They are increased by budding in summer on to plum stocks.

Polygonum (Russian vine) This is a very vigorous twiner capable of ascending a large tree or covering an outbuilding. Its full name is *Polygonum baldschuanicum* and it is deciduous and produces great sprays of small, white or pink-tinted flowers in late summer.

It will grow in most soils but it flowers best in sunny places and can be cut back in spring if it strays too far. Increase is by cuttings in summer and autumn.

Potentilla Some potentillas are herbaceous plants and some are rock plants, but two, *Potentilla fruticosa* and *P. arbuscula* are deciduous shrubs 4 ft (1·25 m) high with yellow flowers which are at their best in early summer but continue almost till autumn. *P. fruticosa* has numerous varieties such as Katherine Dykes, with larger, deeper yellow flowers; *vilmoriniana* with silvery leaves and pale yellow flowers and *veitchii*, with white flowers. *P. arbuscula* is shorter and more spreading in habit with deep yellow flowers and silvery leaves in the variety *beesii*. Elizabeth is a fine hybrid between these two species, intermediate in height and with light yellow flowers. All are excellent because of their moderate size, long flowering season and hardiness.

They like sunny places and prefer well-drained soils but there are few soils in which they cannot be grown. They can be cut back quite hard each spring and are increased by cuttings of firm young growth in a frame in summer.

Prunus, see Almond, Cherry, Peach and Plum

Pyracantha (Firethorn) These evergreen shrubs are grown primarily for their fine crops of berries in autumn but they also have good foliage and their clusters of small white flowers make an effective display around mid-summer. They are frequently trained against walls, though they can equally well be grown as bushes in the open. The most popular is *Pyracantha coccinea lalandei* with large orange-scarlet berries. *P. atalantioides* has smaller crimson berries and *P. rogersiana flava* has yellow berries.

All are easily grown in almost any soil and will succeed in sunny or shady places. When grown against walls, badly placed shoots should be removed or shortened immediately after flowering. Propagation is by seed in spring or by cuttings of firm young growth in a frame in late summer.

Pyrus This is the genus to which the pear belongs and fruiting pears do make highly ornamental trees, but one kind, *Pyrus salicifolia pendula*, is grown solely for its weeping habit and its silver-grey leaves, its flowers being sparsely produced. It will grow in any reasonably fertile soil in an open situation and can be pruned in winter to improve its shape and to prevent the

branches from becoming overcrowded. Increase is by grafting or budding on to pear stocks.

Quick, see Crataegus

Redwood, Dawn, see Metasequoia

Rhododendron All the shrubs commonly known as azaleas are, in fact, rhododendrons and in catalogues may be found under either name. Here, however, I have kept them apart so that under this heading only the evergreen rhododendrons, commonly so called, are included. They are a splendid lot of shrubs, many of them extremely showy in bloom, with a peak display period in late spring, though there are rhododendrons which bloom from the early part of the year until after mid-summer. Some of the best for general garden planting are the hardy hybrids making big rounded bushes up to 10 ft (3 m) high, covered with large clusters of flowers in a variety of colours from white, pale pink, mauve and cream to crimson, purple, scarlet and apricot. Typical of these are Pink Pearl, Betty Wormald, White Pearl, Cynthia, Britannia, Susan, Blue Peter, Purple Splendour and Dairymaid.

There are other much smaller kinds such as *praecox*, 4 ft (1·25 m) high, with pale rose flowers in early spring; Blue Tit, 3 ft (1 m), with small blue flowers; *Rhododendron williamsianum*, 3 ft (1 m), with bell-shaped pink flowers; Elizabeth, deep scarlet, 3 ft (1 m), and many more.

Almost all rhododendrons dislike lime and chalk. They thrive on moderately acid soils, but the hardy hybrids will grow in almost any soil that is not actually alkaline. They like peat and leafmould and benefit from annual topdressings of either of these applied at any time of year. They do not need pruning, except for the removal of faded flowers before seed commences to form. They can be transplanted even when quite large, which means that rearrangement can take place if the garden has to be replanned.

All can be increased by layering in late spring. Nurserymen grow many selected varieties by grafting on to seedlings of *R. ponticum*, the common mauve-flowered species, and suckers from such plants should be removed since they will be of this species and will swamp the garden variety if permitted to remain. Seed of most kinds germinates freely in peat and sand in a frame or greenhouse in spring. Species come true from seed but garden varieties may show considerable variation. Seedlings may take a number of years to reach flowering size.

Rhus (Stag's-horn sumach) There is only one kind worth planting in the garden and that is a highly decorative small tree of open-branched habit with long fern-like leaves and curious horn-like spikes of velvet red fruits which look more like flowers. Its name is *Rhus typhina* and it has a variety, *laciniata*, in which the leaflets are deeply divided and even more fern like. The leaves of both turn to brilliant shades of yellow, orange, scarlet and crimson before they fall in the autumn and the fruits remain on the tree long after this. This tree soon grows to 10 ft (3 m) high and spreads by suckers which can be dug up with roots in autumn or winter and planted on their own. In any event suckers are best removed as they can become a nuisance by converting one tree into a thicket.

Rhus is not fussy about soil but it likes a sunny position. For the shrub often known as *Rhus cotinus*, see *Cotinus*.

Ribes (American currant) This gay and vigorous deciduous shrub, the full name of which is *Ribes sanguineum*, is one of the first to flower in the spring and it is very easy to grow. Its short, hanging trails of pink or carmine flowers are very freely produced. One of the best varieties is Pulborough Scarlet. All varieties soon make big bushes 8 ft (2·5 m) high and will grow anywhere in heavy or light soil, chalk or peat, sun or shade. They can be increased by cuttings in autumn and can be pruned after flowering as hard as is necessary to keep bushes from growing too large.

Rock rose, see Cistus

Romneya (Californian tree poppy) These lovely plants are half shrubby, half herbaceous. Their 6-ft (2-m) stems become firm and almost woody as the summer advances but are usually killed back to ground level in winter and a new lot appears the following spring. The flowers come in late summer and are huge white poppies, each with a central boss of golden stamens. The foliage is blue grey. Though there are several kinds, they do not differ much from a garden standpoint.

All like sun and the best of drainage and

Rhus typhina, **grown primarily for its brilliant autumn tints**

Romneya coulteri

will thrive in very poor, gravelly soils. They are raised from root cuttings in winter, but are rather difficult to transplant, so are grown in pots until planting-out time in spring or autumn.

Rose of Sharon, see Hypericum

Rosemary Evergreen shrubs with narrow aromatic leaves and small lavender-blue flowers in spring. The botanical name is *Rosmarinus*. The best kind is *R. officinalis*, a bushy, erect plant about 4 ft (1·25 m) high. There are several varieties, of which Corsican Blue is one of the most desirable because of the brighter and deeper colour of its flowers. *R. lavandulaceus*, also known as *R. o. prostratus*, is a prostrate shrub which can be planted at the top of a terrace wall or bank to trail downwards. It is very attractive but not very hardy.

All rosemaries like warm, sunny places and well-drained soils and all can be increased by cuttings of firm young growth in a frame in summer.

Rosmarinus, see Rosemary

Russian vine, see Polygonum

St John's wort, see Hypericum

Salix, see Willow

Santolina (Lavender cotton) Low-growing evergreen shrubs with aromatic leaves and small yellow flowers in summer. The most popular kind is *Santolina chamaecyparissus nana*, a dwarf form with silvery-grey leaves which may attain a height of 2 ft (60 cm) but can easily be kept to half that if it is clipped hard back each spring. It makes a fine edging for large beds. *S. virens* is similar in habit but has bright green leaves. Both like

sunny places and prefer well-drained soils. They can be increased by cuttings in summer or autumn or by division in autumn.

Scottish heather, see Calluna

Sea buckthorn, see Hippophaë

Senecio This is a family that contains all kinds of strange relations, the common groundsel and the cineraria, the ragwort and the dusty miller. But there is also one excellent evergreen shrub, *Senecio greyii*, 4 ft (1·25 m) high with grey, rounded leaves and masses of bright yellow daisy flowers in mid-summer.

It is fairly hardy but likes a sunny place and well-drained soil. If it gets too big it can be cut back moderately in spring. Cuttings of firm young shoots root readily in a frame in summer.

Skimmia These evergreen shrubs are useful because they will grow well in shade and any reasonably good soil. They are slow growing, have good dark green foliage and clusters of small white fragrant flowers in late spring or early summer followed by shining scarlet berries. The kind most commonly grown is *Skimmia japonica* and in this there are two sexes, only the female bushes producing berries and then only if there is a male bush nearby for fertilization. But another – a species named *S. reevesiana* (or sometimes *S. fortunei*) – is bisexual and so every bush will produce berries. *S. japonica* is the taller and may eventually reach 5 ft (1·5 m). *S. reevesiana* is about 2 ft (60 cm) high. Both can be increased by cuttings of firm young growth in summer in a frame or by layering some of the stems in late spring.

Smoke tree, see Cotinus

Snowball tree, see Viburnum

Snowy mespilus, see Amelanchier

Southernwood, see Artemisia

Spanish broom, see Spartium

Spartium (Spanish broom) This is a very good flowering shrub because it is easy to grow and flowers from mid to late summer when not many shrubs are in bloom. There is only one kind, *Spartium junceum*, and it makes a big, rather gaunt bush as much as 10 ft (3 m) high if left to its own devices. It can be kept smaller and more compact if pruned in spring by shortening the stems produced the previous year. These stems are green and rush-like and the flowers, like those of a broom in shape, are bright yellow and scented.

The Spanish broom will grow in any soil but particularly likes. light, well-drained soils. It grows well near the sea and likes sun. It can be increased by seed sown in spring.

Spindle tree, see Euonymus

Spiraea (Bridal wreath) There are a lot of different spiraeas and they are all very easily grown deciduous shrubs, some being inclined to spread too quickly and take

Senecio greyii

Skimmia japonica

charge of the garden if not checked. This criticism does not apply to the best kinds which include *Spiraea thunbergii* and *S. arguta*, two very similar shrubs about 4 ft (1·25 m) high, with slender, twiggy growth wreathed in tiny white flowers in spring. *S. vanhouttei* grows to 6 ft (2 m) and produces abundant clusters of white flowers in late spring and early summer. *S. veitchii* has long, arching branches covered in white flowers in summer. One of the best later summer-flowering kinds is *S. bumalda* Anthony Waterer, only about 3 ft (1 m) in height, it has carmine flowers which are produced in flat heads.

All will grow in practically any soil. They prefer open, sunny places but will also grow in shade. The spring-flowering kinds can be pruned after flowering when some of the stems can be cut right out to thin the framework. The summer-flowering kinds recommended are not improved by pruning except Anthony Waterer which can be cut to within 6 in (15 cm) of soil level in March. All can be increased by cuttings in mid- to late summer and *S. japonica* also by dividing bushes in autumn or winter.

Spiraea, Blue, see Caryopteris

Spruce The botanical name for spruce is *Picea* and most kinds make large evergreen trees, more suitable for estates and forestry than for garden planting. But one kind, *Picea pungens glauca*, has such beautiful blue-grey leaves, especially well coloured in spring, that it is a popular garden tree even though it may have to be replaced after 15 or 20 years if it gets too big. It will grow in any reasonably good soil and sunny position and is increased by grafting.

Stag's-horn sumach, see Rhus

Sumach, see Cotinus and Rhus

Sycamore, see Acer

Syringa, see Lilac and Philadelphus

Tamarisk, see Tamarix

Tamarix (Tamarisk) Graceful deciduous shrubs with feathery sprays of white or pink flowers. They like light, well-drained soils and, though they are quite suitable for planting in inland gardens, they have a special value near the sea as they will withstand a lot of salt-laden wind. One of the loveliest is *Tamarix pentandra*, which has pink flowers in summer. The quality of its flower-plumes is improved if all stems are cut back to a few inches each spring. *T. tetrandra* has pink flowers in late spring and pruning must be delayed until the flowers have faded. Another, *T. gallica*, pale pink, flowers in late summer but is not as decorative as the others. It is, however, one of the best for planting as a windbreak near the

sea. All can be increased by cuttings in autumn.

Taxus, see Yew

Thorn, see Crataegus

Thuja (Arbor-vitae) The name is often spelt thuya. These are fast-growing, evergreen cone-bearing trees closely resembling cypress and useful for similar purposes. *Thuja plicata* and *T. occidentalis* are much planted as hedges or screens and they have various garden forms which are also useful. Of these, Rheingold is outstanding because of its slow growth and good golden-bronze colour. Cultivation is as for cypress.

Tree lupin, see Lupinus

Tree mallow, see Lavatera

Tree peony, see Paeonia

Ulex (Gorse) The common gorse, *Ulex europaeus*, is a wonderfully decorative shrub but it is so common and so readily distributes itself by seed that it is not worth planting in the garden except as a hedge, for which in sandy soils it is excellent. It has, however, a double-flowered variety, *floreplenus*, which is even more spectacular when in flower in spring, and which produces no seed. It grows 4 ft (1·25 m) high and can be pruned, if desired, after flowering. It is increased by cuttings in summer.

Venetian sumach, see Cotinus

Veronica, see Hebe

Viburnum (Guelder rose, snowball tree, laurustinus) These are fine hardy shrubs, most of which are deciduous but a few are evergreen. One of the most popular, *Viburnum opulus*, is a British wild plant, the guelder rose. In gardens it is usually represented by one of its varieties, either *sterile*, known as the snowball tree because the white flowers in early summer are carried in ball-like heads, or *compactum*, which has flat heads of white flowers followed by clusters of currant-red berries and is only 5 ft (1·5 m) high against the 10 ft (3 m) or more of the guelder rose and snowball tree. *Viburnum fragrans* produces its small clusters of pinkish-white, very fragrant flowers in winter, whenever the weather is mild. *V. carlesii* is also fragrant but its domed heads of white flowers do not open until mid-spring. A hybrid from it, *V. carlcephalum*, has much larger flower clusters.

All the foregoing are deciduous. *V. burkwoodii*, which closely resembles *V. carlesii* in flower, may be evergreen in a mild winter, but if the weather is cold it loses most of its leaves.

True evergreens are *V. tinus*, *V. davidii*

and *V. rhytidophyllum*. The first is known as laurustinus and is much like a Portugal laurel in leaf but has clusters of white flowers, tinged with pink, during winter and early spring. It does well in town gardens and will make a dense bush 8 to 10 ft (2·5 to 3 m) high.

Viburnum davidii is only about 3 ft (1 m) high with large, leathery, shining leaves and flat clusters of white flowers which are followed by turquoise blue berries if two or more bushes are planted together to ensure fertilization.

Viburnum rhytidophyllum has the largest leaves of all, 6 or 7 in (15 to 18 cm) long, dark green above, covered with yellow hairs beneath. It makes a bush 10 ft (3 m) high and has flat heads of yellowish flowers in early summer followed by berries which change from red to black.

Viburnum plicatum is like a smaller version of *V. opulus sterile* and, because it comes from Japan, is often known as the Japanese snowball. It has a variety named *tomentosum* in which the flowers are carried in flat clusters along almost horizontal branches, and another named *mariesii* in which this feature is even more pronounced.

All can be grown in any reasonable soil. Most like open, sunny positions but *V. tinus* and *V. davidii* will grow in shade. Most require little or no pruning, but *V. plicatum tomentosum* is improved if the top is cut out occasionally to exaggerate the natural, spreading habit of the plant. *V. tinus* can be trimmed after flowering and again in summer if it is grown as a hedge or screen, a purpose for which it is very suitable.

All can be increased by cuttings in summer and *V. fragrans* by layers which often grow naturally all round the bush and can be dug up in autumn or winter.

Vinca (Periwinkle) Trailing evergreens very useful for covering the ground in shady places, growing well beneath trees and tall shrubs. There are two principal kinds, the greater periwinkle, *Vinca major*, which grows 18 in (45 cm) high and quickly spreads over several yards of ground, and the lesser periwinkle, *V. minor*, a much neater, more manageable plant, 6 in (15 cm) high and spreading less rapidly. Both have blue flowers in spring and both have varieties with yellow-variegated leaves which are very decorative. In addition, *V. minor* has a number of other varieties with white or purple, single or double flowers.

All are very easily grown in practically any soil and place. They can be increased by division in autumn or winter and can be cut back after flowering.

Vine, see Vitis

Virginia creeper, see Parthenocissus

Vitis (Vine) The grape vine is named *Vitis vinifera* and is a suitable climber for sunny

Vitis coignetiae

Yucca filamentosa **a plant of great architectural merit**

Salix matsudana tortuosa (Willow)

walls particularly the variety *purpurea* which has purple leaves. The hybrid, Brandt, has leaves that turn crimson and purple before they fall in autumn. Both need wires, trellis or something of the kind for their tendrils to cling to. The very vigorous *V. coignetiae* with large rounded leaves that colour brilliantly in the autumn, is better grown over a shed or outbuilding or allowed to climb

into a tree. All vines can be pruned in winter by shortening the growth made the previous summer to within a few inches of the main vines. All grow in any reasonably fertile soil and are particularly happy on chalk or limestone. See also Parthenocissus.

Weigela These useful and easily grown shrubs are often known as diervilla; all are deciduous and flower in early summer, carrying their tubular blooms along arching branches. There are several varieties, Bristol Ruby, Newport Red and Eva Rathke with deep carmine flowers; *styriaca* with rose flowers; Abel Carrière, pink, and *variegata* with pale pink flowers and white-variegated leaves.

All grow 6 or 7 ft (2 to 2·5 m) high and are very easy to manage in practically any soil and position. They can be pruned immediately after flowering when the old flowering branches are cut back as far as non-flowering stems on young shoots. Increase by cuttings in summer or autumn.

Wig tree, see Cotinus

Willow The botanical name of willow is *Salix*. All are quick-growing trees, thriving in most soils, but often becoming too large for gardens. Most popular is the golden-barked weeping willow, *Salix chrysocoma*, which will soon reach a height of 30 ft (9 m). *S. matsudana tortuosa* is less spreading and has curiously twisted branchlets. *S. alba vitellina* is grown for the orange colour of the young bark and *S. a. chermesina* for its red bark. For best effect both are pruned hard each spring. Increase by cuttings in autumn.

Winter sweet, see Chimonanthus

Wisteria (Wistaria) Hardy twining plants with long trails of pea-type flowers in late spring and early summer. They are admir-

able for covering large areas of walls or for training over pergolas or along trellis work. Alternatively, by annual pruning in summer they can be converted to an almost shrub-like habit or trained as standards.

The most vigorous kind is *Wisteria sinensis*, the Chinese wisteria, which is capable of climbing to 30 ft (9 m) or more. Typically bluish lilac in colour, it has a white variety and a double-flowered variety with deeper purple flowers. The Japanese wisteria, *W. floribunda*, is less vigorous, seldom over 15 ft (4·5 m) high and it has numerous varieties which can be violet blue, white, pink, and double. One named *macrobotrys* (or *multijuga* in some catalogues) has extra fine lilac and purple flowers in trails up to 3 ft (1 m) long.

All like a sunny place and fairly rich soil though they will grow in almost any soil. They flower most freely if pruned every year in mid-summer, when all young growths not actually needed to extend the coverage of the plant are cut back to four or five leaves. If desired, in winter, these summer-pruned stems can be further shortened to 2 in (5 cm). It is by starting this kind of pruning on quite young plants and applying it to practically every growth that shrub-like specimens or standards are formed.

Wisterias can be raised from seed but it is better to increase good varieties by layering in spring or early summer.

Witch hazel, see Hamamelis

Yew The botanical name for yew is *Taxus*, the common English yew being *Taxus baccata*. It makes a fine hedge, notable for its dark green colour, and stands clipping well, for which reason it is much used in topiary work. It has a golden variety named *semperaurea*. The Irish yew is *T. b. fastigiata*, a variety distinguished by its broadly columnar habit and this also has a golden-leaved variety.

All yews will grow in practically any soil and place. The common yew can be raised from seed but garden varieties must be increased by cuttings in summer or autumn.

Yucca (Adam's needle) Striking evergreen plants with large rosettes of stiff, sword-shaped leaves and, in summer, tall spikes of bell-shaped, creamy-white flowers. They thrive best in well-drained soils and sunny, fairly sheltered places. One of the hardiest and most beautiful is *Yucca filamentosa* with flower spikes 4 ft (1·25 m) high. A variety of this has leaves striped with grey and gold. One of the largest is the true Adam's needle, *Y. gloriosa*, 6 ft (2 m) or more in height. No pruning is required except for the removal of the faded flower spikes. Increase is by offsets removed carefully with roots in early spring.

Roses

Roses like sun and free movement of air and do not succeed so well in the shade or in very enclosed places where the air is confined. They can be grown on any soil that is in reasonably good condition and they thrive on generous feeding, for the very finest roses are produced on strong young stems. There is a natural tendency for rose stems to lose vigour as they age and the main object of pruning roses is to get rid of old growth before it begins to die and to maintain a constant supply of good new growth to take its place. Good, fertile soil helps to this end.

Ground is prepared for roses by thorough digging just as it is for other permanent plants such as shrubs and trees. If manure is available it can be dug in freely. If no manure is available, peat can be used instead, or compost made from well-rotted garden refuse. Turves, buried grass-side downwards under 8 to 10 in (20 to 25 cm) depth of soil, will rot slowly and provide an excellent basis for the rose bed. Coarse bonemeal and hoof and horn meal can be sprinkled through the soil as it is dug with the same object of supplying plant food for a long period.

Some very vigorous roses are grown exactly like shrubs, either as individual bushes or in a border together with other shrubs, but most of the popular garden roses are usually grown as display plants on their own. They are very suitable for this purpose because they flower freely over a long period and may be compared, in this respect, with good bedding plants such as the geranium and dahlia, but whereas these must be removed each autumn and replaced each spring, the rose remains permanently in place.

These free-flowering bedding roses are of two main types, the hybrid tea or large flowered, and the floribunda or cluster flowered, but as breeders are constantly crossing one type with the other in their efforts to get new and better varieties, the division between the two types is getting progressively more blurred.

Hybrid tea or large-flowered roses have shapely flowers carried either one per stem or in small clusters in which one flower opens well ahead of the others. Successive batches or flushes of flowers are produced, but the first, in early summer, is the most abundant and after this there may be quite long gaps between the successive flushes of bloom.

Floribunda or cluster-flowered roses are smaller individually and often, though by no means always, less shapely, but there are many more of them and often all the flowers in a cluster open at the same time. They flower in flushes but these come more rapidly so that the effect is of a more continuous display. To give colour in the garden the cluster-flowered roses are superior to the large-flowered roses but they lack their charm and individual quality of bloom.

Shrub roses The term shrub rose is applied to any rose too big to be used conveniently in a bed of massed roses. Some shrub roses are really strong-growing floribundas, but some are very old roses that have survived from earlier times and some are wild, or species roses. These wild roses have single flowers which are sometimes followed by shapely, highly coloured fruits or heps.

Wild roses usually have a fairly short flowering season and this is also true of some shrub roses, but others flower in flushes from early summer until autumn like large-flowered and cluster-flowered roses. These are distinguished from the others as repeat-flowering shrub roses.

Climbing roses Climbing roses are of several different kinds. Some are simply extra-vigorous forms of ordinary bush roses and these always carry the name of the rose from which they originated prefixed by the word 'Climbing'. Thus, Climbing Madame Butterfly is an extra vigorous form of the popular pink hybrid tea rose, Madame Butterfly. Its flowers are exactly like those of Madame Butterfly, but its stems are so long that they can be trained to cover a sizeable wall or fence. One cannot have everything, however, and as a rule the climbing sports, as they are called, do not flower so freely nor so continuously as the bush roses from which they originated.

Ramblers Rambler roses are climbing roses with very flexible stems which carry their usually rather small flowers in large clusters. Most of them have only one flush of flowers each summer. They are very impressive for a few weeks in mid-summer but there is little display afterwards.

Repeat-flowering climbers Again breeders have tried to get the best of both worlds by crossing climbers of different types to get new varieties with large flowers freely produced over a long season. These are called repeat-flowering climbers and they usually have stiffer stems than the ramblers.

Standards Left to grow naturally all roses would start to branch from ground level. For some purposes gardeners prefer a head of branches on a stout bare stem and this

Rambling roses can be attractively trained to form a colonnade

they obtain by budding a garden rose on to a specially grown stem of a wild rose. If the head of branches is on top of a stem $3\frac{1}{2}$ ft ($1\cdot1$ m) or more in height it is called a full standard; if the stem is only 2 to $2\frac{1}{2}$ ft (60 to 75 cm) high, a half standard, and if the head is formed with a climbing or rambler rose it is called a weeping standard.

Miniatures These have very small leaves and flowers and, as a rule, make quite small bushes, though there are some that are taller or even climbing in habit. The bushy varieties are useful for edging and for massing in small beds and some gardeners also like to plant them in rock gardens though they are really rather too sophisticated to be grown with wild plants.

Other Types There are numerous old roses classified under such names as China, damask, gallica, moss, Provence and sweet briar. These are generally lumped together as old garden roses.

Planting and Aftercare

Rose planting differs little from the planting of shrubs and the season is the same as that for deciduous shrubs, namely from autumn to spring. This is for plants lifted from the open ground. If, however, plants are obtained in containers from which they can be moved without disturbing the soil around the roots, they can be planted at any time.

Roses planted for massed display in beds or borders are spaced $1\frac{1}{2}$ to 2 ft (45 to 60 cm) apart, but vigorous shrub roses may be as much as 4 or 5 ft ($1\cdot25$ to $1\cdot5$ m) apart and climbers against a wall or frame can easily fill 8 or 10 ft ($2\cdot5$ to 3 m) each.

How roses are bought Nurserymen nearly always sell year-old plants, known as maidens. These will have from two to five stems all coming from about the same point close to the roots. This is because the plant has been produced by joining a growth bud of the variety required to a rootstock of a quite different rose, chosen for its vigour and ease of increase. The root, known as the stock, is subsequently prevented from making any shoots of its own but passes all its sap through the bud grafted upon it. The point where bud (or scion) and root (or stock) were joined, known as the union, can always be detected because this is the place from which the top growth starts. When planting it is desirable to keep this point of union just below the surface of the soil. The particular form of grafting used to join bud and stock is known as budding.

Pruning roses The pruning of roses can

be made to appear complicated but is in reality very simple. When roses are first planted all stems are pruned severely, which means that all are cut to a length of 3 or 4 in (8 or 10 cm) at most. This can be done when the rose is put in but as a rule is left until early spring as a precaution in case there is some dying back or withering after planting.

In subsequent years pruning can be done at any time between mid-autumn and early spring, or for ramblers in late summer or early autumn as soon as the flowers have faded. The object, as I have already explained, is to keep up a supply of strong young growth and to get rid of worn-out old growth. With the most vigorous ramblers such as American Pillar, Dorothy Perkins and Excelsa, this can be reduced to a simple formula. Each year, as soon as the flowers fade, cut out all the stems that have just flowered and train the young non-flowering stems in their place.

With less vigorous climbers a little more inspection of growth is needed. A lot of the old flowering stems can be cut out but not all because some will be carrying good new shoots as well. Cut these back to the best of the new shoots and shorten some of them by a foot or so especially if thin or weak.

With bedding roses, whether large flowered or cluster flowered, start by cutting out all old stems that are carrying little or no new growth and also any that look diseased. Then shorten the young stems that are left, the longest and strongest on the cluster-flowered varieties, by about one-third their length, the weaker ones by a half or two-thirds.

This final pruning can be a little more severe for large-flowered varieties, especially if exhibition quality blooms are required. Then the best stems can be shortened by half or even two-thirds, the thinner ones cut back to 3 or 4 in (8 or 10 cm) or even removed altogether.

Shrub roses are simply thinned out, some of the older stems being removed and some of the younger ones shortened if the bushes are getting too big.

Suckers When roses are budded only the top growth will produce the required flowers. If shoots are allowed to grow from the roots, or even from the main stem of the plant below the point of budding (visible as a distinct swelling) they will be from the root-stock and will produce wild rose flowers instead of garden rose flowers. All such suckers must, therefore, be cut out directly they are seen and right back to the root from which they grow. Any growth from the main stem of a standard rose will be a sucker and should be removed.

Feeding roses Roses repay regular and generous feeding. Every winter or early spring some manure or rotted vegetable compost should be spread over the beds. In early spring they should have a top-dressing of peat and bonemeal or a good

1. Established hybrid tea roses can be cut back by about two-thirds and the centre of the bush kept open.

2. Newly planted roses are cut hard back. This is usually done in the spring after autumn planting.

3. Rose suckers should be removed as close to the stem as possible.

4. Mulching rose beds with manure will enrich the soil and keep down weeds

Rose blackspot is best controlled by applying benomyl or triforine

fish manure or bonemeal and dried blood. These will supply the basic food but, even so, more is almost certain to be needed and can be given as a compound fertilizer two or three times in late spring and summer. National Growmore will do at 2 oz (55 g) per square yard each time, or a proprietary rose fertilizer may be used according to the manufacturer's instructions.

Keeping roses healthy Roses also benefit from routine spraying to keep down pests and diseases which can weaken or disfigure them. A systemic insecticide (i.e. one that enters the sap) such as menazon, dimethoate or formothion will take care of most of the pests if applied once a month during the growing season. Thiram or maneb applied once a fortnight from late spring until early autumn will look after most of the diseases, but it is important to get the first spray on before black spot, the most troublesome of rose diseases, starts to spread. Alternatively, a systemic fungicide such as benomyl or triforine can be used monthly.

Really that is all there is to rose growing except to cut off all the faded flowers, with a few inches of stem, regularly in summer to keep the plants growing and flowering.

Recommended Roses

Varieties are very numerous and constantly added to by the introduction of new seedlings, some of which extend still farther the colour range or variety of form of the rose. New varieties inevitably cost more than the older ones, which have been more widely distributed and are grown by most nurserymen. The older varieties also have the advantage that any fault or weakness will have been revealed and their true garden value can be more accurately assessed. The wisest plan therefore is to base a rose garden on well tried varieties but to include a few new ones, to be added in small numbers annually, so that the most desirable can be identified and planted in greater quantity. Nursery catalogues give long descriptive lists of roses and the Royal National Rose Society also helps by publishing annually in its excellent *Year Book* (which is sent free to all members) an analysis of the most popular roses based on the votes of a number of experts both professional and amateur. However, what happens in other gardens is not always an accurate guide to the way a rose will behave in one's own garden as varieties react differently to different conditions.

The following lists are simply suggestions of a few roses that have given widespread satisfaction. They are not put forward as exhaustive or even as representing the best.

LARGE FLOWERED

Beauté Yellow flushed with apricot, flowers full and well shaped but little fragrance. Medium height, bushy habit.

Blue Moon Shapely lavender-blue flowers, nicely fragrant. Medium height and branching habit.

Eden Rose A very glowing pink with even brighter reverse. A big, full, shapely rose with good fragrance. Medium height, branching habit.

Ena Harkness A shapely, full-petalled, bright crimson rose with moderate fragrance. Medium height and bushy habit.

Fragrant Cloud Large, very full, geranium-like flowers, powerfully scented and freely produced. Medium height and bushy habit.

Gail Borden Very large, full, bright pink and gold flowers, moderately scented. Medium height and bushy habit.

Gavotte Light rose-pink flowers, paler outside, full and shapely. Fragrant. Medium height and bushy habit.

Gold Crown Large, full-petalled, deep yellow flowers. Rather tall bushy habit.

Grand'mère Jenny Very large, full, soft yellow flowers flushed with pink. Some fragrance. Tall, bushy habit.

Josephine Bruce Shapely, full-petalled, rich crimson flowers with plenty of fragrance. Medium height, bushy habit.

King's Ransom Shapely yellow flowers of medium size freely produced and with moderate fragrance. Medium to tall, bushy habit.

Margaret Clear pink with lighter reverse, full, shapely, moderately fragrant flowers. Medium height, bushy habit.

McGredy's Yellow Large, full, light yellow flowers with moderate fragrance. Tall, well-branched habit.

Mischief Medium-size, shapely orange and vermilion flowers freely produced and fully fragrant. Medium height, bushy habit.

Mojave Coppery-orange flowers rather lacking in substance, very sweetly scented. Medium height, bushy habit.

Mrs Sam McGredy Coppery-orange and rose flowers. Good fragrance. Medium height, bushy habit.

My Choice Shapely, soft carmine and gold flowers, fully fragrant. Medium height, bushy habit.

Peace Very large, full, lemon-yellow flowers edged with pink. Not much fragrance. Very vigorous, tall and well branched.

Perfecta Shapely, full-petalled flowers, ivory edged with rose. Not much fragrance. Rather tall, erect habit, not much branched.

Piccadilly Large, shapely orange-scarlet and yellow flowers, moderately scented. Medium height, bushy habit.

Picture Shapely warm pink flowers, only

Dearest (Cluster flowered)

slightly scented. Medium height, bushy.

Pink Favourite Large, full, shapely rose-pink flowers, not much scent. Medium height, bushy habit.

Prima Ballerina Large, full, shapely pink flowers. Very fragrant. Medium height, branching habit.

Rose Gaujard Large, full flowers, white or cream heavily flushed with carmine. Moderate fragrance. Rather tall, branching habit.

Silver Lining Large, shapely and full, soft rose flowers paling to white at the base and delightfully fragrant. Medium height, branching habit.

Stella Large, very shapely carmine flowers shading to near white. A very beautiful rose which has little fragrance. Rather tall, branching habit.

Super Star Very shapely, full, bright vermilion flowers, moderately fragrant. Medium height, branching habit.

Sutter's Gold Medium-size, rich yellow flowers shaded with red, fully fragrant. Rather tall, upright habit.

Wendy Cussons Large, full, shapely, deep cerise flowers, richly fragrant. Medium height, branching habit.

CLUSTER FLOWERED

Allgold Deep yellow, semi-double, fragrant flowers in good clusters. Medium height.

Anna Wheatcroft Soft vermilion flowers that are nearly single. Slightly fragrant. Medium height.

Chanelle Shell pink paling to light peach. Fragrant. Rather tall.

Circus Flowers yellow at first deepening to orange flushed with carmine, borne in large clusters. Fragrant. Medium height.

Dearest Large, sweetly scented, salmon-pink flowers. Medium height.

Elizabeth of Glamis Large, shapely, sweetly scented orange-salmon flowers. Medium height.

Europeana Blood red flowers of fair size produced in large clusters. Slightly fragrant. Medium height.

Evelyn Fison Brilliant scarlet flowers in large clusters. Slightly fragrant. Medium height.

Frensham Light crimson flowers of good size, very freely produced. Slightly fragrant. Tall and very vigorous.

Honeymoon Fragrant, canary-yellow roses of good size and substance. Light green foliage. Rather tall habit.

Iceberg Shapely, pure white flowers very freely produced. Moderately fragrant. Rather thin growth but tall habit.

Korona Large, semi-double, flame-scarlet flowers, very freely produced. Slightly fragrant. Rather tall habit.

Lilli Marlene Rich crimson, slightly scented flowers very freely produced in large clusters. Medium height.

Marlena Blood-red flowers very freely produced on a low and well-branched bush.

Masquerade Flowers at first yellow, gradually changing through pink to carmine. Slightly fragrant. Freely produced in large clusters. Rather tall and very vigorous.

Orangeade Tangerine, semi-double, slightly scented flowers. Under medium height.

Orange Sensation Fairly large, bright orange-red, fragrant flowers very freely produced. Medium height.

Paddy McGredy Large, full, fragrant, shapely deep rose flowers in good clusters. Rather below medium height.

Paprika Bright turkey-red flowers in large clusters. Medium height.

Queen Elizabeth Large, shapely, slightly fragrant salmon-pink flowers. Very tall, vigorous habit.

Rosemary Rose Large, double, flat-topped flowers of currant red with purple foliage. Medium height.

Vera Dalton Large, well-formed, slightly fragrant, rose-pink flowers. Medium height.

Woburn Abbey Large, well-formed, fragrant deep orange flowers. Medium height.

Zéphirine Drouhin (Climber)

CLIMBING ROSES

Climbing Crimson Glory Large, fully double, fragrant, deep crimson flowers, freely produced in early summer, with some more in early autumn.

Climbing Ena Harkness Large, fully double, fragrant, bright crimson flowers, freely produced in early summer, with some more in early autumn.

Climbing Etoile de Hollande Large, fully double, very fragrant, crimson flowers, freely produced in early summer, with some more in early autumn.

Climbing Golden Dawn Large, fully double, very fragrant light yellow flowers, freely produced in early summer, with some more in early autumn.

Climbing Madame Caroline Testout Very large, fully double, slightly fragrant pink flowers, freely produced in early summer, with some more in early autumn.

Climbing Mrs Sam McGredy Large, double, fragrant, coppery-orange and rose

flowers, freely produced in early summer, with some more in early autumn.

Danse du Feu Medium-sized, double, orange-scarlet flowers all summer.

Golden Showers Large, fully double, fragrant yellow flowers all summer.

Madame Gregoire Staechelin Large, double, very fragrant carmine and pink flowers in early summer.

Mermaid Large, single, fragrant soft yellow flowers all summer.

Parkdirektor Riggers Large, semi-double blood-red flowers all summer.

Royal Gold Large, double, fragrant deep yellow flowers all summer.

Zéphirine Drouhin Large, double, very fragrant clear pink flowers all summer. Thornless.

RAMBLER ROSES

Albéric Barbier Double, fragrant creamy-white flowers in early summer. Nearly evergreen leaves.

Albertine Fairly large, coppery pink, very fragrant flowers in early summer.

American Pillar Single, rose and white flowers in large clusters in mid-summer.

Dr W. Van Fleet (Rambler)

Nevada (Shrub)

Chaplin's Pink Climber Fairly large, semi-double, bright pink flowers which are borne in large clusters in mid-summer.

Crimson Shower Semi-double, crimson flowers in large clusters throughout late summer.

Dr W. van Fleet Fairly large, pale pink, fragrant flowers in mid-summer.

Dorothy Perkins Small, double, shell-pink flowers in large clusters in mid-summer.

Emily Gray Fairly large, double, apricot flowers in early summer. Beautiful glossy foliage.

Excelsa Small, double, crimson flowers in large clusters in mid-summer.

New Dawn Very like Dr W. van Fleet, but flowers all summer.

Paul's Scarlet Climber Fairly large, semi-double, scarlet flowers in clusters in mid-summer.

Sanders' White Small, double, fragrant white flowers in large clusters in late summer.

Violetta Small, double, lavender-purple flowers in large clusters in mid-summer.

SHRUB ROSES

Blanc Double de Coubert Semi-double, very fragrant, white flowers all summer. 6 ft (2 m).

Bonn Large, double, light scarlet flowers with musk fragrance, all summer. 5 ft (1·5 m).

Celestial Double, shell-pink, fragrant flowers in early summer, grey-green leaves. 7 ft (2·25 m).

Chinatown Large, double, light yellow, slightly fragrant flowers all summer. 6 ft (2 m).

Cornelia Double, rose-pink and salmon, very fragrant flowers in clusters all summer. 5 ft (1·5 m).

Elmshorn Double, rose-pink and salmon, fragrant flowers in clusters all summer. 5 ft (1·5 m).

Felicia Double, shell-pink flowers in large clusters all summer. 5 ft (1·5 m).

Frühlingsgold Large, semi-double, creamy-yellow flowers in June. 8 ft (2·5 m).

Frühlingsmorgen Large, single, cream and pink flowers in June. 6 ft (2 m).

Kassel Semi-double, cherry-red flowers in large clusters all summer. 5 ft (1·5 m).

Madame Hardy Large, double, white flowers in June and July. 6 ft (2 m).

Magenta Large, double, very fragrant, lilac-purple flowers all summer. 4 ft (1·25 m).

Maiden's Blush Double, fragrant, flesh-pink flowers in June and July. 5 ft (1·5 m).

Maigold Large, semi-double, deep yellow flowers all summer. 7 ft (2·25 m).

Nevada Large, semi-double, creamy-white flowers, freely produced in June, with some more in August or September. 7 ft (2·25 m).

Penelope Semi-double, pale apricot-pink, fragrant flowers all summer. 6 ft (2 m).

Rosa gallica versicolor **(Shrub)**

Prosperity Pink buds opening to double, white, fragrant flowers all summer. 6 ft (2 m).

Rosa cantabrigiensis Single, soft yellow flowers in May and June. 8 ft (2·5 m).

Rosa gallica versicolor Semi-double, red flowers freely striped with white. June flowering. 3 ft (1 m).

Rosa moyesii Geranium (Shrub)

Rosa moyesii Geranium Single, crimson flowers in June. Blue-grey leaves tinged with shaped, scarlet heps. 8 ft (2·5 m).

Rosa rubrifolia Small, single, rose-pink flowers in June. Blue-grey leaves tinged with pink and purple. 7 ft (2·25 m).

Scarlet Fire Large, single, bright scarlet flowers in June and July. 7 ft (2·25 m).

Wilhelm Double, light crimson flowers in large clusters all the summer. 6 ft (2 m).

Hardy Herbaceous Perennials

Hardy herbaceous perennials are semi-permanent occupants of the garden but few of them will remain in one place for anything like so long as trees or shrubs. Many of them spread quite quickly, forming clumps of ever increasing size, and in doing so they tend to starve themselves out. To counteract this they must be lifted and replanted every few years and each time this is done the clumps are split up into numerous pieces, the older parts in the centre of the clump being discarded, the younger outside portions being replanted or given away to friends. This periodic replanting gives the opportunity for rearrangement or even complete remodelling of those parts of the garden mainly or entirely devoted to hardy herbaceous perennials.

Since they grow quickly, most will make their maximum effect in the second year after planting and many will give a very good account of themselves the first year. They are, therefore, much quicker in making a display than trees and shrubs.

Partly for this reason, and partly for economy of space in the rather small gardens which are common today, hardy herbaceous perennials are often combined with shrubs, the latter providing a more permanent background to the changing pattern of the herbaceous plants in front or between. For even further variety and to maintain continuity of colour, annuals and bedding plants may be introduced as well.

A traditional herbaceous border

The traditional way of using herbaceous perennials is in a border confined to them and therefore called an herbaceous border. In this the plants are grouped, several of a kind together, to produce a bold patchwork of colour, irregular yet balanced. For the best effect a fairly wide border is needed, 8 ft (2·5 m) at least and preferably 10 or 12 ft (3 or 4 m). In narrower borders many of the larger plants must be planted singly and the effect will almost inevitably be more confused.

An alternative to the herbaceous border is the island bed or beds. These beds may be of any shape and size, separated, as a

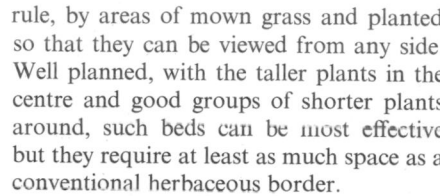

Herbaceous perennials can be divided with two garden forks used back to back.

As the foliage dies back in the autumn, herbaceous plants can be cut hard back.

Fertilizer is best applied in spring

rule, by areas of mown grass and planted so that they can be viewed from any side. Well planned, with the taller plants in the centre and good groups of shorter plants around, such beds can be most effective but they require at least as much space as a conventional herbaceous border.

Methods of propagation Many herbaceous perennials can be readily raised from seed sown in February or March under glass, or in April or May outdoors. As a rule the seedlings will not bloom until their second year, and in the case of some kinds, such as delphiniums, lupins and phlox, which have been highly developed in gardens, the seedlings may vary considerably, especially in flower colour, from their parents.

For this reason selected varieties are usually increased by division of the roots at planting time, or by cuttings. Either way, every characteristic of the parent will be preserved. As a rule divisions will flower in their first year but cuttings may take longer.

Planting and Aftercare

With care herbaceous plants may be transplanted at almost any time of the year but the safest period is early spring and the next best is early autumn and so these are the two seasons when nurserymen do most of their despatching. Bearded or flag irises, however, may be despatched in mid-summer as they are then making roots and transplant well.

The taller herbaceous plants usually need some support as they grow. Canes and encircling ties can be used, or special plant supports, but one simple, cheap and effective method is to use twiggy branches, such as those sold for pea supports. Cut these to the required length, a few inches below the full height of the plant, and push two or three of them into the ground around each plant in spring while growth is still short. Then, as growth continues, the shoots will find their own support between the twigs, at the same time screening them from view.

Hardy herbaceous plants suffer from few pests and diseases and require a minimum of care. For the sake of tidiness, faded flowers or flower spikes should be cut off and in the autumn all growth, except of evergreen plants such as kniphofias and irises, can be cut off an inch or so above ground level, leaving the border clear for a thorough cleaning, best done by pricking the surface lightly with a fork.

Many herbaceous plants are so sturdy that they will grow in any reasonable soil without feeding, but for best results some feeding is desirable. Rotted animal manure, garden compost or peat can be spread thinly between the plants in early spring and then, a few weeks later, the soil can be dusted with any good general garden fertilizer. Further topdressings of fertilizer can be given to special plants at intervals of a few weeks during the spring and summer.

Roses in a traditional setting

Recommended Herbaceous Perennials

Acanthus (Bear's breeches) Handsome plants with big thistle-like leaves and stiff spikes of dull purple and white flowers in late summer. They are very easy to grow in almost any soil and a sunny or partially shady place. Roots spread outwards throwing up new shoots as they go, so that it is the easiest thing in the world to increase these plants simply by digging up any outlying piece with roots attached. It may, in any case, be necessary to do this to prevent the plants from spreading too far.

The two best kinds are *Acanthus mollis*, with broadly-lobed leaves, and *A. spinosus*, with more deeply and sharply divided leaves. Both are about 4 ft (1·25 m) tall.

Achillea (Yarrow, milfoil) One of the commonest milfoils is a troublesome lawn weed but it has produced better varieties with carmine instead of white flowers. One of the best is *Achillea millefolium* Cerise Queen which has ferny leaves, bright carmine flowers in early summer and grows 18 in (45 cm) high.

Quite different in appearance is *A. ptarmica* which grows 3 ft (1 m) high and has white flowers in small clusters all summer. A very good variety of this, named The Pearl, has double instead of single flowers. The most handsome kind is *A. filipendulina* which has flat heads of yellow flowers on 4-ft (1·25-m) stems from mid-summer. An especially good form of this is named Gold Plate. Two other kinds, *A. clypeolata* and *A. taygetea*, resemble the last but on a smaller scale and with the added attraction of silvery foliage. There are also hybrids with flat heads of flowers. Coronation Gold is yellow, 2½ ft (75 cm) high and flowers non-stop all summer; Moonshine is sulphur yellow in early summer and has grey leaves.

Most of these achilleas are very hardy and almost indestructible plants for any soil and place, but the grey-leaved kinds are a little more fussy and prefer a well-drained soil and sunny place. All can be increased by division in spring or autumn.

Aconitum (Monkshood) The popular name monkshood was given to aconitum because the flowers look a little like the hoods or cowls worn by monks. These flowers are borne in long narrow spikes and are mostly blue or purple but one species, *Aconitum lycoctonum*, is pale yellow. One of the best kinds for the garden is *A. napellus* Spark's Variety with deep purple flowers on 3-ft (1-m) stems in mid-summer; another is *A. bicolor*, of similar height and with blue and white flowers. Bressingham Spire has particularly well-filled flower spikes, violet-blue in colour. *A. fischeri* flowers in autumn, is light blue and 3 ft (1 m) high.

All will grow well in any reasonably good soil and sunny or partially shaded position. All can be divided in spring or autumn.

Heleniums (red) and Solidago (yellow)

Acanthus spinosus

Achillea **Coronation Gold**

Alchemilla mollis and Hosta sieboldiana

African lily, see Agapanthus

Agapanthus (African lily) These showy plants are not really lilies nor do they make bulbs like true lilies, but they do make mats of fleshy white roots which dig deeply into the soil and enable the plants to survive even in quite dry places. But to see African lilies at their best they should be grown in good, fertile, well-drained soil and a warm sunny place; then they will produce fine clumps of their rather fleshy, strap-shaped leaves and good heads of blue, mauve or white flowers in summer. The largest heads on 3-ft (1-m) stems are produced by *Agapanthus africanus*, but it is not very hardy and in many places is best grown in pots or tubs and removed to a greenhouse or sun room in winter. *A. campanulatus* and the Headbourne Hybrids derived from it are much hardier and are available, in height, from 1 to 3 ft (30 cm to 1 m) and in colour from white and light blue to deep violet blue. All can be increased by seed or division in spring but plants should not be disturbed frequently.

Ajuga (Bugle) These are mat-forming plants which can be used in beds and borders, to carpet the ground beneath shrubs, or in the rock garden, though there they must be placed with care, lest by their rapid spread they smother less vigorous plants. The kind commonly grown is *Ajuga reptans* which is quite prostrate and, in late spring, carries 6-in (15-cm) spikes of blue flowers. In the common form the leaves are green, but in the variety *multicolor* they are bronze, yellow and red, and in *variegata* green and cream.

All will grow readily in almost any soil and place and can be easily increased by division at practically any time of year.

Alchemilla (Lady's mantle) *Alchemilla mollis* is a foot-high plant grown primarily for its soft grey-green leaves which make a pleasant foil for the bright colours of more showy plants. The small yellow flowers are produced in loose sprays in early summer.

It will grow in any reasonable soil and open or partially shaded place, and is readily increased by division in spring.

Alkanet, see Anchusa

Alstroemeria (Peruvian lily) These plants are not true lilies, nor do they form bulbs, like lilies, but make mats of rather fleshy roots. These need to be planted about 5 in (13 cm) deep in good, well-drained soils and warm, sunny places. They may not produce a great deal of growth the first year but once established can spread rapidly. The easiest and hardiest is *Alstroemeria aurantiaca* with loose heads of bright orange flowers on slender 3-ft (1-m) stems in mid-summer. The Ligtu Hybrids have a much wider colour range, including many delicate shades of pink, salmon and apricot as well as flame.

All can be grown from roots planted in spring and also from seed sown in a greenhouse or frame in spring but it is sometimes difficult to transplant seedlings of the Ligtu Hybrids safely. The best method is to sow two or three seeds in a 3-in (8-cm) pot and allow the seedlings to remain in this for a year, then plant the whole potful undisturbed.

Anaphalis (Pearly everlasting) Attractive grey-leaved plants for the front of the border. One, *Anaphalis margaritacea*, is called pearly everlasting because of its clusters of small, silvery flowers which can be dried for winter use. The plant grows a foot (30 cm) or slightly more in height. *A. triplinervis* has larger leaves and makes a low, spreading plant about 8 in (20 cm) high.

Both like sunny places and well-drained soils and can be increased by careful division in spring.

Anchusa (Alkanet) Imagine a forget-me-not 4 ft (1·25 m) high with flowers to scale and you have some idea of what *Anchusa italica*, the best kind, looks like. There are several garden varieties of it but all have blue flowers and they differ principally in the precise shade of blue. All flower in early summer. The plant commonly called *A. caespitosa* is really *A. angustissima*; it resembles *A. italica* on a much smaller scale, being only about 15 in (38 cm) high, and it flowers from late spring to mid-summer.

Both plants like well-drained soils and open, sunny positions and neither is very long lived. They can be raised from seed, but selected forms of *A. italica* are usually grown from root cuttings inserted in sandy soil in winter or early spring and started into growth in a frame or greenhouse.

Anemone (Windflower) There are a great number of anemones but the only one that is commonly grown as an herbaceous plant is the Japanese anemone, *Anemone japonica* of catalogues though more accurately it should be called *A. hupehensis*. This is a fine plant with white, pink or rose flowers on 3- to 4-ft (1- to 1·25-m) stems in autumn. It is very hardy and capable of growing in most soils and sunny or shady places but it is often a slow starter and so it is one of the few herbaceous plants which should be left undisturbed for as long as possible. Give it plenty of room and it will gradually creep about, forming an ever-enlarging carpet of its three-parted leaves from which the thin but stiff flower stems are thrown up in late summer. It is increased by division in spring or autumn.

Anthemis (Golden marguerite) There are several different kinds of anthemis but the most popular and best for the garden is *A. tinctoria*, a very bushy plant with grey ferny leaves and yellow daisy flowers. It grows 2 or 3 ft (60 cm to 1 m) high and flowers most of the summer. There are several varieties differing in size and shade. E. C. Buxton's Variety is the palest, a sulphur yellow; Beauty of Grallagh, the biggest and deepest yellow, and the most popular and probably best garden variety is Grallagh Gold, which is bright yellow. Very different from these is *A. cupaniana*, a sprawling plant with finely divided grey leaves and white daisy-type flowers, like marguerites, which are freely produced in late spring and early summer.

All like sunny places and well-drained soils and can be increased by cuttings in early summer.

Anthericum (St Bernard's lily) The full name of this plant is *Anthericum liliago*. It is not really a lily nor does it look much like one for it makes tufts of grassy leaves among which grow, in early summer, slender, foot-high stems bearing starry white flowers. It is not fussy about soil but it likes an open, sunny situation. It is easily increased by division in spring or summer.

Aquilegia (Columbine) Exquisitely graceful flowers, often with long, nectar-filled spurs which add to their charm. Aquilegias are hardy perennials but not, as a rule, long lived, though they usually leave plenty of self-sown seedlings around as replacement. Colours are varied and usually delicate, though there are also quite strong blues and reds. As a rule mixed colour strains are sold, two of the best being Mrs Scott-Elliott's Hybrids and McKana Hybrids. Both are about 2½ ft (75 cm) high but there are also shorter kinds. They flower in late spring and early summer.

All will grow in any reasonably well-drained soil and sunny or partially shady position. They are readily raised from seed sown outdoors in spring or as soon as ripe in summer.

Armeria (Thrift) Most of the thrifts are plants for the rock garden but the variety known as Bees' Ruby is a useful plant for the front of an herbaceous border. It makes a tuft of narrow leaves and the almost globular heads of carmine flowers are carried on 18-in (45-cm) stems in late spring and early summer. It likes well-drained soils and sunny places and is increased by division in spring or autumn.

Artemisia There are a great many artemisias and their names are rather confused. Many are not very attractive but the best are very beautiful foliage plants. Many have grey or silver leaves and in some kinds the leaves are divided into lace-like patterns. One of the finest of these is *Artemisia schmidtiana*, a 2-ft (60-cm) high plant with silver leaves. *A. ludoviciana* has undivided silver leaves and grows 2 to 3 ft (60 cm to 1 m) high. It spreads rapidly and is one of the most reliable silver-leaved plants for the border.

Very different from these, and much taller, is *A. lactiflora* which produces large and elegant sprays of small creamy-white flowers in late summer, has green divided leaves and grows 5 ft (1·5 m) tall.

Most artemisias like open sunny places and the grey- or silver-leaved kinds prefer light, well-drained soils. *A. lactiflora* will grow happily in almost any soil and in semi-shade. Most can be increased by division.

Anemone hupehensis

Aruncus sylvester

Aruncus (Goat's beard) *Aruncus sylvester* is a vigorous plant with great plumes of tiny creamy-white flowers, like those of an astilbe, in early summer. It grows to 6 ft (2 m) tall and will thrive in almost any soil in sun or shade. It is a particularly good plant for damp places. Increase is by seed, which is often self sown, or by division in spring or autumn.

Aster (Michaelmas daisy) The China aster is an annual plant, correctly known as *Callistephus chinensis*, but there are many other kinds of true asters which are hardy herbaceous perennials. Most familiar of these are the Michaelmas daisies, which are varieties of either *Aster novi-belgii*, which has smooth shiny leaves, or *A. novae-angliae*, which has downy leaves. There are a great number of garden varieties of the first of these species, varying in height from under a foot (30 cm) to as much as 6 ft (2 m), and in colour all the way from white, pale lavender and silvery-pink to deep violet and crimson. Some have single flowers, some more or less double flowers and all bloom in autumn.

Then there are the numerous varieties of *A. amellus*, all about 2 ft (60 cm) high and very bushy, with larger, single flowers in late summer. *A. frikartii* is of this type, though it is not a simple variety of *A. amellus* but a hybrid between it and *A. thomsonii*. It makes a 3 ft (1 m) bush producing light blue flowers with great profusion in late summer.

All these perennial asters are easily grown in almost any soil and fairly open situation but the varieties of *A. amellus* do not transplant quite so easily as other kinds and are best moved in spring. The very vigorous Michaelmas daisies should be lifted and divided annually for best results as they spread so rapidly that they tend to starve themselves out. Division is the best method of increasing all kinds.

Varieties of *Aster novi-belgii* are sometimes severely attacked by a mite which cripples growth and deforms the flowers. It can be killed by spraying occasionally in late spring and summer with dicofol.

Astilbe These graceful plants are sometimes called spiraea, a name which correctly belongs to related shrubby plants. The astilbes, by contrast, are all true herbaceous perennials, dying down to ground level each winter and throwing up a fresh lot of ferny leaves in spring, followed in summer by the feathery plumes of white, pink or crimson flowers. Most are 2 to 3 ft (60 cm to 1 m) high, but the white or pink flowered *Astilbe simplicifolia* is no more than 1 ft (30 cm). It is also a little later in flowering.

Astilbes like damp soil and are often grown at the waterside though they can also be planted in ordinary beds or borders provided these are not too dry. They can be increased by division in spring or autumn.

Balloon flower, see Platycodon

Barrenwort, see Epimedium

Bear's breeches, see Acanthus

Bellflower, see Campanula

Bergenia (Large-leaved saxifrage) Sometimes these handsome plants are called saxifraga, sometimes megasea, but bergenia is correct. They are grown for their large, fleshy, semi-evergreen leaves and clusters of pink, rose or crimson flowers produced in early spring on short stout stems. In some kinds, such as *Bergenia purpurascens* or Ballawley, the leaves turn crimson in the autumn.

They are excellent front-line plants which will grow in almost any soil and sunny or shady place. They can be increased by division in spring or autumn.

Bistort, see Polygonum

Bleeding heart, see Dicentra

Bocconia, see Macleaya

Bugle, see Ajuga

Buphthalmum Easily grown and very hardy plants with yellow daisy flowers in summer. One of the best, *Buphthalmum salicifolium*, is particularly useful because it is only 18 in (45 cm) high, needs no staking, and flowers all the summer. It will grow in any reasonable soil, in sun or partial shade, and is readily increased by division in spring or autumn.

Burning bush, see Dictamnus

Campanula (Bellflower) There are a great many kinds of campanula, some being rock plants, some biennials for bedding, some greenhouse plants and some hardy herbaceous plants. Of these last, the three best are *Campanula persicifolia*, *C. lactiflora* and *C. glomerata*.

Campanula persicifolia carries its broadly bell-shaped flowers up long slender stems in early summer. There are single- and double-flowered forms and white and blue varieties of each. The average height is 2½ ft (75 cm).

Campanula lactiflora is taller, 4 to 5 ft (1·25 to 1·5 m), with smaller flowers in loose sprays all summer. Normally light blue, there is also a lilac-pink variety named Loddon Anna and one named Pouffe, which is quite different in habit, making a compact mound about 9 in (23 cm) high covered with light blue flowers.

Campanula glomerata carries its purple flowers in a close cluster at the tops of 18-in (45-cm) stems in early summer. A fine, deep-coloured variety of this is named *dahurica*.

All are very easily grown in any reasonable soil and sunny or partially shady position and all can be increased by division in spring or autumn.

Cape fuchsia, see Phygelius

Cape gooseberry, see Physalis

Catananche (Cupid's dart) *Catananche caerulea* is a pretty little blue-flowered plant rather like a dwarf cornflower. It is quite hardy and can be grown in any sunny place provided the soil is reasonably well drained. The flowers, on 2-ft (60-cm) stems, are produced most of the summer. The best variety is *major* and there is also one named Perry's White, with white flowers. Increase is by division in spring.

Catmint, see Nepeta

Centaurea (Cornflower) The common blue cornflower is a centaurea but is an annual and so is described under that heading. Other kinds of centaurea are hardy perennials, one of the commonest in gardens being *Centaurea montana* with grey leaves and blue cornflowers on 18-in (45-cm) stems in late spring. *C. dealbata* has silvery leaves and pink flowers on 2-ft (60-cm) stems all summer; *C. macrocephala* has yellow flowers in early summer and is 4 ft (1·25 m) high, as is *C. ruthenica*, a more slender plant with lemon flowers also in early summer.

All are easily grown in almost any soil

and sunny place; indeed *C. montana* often spreads so quickly as to become rather a nuisance. They can all be increased by division in spring or autumn.

Centranthus (Red valerian) Although *Centranthus ruber* can be found growing wild on cliffs and walls in many parts of the country it is well worth cultivating in the garden for the beauty of its clusters of small red, pink or white flowers, freely produced on 2-ft (60-cm) stems in early summer, even in the hottest, driest places. It makes an excellent companion for the blue catmint (*Nepeta faassenii*) and thrives in similar sunny places and well-drained soils. It produces seed freely and usually self-sown seedlings appear in great number but may vary in the colour of their flowers. Especially good varieties are therefore best increased by careful division in the spring or by cuttings in spring or early summer.

Chinese lantern, see Physalis

Christmas rose, see Helleborus

Chrysanthemum (Shasta daisy, moon daisy) The plants that are commonly thought of as chrysanthemums are not, on the whole, very hardy, and many varieties are exclusively grown for flowering under glass. However, there are also varieties which are more suitable for growing outdoors, either because they flower in summer or early autumn, before there is risk of serious frost to damage their flowers, or because they are tougher and more frost resistant. This last group includes the Korean chrysanthemums and varieties bred from *Chrysanthemum rubellum*. These flower from mid-summer to mid-autumn, have a wide colour range from white, lemon and pale pink to coppery orange and crimson, and spread rapidly into bushy plants 2 to 3 ft (60 cm to 1 m) high. Some have single flowers, some double, and all grow freely in any reasonably good and well-drained soil and a sunny position. They are often grown, like other chrysanthemums, from cuttings taken in late winter or early spring and rooted in a greenhouse or frame, but they are even more easily increased by splitting up the roots in spring, like those of any other herbaceous plant.

This can also be done with the larger-flowered varieties of early-flowering chrysanthemum, which resemble the greenhouse chrysanthemums in almost everything but their time of flowering; but it is not so successful. Better plants, producing flowers of superior quality, are obtained by taking cuttings which are treated just like those of the greenhouse chrysanthemums, except that the plants are hardened off for planting outdoors in mid- to late spring in good soil and a sunny place. Usually the growing tips of the plants are pinched out a week or so after planting to encourage early

Chrysanthemum maximum Thomas Killin

branching; and later on, if large flowers are desired, only one flower bud is retained on each stem, all others being removed at an early stage of development. Flowering is in late summer and early autumn.

In mild places and well-drained soils the early-flowering chrysanthemums will survive the winter outdoors, but in colder districts they are lifted in autumn, the top growth cut off and the roots placed close together in boxes with a little soil, to be over-wintered in a frame or greenhouse. It is from these 'stools', as they are called, that cuttings are taken in the spring.

In addition to these florist's chrysanthemums, there are several other kinds of chrysanthemum which are genuinely hardy herbaceous perennials to be grown along with other plants of this class. Most important of these are the varieties of *C. maximum*, the Shasta daisy. These are the big white daisies, also called moon daisies, that bloom in midsummer and are so useful for cutting as well as for garden display. Some have single flowers, some semi-double or fully double flowers, and although all are hardy, some of the double-flowered varieties, such as Esther Read and Horace Read, are not so robust as the singles and do not relish a cold, wet soil in winter. The singles, by contrast, will grow practically anywhere and seem almost indestructible. All like sunny places, though they will survive in shade, and all can be increased by division in spring, the single-flowered kinds also by seed though seedlings may vary in quality.

Clary, see Salvia

Clematis In addition to the well-known climbing clematis there are a few, far less

familiar, hardy herbaceous kinds, so very different in appearance from the climbers that the gardener might well wonder where the connection lay. One of the best is *Clematis heracleifolia*, 3 ft (1 m) high with clusters of little, pale blue, tubular flowers in late summer and autumn. A variety of this named *davidiana* has sweetly scented flowers and so has the taller, white-flowered *C. recta*.

All will grow in any reasonable soil and open position and can be increased by division or cuttings in spring.

Columbine, see Aquilegia

Coneflower, see Rudbeckia

Convallaria (Lily of the valley) These sweetly scented spring flowers are grown from fleshy rhizomes or crowns which are best planted in autumn. Space them about 4 in (10 cm) apart and just cover them with soil, preferably in a shady or semi-shady place, though lily of the valley will grow in full sunshine provided the soil is moist.

It does best in fairly rich soil with plenty of leaf mould or peat. In addition to the familiar white kind there is a variety with rather washy pink bells. Lily of the valley is increased by division in spring.

Coral bells, see Heuchera

Coreopsis Some kinds of coreopsis are annuals but there are also a few perennials of which one of the hardiest is *Coreopsis verticillata*. This has very narrow leaves on thin, branching stems, grows about 2 ft (60 cm) high and covers itself with small yellow flowers throughout the summer. It is a very pretty plant for the front of a bed or border. *C. grandiflora* has much larger flowers, also yellow, produced continuously all summer and in early autumn, but it is apt to flower itself to exhaustion and is seldom a long-lived plant. There are superior varieties of it with even larger flowers and one, named Sunburst, which produces some double flowers. *C. auriculata* is similar to *C. grandiflora* but there is a deep crimson blotch at the base of each petal.

All like sunny places and well-drained soils. They can be increased by division in spring.

Cornflower, see Centaurea

Cortaderia (Pampas grass) This is one of the most handsome of all grasses, up to 8 ft (2·5 m) tall in some varieties, though there are also shorter kinds. *Cortaderia argentea* is the best for general planting and its silvery plumes are a familiar sight in late summer or early autumn. It is quite hardy in all well-drained soils but thrives best in warm, sunny places. It should only be transplanted in spring when it can be divided.

Cranesbill, see Geranium

Crocosmia *Crocosmia masonorum* is a very showy plant, much like a large montbretia. It grows 3 ft (1 m) high, has sword-shaped leaves and arching sprays of orange-red flowers in late summer. It is not very hardy, needs a warm, sunny, sheltered place and well-drained soil. In cold districts it can be lifted in autumn and over-wintered in a frame. Increase is by division in spring.

Cupid's dart, see Catananche

Day lily, see Hemerocallis

Dead nettle, see Lamium

Delphinium There are two main types of delphinium for the herbaceous border or bed, those that produce their flowers in long spikes, known as the elatum varieties, and those that have branching sprays of flowers, known as the belladonna varieties. The former make the boldest display and have been most highly developed by plant breeders. They make magnificent plants for the middle or back of the border. Belladonna delphiniums are shorter and more graceful and may be used to break up the heavier masses of bloom in the garden and for cutting.

The elatum varieties range in height from 3 to 7 ft (1 to 2·25 m) and in colour from white and palest mauve through all shades of blue to intense purple. There are also varieties with pink or lilac flowers. Most of the popular kinds have semi-double flowers but there are also single delphiniums and a few that are fully double.

The colour range in the belladonna type is similar but there are not nearly so many varieties and most have single flowers,

though there are also some semi-doubles.

All these delphiniums flower in early summer and sometimes give a second display in late summer or early autumn. They like fairly rich but well-drained soils and open sunny positions and are seldom long lived. Every two or three years they should be renewed from seed or cuttings. Seed is best sown as soon as it is ripe in late summer, in a frame or greenhouse, but alternatively it can be sown in spring. The seedlings are pricked off into boxes and later potted singly to be grown on into sturdy plants which can go outside in spring or early summer. Seedlings usually flower late the first summer and often differ considerably in colour, flower shape and height from their parents.

Cuttings are prepared from young shoots in spring, severed low down where they are firm and solid (larger shoots tend to be hollow) and are inserted in sandy soil in a frame. By early summer they should be well rooted and ready for planting out. Plants grown from cuttings will resemble their parents in every respect.

Another way of increasing delphiniums is by splitting up the old plants in spring, but plants grown in this way are seldom so healthy and vigorous as those grown from seed or cuttings.

Dianthus (Pink) Many kinds of dianthus are such small creeping or tufted plants that their proper place is the rock garden, but the garden pinks or varieties of *Dianthus*

Echinops sphaerocephalus

plumarius, and their near allies, the numerous varieties of *D. allwoodii*, are plants for the front of a bed or border or for any other place where free-flowering plants up to 18 in (45 cm) high are appropriate. The old-fashioned pinks, such as the popular white-flowered Mrs Sinkins and pink Inchmery, both deliciously fragrant, flower in early summer but some modern pinks and all the varieties of *D. allwoodii* have a longer flowering season extending throughout the summer and even into the autumn.

All like open, sunny places and the true pinks are not at all fussy about soil, though they do particularly well on chalk or limestone. Some varieties of *D. allwoodii* are less tolerant and must have really well-drained soils if they are to prove reasonably permanent. All are increased by cuttings taken around mid-summer and some varieties can be carefully divided in spring, but with others it is difficult to get divisions with roots attached.

Dicentra (Bleeding heart) These are very elegant plants with fern-like leaves and erect or arching sprays of pendant flowers in early summer. *Dicentra spectabilis* grows 2 to 3 ft (60 cm to 1 m) high and has pink and white heart-shaped flowers. *D. eximia* is shorter, about 18 in (45 cm) high, with smaller pink flowers. Yet another kind, *D. formosa*, is 15 in (38 cm) high and has rose-pink flowers. All flower in spring and early summer. They will thrive in sun or partial shade in any reasonably well-drained soil and can be increased by division in spring or autumn.

Dictamnus (Burning bush) *Dictamnus albus* is an unusual and handsome plant about 3 ft (1 m) high with spikes of purple or white flowers in early summer. It gets its popular name from the fact that it produces, in warm weather, small quantities of an inflammable gas that will sometimes burn briefly with a blue flame if a match is held to the plant.

It will grow in sun or partial shade in almost any soil and can be increased either by seed sown in spring or by division in spring or autumn.

Dierama (Wand flower) Although *Dierama pulcherrimum* makes corms it is usually treated as an herbaceous perennial, growing plants being transplanted in spring. It is a very graceful plant with grassy leaves and long, slender, arching stems bearing pendant pink, rose, purple or white flowers in late summer. It likes good, well-drained soils and warm, sunny places, and can be raised from seed sown in spring or by careful division also in spring, but it does not really like being disturbed.

Doronicum (Leopard's bane) These are among the earliest flowering of hardy herbaceous plants producing their big yellow daisies in spring. *Doronicum plantagineum excelsum* is 3 ft (1 m) high, *D. caucasicum*, 1 to 1½ ft (30 to 45 cm) and *D. cordatum*, 6 in (15 cm). There is a double-flowered variety of *D. caucasicum* called Spring Beauty.

All are easy to grow in almost any soil and in sun or partial shade. They can be increased by division after flowering or in the autumn.

Dropwort, see Filipendula

Echinacea (Purple coneflower) Handsome plants with large, reddish-purple daisy flowers each with a dark, almost black central disc which adds to their striking appearance. The only kind grown is *Echinacea purpurea*, but it has several garden varieties, one not often seen, with white flowers, another, named The King, with extra large flowers of a particularly fine shade of purple. All are about 4 ft (1·25 m) high and flower in late summer.

They will grow in almost any reasonably well-drained soil and fairly open, sunny place and can be increased by division in spring or autumn.

Echinops (Globe thistle) Striking and easily grown plants with small blue or white flowers crowded into spherical heads. The seed heads are also globular and have a spiky appearance which makes them almost

as attractive as the flowers. Good kinds are *Echinops humilis*, 4 ft (1·25 m) high with good blue flowers; *E. humilis nivalis*, white, and *E. sphaerocephalus* (often listed as *E. ritro*) blue, 4 ft (1·25 m). All flower from mid-summer for several weeks.

Echinops like well-drained soils and sunny places but can be grown almost anywhere as they are very robust plants. They are readily raised from seed sown in spring, from root cuttings in winter or early spring, or by careful division of the roots in spring or autumn.

Epimedium (Barrenwort) These low-growing plants are valued as much for their foliage, which becomes coppery in autumn, as for their loose sprays of white, pale yellow or reddish flowers in spring. *Epimedium sulphureum* is light yellow; *E. alpinum* is red and yellow; *E. grandiflorum niveum* is white. All are 9 to 12 in (23 to 30 cm) high and spread considerably, forming a dense, weed-smothering ground cover. Their appearance is much improved if they are cut with shears to within an inch or so of the ground in early spring. They thrive in shady places but will also grow in the sun. They are not fussy about soil and are increased by division in spring or autumn.

Eremurus (Fox-tail lily) These remarkable and very handsome plants have strap-shaped leaves and long stiff spikes of flowers in early summer. The tallest kind, *Eremurus robustus*, may reach 7 to 10 ft (2·25 to 3 m) and is pale pink. By contrast, *E. himalaicus* has white flowers and is 3 to 5 ft (1 to 1·5 m) high, and *E. bungei* is maize yellow and 2 to 3 ft (60 cm to 1 m) high. There are also garden hybrids, 3 to 5 ft (1 to 1·5 m) high, in various shades of pink, maize, apricot and orange. All have fleshy roots radiating like spokes from a central crown.

They like good, well-drained soil and a sunny place and should be planted in early autumn, 4 in (10 cm) deep with their roots spread out fully. Once established they should be left to grow undisturbed for as long as possible. As they are just a little tender, it is wise, in cold places, to cover the roots with bracken or sand in winter, removing this in the spring.

Seed sown in the spring may germinate rather slowly and seedlings are unlikely to flower for several years. Alternatively, plants can be carefully divided in early autumn.

Erigeron (Fleabane) Easily grown plants with blue, pink or soft orange daisy flowers very like those of Michaelmas daisies but coming earlier in summer. Plants are usually about 2 ft (60 cm) high but there are shorter varieties, especially in the orange shades of which the aurantiaca hybrids, about 1 ft (30 cm) high, are typical. Other good kinds are Charity, pink; Dignity,

mauve; Quakeress, lavender; Darkest of All, violet-blue, and Foerster's Liebling, cerise.

Most are very easily grown in almost any soil and reasonably open position but the orange shades are more difficult and are often short lived. They should be given particularly well-drained, sunny positions. Most can be increased by division in spring or autumn, but the orange shades are best divided in spring only.

Eryngium (Sea holly) Very distinctive plants with stiff, spiny, blue-grey leaves and teasel-like heads, usually blue or violet, though in one kind, *Eryngium giganteum*, they are bone-white. This last, however, is not a good perennial and must be renewed from seed annually, the seedlings flowering in their second year and usually dying thereafter. One of the easiest to grow is *E. planum*, with thimble-size heads of blue flowers in large branching sprays about 4 ft (1·25 m) high. *E. tripartitum* is similar. *E. alpinum* has large blue heads surrounded by steel-blue, finely divided bracts which are very decorative. It is 3 ft (1 m) high. All flower around mid-summer and remain decorative for many weeks; in fact the flowers can be cut and dried for winter use.

They like light, well-drained soils and sunny places and can be increased by seed in spring or by root cuttings in winter or spring.

Euphorbia (Spurge) Most of the spurges have greenish-yellow flowers and so they are not particularly showy, but they make a pleasant foil to the brighter colours of other plants. One of the best is *Euphorbia polychroma*, also known as *E. epithymoides*, an easily grown plant 18 in (45 cm) high with heads of lemon-yellow flowers in spring *E. griffithii* is brighter than most with reddish-orange flowers on leafy 2-ft (60-cm) stems in summer. *E. wulfenii* is almost a shrub, 4 ft (1·25 m) high and as much or more in diameter, with big heads of yellowish-green flowers in spring. All like sunny places, but are not fussy about soil. Division is possible in spring.

Evening primrose, see Oenothera

Everlasting pea, see Lathyrus

False dragonhead, see Physostegia

Filipendula (Dropwort) These plants used to be called spiraea and still are in many catalogues. Most of them are moisture lovers like the closely allied astilbes which they resemble, but one, *Filipendula vulgaris* (or *Spiraea hexapetala*), the Dropwort, grows well in dry places. It makes large rosettes of narrow ferny leaves and has clusters of small creamy white flowers in summer which are converted into tiny balls in the variety *flore pleno*, the best

Eryngium alpinum

form to plant. Other kinds are, however, considerably more beautiful, especially *F. purpurea* (or *Spiraea palmata*) with plumy sprays of crimson flowers on 4-ft (1·25-m) stems in summer, and *F. rubra magnifica* (or *Spiraea magnifica*) with pale pink flowers on 6-ft (2-m) stems.

These are plants for the waterside or for very moist places in sun or light shade. All can be increased by division in spring.

Fleabane, see Erigeron

Fox-tail lily, see Eremurus

Gaillardia Plants with large, very showy flowers of the daisy type, usually scarlet and yellow but in some varieties all yellow, all red, or tangerine. They are 2 to 3 ft (60 cm to 1 m) high but the stems are rather thin and inclined to be weighed down by the large flowers so that some extra support is desirable. This can be given by pushing short twiggy branches into the soil around the plants in spring and letting them grow up through these. They are excellent flowers for cutting.

All like sunny places and well-drained soils. They can be raised from seed sown in a frame or greenhouse in spring but seedlings may show considerable colour variations, so selected garden varieties are usually increased either by careful division in the spring or by root cuttings in winter or early spring.

Galega (Goat's rue) Rather rampant plants worth growing for the freedom with which they flower most of the summer. All make big bushy plants 4 or 5 ft (1·25 to 1·5 m) high and produce little clusters of pea-type flowers which are mauve in *Galega officinalis*, pale blue in its variety *hartlandii*, and pinkish-lilac in Lady Wilson.

All will grow in almost any soil and place, and can be very easily increased by division in spring or autumn.

Geranium (Cranesbill) These plants are quite different from the brilliant scarlet or pink 'geraniums' which are used for display outdoors and are removed to a greenhouse in winter. These bedding geraniums are not, in fact, true geraniums at all, but pelargoniums, a related genus. The true geraniums are hardy plants mostly with blue, purple or crimson flowers. *Geranium* Johnson's Blue with blue flowers is one of the best for the border. It grows 18 in (45 cm) high and flowers in summer. So does *G. pratense* which has a very attractive variety named *flore pleno*, with double lavender-blue flowers. *G. endressii*, 18 in (45 cm) high, has pink flowers all summer. *G. phaeum*, 2 ft (60 cm) high, is called mourning widow because of its almost black flowers; *G. armenum*, similar in height, is vivid magenta, and *G. macrorrhizum* makes wide, low mounds of scented leaves which make excellent ground cover, and has small pink flowers in late spring. There are numerous other kinds.

All grow readily in any reasonable soil

and like an open, sunny place. *G. pratense* is particularly good on chalk. All can be increased by division in spring or autumn.

German catchfly, see Lychnis

Geum Easily grown plants with an exceptionally long flowering season. The border geums are mostly varieties of *Geum chiloense* which has bright scarlet flowers on 2-ft (60-cm) stems all summer. Garden varieties of this differ in having larger, semi-double flowers, scarlet in Mrs Bradshaw, yellow in Lady Stratheden, and coppery orange in Fire Opal. *G. borisii* is a smaller hybrid, 1 ft (30 cm) high with single orange-red flowers.

All like well-drained soils and warm, sunny positions. They can be raised from seed sown in a frame or greenhouse in spring and some strains of seed give remarkably uniform seedlings. Nevertheless, to keep selected garden varieties absolutely true to type they must be increased by division, best done in spring.

Globe flower, see Trollius

Globe thistle, see Echinops

Goat's beard, see Aruncus

Goat's rue, see Galega

Golden drops, see Oenothera

Golden marguerite, see Anthemis

Golden rod, see Solidago

Gypsophila Some kinds of gypsophila are annuals or rock plants, but one, *Gypsophila paniculata*, is a hardy herbaceous perennial which makes a big dome-shaped plant 3 ft (1 m) high, with slender but stiff stems,

Geranium endressii

narrow grey-green leaves and clouds of tiny white flowers from mid to late summer. Some varieties have little double flowers, one of the best being Bristol Fairy. There are also pale pink varieties such as Rosy Veil, single, and Flamingo, double, but these are weaker and more sprawling in habit. All have long tap roots and should be disturbed as little as possible.

They will grow in any reasonably well-drained soil and sunny place but prefer chalky soils. The single-flowered kinds can be raised from seeds though there may be some colour variation in seedlings. Doubles are usually grafted on to roots of single-flowered seedlings though they can also be grown from summer cuttings in a frame or propagator.

Helenium These are easily grown plants with clusters of broad-petalled, daisy-type flowers very freely produced from midsummer to early autumn. The colour range is from yellow to wallflower red, often with one colour splashed on the other. Good varieties of *Helenium autumnale* are *pumilum magnificum*, yellow, 3 ft (1 m); Madame Canivet, yellow and bronze, 3 ft (1 m); Moerheim Beauty, wallflower red, 4 ft (1·25 m), and Riverton Gem, yellow splashed bronze-red, 5 ft (1·5 m). All will grow in almost any soil and reasonably open place and can be increased by division in spring or autumn.

Helianthus (Sunflower) There are annual as well as perennial sunflowers and the latter are excellent plants for the middle or back of the border. Among the best are Loddon Gold, 5 ft (1·5 m) high with large, double, golden-yellow flowers in mid to late summer; *maximus*, 4 ft (1·25 m) high with single yellow flowers in late summer, and Monarch, 7 ft (2·25 m) high with large, deep yellow, black-centred flowers in early autumn. With the exception of Monarch, which needs well-drained soil and a warm, sunny position, all are very easy to grow in almost any soil and place. They can be increased by division in spring or autumn.

Heliopsis These vigorous plants closely resemble sunflowers and have similar showy yellow flowers from mid to late summer. *Heliopsis scabra* has provided some of the best varieties such as Loddon Plume and *incomparabilis*, both with deep yellow double flowers on 3- to 4-ft stems. There are several more of similar appearance.

All are easily grown in practically any soil and an open, fairly sunny place and are increased by division in spring or autumn.

Hellebore, see Helleborus

Helleborus (Christmas rose, Lenten rose, hellebore) All the hellebores are early-flowering plants, some varieties of the Christmas rose, *Helleborus niger*, opening their white- or red-spotted, saucer-shaped

flowers in winter, and the latest of the family, the Lenten rose, *H. orientalis*, starting a month or so later and continuing in bloom right through the spring. There are many varieties of the Lenten rose, with flowers varying from white and pale pink to deep maroon, and they are a little longer stemmed than those of the Christmas rose, about 18 in (45 cm) against the 12-in (30-cm) average of *H. niger*. Even larger is the Corsican hellebore, *H. corsicus*, 3 ft (1 m) high with handsome, deeply divided leaves and large clusters of pale green flowers in late winter.

All like good soil and cool, shady places. They can be raised from seed sown in spring but it may be several years before the seedlings flower. Plants can be carefully divided after flowering but hellebores do not like disturbance and it may be a year or so before they settle down again into free and regular flowering.

Hemerocallis (Day lily) These are very easily

Helleborus corsicus

grown plants with lily-like flowers which individually last only one day but are produced freely in succession from mid-summer for several weeks. The flowers are produced in clusters on stems 2 to 3 ft (60 cm to 1 m) long and the colour range is from lemon yellow, through orange to deep mahogany crimson.

All will grow in practically any soil and sunny or partly shaded position, and can be increased by division in spring or autumn or by seed in spring, though seedlings are likely to vary in colour.

Heuchera (Coral bells) These plants, mainly derived from *Heuchera sanguinea*, make low mounds of rounded leaves from which the loose sprays of small white, pink or red flowers grow on slender stems from mid-summer onwards for several weeks. There are numerous garden varieties such as Bressingham Hybrids in mixed colours;

Kniphofia uvaria Bee's Lemon

Pluie de Feu, coral red, and Scintillation, pink, all about 2 ft (60 cm) high. *Heuchera tiarelloides*, white, is only 1 ft (30 cm) high and flowers in early summer.

All will grow in any reasonable soil and in sun or partial shade, and all can be increased by division in spring or autumn.

Himalayan poppy, see Meconopsis

Hosta (Plantain lily) These plants are grown primarily for their large and very handsome leaves, though in some kinds the spikes of tubular flowers are quite attractive. *Hosta sieboldiana* has broad blue-grey leaves and white flowers. *H. undulata* has wavy leaves, which are light green splashed with white. *H. lancifolia* has narrower leaves, and deep lilac flowers. *H. plantaginea*, with broad yellowish-green leaves and white flowers on 2½-ft (75-cm) stems is the most showy in bloom. *H. fortunei* has blue-green leaves and blue-mauve flowers and has several good varieties including one oddly named *albo picta* with leaves that are pale green edged with deep green.

All will thrive in sun or shade in practically any soil, but are seen at their best in fairly rich, slightly moist soils. They can be increased by division in spring or autumn.

Incarvillea Remarkable plants with showy trumpet flowers similar in shape to those of the greenhouse gloxinias. They are quite hardy and the tuberous roots should be planted in a sunny place in rather rich, but well-drained soil. *Incarvillea delavayi* has rosy-red flowers and is 2 ft (60 cm) high; *I. grandiflora* is deeper in colour and shorter, and Bees Pink is shell pink. All flower in early summer and can be increased by careful division in the spring.

Inula Plants with large, yellow daisy flowers produced for long periods in summer. *Inula ensifolia* makes a bushy little plant no more than 9 in (23 cm) high; *I. orientalis*, also known as *I. glandulosa*, is 2 ft (60 cm) high, as is the orange-yellow *I. royleana*, and *I. helenium* as much as 5 ft (1·5 m).

All are hardy and easily grown in any reasonable soil and an open position. Increase is by division in spring or autumn.

Iris The popular bearded, or German irises, have fleshy, root-like stems known as rhizomes, which lie flat on the surface of the ground. From these grow the sword-shaped leaves and, in late spring or early summer, the flower stems, which vary in height from 2 to 5 ft (60 cm to 2·5 m). The flowers have a wide colour range including many shades of blue, yellow, orange, copper bronze, and purple. These fine irises will grow in almost any soil but they particularly like chalky soils which have been well cultivated. They will survive in shade but are seen at their best in full sun. All can be increased by division in spring or autumn or, better still, immediately after flowering about mid-summer.

The Siberian iris, *Iris sibirica*, also flowers in early summer but is a more elegant plant which makes clumps of long narrow leaves and carries its flowers on slender stems 3 to 4 ft (1 to 1·25 m) high. These flowers, individually smaller than those of the German iris, may be white, lavender blue, or violet purple. This iris will grow almost anywhere but is particularly happy near water. It can be divided in spring or autumn.

There are also dwarf spring-flowering irises which can be planted at the front of a border. They are known as Crimean irises and are varieties of *I. chamaeiris*. They are about 1 ft (30 cm) in height and colours range from white, lemon and lavender to deep yellow and purple. They like similar conditions to the German iris and can be divided in spring or autumn.

Jacob's ladder, see Polemonium

Jerusalem cross, see Lychnis

Kaffir lily, see Schizostylis

Kniphofia (Red-hot poker, torch lily) Many kinds of kniphofia really do produce flower spikes that justify the popular name, red-hot poker. In *K. uvaria*, the commonest kind, they are scarlet and yellow, carried on stout bare stems 4 ft (1·25 m) high. They are at their best from mid- to late summer. Others, while having the typical poker shape, are not red. In *K. galpinii* they are orange and carried on quite slender stems only about 2 ft (60 cm) high. In Maid of Orleans they are creamy white on 3-ft (1-m) stems, and this fine variety continues to flower from mid-summer to autumn. There are tall varieties of kniphofia, up to 7 ft (2·25 m) high, and one very popular variety, named Royal Standard, which has red and yellow flower spikes on 5-ft (1·5-m) stems, blooms about a month earlier than those of *K. uvaria*.

All like fairly rich soils, well drained in winter, but not dry while the flower spikes are forming in summer. They should be given a sunny place. All can be increased by division in spring or autumn.

Knotweed, see Polygonum

Lady's mantle, see Alchemilla

Lamium (Dead nettle) The common dead nettle is a pretty but troublesome weed but *Lamium maculatum* is a useful carpeting

Lamium maculatum aureum the golden-leaved form of the dead nettle

plant for the front of a bed or border or for covering rough banks or the ground between shrubs. It is only about 9 in (23 cm) high but spreads indefinitely, and it has little reddish-purple flowers produced most of the year, and dark green, nettle-shaped leaves, each with a broad creamy-white stripe down the middle. It will grow anywhere and can be increased by division at practically any time. A yellow-leaved variety named *aureum* is attractive but less vigorous.

Large-leaved saxifrage, see Bergenia

Lathyrus (Everlasting pea) *Lathyrus latifolius* is a climber, allied to the sweet pea, which dies down each autumn but shoots up again in the spring from fleshy roots. The flowers are produced from mid-summer onwards and are smaller than those of the sweet pea and not scented. They may be white, pink or rosy red.

It is very easily grown in almost any soil and sunny position and can be increased by seed sown in spring outdoors or in a frame, but seedlings may differ somewhat in colour or quality of flower, so specially selected forms are increased by careful division in spring.

Lenten rose, see Helleborus

Leopard's bane, see Doronicum

Liatris The reddish-purple flowers of these plants are borne in mid- and late summer in stiff, narrow spikes, a peculiarity being that they start to open from the top downwards. There are several kinds, such as *Liatris spicata*, *L. callilepis*, and *L. pycnostachya*, but they do not differ greatly in appearance. A particularly attractive garden variety named Cobald has deeper purple flowers.

All are 2 to 3 ft (60 cm to 1 m) high and thrive in sunny places and soils containing enough humus to ensure that they do not dry out rapidly in hot weather. The tuberous roots should be planted in spring so that they are just covered with soil. Plants can be increased by careful division in spring.

Ligularia These sturdy plants with yellow daisy flowers in summer were at one time called senecio and are still listed under that name in some nursery catalogues. *Ligularia clivorum* carries its very large flowers erect in open clusters on stout 3-ft (1-m) stems, whereas in *L. przewalskii* the flowers are smaller and crowded on a narrow, tapering spike 4 ft (1·25 m) high. Both will grow in ordinary soil, but *L. przewalskii* prefers rather moist soil. There are several selected varieties of *L. clivorum* including Desdemona with purplish leaves and stems.

All will thrive in sun or partial shade and can be increased by division in spring or summer.

Lily of the valley, see Convallaria

Limonium (Statice) Some kinds of limonium are annuals which must be renewed from seed every year but there are also good perennial kinds of which the best for the garden is *Limonium latifolium*. It grows 2 ft (60 cm) high and in late summer produces big, spreading sprays of tiny lavender flowers. These sprays may be cut and dried for winter decoration.

This limonium thrives in sunny places and well-drained soils. It is increased by root cuttings in winter or early spring, or by seed in spring.

Linaria (Toadflax) Some kinds of linaria are annuals to be renewed each year from seed, and some are rock garden plants, but there is also one good hardy border plant, *Linaria purpurea*. It has very narrow leaves and produces slender spikes of purple or pinkish flowers, 3 to 4 ft (1 to 1·25 m) high, throughout the summer. It will grow almost anywhere and often seeds itself about in warm, sunny places. Plants can be divided in spring or autumn.

Lobelia The most familiar lobelias, the creeping blue-flowered kinds, are summer bedding plants too tender to live outdoors in winter, but there are other very different kinds which are reasonably hardy and are good plants for the border. *Lobelia fulgens* has vivid scarlet flowers carried on 3-ft (1-m) long, slender spikes in late summer and early autumn, and beetroot-red leaves. *L. vedrariensis*, has violet-blue flowers in more crowded spikes produced over an equally long period of time.

Both thrive in good rich soils, well drained in winter. They may not prove fully hardy in cold districts or on wet soils and are then best lifted in autumn and removed to a frame or greenhouse for the winter. They are very easily increased by division in the spring.

Loosestrife, see Lysimachia and Lythrum

Lungwort, see Pulmonaria

Lupin, see Lupinus

Lupinus (Lupin) The border lupins are all varieties of *Lupinus polyphyllus*, a splendid early summer-flowering plant with stout spikes of flowers on 4-ft (1·25-m) stems and in a wide variety of colours. The finest kinds are known as Russell lupins because they were first raised by Mr George Russell of York. The flower spikes of these are more solidly filled with bloom than those of the older types of lupin and they are often in two contrasted colours.

Lupins like well-drained soils and sunny places and they do not thrive well on chalk or lime, on which their leaves tend to turn yellow and die off. They are seldom long-lived plants and need to be frequently renewed, either from seed sown in spring

Lupinus polyphyllus

or early summer or from cuttings taken in the spring. Seedlings are likely to vary in colour, but plants from cuttings reproduce exactly the characteristics of their parents.

Lychnis (Maltese cross, Jerusalem cross, rose campion, German catchfly) There are many different kinds of lychnis and not all are hardy perennials. *Lychnis chalcedonica* is the Maltese cross or Jerusalem cross, a striking plant with greyish leaves and stiffly erect 2-ft (60-cm) stems carrying heads of vivid scarlet flowers in early summer. *L. coronaria* is the rose campion, sometimes known as agrostemma, similar in height to the last but more branched, with even greyer leaves and magenta-crimson flowers in early summer. *L. viscaria* is the German catchfly, a plant 18 in (45 cm) high with rose-carmine flowers in late spring and early summer. It has a double-flowered form, known as *splendens plena*, which is even better.

All these kinds like sunny places and well-drained soils. *L. chalcedonica* and *L. coronaria* are readily raised from seed and often seed themselves about so freely as to become a nuisance. *L. viscaria splendens plena* is increased by division, in the spring.

Lysimachia (Loosestrife) There are several different kinds of lysimachia for the border and most have erect spikes of yellow flowers in early summer. In *Lysimachia vulgaris* these spikes are stiff and narrow, in *L. punctata* they are looser and more graceful. Both kinds are 3 ft (1 m) high and will grow in almost any soil and situation. A kind that needs a little more care and should be given a sunny position and well-drained soil is

Meconopsis betonicifolia

L. clethroides with short spikes of white flowers in late summer. All can easily be increased by division in either spring or autumn.

Lythrum (Purple loosestrife) These plants are as easily grown as the yellow loosestrifes or lysimachia, but they have slender 3-ft (1-m) spikes of magenta flowers around mid-summer. The two best kinds are *Lythrum salicaria*, about 4 ft (1·25 m) high, and *L. virgatum*, 2½ to 3 ft (75 cm to 1 m). Both have improved garden varieties with brighter, purer colours. They can be increased by division in either spring or autumn.

Macleaya (Plume poppy) The plant correctly known as *Macleaya cordata* is, in gardens, more usually called by its old name *Bocconia cordata*. It is grown for its large, almost circular, greyish leaves and tall sprays of small buff-coloured flowers in late summer. It will grow in any reasonable soil and sunny position and can be increased by division in spring.

Maltese cross, see Lychnis

Marguerite, Golden, see Anthemis

Meadow rue, see Thalictrum

Meconopsis (Himalayan poppy, Welsh poppy) Although the various kinds of meconopsis are all herbaceous plants, by no means all are perennials and very few fit comfortably into the ordinary herbaceous border or bed. They demand special conditions and need to be grown in specially prepared places. Most must be frequently, even annually, renewed from seed, and at least one, *Meconopsis cambrica*, does this for itself so freely and easily that it can become a nuisance. Yet the family is well worth persisting with for it contains some plants of quite exceptional beauty. The best known of these is the Himalayan poppy, *M. betonicifolia*, with sky-blue

flowers on 3-ft (1-m) stems in early summer. It is readily raised from seed sown in a frame or cool greenhouse in sandy peat in spring. The seedlings must be planted out in a partially shaded place in deep, well-drained but not dry soil, containing plenty of peat or leaf mould. They will flower in their second year and may prove impermanent thereafter, particularly if they get too dry in summer or too wet in winter. *M. grandis* is similar with finer flowers.

There are other interesting kinds requiring similar treatment, notably the Chinese yellow poppy, *M. integrifolia*, 3 ft (1 m) high with large primrose-yellow flowers, and the Nepal poppy, *M. napaulensis*, which has handsome leaves clothed in tawny hairs and flowers which may be anything from a rather washy mauve to a glorious rose. Both flower in early summer, and as *M. integrifolia* invariably dies after flowering, a fresh stock of it must be raised annually from seed.

The Welsh poppy, *M. cambrica*, is a perennial about 1 ft (30 cm) high with yellow or orange flowers in summer. It likes cool, partially shaded places such as light woodland but is not fussy about soil and is one of the easiest kinds to grow.

Michaelmas daisy, see Aster

Milfoil, see Achillea

Monarda These easily grown plants bear clusters of scarlet, pink, mauve or purple flowers in mid- and late summer, and their abundant leaves are aromatic. There are numerous varieties, mostly of *Monarda didyma*, and these include Cambridge Scarlet, bright scarlet; Croftway Pink, pale pink, and Blue Stocking, violet purple. All are about 3 ft (1 m) high, spread quite rapidly and will thrive in practically any soil and a reasonably open position. They are readily increased by division in spring or autumn.

Monkshood, see Aconitum

Moon daisy, see Chrysanthemum

Mullein, see Verbascum

Nepeta (Catmint) Free-flowering plants for the front of the border or bed. The commonest kind is *Nepeta faassenii* which has slender 15-in (38-cm) spikes of lavender-blue flowers all the summer. Six Hills Giant is taller and may reach 3 ft (1 m) in good soil. Both have pleasantly aromatic leaves.

They like well-drained soils and sunny places, and in wet soil may rot away in winter but otherwise are perfectly hardy. If they are cut back each spring to within a few inches of ground level the habit is improved. Spring is the best season for planting and plants can then be divided.

Obedient plant, see Physostegia

Oenothera (Evening primrose, golden drops) The commonest evening primrose is a British wild plant which should only be admitted to the rougher parts of a garden as it is apt to seed itself about too freely, especially in light, sandy soils. It has pale primrose flowers, individually short-lived, but produced in succession in summer. It flowers in the second year from seed and dies thereafter so that it is necessary to raise it afresh from seed every year.

Far better as garden plants are the varieties associated with *Oenothera fruticosa* and *O. tetragona*, both good perennials, 18 to 24 in (45 to 60 cm) high, bearing a profusion of bright yellow flowers in late summer. Fireworks, with red buds, is particularly showy.

A useful sprawling kind for the front of the border is *O. missouriensis*. It has big lemon-yellow flowers in late summer and early autumn.

All like well-drained soils and sunny places and can be increased by seed sown in spring or early summer or, the perennial kinds, by division in spring.

Omphalodes (Creeping forget-me-not, blue-eyed Mary) Some kinds are rock plants but *Omphalodes verna* is a sprawling herbaceous

Monarda didyma Croftway Pink

plant with rather coarse, rounded leaves and loose sprays of small blue flowers, like forget-me-nots, in spring. It will grow practically anywhere, in sun or shade, and is a useful carpeting plant for the border or shrubbery. It is easily increased by division in spring or autumn.

Paeonia (Peony) There are both herbaceous and shrubby peonies; the two most familiar herbaceous kinds are the common peony, *Paeonia officinalis*, which has crimson, pink or white flowers, usually very full and double, in late spring, and the Chinese peony, *P. albiflora*, which is at its best a week or so later in early summer and has a wide range of colours and flower forms. There are single-flowered varieties, semi-doubles and full doubles and colours go all the way from white and delicate pink, through deeper pink, salmon pinks, rose and scarlet to intense crimson. All are fragrant. Both the common and the Chinese peony are about 3 ft (1 m) high.

They like reasonably good soils and sunny places, can be planted in spring or early autumn and are increased by careful division when transplanting but should be left undisturbed as long as possible as they are often rather slow to re-establish themselves. Quality of flowers is improved if a little well-rotted manure or garden compost is spread around the plants each spring.

Pampas grass, see Cortaderia

Papaver (Poppy) Many of the poppies are annuals or biennials but the Oriental poppy, *Papaver orientale*, is a true hardy herbaceous perennial which will live for years in light soils, though it may prove impermanent where drainage is poor in winter. The flowers are very large and showy, scarlet, pink or white, carried on 2½-ft (75-cm) stems in early summer.

This poppy likes a sunny place and is readily raised from seed sown in spring, but seedlings often vary in colour from their parents, so selected garden varieties are increased by root cuttings in spring or early autumn.

Pearly everlasting, see Anaphalis

Penstemon On the whole these are not very hardy plants but they are very readily grown from summer cuttings and so, in cold districts, it is best to root some cuttings in a frame late each summer and over-winter them in the frame in case the outdoor parent plants die. Penstemons carry their showy tubular flowers in spikes and continue to flower from mid-summer until autumn. *Penstemon heterophyllus* makes a bushy plant 1 ft (30 cm) high and has blue flowers; it is one of the hardiest. Garnet is a larger plant, to 2 ft (60 cm), with deep red flowers; Evelyn is similar but pink and Mydleton Gem is carmine. There are many

more and, if seed of *Penstemon gloxinioides* is purchased, a variety of colours will be obtained. Selected varieties must be grown from cuttings. All like good, well-drained soil and warm, sunny places.

Peony, see Paeonia

Peruvian lily, see Alstroemeria

Phlox The herbaceous phlox is one of the most popular of summer-flowering plants. It flowers in the latter part of the summer and carries its sweetly scented flowers in large, more or less conical heads. There are a great many varieties ranging in height from 1 to 4 ft (30 cm to 1·25 m), and in colour from white, palest pink and mauve to vivid scarlet, crimson and deep purple.

All are easily grown in almost any soil, though the quality of the flowers is best in moderately rich soil. Plants will thrive in full sun or partial shade and can be planted in spring or autumn. Increase is by division at planting time or by root cuttings in winter or spring.

The phlox is sometimes attacked by eelworms which make the stems gouty and the leaves narrow and distorted. As the eelworms live in the upper parts of the plant it is often possible to raise a clean stock from infected plants by taking root cuttings, but the resultant plants should be given a new place or they will soon become re-infested.

Phygelius (Cape fuchsia) There is a curious upside-down look about the curved orange-red flowers of this uncommon hardy plant. In the open it grows about 4 ft (1·25 m) high but against a wall it will often behave like a climber, and ascend to a height of 7 or 8 ft (2·25 to 2·5 m). The flowers come in late summer and early autumn.

The Cape fuchsia likes a warm, sunny spot and well-drained soil. It is increased by division in the spring.

Physalis (Cape gooseberry, Chinese lantern) These plants are grown for the decorative

Papaver orientale

effect of their orange berries enclosed in an orange bladder which, as it ripens, becomes net-like so that the berry is seen like a light in a lantern. There are several kinds, but the best is *Physalis alkekengi* which is often listed in nursery catalogues as *P. franchetii*. It grows 2 ft (60 cm) high, has white flowers in summer and likes good, well-drained soil and a warm, sunny position. It is increased by division in the spring.

Physostegia (False dragonhead, obedient plant) *Physostegia virginiana* is sometimes called the obedient plant because its rose-coloured tubular flowers, which stand out from the flower stems to form short spikes, can be moved from side to side as though on a hinge and will stay where they are put. The common form is 4 ft (1·25 m) high and inclined to be untidy, but there is a much better dwarf form, known as Vivid, only 1 ft (30 cm) high with bright rosy-red flowers.

Both tall and short kinds flower in early autumn, will grow in any reasonable soil and open position and can be easily divided.

Physalis alkekengi

Polygonum bistorta superbum

Pink, see Dianthus

Plantain lily, see Hosta

Platycodon (Balloon flower) The popular name of this unusual plant refers to the flower buds which look like small inflated balloons. They expand into showy, bell-shaped, light blue or white flowers like those of some campanulas. The flowering season is late summer and the height of *Platycodon grandiflorum* is 18in (45cm), but there is a lower growing, blue-flowered variety named *mariesii* which is only 9in (23cm) high.

All like sunny places and fairly rich but reasonably well-drained soils. They can be increased by division in spring.

Plume poppy, see Macleaya

Polemonium (Jacob's ladder) This pretty plant gets its popular name from the laddered appearance of its elegant, ferny leaves. The light blue or white flowers are borne in 18-in (45-cm) spikes in early summer.

The plant will thrive in sun or shade in almost any soil. It is easily increased by division in spring or autumn or by seed in spring or early summer; indeed it often seeds itself about so freely that it has to be thinned out rather than further increased.

Polygonatum (Solomon's seal) Graceful plants which will grow in quite densely shaded places as well as in more open situations. The creamy-white tubular flowers hang along the upper half of the arching stems in late spring and early summer. There are two kinds, *Polygonatum officinale* and *P. multiflorum*, both 2 to 3ft (60cm to 1m) high, but the latter has the larger flowers and is the better garden plant.

They will thrive in any reasonable soil and can be increased by division of the fleshy roots in spring or autumn.

Polygonum (Bistort, knotweed) Some of the polygonums spread so rapidly by underground stems that they soon become a nuisance but this is not true of the bistort, *Polygonum bistorta*, a plant which makes a dense carpet of growth from which arise, in late summer, slender 2-ft (60-cm) stems terminating in short spikes of pink flowers. A more decorative variety, known as *superbum*, has deeper rose flowers. Another good kind is *P. campanulatum* which spreads rapidly over the surface, has greyish-green leaves and branching sprays of blush pink flowers in late summer and early autumn.

Both kinds like rather moist soils and will grow in sunny or partially shady places. They are very easily increased by division.

Poppy, see Papaver

Poppy, Himalayan, see Meconopsis

Poppy, Welsh, see Meconopsis

Potentilla Some potentillas are shrubs and some are rock plants but the numerous varieties and hybrids of *Potentilla atrosanguinea* are very showy herbaceous plants for the front or middle of the border. They range in height from the sprawling, foot-high Gibson's Scarlet, with brilliant scarlet flowers, and *P. nepalensis* Miss Willmot, cherry rose, smaller flowered but very showy, to the 2-ft (60-cm), orange-flame William Rollison.

All flower most of the summer, enjoy sunny places, are not fussy about soil and are increased by division in spring or autumn.

Pulmonaria (Lungwort) These plants make low clumps of leaves which in some kinds are handsomely spotted with pale green or silver. In early spring they produce clusters of small flowers on 9-in (23-cm) stems, blue in the case of *Pulmonaria angustifolia*, pink or rose changing to purple in *P. saccharata*, which has the most heavily silver-spotted foliage, brick red in *P. rubra*. A particularly good variety of *P. angustifolia* is named Munstead Blue.

All are very easily grown in almost any soil and sunny or shady position, and all can be increased by division in spring or autumn.

Purple coneflower, see Echinacea

Purple loosestrife, see Lythrum

Pyrethrum Plants making clumps of ferny leaves from which, in early summer, grow 2-ft (60-cm) stems, each terminated by a large daisy-type flower which may be single or double, white, pink, rose, scarlet or crimson. They are first class for cutting and also make a good display in the garden.

They like good, well-drained soils and sometimes prove impermanent in ground

that lies wet in winter. They can be planted in spring or in summer immediately after flowering and are increased by division when planting.

Red-hot poker, see Kniphofia

Red valerian, see Centranthus

Rodgersia Plants with handsome bronzy leaves, often deeply divided like those of a horse chestnut, and branching sprays, 3 to 4ft (1 to 1·25m) high, of small flowers around mid-summer. These flowers are pink in *Rodgersia pinnata* and *R. aesculifolia* and white in *R. tabularis*.

They all like damp soil but will also grow in ordinary soil provided it contains enough humus to prevent it drying out badly in summer. They will grow in sun or partial shade. Divide in spring or autumn.

Rose campion, see Lychnis

Rudbeckia (Coneflower) These plants belong to the daisy family and have big yellow flowers rather like sunflowers but in some kinds the central disk is raised and cone-shaped. This characteristic is particularly well marked in the popular variety Herbstsonne, which grows 7ft (2·25m) high and has lemon-yellow, green-coned flowers. Golden Glow, which is even taller, has double flowers of similar colour, but Goldsturm is only 3ft (1m) high, and has a black, nearly flat central disk to its orange-yellow flowers. All flower in late summer and early autumn.

They like sunny places and will grow in practically any soil. They can be increased by division in spring or autumn.

Sage, see Salvia

St Bernard's lily, see Anthericum

Salvia (Sage, clary) The scarlet salvia is a tender bedding plant and the common sage is a sub-shrub, but there are other kinds of salvia which are hardy herbaceous perennials. One of the best of these is *Salvia superba*, a bushy plant, 3ft (1m) high, with slender violet-blue flower spikes in late summer. There are shorter varieties, one named Lubeca, 2ft (60cm) high, another named East Friesland, only 1½ft (45cm). All are easily grown in any reasonable soil and open place and are increased by division in the spring or autumn.

The clary, *S. sclarea*, grows 3 to 4ft (1 to 1·25m) high and has large leaves and spikes of mauve or lilac flowers in mid-summer. A variety with finer flowers is named *turkestanica*, but neither this nor the ordinary form are very long lived and they are usually treated as biennials to be raised each year from seed sown in late spring, allowed to flower the following year and then discarded.

Salvia patens has tuberous roots and gentian-blue flowers on 3-ft (1-m) spikes in late summer, but it is not very hardy and in cold places or on poorly drained soils it is best to place the roots in a greenhouse or frame each autumn and leave them there until the spring.

Saxifrage, Large-leaved, see Bergenia

Scabiosa (Scabious) The sweet-scented scabious is an annual, but the Caucasian scabious, *Scabiosa caucasica*, is a useful perennial for well-drained or chalky soils. Its flowers are blue or white, produced continuously from mid-summer to autumn on 2½-ft (75-cm) stems which are ideal for cutting. It likes open, sunny places and can be increased by careful division in spring, which is also the best planting season.

Scabious, see Scabiosa

Schizostylis (Kaffir lily) This is a plant that creeps about by stems (or stolons) just beneath the surface so that, in a favourable warm, sunny place and well-drained but not too dry soil, a few plants will soon form a sizeable colony. The leaves are narrow and the flowers are borne in erect spikes 1 to 1½ ft (30 to 45 cm) high all autumn and well into the winter if the weather is mild. The common form is scarlet but there are also pink varieties of which the best is Viscountess Byng. *Schizostylis coccinea* (its full botanical name) should be planted in spring and is easily increased by division when replanting.

Sea holly, see Eryngium

Sedum (Stonecrop) Most of the stonecrops are rock garden plants but a few are sufficiently tall for the herbaceous border or bed. *Sedum spectabile* is a particularly useful plant with fleshy grey-green leaves and large flat heads of small pink flowers on 18-in (45-cm) stems in late summer and early autumn. *S. telephium* is similar in habit but duller in colour but the hybrid between this and *S. spectabile*, named Autumn Joy, is an excellent plant with large, flat heads of salmon-pink flowers deepening to bronze red as they age. *S. maximum* is taller, about 2 ft (60 cm), with greenish-yellow flowers in late summer. This is not a very good plant but it has an attractive variety named *purpureum* with reddish-purple leaves.

All like sunny places and will thrive in any reasonably well-drained soil. They can be increased by division in spring or autumn.

Shasta daisy, see Chrysanthemum

Sidalcea These plants are grown for their long, slender spikes of pink, mallow-like flowers in the latter half of the summer. There are numerous varieties and as the plants set seed freely and this often comes up of its own accord all over the place, giving seed-lings of slightly varying height and colour, it is easy to raise more varieties at home. Heights range from 2 to 5 ft (60 cm to 1·5 m), colours from pale silvery-pink to rosy-carmine.

Sidalceas will grow in almost any soil and reasonably open place and can be increased by division in spring or autumn or by seed sown in spring.

Soapwort, see Saponaria

Solidago (Golden rod) Very easily grown plants with branching sprays of tiny yellow flowers in late summer and early autumn. There are numerous varieties differing in height and shade of yellow; Tom Thumb, deep yellow, 1½ ft (45 cm); Goldenmosa, light yellow, 3 ft (1 m), and Golden Wings, bright yellow, 5 to 6 ft (1·5 to 2 m).

All will grow in practically any soil and open or partially shaded place and can be increased by division in spring or summer. Self-sown seedlings often appear freely but may be inferior to their parents.

Solomon's seal, see Polygonatum

Spiderwort, see Tradescantia

Spiraea, see Aruncus, Astilbe and Filipendula

Spurge, see Euphorbia

Stachys (Lamb's ear) *Stachys lanata* is a plant with leaves so densely covered with silky grey hairs that they feel soft and woolly like an animal's coat. Purplish flowers are produced on 18-in (45-cm) stems in early summer but they add nothing to the beauty of the plant. A variety named Silver Carpet has actually been introduced which never flowers and this is considered an advantage. This stachys can be grown anywhere and is increased by division at any time.

Statice, see Limonium

Rodgersia aesculifolia

Stokesia The aster-like flowers of *Stokesia laevis* come in early autumn and are produced on a plant 1 ft (30 cm) high, very suitable for the front of a border or bed. The flowers may be lavender, lilac or light blue. It is a plant which likes a sunny place and well-drained soil. Divide in spring.

Stonecrop, see Sedum

Sunflower, see Helianthus

Thalictrum (Meadow rue) Very elegant plants, the foliage of which is small and fern like, the flowers carried in loose sprays or little fluffy heads. The loveliest is *Thalictrum dipterocarpum*, 5 to 6 ft (1·5 to 2 m) high, with nodding lilac and yellow flowers produced in open sprays in the latter half of summer. There is a good double-flowered form known as Hewitt's Double. *Thalictrum glaucum* is 4 ft (1·25 m) tall, has grey-green leaves and pale yellow flowers at mid-summer. *T. aquilegifolium* is about 3 ft (1 m) high and has fluffy purple flowers in late spring. *T. adiantifolium* is no more than 1½ ft (45 cm), has greenish-yellow flowers in summer and leaves like maidenhair fern.

All like reasonably good well-drained soils and sunny places. A little shelter is desirable for *T. dipterocarpum*. Most can be increased by division in spring but *T. dipterocarpum* is best raised from seed in spring.

Thrift, see Armeria

Toadflax, see Linaria

Tradescantia (Spiderwort) The flowers of the spiderwort are unusual in having only three petals. They are produced on 2-ft (60-cm) stems in continuous succession throughout the summer. The common kind, *Tradescantia virginiana*, has blue

Trollius **Earliest of All**

flowers, but there are several garden varieties such as J. C. Weguelin, lavender blue; Osprey, white and blue, and *rubra*, rosy red.

All are easily grown in almost any soil and place and can be increased by division in spring or autumn.

Trollius (Globe flower) The flowers are like very large, unusually globular buttercups and those of *Trollius europaeus* come in late spring before the main flush of hardy plants. They are lemon yellow and carried on 2-ft (60-cm) stems. *T. ledebourii* flowers a month later in early summer and has more open orange flowers on 2½-ft (75-cm) stems. There are also numerous hybrids with names like Earliest of All, Golden Queen and Orange Princess, which adequately describe their particular qualities.

All like good, rich, rather moist soils and will grow in either sunny or partially shaded places. They can be increased by division in spring or autumn.

Valerian, Red, see Centranthus

Verbascum (Mullein) Some mulleins are impermanent and must be renewed annually from seed, but a few are perennials, though even these may not live for many years. All are grown for their rosettes of large, handsome leaves and tall, narrow spikes of flowers. Some kinds, such as *Verbascum thapsus* and *V.* Broussa, have their leaves and stems densely clothed in silvery hairs which is an additional attraction to their yellow flowers. Both these are biennials and should be renewed annually by seed sown in late spring, to give flowering plants the following year. One of the smallest is *V. phoeniceum*, a good perennial with 2-ft (60-cm) spikes of purple flowers in early summer. Good perennial varieties of medium height, 3 to 4 ft (1 to 1·25 m), and summer flowering are Gainsborough, lemon; Cotswold Beauty, amber; Pink Domino, mauve pink, and Cotswold Queen, bronze.

All like well-drained soils and sunny places and the perennial garden varieties are increased by root cuttings in winter or spring.

Verbena Most verbenas are more or less tender bedding plants, often treated as annuals, but there are two good perennial kinds for the herbaceous border or bed. *Verbena rigida* (also known as *V. venosa*) produces 1-ft (30-cm) spikes of purple flowers in late summer and *V. bonariensis* is a taller plant of open, rather gaunt habit with clusters of small purple flowers in late summer and early autumn.

Both like well-drained soils and warm, sunny places. They are increased by division or seed in spring.

Veronica Many kinds of veronica are rock plants but there are also some excellent hardy herbaceous perennials all with narrow spikes of flowers. One of the best is *Veronica longifolia subsessilis*, 18 in (45 cm) high and bearing its violet-blue flowers in late summer. *V. incana* has grey leaves and foot-high spikes of purple flowers after mid-summer. *V. spicata* is about 18 in (45 cm) high and has blue, purple or pink flowers throughout the latter half of summer. *V. gentianoides* is the earliest, producing its spikes of china-blue flowers in May. It has a variety with attractive white-variegated leaves. The tallest kind is *V. virginica*, with nearly white flowers carried on 6-ft (2-m) spikes in late summer.

All will grow in any reasonable soil and fairly open place. They can be increased by division in spring or autumn.

Wand flower, see Dierama

Welsh poppy, see Meconopsis

Windflower, see Anemone

Yarrow, see Achillea

Yellow loosestrife, see Lysimachia

Growing Rock Plants

There is no special definition of a rock plant except that it must be a plant suitable for growing in rocky places. Mountain plants naturally come into this category and are generally referred to as alpines, though they come from all parts of the world and not simply from the European Alps. But alpines are only one category of rock plants which include, also, many plants from low altitudes, from rocky coasts, cliffs and waste places and even from woodlands and other non-rocky places. The essential qualification for a good rock plant is that it does not grow too big, for a great many of the natural dwellers in rocky places are plants which have kept close to the ground in order to escape from the effects of wind and a few rampant plants let loose among them can soon smother the lot.

There is no need to have a rock garden in order to grow rock plants. Most will thrive

The winding path of a country garden

equally well on dry walls built without mortar and with a substantial core or backing of soil, or in raised beds retained by walls, or even in flat beds well supplied with grit and stone to give the sharp drainage that most rock plants like. A few of the choicest, most difficult alpine plants often take so unkindly to garden conditions that the enthusiasts who grow them do so in pots or pans and keep their treasures in frames or unheated greenhouses much of the time. However, there are plenty of rock plants which are as easy to grow as any other garden plants and some of them are capable of making a very fine display and bringing to the garden a special miniature beauty of their own.

Rules for Rock Garden Construction

If you decide to build a rock garden there are a few rules it is wise to observe. The site should be open and, in particular, should not be overhung by trees. Not many rock plants really like shade and those that do can be accommodated on the north-facing side of the rock garden. Trees are bad because the falling leaves in autumn tend to smother the small rock plants.

Good drainage is essential for most rock plants. If the rock garden is built above normal ground level there should be no difficulty in getting rid of surplus water, but if any excavation has to be done it may well be necessary to dig a soakaway, that is a large hole filled with rubble and topped up with soil, to catch drainage water and allow it to find its way harmlessly into the subsoil.

The Compost Some rock plants will grow well in ordinary garden soil but many of the choicer kinds need a more gritty compost. Coarse sand and small stone chippings, up to about ¼-in (0·5-cm) size, can be added to the existing soil, as can peat. As a general guide one part of sand, one of stone chippings and two of peat to six or eight parts of soil will make a satisfactory mixture for a great many plants, but this can be varied to meet special needs.

Choosing and Positioning Rocks Limestone and sandstone are the best rocks because they are moderately porous and plant roots take kindly to them, spreading themselves over any buried surface in search of moisture. Limestone and sandstone also weather pleasantly and very beautiful weatherworn limestone can be purchased, though it is usually rather expensive.

The rock garden will look more attractive if it can be irregular in contour, with a miniature hill or two separated by valleys, rather than a plain mound. For the same reason the rocks should be well embedded in the soil and not just laid on top. They should give the impression of being natural – part of an outcrop of rock, most of which lies hidden beneath the surface. Much natural rock is stratified, which means that

it lies in layers of various thickness one on top of another. These layers are by no means always horizontal but may be tilted at all kinds of angles as a result of ancient upheavals as the crust of the earth was being formed. Sometimes different angles of strata are to be found close together but more usually all the strata in a particular area will have the same tilt. This is certainly the best pattern to follow in the garden and, cleverly done, will help more than anything else to give an appearance of rightness and inevitability to the finished construction. Any angle can be chosen but usually a moderate tilt is most effective and easier to manage than a very acute one.

Artistic Expression There are no rules for the actual design of the rock garden, which can express the artistic ideas and imagination of its creator. A fairly simple method which can give excellent results is to start from the bottom and build upwards in a series of irregular steps following the contours of the ground and forming pockets and shelves of soil in which plants can be established. As building proceeds see that soil is firmly packed beneath and under the rocks so that there are no hollow places nor any likelihood of subsidence. Do not place each rock hard against its neighbour, but leave soil-packed crevices, for in these many plants will thrive.

Alternatives to the Rock Garden

The Rock Bed An alternative to the mounded rock garden is the flat, or nearly flat, rock bed. Unless the situation is naturally very well drained it will be wise to excavate 2 ft (60 cm) of soil and put 6 to 8 in (15 to 20 cm) of brickbats or hard rubble in the bottom for drainage. Then return the soil, mixed with sand, stone chippings and peat, and sink some rather wide but not very deep stones into it so that they just protrude above the surface. They need not be very close together nor need they follow any particular pattern but the soil between

When constructing a dry wall the plants should be inserted as the building of the wall progresses

them should be completely covered with stone chippings of the same character as the rock itself. The finished bed will look like one of those areas of moraine one can see in the mountains, where finely ground rock has slid down and nearly covered larger pieces of rock. Such a bed, well planted with small, tufted and creeping plants, can look most attractive.

The Dry Wall Yet another alternative to a rock garden is a dry wall, which is a wall built without mortar. Such walls are used in many parts of the country by farmers and are usually well clothed with small plants and moss. The farm walls, however, only have the soil that has been packed between the stones or has lodged there with the passage of time. More soil is required if a wide variety of plants is to be grown and this can be done either by using the wall to support a terrace of soil or by making a double wall with a core of soil in the space between.

Trough gardens are particularly welcome where there is no room for a rock garden

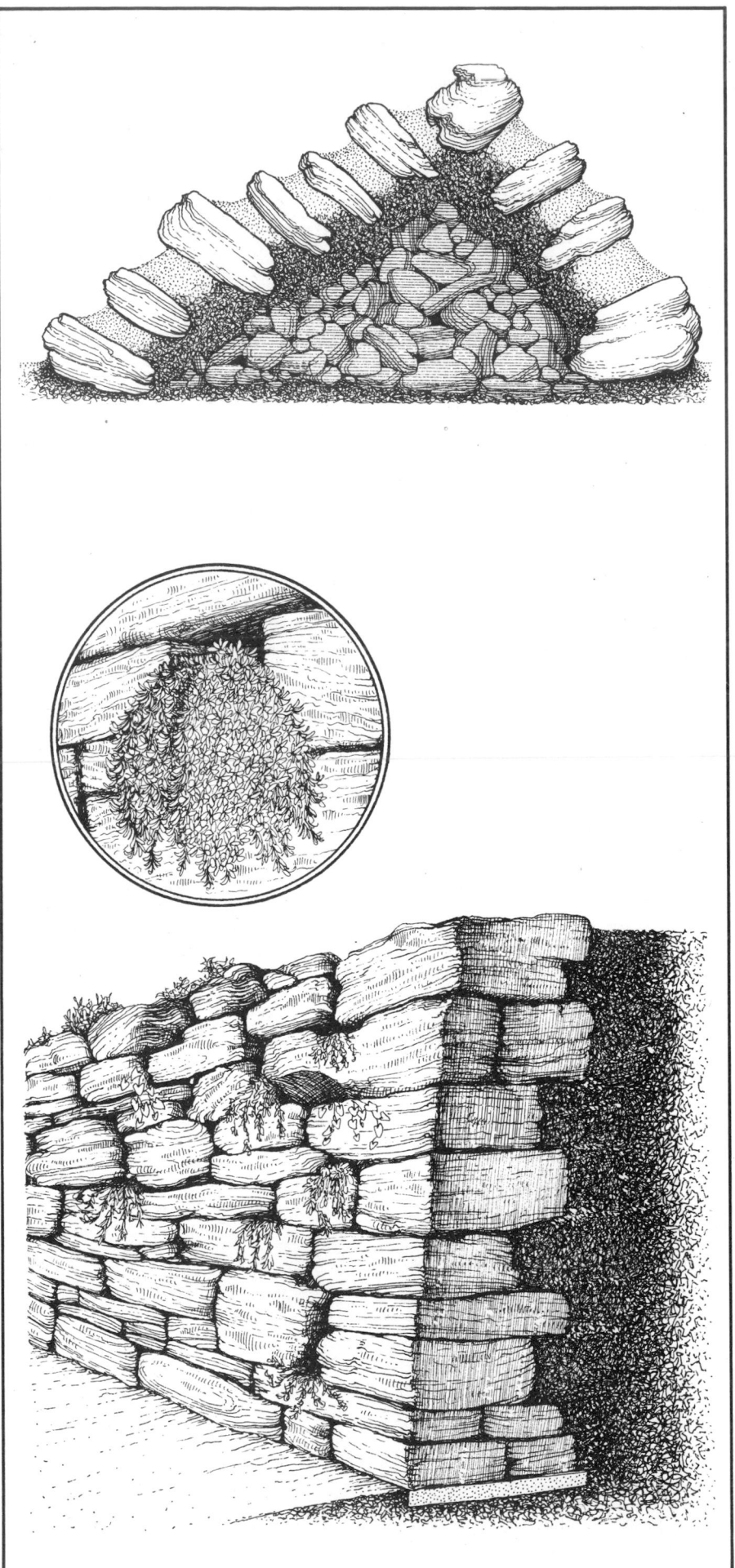

A rock garden can be constructed on a flat site by making a mound of rubble. The mound is well firmed, covered with finer rubble and an 18-in (45-cm) layer of soil is then added. Rocks are sunk into the soil at a slight backward angle, care being taken to keep the strata lines running in the same direction

Dry walls may be constructed from dressed or random stone or even broken paving slabs.

Construction: A 3-in (8-cm) trench should be taken out at the base of the soil terrace and the first course of stone bedded into cement on the floor of the trench. Walls above 2 ft (60 cm) in height should be given a slight backward tilt for added strength. The wall is built up, inserting those plants required to grow in it as building progresses. The stones are bonded as are bricks and a thin layer of soil is used instead of cement

Either way, soil should be well packed between and behind the stones to give them stability and to enable plants to grow un-impeded. If dry walls are more than a couple of feet high it is usually wise to give them a slight backwards or inwards slope, known as a batter, to give them greater stability and reduce the likelihood of their being pushed out by the weight of soil behind.

The Raised Rock Bed A development of the double dry wall with its core of soil is the raised rock bed. It can be of any size but as a rule it is most convenient to have a bed between 2 ft and 3 ft (60 cm to 1 m) high and not more than 6 ft (2 m) wide as the whole surface of this will then be in easy reach from either side without scrambling. The details of soil and building are exactly the same as for dry walls.

Some very low-growing rock plants can be planted in crevices between paving slabs provided their roots can penetrate freely into good soil beneath.

Advice on Planting

Nurserymen usually grow rock plants in small pots and as they can be moved from these without root disturbance they can be planted at practically any time of year. Spring is a favourable time but it is often convenient to buy rock plants in flower when one can see exactly what one is getting, and there is nothing against this provided the plants are carefully turned out of their pots and, if the weather is dry, are watered for a week or so until they are established.

Recommended Rock Plants

Acaena These are carpeting plants which are useful as ground cover and also for growing in the crevices between paving slabs since they do not mind being walked on. Their small flowers are followed by curious little brown or reddish seed heads but it is for their little leaves that these plants are mainly grown. These are grey green in *Acaena buchananii*, green in *A. novae zealandiae* and bronzy in *A. microphylla*. All will grow in any reasonable soil in sun or semi-shade.

Achillea (Yarrow) In addition to the larger achilleas, which are plants for the herbaceous border or bed, there are a number of smaller kinds which are admirable little plants for the rock garden. They are mat-forming plants with flattish clusters of small flowers, sulphur-yellow in *Achillea* King Edward; deep yellow in *A. tomentosa*; white, with silvery leaves in *A. argentea*. They mostly flower in late spring and early summer but King Edward is rarely without some flowers all the summer.

All are easily grown in sunny places and well-drained soils and are increased by division in spring or autumn.

Aethionema (Stone cress) These are really tiny shrubs, but far too small for the shrub garden, and their proper place is the rock garden or dry wall. In time they will make foot-wide mounds of slender 9-in (23-cm) stems closely set with narrow leaves and surmounted in spring by clusters of small pink flowers. One of the finest is Warley Rose, as it is neater and more compact in habit than most and has brighter pink flowers.

This variety must be raised from cuttings in a frame in mid-summer but the wild species, such as *Aethionema grandiflorum* and *A. pulchellum*, can be raised from seed sown in spring. All like light, well-drained soils and sunny places.

Alyssum (Gold dust) The sweet alyssum, *Alyssum maritimum*, with white honey-scented flowers all summer, is an annual and though it can be grown in the rock garden it can seed itself about so freely as to become a nuisance. The kind most commonly grown in rock gardens and on walls is yellow alyssum or gold dust, *A. saxatile*, a vigorous tufted plant 9 in (23 cm) high with fine clusters of small yellow flowers in spring. In addition to the common form, with deep golden-yellow flowers, there is an even better variety, named *flore pleno*, with double flowers, and a lemon-yellow, single-flowered variety named *citrinum*.

The double-flowered kind must be raised from cuttings in a frame in spring but the single-flowered kinds can be readily raised from seed, though there may be some variation in the flower colour of the seedlings. Often the plants seed themselves about freely. All like sunny places and well-drained soils.

American cowslip, see Dodecatheon

Androsace Delightful mountain plants, some cushion forming, some trailing, but all with neat little heads of rounded pink or white flowers like pieces of confetti. They like sun and sharp drainage and are completely happy sprawling over the face of a terrace wall or a small boulder in the rock garden. Two of the best are *Androsace lanuginosa*, a trailing plant, and *A. sarmentosa*, which increases its soft hummocks of growth by pushing out short runners in all directions. Both carry their pink flowers on 5-in (13-cm) stems in late spring or early summer. They can be increased by division in spring.

Anemone (Windflower) The Japanese anemone is too big for the rock garden and the brilliantly coloured varieties of *Anemone coronaria*, the poppy anemone so popular as a cut flower in early spring, may be considered a little too sophisticated, though they are sometimes planted. But there is nothing wrong with either *A. apennina* or *A. blanda* as rock garden plants, for both make low clumps of deeply divided leaves smothered in early spring by fragile blue, pink or white flowers. They are grown from little tubers which can be purchased in early autumn and planted 2 in (5 cm) deep in soil containing plenty of peat or leafmould and, for preference, a sunny place, though they will grow in partial shade. They are increased by separating out the clusters of tubers in summer. For the plant often known as *A. pulsatilla*, see *Pulsatilla*.

Aquilegia (Columbine) Most of the columbines are for the herbaceous border or wild garden, but a few are sufficiently small for the rock garden. One of the best of these is *Aquilegia glandulosa*, 9 in (23 cm) high with light blue and white flowers of the typical columbine shape in early summer.

It likes a sunny place and a well-drained but cool soil containing plenty of grit and peat or leafmould. It can be increased by seed in spring.

Arabis One of the most popular of all white-

Armeria maritima

flowered trailing plants is *Arabis albida*. It flowers in spring and makes a first-rate companion for the blue and pink aubrieta on walls, rock gardens and banks. There is a double-flowered form which is even more effective than the more common single, and also a pink variety named *rosea* or Rosabella.

All like sunny places and will grow in almost any soil. The singles can be raised from seed sown in spring but the double-flowered variety must be increased by cuttings in a frame in late spring or early summer.

Arenaria No plant makes a closer carpet of shiny bright green leaves than *Arenaria balearica*. It makes excellent ground cover for small bulbs and is also very attractive when covered in spring in its own white flowers. *Arenaria caespitosa* makes low, moss like mounds and is particularly useful in its golden-leaved variety *aurea*. Quite different in character is *A. montana*, a trailing plant with quite large white flowers rather like those of the native stitchwort. *A. balearica* grows best in rather moist soil but the others grow well in ordinary soil and an open position. All can be increased by division in spring or autumn.

Armeria (Thrift) Tufted plants with narrow, grass-like leaves and almost globular heads of small pink or red flowers in late spring and early summer. The best kind for the rock garden is *Armeria maritima* which itself has pale pink flowers but has produced garden varieties with deeper carmine flowers and also a white-flowered form.

All are accustomed to growing in very stony places in full sun and this is what they like, though they will grow almost anywhere. They can be increased by division in the spring.

Aster Most of the perennial asters are far too big for the rock garden but there are a few exceptions, notably *Aster alpinus*, 9 in

Cyclamen neapolitanum

(23 cm) high with mauve daisy-like flowers in late spring and early summer; *A. sub-caeruleus*, 1 ft (30 cm) high with bright blue flowers at the same period, and *A. yunnanensis*, 18 in (45 cm) high, with deep blue flowers around mid-summer.

All will grow in any sunny place and reasonably well-drained soil and can be increased by division in spring.

Aubrieta (Rock cress) One of the most popular of spring-flowering, trailing plants for rock garden or dry walls and an essential companion for white-flowered arabis and yellow alyssum. The aubrieta is typically a blue-flowered plant but there are also pink-, purple- and crimson-flowered varieties. Plants can easily be raised from seed sown in spring but seedlings vary in colour for which reason selected garden

Campanula carpatica

varieties are increased by cuttings of young shoots in a frame about mid-summer.

Aubrietas like sunny places and will grow in practically any soil, though they particularly like soils containing lime or chalk.

Bellflower, see Campanula

Bellis (Daisy) *Bellis perennis* is the common daisy of lawns, not to be admitted to the garden in its wild form, but it has produced double-flowered varieties, some with much larger flowers, these being used for spring bedding displays, and one, named Dresden China, with tiny double pink flowers which look exquisite in the rock garden. Oddly enough it is not a particularly easy plant to grow, needing good drainage, a sunny place and freedom from the competition of more vigorous plants which can easily overrun it. Increase is by division at almost any time.

Broom, see Cytisus and Genista

Campanula (Bellflower) There are tall campanulas for the border and small, tufted or trailing campanulas for the rock garden. One of the best of these is *Campanula portenschlagiana* (syn. *C. muralis*) with innumerable deep blue bell-shaped flowers from mid- to late summer. At this season it is one of the best plants for the rock garden. *C. poscharskyana* spreads even more rapidly, has pale, more widely open flowers and starts to flower earlier. *C. cochlearifolia*

(syn. *C. pusilla*) hangs its little blue or white flowers on slender 4-in (10-cm) stems in early summer, and *C. garganica* makes a carpet of growth studded with starry light blue flowers in summer. *C. carpatica* is larger than any of the foregoing, with quite big cup-shaped flowers held erect on 9-in (23-cm) stems in mid-summer. There are light blue, dark blue and white-flowered varieties. Catalogues contain the names of a great many more campanulas, many of them raised in gardens.

Most are easily grown in full sun or partial shade and any reasonably porous soil. They are increased by division in spring or autumn.

Candytuft, see Iberis

Catchfly, see Silene

Cerastium (Snow in summer) These grey-leaved plants with abundant white flowers in early summer spread so rapidly that they can be a menace in the rock garden, taking complete charge and smothering all less vigorous plants. Yet for covering rough places quickly they have a use, and they will grow in the poorest soils and driest places. The kind most commonly grown is *Cerastium tomentosum*, but *C. biebersteinii* is equally effective and a little less invasive. Both can be increased by division at practically any time.

Cheiranthus (Wallflower) Most of the wallflowers are used for bold displays of colour in spring bedding schemes and are too big and too impermanent for the rock garden, but there are one or two exceptions including *Cheiranthus* Harpur Crewe, a bushy little plant, 1 ft (30 cm) high, with double yellow flowers in spring. It likes sandy, well-drained soils and sunny places, and can be increased by cuttings in spring or summer.

Chiastophyllum *Chiastophyllum oppositifolium*, often known as *Cotyledon simplicifolia*, is a good plant for a sunny crevice or shelf in the rock garden. It makes a rosette of fleshy leaves from which arise in late summer little arching stems laden with bright yellow flowers, the whole no more than 6 in (15 cm) high. It is increased by division in the spring.

Columbine, see Aquilegia

Convolvulus There is only one kind of convolvulus that properly belongs in the rock garden and this is a bushy little plant about 1 ft (30 cm) high with silvery leaves and white flowers in summer, named *Convolvulus cneorum*. It needs a rather sheltered, sunny place as it is none too hardy. It likes well-drained soil and is increased by cuttings in summer.

Corydalis (Fumitory) *Corydalis lutea* is a

pretty little foot-high plant with elegant fern-like foliage and sprays of yellow flowers in summer. In gardens it usually spreads itself by seed and can become rather a nuisance but is a useful plant for clothing walls and rocky, difficult places. It will grow in sun or partial shade and seems able to survive with a minimum of soil. More garden worthy are *C. cheilanthifolia*, with showy yellow flowers, and *C. cashmeriana* with peacock-blue flowers. The last named needs a lime-free, rather peaty soil and protection from strong sunshine.

Cotula Carpeting plants which, like acaena, have the merit of being completely prostrate and able to withstand quite a lot of wear so that they are suitable for planting in the crevices between paving slabs. The kind commonly planted is *Cotula squalida*, with small, divided green leaves. It will grow in any soil in sun or semi-shade and can be increased by division at almost any time.

Cotyledon, see Chiastophyllum

Cranesbill, see Geranium

Cyclamen In addition to the large-flowered cyclamen, which are popular pot plants for the greenhouse and are sold in great numbers in florists' shops around Christmas, there are some which are quite hardy and suitable for the rock garden, wild garden or woodland. One of the best and easiest to grow is *Cyclamen neapolitanum*, (syn. *C. hederaefolium*) with dark green leaves handsomely marbled with white, and small pink flowers on 4-in (10-cm) stems in early autumn. *C. coum* is still smaller and produces its deep crimson flowers in late winter or early spring, and *C. europaeum* its rather lighter red flowers in late summer.

All produce corms, like the greenhouse cyclamen, and these are sometimes sold dry. It is not the best way to start, however, as sometimes these dry corms fail to grow. The corms are best started into growth in seed boxes filled with damp peat and placed in a greenhouse or frame, the young plants not being planted out until the spring. A better

Dodecatheon meadia

Dianthus hybrid

way to start is to purchase growing plants in (or tapped out of) pots. Once established in the garden in a partially shaded place they often spread freely by self-sown seed if well supplied with peat or leafmould. They should be left undisturbed as long as possible.

Cytisus (Broom) Most of the brooms are big shrubs but one or two are sufficiently small to be grown in the rock garden. *Cytisus beanii* makes a little bush about 1 ft (30cm) high smothered in yellow flowers in spring. *C. kewensis* produces showers of arching stems, the whole no more than 15 in (38cm) high but possibly spreading over two square yards of ground, with pale yellow flowers in spring. *C. purpureus* creeps about by underground stems but remains low to the ground and bears rather dull purplish flowers in late spring. All like sunny places and are not fussy about soil.

Daisy, see Bellis

Daphne Many daphnes are too big for the rock garden but *Daphne blagayana* is a prostrate shrub which likes to grow with stones holding its sprawling stems to the soil. The creamy-white flowers come in spring and are intensely fragrant. So are the pink flower clusters of *D. cneorum*, a little shrublet 12 in (30cm) high, flowering in spring.

Both like a sunny place and well-drained soil and can be increased by layering the stems in late spring, or *D. cneorum* by summer cuttings.

Dianthus (Pink) A great many of the smaller kinds and varieties of dianthus make excellent rock plants. Three of the best are the maiden pink, *Dianthus deltoides*, a trailing plant with masses of rosy-red flowers from mid-summer onwards for several weeks; the Cheddar pink, *D. caesius*, or *gratiano politanus*, a tufted plant with soft pink flowers in late spring, and *D. neglectus*, which makes close cushions of narrow leaves on which sit, in early summer, the almost stemless rose flowers with buff reverse.

All these, and the many other kinds offered in the catalogues of rock garden specialists, thrive in sunny places and gritty well-drained soils. Most do well on limestone or chalk. The species can be raised from seed but specially selected garden varieties are increased by cuttings in early summer or by careful division in spring.

Dodecatheon (American cowslip, shooting star) Pretty plants for damp but open places, particularly around pools or at the side of streams in the rock garden. Despite the popular name they have little resemblance to cowslips, the rosy-purple or white petals of the flowers being turned back like those of a cyclamen. They are, however, carried on bare 12-in (30-cm) stems rather in the manner of a cowslip and they appear in late spring. The best method of increase is by seed sown in a greenhouse or frame in spring. *Dodecatheon meadia* is the easiest.

Gentiana acaulis

Edelweiss, see Leontopodium

Erinus A little rosette-forming plant which will establish itself in a wall and other stony places with little or no soil and produce short spikes of purple flowers in spring. The kind cultivated is *Erinus alpinus* which has a white variety, *albus*, and a carmine variety, Dr Hanele. This last must be increased by division but the others can be raised from seed and usually spread naturally by self-sown seedlings.

Erodium (Heron's bill) Pretty little plants most of which either make small hummocks or spreading carpets of growth. *Erodium corsicum* has grey leaves and rose-pink flowers throughout the summer. *E. reichardii roseum* makes a mat of soft green leaves studded with pink flowers from late spring to autumn.

These and other kinds can be grown in any reasonably well-drained soil and open position and they are readily increased by division in spring or autumn.

Erysimum Bushy plants closely allied and similar in appearance to wallflowers. The best are *Erysimum alpinum* Moonlight with pale yellow flowers, and *E. linifolium*, bright purple, both flowering in spring and early summer.

They like sunny places and well-drained soils and grow well on chalk or limestone.

Increase by cuttings in spring or summer, or *E. linifolium* by seed in spring.

Evening primrose, see Oenothera

Flax, see Linum

Fumitory, see Corydalis

Genista (Broom) Most of the genistas are too large for the rock garden but a few, such as *Genista lydia* and *G. tinctoria flore-pleno* are useful rock garden shrubs. The first makes a low, wide-spreading bush of arching branches covered in bright yellow flowers in early summer. *G. tinctoria flore-pleno* is practically prostrate and will spread for several feet, smothering itself with double yellow flowers in early summer.

These and other kinds of genista like well-drained soils and sunny places and can be increased by cuttings in summer, and *G. tinctoria* also by careful division in autumn or early spring.

Gentian, see Gentiana

Gentiana (Gentian) Almost all the gentians that matter from the garden standpoint are low-growing, spreading plants. The one notable exception is the willow-leaved gentian, *Gentiana asclepiadea*, which makes slender arching stems 18 in (45 cm) or so in height, bearing purple or white blooms in summer. It is a plant for cool, partially shady places.

Most of the other kinds like sunny, open places in soil containing plenty of peat or leafmould as well as gritty sand to keep it open.

Gentiana acaulis is typical of the family, making spreading tufts of growth on which the large, deep blue flowers sit in spring. It is one of the few kinds that does well on chalky soil. *G. verna* is much smaller, even brighter in colour, and more difficult to grow. It dislikes lime in any form. There are several summer-flowering kinds with clusters of purple flowers and for early autumn there is the lovely Chinese gentian, *G. sino-ornata*, with deep sky-blue flowers. It also dislikes lime and will grow in practically pure peat and sand. *G. macaulayi*, a vigorous hybrid between *G. sino-ornata* and *G. farreri*, has a white throat and needs the same treatment.

Easier to manage are the summer-flowering gentians such as *G. freyniana, G. lagodechiana* and its variety *septemfida*. These are semi-trailing plants with clusters of deep blue flowers and they will grow in the ordinary rock garden soil mixture without difficulty.

All these gentians can be increased by careful division in spring and most can also be raised from seed sown in a greenhouse or frame in spring.

Geranium (Cranesbill) In addition to the popular bedding geraniums, which are really pelargoniums, and the quite large hardy geraniums for the herbaceous border or bed, there are several much smaller kinds that can be grown in the rock garden. One of the best is *Geranium subcaulescens*, a trailing plant with 6-in (15-cm) stems, carrying, in early summer, remarkably bright rose-purple flowers. *G. sanguineum* makes mats of growth, studded in spring and summer with magenta flowers, but it is apt to be invasive. A better plant is a less vigorous variety of it named *lancastriense*, with clear pink flowers.

All are readily grown in any reasonable soil and open position, and can be increased by division in spring or autumn.

Geum Most of the geums are for the herbaceous border rather than for the rock garden, but the foot-high *Geum borisii*, with orange-red flowers from late spring to autumn, is suitable for both, and the prostrate yellow-flowered *G. reptans* is definitely a rock plant. It flowers in early summer and likes a sunny place and very gritty, sharply drained soil. *G. borisii* will grow in any reasonably well-drained soil. Both can be increased by division in spring.

Gold dust, see Alyssum

Gromwell, see Lithospermum

Gypsophila These are also primarily border plants but *Gypsophila repens* is a slender, trailing plant with grey-green leaves and showers of small white flowers in late spring and early summer. It has an even prettier

Geranium subcaulescens

pink variety named *rosea*. This is a plant for sunny crevices and shelves in the rock garden or on the face of a wall. It will grow in any reasonably well-drained soil, but particularly likes chalk and limestone. It can be increased by seed sown in spring.

Helianthemum (Rock rose, sun rose) Bushy, sprawling plants admirable for planting on sunny rock gardens or dry walls. The flowers do not last long but are constantly replaced, so that a plant will remain highly decorative for many weeks in late spring and early summer. The colour range is from white and pale yellow to orange, copper and crimson. Most varieties have single flowers, but a few, such as Jubilee, yellow, and Fireball, crimson, are double. Habit is improved by trimming the young growth with shears or secateurs after flowering, but do not cut back into the hard old wood.

All can be increased by cuttings in summer in a propagating frame and seed may also be sown in spring, but seedlings are likely to vary greatly in colour and quality of flower. It is better to increase from cuttings to obtain uniform plants.

Heron's bill, see Erodium

Houseleek, see Sempervivum

Hypericum (St John's wort) Shrubby or trailing plants, some of which make excellent rock plants. The best for this purpose are *Hypericum olympicum*, 1 ft (30 cm) high with pale yellow flowers; *H. repens*, with thin, wiry stems and deep yellow flowers; *H. coris*, which in appearance is intermediate between the last two, and *H. fragile*, 6 in (15 cm) high, with pale gold flowers.

All thrive in any ordinary soil and open, sunny position, and can be increased by seed sown in spring, or some kinds by careful division, also in spring.

Iberis (Candytuft) There are both annual and perennial candytufts and it is the latter that are good rock plants. They are equally suitable for a sunny rock garden or dry wall. They grow about 9 in (23 cm) high, have evergreen foliage, and white flowers in late spring.

One of the best varieties is *Iberis sempervirens* Snowflake. The lowest growing kind is *I. saxatilis*, which often does not exceed 3 in (8 cm) in height, though it can spread quite a lot. *I. gibraltarica* is taller and has lilac-pink flowers but is less hardy and reliable than the others.

All can be grown from seed, though seedlings are unlikely to flower before their second year and may vary a little in quality. Alternatively, cuttings can be rooted in a frame in summer and will exactly reproduce the qualities of the parent plant.

Kenilworth ivy, see Linaria

Leontopodium alpinum

Leontopodium (Edelweiss) *Leontopodium alpinum* is a rock plant with narrow grey leaves, and tiny flowers surrounded by star-shaped clusters of bracts which are densely clad in white down. It is grown more for sentiment and because of the many legends attached to it than for its beauty, though it is not unattractive in a quiet way. It should be given an open, sunny place in well-drained soil and will benefit from the protection of a pane of glass in winter, supported a few inches above it, to ward off rain. Propagation is by division in spring.

Lewisia Very attractive plants bearing fine sprays of flowers above flattish rosettes of leaves. Some kinds are rather difficult to grow, but there is a race of garden hybrids which will grow well in sunny places and gritty, well-drained but not dry soils. They are ideal plants for the crevices in a dry wall with an ample body of soil behind it. The fine flowers of these hybrids are in shades of peach, apricot, salmon and pink, and are borne on 9- to 12-in (23- to 30-cm) stems in late spring and early summer.

As a rule the plants are not very long lived, but they can be renewed fairly easily from seed sown in a frame or greenhouse in spring.

Linaria (Toadflax, Kenilworth ivy) Two very different kinds of toadflax may be grown in rocky places. One, a true mountain plant, is *Linaria alpina*, which might be likened to a tiny antirrhinum, with slender 4-in (10-cm) spikes of purple or shrimp-pink flowers in summer. It likes sunny places and gritty soils, and is raised from seed sown in a frame or greenhouse in spring.

The other, *Linaria aequitriloba*, has been renamed *Cymbalaria aequitriloba* and may be found so listed in some catalogues. It is a carpeter with little lavender flowers sitting on the close carpet of rounded leaves. It is an excellent plant to grow in the crevices between paving slabs and it will thrive in

sun or shade in any reasonable soil. Increase is by division at almost any time.

Linum (Flax) *Linum perenne* is a slender, elegant plant with pale blue flowers produced in summer in loose sprays on 18-in (45-cm) stems. *L. narbonnense* is very like it, but a shade deeper in colour. *L. flavum* is about 9 in (23 cm) in height and it has more compact clusters of bright yellow flowers, and the so-called tree flax, *L. arboreum*, is a tiny bushling of 9 to 12 in (23 to 30 cm), otherwise very much like the last. Gemmell's Hybrid, probably a hybrid between these last two species, is a particularly good form of yellow-flowered flax and probably the best for general planting.

All these flaxes like sunny places and well-drained soils. They can be raised from seed sown in a frame or greenhouse in spring, or *L. arboreum* by cuttings in a frame in summer; a method which is essential for Gemmell's Hybrid as it is variable in colour and flower quality if raised from seed.

Lithospermum (Gromwell) One of the loveliest of pure blue flowers for the sunny rock garden, rock bank or dry wall is

Lithospermum diffusum

Oenothera missouriensis

Lithospermum diffusum, also known as *L. prostratum*, a trailing plant with flowers individually quite small, but so blue and produced so freely in late spring and early summer that there are few plants to equal it for beauty at this season. The two finest varieties are Heavenly Blue and Grace Ward.

All need a lime-free and well-drained soil, but otherwise are not in the least difficult to grow. Increase is by cuttings in a frame in summer.

Mentha This is the botanical name for mint, few kinds of which should be allowed anywhere near a rock garden, but one kind, the Corsican mint, *Mentha requienii*, is a useful carpeter for cool, rather moist places. It can be used over small bulbs or in the crevices between paving slabs where it will emit its strong minty aroma when walked on. It is increased by division in spring.

Moss pink, see Phlox

Oenothera (Evening primrose) Some kinds of evening primrose are far too large and coarse for the rock garden, but there are exceptions. *Oenothera missouriensis* is a trailing plant with large, pale yellow flowers in late summer and autumn which will grow in any reasonable soil and sunny place and is quite at home in a rock bed or rock garden. Divide or sow seed in spring.

Omphalodes *Omphalodes verna*, described on page 66 is rather too rampant for most rock gardens, but two other kinds with a much neater habit are worth growing in this part of the garden. *O. cappadocica* has blue-grey leaves and sprays of small blue forget-me-not flowers in spring and is not fussy about soil. It will grow well in sun or semi-shade. *O. luciliae* is more tufted in habit with blue-grey leaves and azure-blue flowers on 6-in (15-cm) stems in late spring. It enjoys sun and well-drained but not dry soil; slugs are very fond of it. Both kinds can be increased by division in spring.

Onosma These are very distinctive plants to grow in the crevices of a dry wall, or in a sunny rock garden with perfect drainage. They grow especially well on chalk and limestone. *Onosma tauricum* carries golden-yellow flowers above its tufts of downy, grey-green leaves. The flowers are tubular and carried in curling spikes in early summer. One of the easiest to grow, it has the common name of golden drops. *O. alboroseum* with white flowers that change to pink as they age is more resentful of excess moisture, especially in autumn and winter. Both kinds can be increased by seed in spring.

Oxalis Sun-loving plants for the rock garden or, in the case of *Oxalis floribunda* (it is often called *O. rosea*), as an edging to beds. The two best rock garden kinds are *O. enneaphylla* and *O. adenophylla*, rather similar plants with clustered flowers in summer, white in the first, pink-flushed in the second, sitting close down on the tufted blue-grey leaves.

They need the best possible drainage and rather light, gritty soil and plenty of leaf-mould or peat to retain moisture in summer without becoming too waterlogged in winter. *O. adenophylla* likes full sunlight while *O. enneaphylla* prefers a light place which will not be scorched by too much direct sunshine.

By contrast *O. floribunda* will grow in any warm, sunny place and does not mind how poor the soil is. Its bright rose flowers in loose sprays are produced all the summer. It can be easily increased by division in spring, and *O. enneaphylla* can also be carefully divided, but *O. adenophylla* can be increased only by seed.

Papaver (Poppy) The only poppy for the rock garden is a mountain kind named *Papaver alpinum*, a charming little plant like a miniature Iceland poppy, with fragrant white, yellow or orange flowers on 4-in (10-cm) stems in summer. It seldom sur-

Polygonum affine

vives for long, but since it reproduces itself from seed in well-drained, gritty soil, it is not difficult to maintain a succession of plants. It must have a sunny place.

Pasque flower, see Pulsatilla

Penstemon There are several small penstemons worth growing in the rock garden, notably *Penstemon heterophyllus*, a plant with sturdy 15-in (38-cm) spikes of blue flowers all summer; *P. scouleri*, a more compact plant with lilac-blue flowers on 9-in (23-cm) stems in late spring and early summer; *P. rupicola*, almost prostrate and with ruby-red flowers.

All like well-drained soils and sunny rather sheltered places, and can be increased by cuttings in summer or seed in spring.

Phlox (Moss pink) The moss pink *Phlox subulata*, is a mat-forming plant with narrow leaves and mauve, pink, rose or white flowers in late spring. There are numerous garden varieties and all are easy to grow in reasonably open places and almost any soil. *P. douglasii* is more compact in habit and needs well-drained, rather gritty soil. It has numerous excellent varieties. *P. divaricata* is a taller plant with 9-in (23-cm) stems bearing loose clusters of mauve or lavender flowers, which are a good clear blue in the variety *laphamii*, in spring and early summer.

Varieties of *P. subulata* and *P. douglasii* are best increased by cuttings in summer, *P. d. laphamii* by division in spring. The species also grow from seed but seedlings may vary in flower colour.

Pink, see Dianthus

Polygonum (Knotweed) There are vigorous climbing polygonums and herbaceous kinds that do not seem to know where to stop, but there are also a couple of small mat-forming kinds that are excellent for the rock garden or wall. One of these is *Polygonum vacciniifolium*, with little slender spikes of pink flowers and the other, *P. affine*, with rather stouter spikes of rose or carmine flowers. Both flower in late summer and early autumn, like sunny places and are not at all fussy about soil. They can be increased by division in the spring.

Poppy, see Papaver

Potentilla There are several small potentillas suitable for the rock garden. One of the best is *Potentilla tonguei*, a creeping plant with orange-buff flowers from mid-summer to autumn. *P. alba* makes a wide-spreading carpet of leaves studded with white flowers all summer. Both *P. aurea* and *P. verna nana* have bright yellow flowers, most effective in a double-flowered variety of *P. aurea* named *flore pleno*.

All these will grow in any reasonably well-drained soil and open position and can be increased by division in the spring.

Primrose, see Primula

Primula (Primrose) In addition to the wild British primrose, which has produced various coloured and double-flowered varieties of garden merit, and the polyanthus, which is a cluster-flowered form of primrose, there are a number of other hardy primroses which are excellent plants for the rock garden, the side of a pool or woodland. *Primula juliae* is a mat-forming plant with almost stemless deep carmine flowers. It has given a whole race of hybrids with the British primrose, all pink or magenta in colour and often collectively known as *P. juliana*. Wanda, crimson magenta, is one of the best known and a first-class plant.

The drumstick primrose, *P. denticulata*, has mauve, pink or white flowers in an

Bog primulas

almost spherical head on 5-in (13-cm) stems in spring, and will grow anywhere, though it has a preference for rather damp spots. So has *P. rosea*, a brilliant little spring flower for the waterside with intense deep rose flowers on 3-in (8-cm) stems.

The candelabra primroses, which include *P. japonica*, *P. pulverulenta* and *P. helodoxa*, are also plants for damp places. They will thrive along the sides of drainage ditches in leafy or peaty soils and are also at home in the woodland. Their pink, magenta or, in *P. helodoxa*, yellow flowers, are produced in candelabra-like sprays 2 ft (60 cm) high.

The Tibetan cowslip, *P. florindae*, will actually grow in shallow water, though it is better in the bog garden where it is damp but not actually covered with water. The same is true of the Sikkim cowslip, *P. sikkimensis*. Both have big heads of nodding yellow flowers like giant cowslips.

Pulsatilla vulgaris

For drier places, such as ledges or crevices in the rock garden, there is *P. marginata*, with heads of lavender-blue flowers, *P. edgeworthii*, also lavender-flowered, both out in early spring, and the numerous varieties of *P. auricula* which are much easier to manage and can be grown as edgings to flower borders if there is no room for them in the rock garden.

All these hardy primroses can be increased by careful division in spring, also by seed sown as soon as ripe or also in spring. Many kinds will spread themselves by self-sown seed.

Pulsatilla (Pasque flower) The beautiful *Pulsatilla vulgaris* was for long known as *Anemone pulsatilla*, and may still be found so listed in some nursery catalogues. It makes a low clump of softly hairy leaves from which, in spring, grow 9-in (23-cm) stems bearing large mauve-purple flowers followed by tangled, silken seed heads. There is considerable variation in colour from pale reddish forms to blue purple, but all are beautiful.

This is a plant that grows naturally on chalk downs. It likes open, sunny places and well-drained soils, and it can be increased by seed, but because of the colour variation specially selected forms are increased by careful division of the roots in spring after flowering.

Ramonda Very distinctive plants for shady places in soil containing plenty of peat or leafmould. They make flat rosettes of leathery leaves from the centres of which the 6-in (15-cm) flower stems are produced in late spring. The most popular kind is *Ramonda myconi* with bluish-lilac flowers. *R. nathaliae* is nearer to blue and there are also white and pinkish forms.

All like to grow on their sides in vertical crevices so that water does not collect in their rosettes; they do well facing north. Increase is by seed in spring or leaf cuttings in early summer.

Raoulia One of the most beautiful carpeting plants but not one of the easiest to grow. *Raoulia australis* makes a completely flat mat of shiny silver leaves and can be used over choice rock garden bulbs, but it does

require a gritty, well-drained yet not dry soil. It is increased by division in the spring.

Rhodohypoxis Another little beauty that is not easy to grow well, *Rhodohypoxis baurii* makes tiny tufts of narrow leaves and bears its white, pink or carmine flowers like brightly coloured moths, on 3-in (8-cm) stems in summer. It needs peaty, lime-free soil with plenty of moisture while it is growing in late spring and summer but no excess of water in winter. It should only be moved in spring and can be divided then or grown from seed sown in moist peat and sand.

Rock cress, see Aubrieta

Rock rose, see Helianthemum

St John's wort, see Hypericum

Saponaria (Soapwort) The most popular kind is *Saponaria ocymoides*, a spreading plant for sunny banks, rock gardens or walls. It grows rapidly and around mid-summer covers its loose mounds of growth with bright pink flowers.

It likes sunny places, will grow in almost any soil and is readily increased by division in spring or autumn.

Saxifraga (Saxifrage) There are a great many different kinds of saxifrage and they vary so much in appearance that it is not immediately obvious that all are related. From the garden standpoint four groups are most valuable – the silver saxifrages, the cushion saxifrages, the mossy saxifrages, and the London prides.

The first two are plants for sunny crevices and ledges in the rock garden or dry wall. The silver saxifrages make flattish rosettes of leaves, often silvered all over or along the edges, and they produce clusters or sprays of flowers, usually white, though there are pink and even yellow varieties. One of the loveliest is Tumbling Waters with arching 2-ft (60-cm) flower sprays in early summer.

The cushion saxifrages make low hummocks of usually greyish leaves which often have a hard and spiky feel. The flowers, which may be white, pink or pale yellow, are produced in early spring on 1- to 3-in (2·5- to 8-cm) stems. Typical of this lovely group is Cranbourne, with flowers the colour of apple blossom; *Saxifraga burseriana*, pure white, and *S. elizabethae*, yellow, but there are many more.

Both the silver and the cushion saxifrages thrive in well-drained, gritty soils, preferably containing plenty of limestone chippings, and they like open places.

By contrast, the mossy saxifrages thrive in ordinary soils and do not object to shade. They make soft, low mounds of much divided green leaves and carry sprays of white, pink or red flowers on 6- to 9-in

(15- to 23-cm) stems in spring. They can be grown in the rock garden, but are equally good for edging a bed or border. Typical kinds are James Bremner, white; Winston Churchill, pink, and *sanguinea superba*, crimson.

The London prides are best known by the common London pride *Saxifraga umbrosa*, a plant with rosettes of green leaves and loose 1-ft (30-cm) sprays of small pink flowers in early summer. It will grow anywhere in sun or shade. It is splendid on walls, in shady borders and in big rock gardens, but in small rock gardens a better plant is the small London pride, *S. u. primuloides*, which is at its most beautiful in Ingwersen's Variety. This is only 6 in (15 cm) high and has deep pink flowers in late spring.

Almost all saxifrages can be increased by division in spring and most can also be raised from seed sown in a frame or greenhouse in spring, though it may be a year or two before seedlings attain flowering size, and they may vary in flower colour from their parents.

Saxifrage, see Saxifraga

Sedum (Stonecrop) Succulent plants, many of which are quite hardy and can be grown on sunny rock gardens, dry walls, banks, etc. Most will grow in quite poor and dry soils. Some, such as *Sedum spathulifolium*, with yellow flowers, and *S. spurium*, with pale pink flowers in summer, are quite prostrate plants which can cover a considerable area in time. Others are more tufted. One of the smallest in leaf is *S. hispanicum*, a creeping plant with blue-grey leaves so small that the plant almost looks like a moss. This and similar small kinds such as *S. lydium*, with reddish bronze leaves, and *S. dasyphyllum*, with blue-grey leaves, can be planted in the crevices between paving slabs.

Most stonecrops can be increased by division in spring or autumn, but a few, including *S. caeruleum* with small pale blue flowers, are annuals grown from seed sown in spring.

Sempervivum (Houseleek) The sempervivums do flower but they are grown primarily for the decorative merit of their rosettes of succulent leaves which are variously coloured and sometimes covered with a cobweb-like network of hairs. One of the best of these cobweb houseleeks is *Sempervivum arachnoideum*. It has small rosettes not much over $\frac{1}{2}$ in (1 cm) in diameter in contrast to the 3-in (8-cm) rosettes of the common houseleek, *S. tectorum*.

Many more varieties will be found in catalogues and all will grow well in hot, dry places with a minimum of soil once established, though some good loam, alkaline rather than acid, plus a dash of bonemeal and some limestone chippings will get them started. Divide in spring.

Shooting star, see Dodecatheon

Silene (Catchfly) Three silenes are useful rock garden plants. The smallest is *Silene acaulis* which makes tight cushions of growth studded with pink flowers in spring; *S. alpestris* makes carpets of small shining leaves and carries its white flowers on slender 6-in (15-cm) stems in late spring and early summer, and *S. schafta*, a taller, looser plant, is the last to bloom in late summer and early autumn, when it is covered with rose-carmine flowers.

All like sunny places and well-drained soils and can be increased by division in spring.

Sisyrinchium Not all kinds are easy to grow and one of the most beautiful, *Sisyrinchium grandiflorum*, with rush-like leaves and bell-shaped amethyst-purple flowers on slender 9-in (23-cm) stems in early spring, needs a moist yet porous mixture of peat, sand and stone chippings to make it really happy. But *S. angustifolium*, the blue-eyed grass, so called because of its narrow leaves and starry blue flowers, will grow in any reasonably good soil and sunny place where it will often become naturalized and seed itself about freely. It is 9 in (23 cm) high, flowers in early summer and can be increased by seed or division in spring.

Snow in summer, see Cerastium

Soapwort, see Saponaria

Soldanella Very beautiful little plants with small rounded leaves and nodding stems with fringed violet flowers. The two most popular kinds are *Soldanella alpina*, 3 in (8 cm) high and *S. montana*, 3 to 4 in (8 to 10 cm) high. Both need a very porous but not dry mixture of soil, peat and sand or stone chippings and a sunny place. They are not easy plants and are often grown in pans in a frame or unheated greenhouse to protect them against winter wet which can cause them to rot off.

Stone cress, see Aethionema

Stonecrop, see Sedum

Sun rose, see Helianthemum

Thrift, see Armeria

Thyme, see Thymus

Thymus (Thyme) Small perennials with aromatic foliage, suitable for the rock garden, wall and paving. They are either completely prostrate, as in pink-, carmine- or white-flowered *Thymus serpyllum*, or make neat little bushes, as in *T. carnosus* (often listed as *T. nitidus*) and *T. citriodorus*, the lemon thyme, so called because of its distinctive aroma; both have pink flowers.

Saxifraga burseriana Gloria

All like sunny places and well-drained soils and flower in late spring and early summer. The creeping kinds can be divided in spring, the shrubby kinds increased by cuttings in summer.

Toadflax, see Linaria

Veronica Most of the veronicas are shrubs or herbaceous plants, far too big for the rock garden, but a few are small creeping or tufted plants. One of the best is *Veronica prostrata*, a mat-forming plant with little 3-in (8-cm) spikes of bright blue flowers in early summer. *V. catarractae* makes a tiny bush, 1 ft (30 cm) high, with off-white flowers all summer. Both like sunny places but will grow in any reasonable soil. *V. rupestris* is easily increased by division, *V. catarractae* from seed or cuttings.

Viola All violas can be grown in the rock garden, but it is the small-flowered varieties, such as *Viola gracilis*, *V. cornuta* and their varieties, that look most at home there. These are sprawling plants bearing a constant succession of flowers in late spring and early summer. Typical *V. gracilis* has deep violet-purple flowers, typical *V. cornuta*, light blue, but there are numerous garden varieties of each as well as hybrids, ranging in colour from white, cream and lavender to deep yellow and purple.

All like cool, partially shaded places and soils with plenty of leafmould or peat. They can be increased by division in spring or by cuttings in summer.

Wallflower, see Cheiranthus

Windflower, see Anemone

Yarrow, see Achillea

Water can add to the attractions of a garden in several quite different ways. Still water acts as a mirror and provides the gardener with a texture sharply contrasted with that of soil, grass or plants. Moving water is exciting to the eye and pleasant to the ear. And in addition to all this, water is a medium in which a new range of plants can be grown: water plants, or full aquatics, in the deep water and bog plants, or sub-aquatics, in the very shallow water or the wet ground around the pool or stream.

Water can be used as a purely formal feature in pools of circular, oval, rectangular or other geometric formation with or without ornamental fountains, or it can be used informally as streams, waterfalls, cascades and pools of irregular shape. The formal pattern is appropriate when water is used near the house or in conjunction with rose gardens, terraces, patios, patterned beds and other places in which design is important. By contrast water can be used more effectively in informal ways in rock gardens, wild gardens and woodlands where the intention is to achieve a natural appearance.

Scum and blanket weed are less troublesome in shade than in full sun but, nevertheless, it is usually best to site a pool in a fairly sunny and certainly a very light place since good light adds so much to the sparkle of the water and water lilies may refuse to flower if they get no sunshine.

Methods of Retaining Water

However water is used, it must be effectively contained. Leaky pools and streams are a constant source of annoyance and are usually very difficult to repair effectively.

There are four main ways in which water can be retained in pools and streams. One, the traditional method, is to cover bottom and sides with wet, beaten clay, a process known as 'puddling'. In gardens it is seldom practised today partly because of the difficulty of acquiring suitable clay in adequate quantity, partly because the puddling itself is a rural art not easily imparted to those who are unfamiliar with it.

Concrete For reasons just stated, concrete, a modern material the ingredients for which are readily available and which can be prepared by rule-of-thumb methods, took the place of clay, but it is itself now being challenged by two even newer techniques: the use of plastic sheets and of resin-bonded fibre-glass.

Concrete can be prepared at home with all-in ballast (a mixture of sand and gravel), cement and water, or in many districts can be purchased ready mixed and delivered to the site (a very convenient labour-saving method). Ballast is sold by the cubic yard, often referred to simply as the yard, or by the cubic metre, and cement is sold by the hundredweight or ton or in 50kg bags or metric tonnes. A suitable mix for pools is to allow 5cwt of cement to each yard of ballast (or 250kg cement to each cubic metre of ballast).

As a rule a layer of concrete at least 4in (10cm) thick is required for the bottom of a pool and at least 3in (8cm) thick for the sides and it will be wise to increase these thicknesses to 6in (15cm) and 4in (10cm) for large pools and further strengthen them by embedding special reinforcing wire mesh in the concrete. This can be purchased from any dealer in building materials as can the ballast and cement.

Whether one mixes concrete oneself or purchases it ready mixed, the site of the pool must be ready excavated to receive it. Formal ponds often have vertical sides and informal pools usually have sloping sides but there is no rule about this. It is largely a matter of convenience and personal taste, though it should be observed that very shallow pools with a large surface area are more likely to suffer weed problems, particularly from green scum and blanket weed, than those that are deeper. This is because bright light and warmth encourage these growths of algae and the shallow pool heats up more rapidly on sunny days than the deeper pool.

Sometimes shelves are made around the sides of the pools to take plants that like shallow water. Few plants need, or indeed like, more than 2ft (60cm) depth of water and 1ft to 1½ft (30 to 45cm) is sufficient for most water lilies. A great many marginal plants like to have their roots just covered with water but an inch or so is quite sufficient.

If a pool has shallowly sloping sides, well-made concrete can be spread on them without slipping, but for steep slopes or vertical sides, shuttering will be needed. This means pieces of plank temporarily fixed to hold the concrete in place while it is drying.

If reinforcing wire is to be used it should be laid in the bottom and around the sides of the pool before the concrete is put in. Then the wet concrete will completely surround the wire which will become embedded in it and give it greatly increased strength.

Cement contains chemicals which are dissolved out by water and can be harmful to plants and fish. For this reason it is wise to fill a new concrete pool with water, leave it for a week or so and then empty and refill it before planting. An alternative is to paint the surface of the dry concrete with bituminous paint to keep water out of direct contact with it. This helps to ensure that the pool will be waterproof, though this can also be done by adding special waterproofing powders or liquids to the concrete when it is prepared. Ready-mixed concrete can be purchased with a waterproofing compound incorporated.

Plastic Sheets Clearly, the making of a concrete pool involves a great deal of labour. Much of this can be avoided by using plastic sheets or fibre-glass in place of concrete.

Special sheets of P.V.C., sometimes strengthened with nylon, or liners of butyl rubber, can be purchased for pools and they are pre-welded by the supplier so that one sheet covers the whole interior of the pool without the need for joints. The plastic or rubber has some elasticity and the weight of the water on top of it makes it conform closely to the contours of the soil beneath. Care should be taken to get the bottom and sides of the excavation as smooth as possible and to remove any large or sharp stones that might puncture the plastic. Sand can be spread over the bottom and sides to give a smooth, slightly resilient surface for the sheet to lie on.

1. Pool construction:
The pool area can be marked out with slabs but avoid damaging them when excavating.

2. Make sure that the sides and bottom of the excavation are smooth, any sharp stones could puncture the liner.

3. After partially filling with water to settle the lining the edges are tucked away under the edging slabs.

4. When all the edges are tucked under filling is completed

must be shaped to fit the pool which, fortunately, is very light to handle and can be tried in position from time to time as the hole is being prepared.

Plastic sheeting, butyl rubber and fibre-glass contain nothing that is harmful to plants or fish so that stocking can commence immediately the pool is completed.

Making Streams and Cascades Streams and cascades can be made in the same way with concrete, plastic sheeting or pre-formed fibre-glass components. The water can be recirculated from the pool either with small submersible pumps, the simplest way, or with pumps situated outside the pool and drawing water from it through a pipe. Either type of pump can also be used to operate a fountain. It is much better to recirculate water than to draw direct from a mains supply which may be too cold and will, in any case, upset the chemical balance in the pool.

Stocking a New Pool

The best time for stocking pools is in late spring and early summer. Some of the plants require soil in which to root but some are free-floating in the water.

There are two ways of providing soil for those plants that require it; one is to spread soil on the bottom of the pool, either all over or in low mounds here and there, the other is to put the soil in pots or baskets, plant the aquatics in these, and then stand them in the pool, weighting them if necessary to keep them steady. This latter method has considerable advantages in small pools as it makes it much easier to lift the plants out when they require attention or the pool needs cleaning.

Either way, ordinary garden soil can be used but good quality rather stiff loam is better. A small quantity of bonemeal (about 8 oz, 225 g, per bushel) can be added to the loam but other fertilizers are best kept out of the pool and so is animal manure.

The Ideal Way The ideal way to stock a new pool is to put the soil and rooting plants in position and then carefully run in enough water to cover them to a depth of an inch or so. Then, as they start to grow, more water can be added a little at a time until, after three or four weeks, the pool is

When the sheet arrives it should be placed across one end of the pool and carefully unrolled or unfolded across it. It must be large enough to cover bottom and sides, with at least 9 in (23 cm) overlap all round. Water is then run in and the plastic sheet will settle itself snugly in place. Any raw edges can be concealed with stones, soil, turves or creeping plants.

Fibre-glass Resin-bonded fibre-glass is a much stiffer material and is only used to make pre-fabricated pools. This means that the purchaser is restricted to the sizes and shapes available and, having selected one, must dig a hole to accommodate it. The fibre-glass pool need not rest firmly on the soil at every point but the nearer one can get to this the better; in other words the hole

Water lilies and other aquatics can be planted in baskets of heavy loam with a little bonemeal added

After thoroughly firming the soil cover the surface with coarse gravel; this prevents the soil from floating out

When the plants are well established, fish may be added to the pool

completely filled. Of course this method will not work if shelves have been made for marginal plants, unless the plants are in boxes or baskets and can be stood in the bottom of the pool to begin with, those intended for the margins being lifted to the shelves later. An alternative to this method if it is more convenient to fill the pool straight away, or when adding new plants

to pools already stocked, is to plant in pots or baskets and stand these on bricks to bring them quite close to the surface, later removing the bricks one at a time as the plants grow and require a greater depth of water over them.

Free-floating plants can simply be dropped into the water, perhaps with a small stone tied to the lower end of each to act as an anchor. This should be done when the pool is reasonably well filled with water.

Introducing Fish to the Pool Fish can come in a little later when the plants, both soil-rooting and free-floating, are beginning to get established and provide that shelter which fish must have if they are to thrive. Some of the free-floating plants perform a useful function in supplying oxygen to the water which helps to keep it fresh and in good condition for both plants and fish. Do not overstock pools with either plants or fish. It is impossible to be dogmatic about this but a fair average is not to exceed 4 in (10 cm) of body length, excluding tail, per square foot (30 cm sq) of surface area of water.

Crystal clear water is only possible where it is chemically treated or is constantly being changed. Chemical treatment makes it impossible to grow plants or stock with fish. Though it is possible to grow some plants and to have some fish in water that is moving slowly, as a rule in the garden one must be satisfied with the same water most of the time and that, in turn, means that it cannot be completely clear. The amount of discoloration, weed and scum will, however, depend to some extent on the way in which the pool is stocked. At first there is likely to be a good deal of discoloration, but as plants settle in, the free-floating plants produce their full quota of oxygen, and the fish begin to feed, a balance should be struck and the water should begin to clear.

In summer green scum and the greeny yellow cotton-wool-like growth known as blanket weed may make their appearance. They are natural weeds of still water and, like other weeds, must be removed. This can be done by careful raking or by drawing a sack or a sieve through the water.

Cleaning and Re-stocking a Pool

It should not be necessary to clear a pool every year, but small pools do get overcrowded fairly easily so, every second or third year, preferably in late spring, the pool should be emptied, plants and fish removed to buckets or tubs, the pool itself scrubbed out and then re-stocked. This is the opportunity to divide the plants, throwing away or giving away what is not required and replanting only sufficient to give the pool its correct balance of plants and fish. Do not use chemicals or detergents when cleaning out the pool – just plenty of clean water.

Recommended Aquatic and Waterside Plants

Acorus (Sweet flag) Fragrant, sword-like leaves, margined with pink, yellow and white in the variety *Acorus calamus variegatus*. It likes to grow in wet soil or up to 4 in (10 cm) of water.

Alisma (Water plantain) A plant for the margin of a pool in 2 or 3 in (5 to 8 cm) of water. *Alisma plantago-aquatica* has broad, erect leaves and small pink and white flowers in 2-ft (60-cm) high branching sprays in summer.

Aponogeton (Water hawthorn) The oval leaves of *Aponogeton distachyus* float on the surface like those of a water lily and the roots need to grow in soil not more than 18 in (45 cm) below the surface. It will grow in as little as 4 in (10 cm) of water. The small white flowers are carried in short spikes in late spring and early autumn and are sweetly scented.

Arrowhead, see Sagittaria

Bog arum, see Calla

Bog bean, see Menyanthes

Brandy bottle, see Nuphar

Bulrush, see Scirpus

Butomus (Flowering rush) Only one kind is grown, *Butomus umbellatus*, a plant with narrow reed-like leaves and stout 3-ft (1-m) stems bearing, in late summer, clusters of soft pink flowers. It likes to grow in water 3 or 4 in (8 to 10 cm) deep.

Calla (Bog arum) *Calla palustris* is a miniature relative of the familiar arum lily with little yellow and green flowers on 6-in (15-cm) stems in early summer. It is a plant for the extreme margin of the pool in water no more than 2 in (5 cm) deep.

Caltha (Marsh marigold, kingcup) This is the much-admired plant of damp meadows and streamsides in Britain, with shining green leaves and large, golden-yellow buttercup-like flowers in spring. The common kind is *Caltha palustris* and there is a showy variety with double flowers named *flore-pleno*. Yet another kind with extra large single flowers is *C. polypetala*. All like to grow in damp soil right at the edge of a pool or stream rather than in the water.

Cyperus (Umbrella grass) Rushy plants with brownish flowers borne on short stems surmounted by narrow leaves or bracts arranged like the spokes of an umbrella. *Cyperus vegetus* is 2 ft (60 cm) high, *C. longus*, 3 to 4 ft (1 to 1·25 m). Both grow well in wet soil at the edge of a pool but seed themselves about rather too freely.

Elodea Two useful submerged aquatics to supply oxygen to the water and provide shelter for fish are *Elodea canadensis* and *E. crispa*, but both grow rapidly and may have to be thinned out from time to time. In some catalogues these plants may be listed as anacharis.

Flowering rush, see Butomus

Golden club, see Orontium

Hottonia (Water violet) *Hottonia palustris* is a submerged plant with ferny leaves and sprays of pale lavender flowers a few inches above water level. This is a good oxygenating plant.

Iris Several kinds of iris are excellent water or waterside plants. *Iris laevigata* is 2 ft (60 cm) high and has broad-petalled flowers in white or various shades of blue, purple and pink. It thrives in 2 to 4 in (5 to 10 cm) depth of water as does the tall yellow flag, *I. pseudacorus* with larger flowers. *I. sibirica*, with narrow grassy leaves and elegantly formed flowers on 2½-ft (75-cm) stems, and *I. kaempferi*, similar in height but with much larger, broader-petalled flowers in a range of colour from white to deep purple, like the damp soil near pools or streams but should not be covered with water.

Juncus (Rush) There are a great many kinds of rush, one of the best for the garden pool being *Juncus effusus spiralis*, known as the corkscrew rush because its 18-in (45-cm) high stems are twisted like a corkscrew. It will thrive in damp soil or in 2 or 3 in (5 to 8 cm) depth of water.

Kingcup, see Caltha

Lysichitum (Skunk cabbage) Plants with arum-like flowers in spring followed by large, over-profuse leaves. *Lysichitum americanum*, the kind commonly planted, has large yellow flowers; *L. camtschatcense*, has smaller white flowers. Both can be grown in wet soil near a pool or stream or in 2 or 3 in (5 to 8 cm) depth of water.

Marsh marigold, see Caltha

Mentha (Mint) The water mint, *Mentha aquatica*, has mint-scented leaves and heads of small mauve flowers in summer. It likes the damp soil at the edge of a pool.

Menyanthes (Bog bean) *Menyanthes trifoliata* is a native plant which thrives in shallow pools, pushing up three-parted leaves above the surface and, in midsummer, clusters of white or pinkish flowers. It likes wet soil or up to 4 in (10 cm) of water.

Mimulus (Musk, monkey flower) The yellow musk, *Mimulus luteus*, is an excellent plant for damp soil or an inch or so of water. It

carries its deep yellow flowers on 9-in (23-cm) stems all summer and there are varieties with spotted flowers. *M. ringens* is 18 in (45 cm) high and has flowers of a lavender colour.

Mint, see Mentha

Monkey flower, see Mimulus

Musk, see Mimulus

Myosotis (Water forget-me-not) *Myosotis palustris* is like a paler blue version of the common forget-me-not and it thrives in the damp soil at the edge of a pool.

Myriophyllum Several kinds are grown to supply oxygen to the water and provide shelter for fish. All are completely submerged and have fern-like foliage.

Nuphar (Brandy bottle) These look like water lilies and have similar floating leaves but the flowers are smaller, more globular and bright yellow. The kind commonly grown is *Nuphar luteum*, a British wild plant which is vigorous and spreads rapidly. It will grow in up to 2 ft (60 cm) of water and, unlike water lilies, will open its flowers in shade.

Nymphaea (Water lily) Although they appear to float on the surface of pools, water lilies in fact root, like any terrestrial plant, into soil. There should either be a

A pleasant garden feature using pebbles and a single jet of water

depth of several inches of good loamy soil in the bottom of the pool or each water lily should be planted in a basket or box filled with soil and sunk in the pool. Most water lilies thrive best in water 12 to 18 in (30 to 45 cm) deep. A few, such as the white water lily, *Nymphaea alba*, like water 2 to 3 ft (60 cm to 1 m) deep. By contrast, the pygmy water lily, *N. tetragona*, does not need more than 5 in (13 cm) of water and will grow with even less. Some of the best garden kinds are hybrids, such as James Brydon, red; Escarboucle, crimson, and Rose Arey, pink.

All should be planted in late spring and may be increased by careful division of their fleshy roots at the same season. They are best left undisturbed for several years until they become overcrowded.

Nymphoides (Water fringe) The floating plant often called *Villarsia nymphaeoides* in catalogues should really be *Nymphoides peltatum*. The leaves are rather like those of a water lily on a reduced scale and the clusters of bright yellow, poppy-like flowers have fringed petals. It likes to grow in 12 to 18 in (30 to 45 cm) depth of water.

Orontium (Golden club) The rather stiff shining leaves of *Orontium aquaticum* float on the surface and the flowers are small, yellow and closely clustered on a slender

Sagittaria sagittifolia

white column like the central spadix of an arum lily. The plant will thrive equally well in from about 3 to 18 in (8 to 45 cm) depth of water.

Pickerel weed, see Pontederia

Pontederia (Pickerel weed) A handsome plant for the margin of a pool in 2 or 3 in (5 to 7 cm) of water. *Pontederia cordata* has heart-shaped leaves and 2-ft (60-cm) spikes of light blue flowers in summer.

Reed mace, see Typha

Rush, see Juncus

Sagittaria (Arrowhead) Marginal plants with upstanding arrow-shaped leaves and stiff sprays of white flowers in summer. *Sagittaria sagittifolia* is a native plant 2 ft (60 cm) high which has an even better double-flowered variety sometimes called *flore-pleno* and sometimes *japonica*. It likes 3 or 4 in (8 to 10 cm) depth of water.

Scirpus (Bulrush) This is not to be confused with typha, a plant with cigar-like flower spikes often incorrectly known as bulrush. Scirpus has rushy leaves and rather insignificant clusters of flowers. The best variety for the garden, *Scirpus tabernaemontani zebrinus*, has leaves shaped rather like porcupine quills, banded with green and white. It grows very well in 3 or 4 in (8 to 10 cm) of water.

Skunk cabbage, see Lysichitum

Sweet flag, see Acorus

Typha (Reed mace) The plants many people wrongly call bulrushes. The common reed mace, *Typha latifolia*, is a native plant 6 ft (2 m) high with large cigar-like flower heads in late summer. Better for the garden pool are *T. angustifolia*, with narrower leaves and flower heads on 4-ft (1·25-m) stems, and *T. minima*, only 18 in (45 cm) high. All thrive in 3 or 4 in (8 to 10 cm) depth of water.

Umbrella grass, see Cyperus

Villarsia, see Nymphoides

Water forget-me-not, see Myosotis

Water fringe, see Nymphoides

Water hawthorn, see Aponogeton

Water lily, see Nymphaea

Water plantain, see Alisma

Water violet, see Hottonia

Zantedeschia (Arum lily) The familiar arum lily of florists' shops with its gleaming white spathes, each with a central golden column or spadix, is usually grown in greenhouses but it is sufficiently hardy to be grown outdoors in the mildest parts of the country. Elsewhere it can be put out all summer and brought into protection in the autumn. It grows well in the damp soil around pools and may even spread into the shallow water.

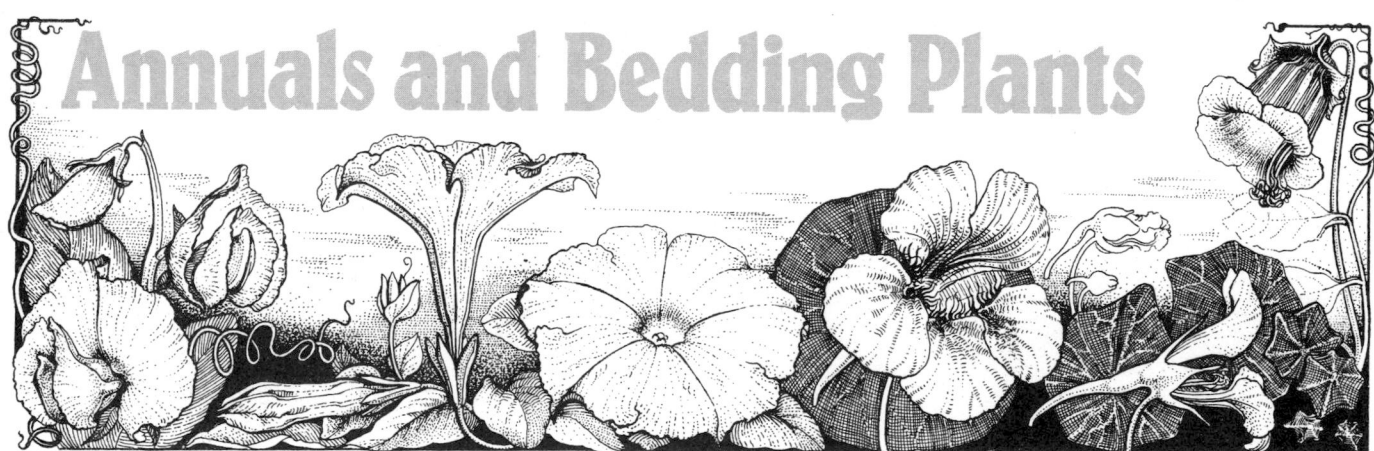

Annuals and Bedding Plants

These might well be called display plants for they are used very largely to supply the garden with extra colour at particular times of the year. As I have explained already, annuals by nature have a short life and a merry one. They grow quickly from seed, produce their flowers followed by seeds to start a new generation, after which they die.

There are many plants, not strictly annuals, which can be reproduced so readily from seed, and come to flowering size in so short a span of time that they are frequently treated in the same way as annuals. I have included some of the best in this chapter but have indicated that they are not true annuals and, under some circumstances, might be

kept from one year to another.

From the garden standpoint annuals are of two kinds, hardy and half hardy, but, as with so many other things in the garden, the distinction between them is not clear cut. Broadly speaking, hardy annuals are those kinds sufficiently resistant to cold to be sown outdoors, usually directly into the

Water adds life to the rock garden

Immediately before planting knock the plants from their boxes and separate them

With potted plants avoid disturbing the root ball when planting

Firm the plant well and leave the soil surface tidy

beds or borders in which they are to flower. This may be done in spring, or in the case of some of the very hardiest, in early autumn, in which case they will germinate quickly, pass the winter as small seedlings and come into flower in late spring or early summer. The spring-sown plants will naturally tend to bloom a little later, the precise time depending partly on the weather, partly on the time of sowing. But in general, annuals have a fairly extended flowering season and if several sowings are made at different times there should be no difficulty in having flowers all the summer.

Half-hardy annuals are similar in every way except that they are not sufficiently tough to stand the cold weather that can be experienced in many places in spring. In mild places they can be sown outdoors just like hardy annuals and even in colder places it may be possible to sow them outdoors in late spring, but then they may start to flower much later or not even have time to flower at all. So in most places they are sown in early spring under glass, are then hardened off, and planted outdoors in late spring or early summer.

'Bedding plant' is a term which includes a great many annuals, especially those kinds that are commonly started under glass and then planted out later on. It also includes many perennial plants, mostly too tender to be left outdoors in winter, but worth growing because of their ability to make a tremendous display for a considerable period. The bedding 'geranium' (it is really a pelargonium) is of this kind and so is the dahlia.

There is a third class of bedding plant which is very useful for spring and early summer display. This is the biennial, or plant treated as such by gardeners. Biennial literally means two-year and indicates that the plant grows from seed the first year, flowers and produces seed the second year and then dies. Despite its two-year cycle the biennial must be raised anew from seed every year if one is to have flowers every year. In this respect it is exactly the same as the annual, the difference being that one

has to wait longer for results. As a rule, seed of biennials is sown outdoors in late spring or early summer. The seedlings are planted a few inches apart in some out of the way part of the garden where they can be grown on undisturbed during the summer. Then, in autumn or very early the following spring, they are transplanted where they are to flower, which they do in spring or early summer, after which they are discarded. Wallflowers, Brompton stocks and forget-me-nots come into this category and

are very useful because they provide extra ground colour in spring when it is particularly needed to set off the spring-flowering bulbs.

Annuals, whether half hardy or hardy, have sufficient points in common for some generalization about their treatment to be useful. Perennial bedding plants, by contrast, are so diverse in character that to generalize about them would be misleading. I have therefore given the necessary instructions for these individually, together with

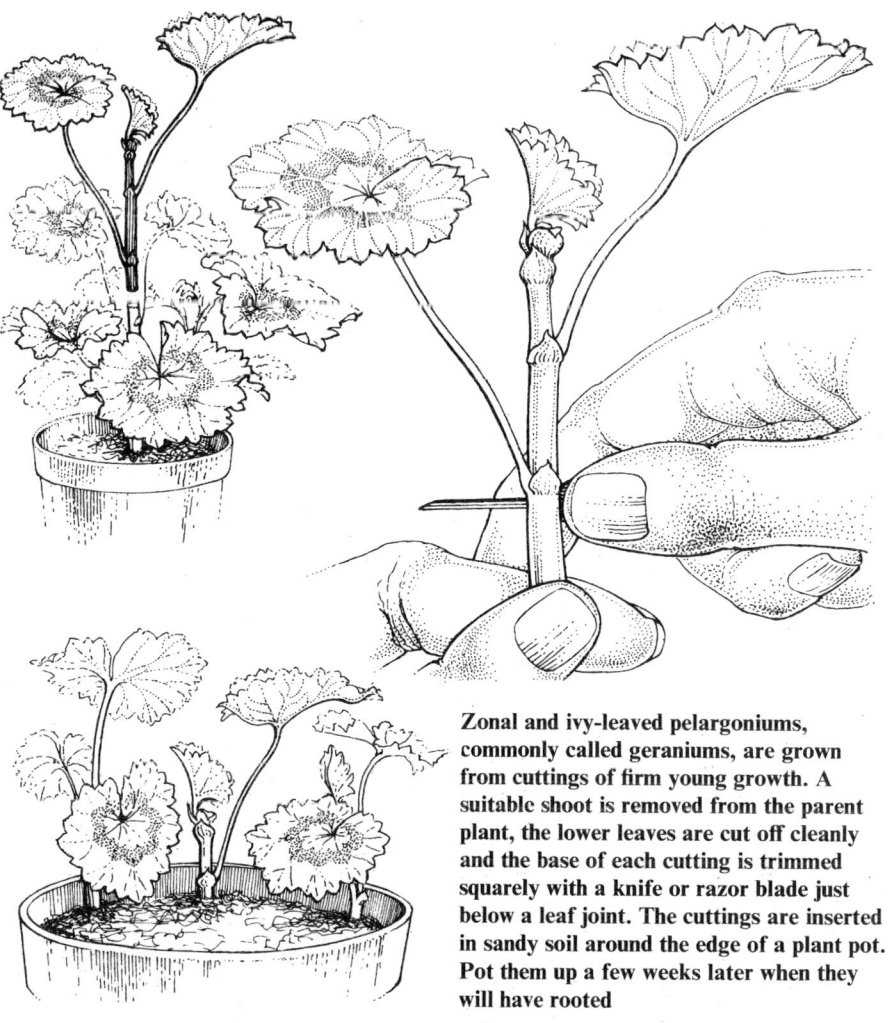

Zonal and ivy-leaved pelargoniums, commonly called geraniums, are grown from cuttings of firm young growth. A suitable shoot is removed from the parent plant, the lower leaves are cut off cleanly and the base of each cutting is trimmed squarely with a knife or razor blade just below a leaf joint. The cuttings are inserted in sandy soil around the edge of a plant pot. Pot them up a few weeks later when they will have rooted

Ageratum houstonianum **Blue Chip**

the name and description of the plant.

What can be usefully said about all these plants is that they have a wide range of utility in the garden. Traditionally they are used for massed displays and the term 'summer bedding' conjures up pictures of great areas of scarlet geraniums or purple petunias, or multi-coloured dahlias in the parks. They can be used in just the same way, on a smaller scale, in gardens, but this is not the only way to use them. A few can be put in here and there amongst the shrubs and herbaceous plants to brighten things up. They can be planted in pots and tubs and window boxes or in baskets suspended from anything that offers a sufficiently substantial support. The smaller kinds can even be used in the rock garden, though I never feel that they look entirely at home there. Many of them are so very obviously man-made plants and the aim in the rock garden should be to simulate nature.

Cultural Requirements Because annual and bedding plants mostly flower for weeks or even months on end, they need a little assistance from the gardener. Most important of all, faded flowers should be removed regularly, not only because this improves the appearance of the plants, but also because it helps them to go on flowering. In dry weather they should be watered, and though they need not be fed while they are actually in growth, it certainly does pay to fork some manure or compost into the soil and give a scattering of bonemeal or fertilizer before sowing or planting them.

Once annuals and biennials have finished flowering they should be pulled up, for they are of no further use. The treatment of perennial bedding plants after flowering will depend on their nature and the facilities available for keeping them.

Recommended Annuals and Bedding Plants

Ageratum One of the most popular of dwarf summer bedding plants and a particular favourite for edging beds. It has masses of small, fluffy-looking, blue, lavender or white flowers and keeps on producing them all the summer. Ageratum is best grown as a half-hardy annual, seed being sown in a warm greenhouse or frame in early spring and the seedlings planted out in late spring where they are to flower. For a really good display space them 6 in (15 cm) apart. They will grow well anywhere but do best in a sunny position.

Althaea, see Hollyhock

Alyssum The sweet alyssum, *Alyssum maritimum*, is a low-growing annual with white, lilac or purple honey-scented flowers, produced during summer. It is a favourite edging plant, often used with blue lobelia, and is raised from seed sown in spring where the plants are to flower. Alternatively seed may be sown in a greenhouse in early spring, the seedlings being pricked off into boxes as they are ready and planted out in late spring.

Amaranthus (Love-lies-bleeding, tassel flower, prince's feather, Joseph's coat) Two kinds are grown primarily as flowering plants, a third as a foliage plant. *Amaranthus caudatus* has long slender trails of crimson or lime-green flowers and is the kind known as love-lies-bleeding or tassel flower. It makes a bushy plant 2 to 3 ft (60 cm to 1 m) high. *A. hypochondriacus* has similar small crimson flowers but in branched, upright spikes, hence the popular name prince's feather. The third kind, *A. tricolor* or Joseph's coat, has large, sometimes deeply lobed leaves in various shades of red, crimson, yellow and green, and is 18 in (45 cm) high.

All three can be grown as half-hardy annuals sown in a warm greenhouse in spring and hardened off for planting out 1 ft (30 cm) apart in a warm sunny place in late spring or early summer. Alternatively, *A. caudatus* and *A. hypochondriacus* can be treated as hardy annuals to be sown outdoors in mid-spring where they are to flower, in which case the seedlings should be thinned or transplanted to at least 9 in (23 cm) apart.

Antirrhinum (Snapdragon) One of the most popular of all summer bedding plants that can be raised easily from seed. The antirrhinum is sometimes called snapdragon because of its peculiar, pouched flowers which can be opened like mouths if they are pinched at the sides but nowadays there are varieties which do not show this typical shape, having, instead, trumpet-shaped or double flowers. There are dwarf, medium and tall varieties from 6 in (15 cm) to 3 ft (1 m) in height, and a wide colour range, including some very bright shades of scarlet and flame as well as pink, yellow, apricot, orange and white. Antirrhinum seed is usually sown in a warm greenhouse in late winter, the seedlings being pricked off into boxes in early spring and gradually hardened off for planting out in late spring. Alternatively, seed sown in early autumn will give seedlings that can be overwintered in an unheated frame and planted out in spring.

These plants are really perennials and in mild places and well-drained soils will occasionally live for years, but it is more satisfactory to treat them as half-hardy annuals.

Antirrhinums succeed best in a sunny, open place and a well-drained soil. If rust disease is troublesome, as it may be in hot, dry places, plants should be sprayed frequently with a copper fungicide, or special rust-resistant varieties of antirrhinum should be grown. The disease causes rusty-looking raised spots to appear on the undersides of the leaves and plants may wither and die as a result.

Arctotis These are amongst the loveliest of South African daisies, mostly with long stems which make them useful for cutting. Though most are rather short-lived perennials in warm places, the best-known kinds are treated as half-hardy annuals and are raised anew each year from seed which is sown in a warm greenhouse in early spring, the seedlings being pricked off into boxes as soon as large enough to handle and planted outdoors in a sunny place in late spring.

One of the loveliest kinds, *Arctotis grandis*, has flowers which are silvery white above and very pale blue beneath. There are also hybrid strains with flowers of various colours, including yellow, orange, red and wine. See also Venidium.

Aster (Callistephus) This is one of the names that has caused a lot of confusion, for the showy annuals most gardeners know as asters are *Callistephus* to the botanists and the botanists' asters are what gardeners call Michaelmas daisies. There are a great many varieties of annual aster, some with single, some with double flowers. The doubles are further subdivided according to the character of their flowers, the very shaggy, narrow-petalled kinds being known as ostrich plume asters, the neater and broader-petalled kinds as comet asters. There are also miniatures, varieties with very compact flowers, and many more types with a height range from 1 to 3 ft (30 cm to 1 m).

All are raised from seed sown in a greenhouse or frame in early spring, or outdoors in mid- to late spring. Glasshouse-raised seedlings are pricked off into boxes and hardened off for planting out in late spring. The single-flowered kinds will tolerate some shade, but in general annual asters like open places. They are not fussy about soil.

Balsam, see Impatiens

Begonia There are a great many different kinds of begonia, but for summer display outdoors the most popular are the many varieties of *Begonia semperflorens*. Although these are perennials which can be kept for a long time in a greenhouse, when used outdoors they are treated as half-hardy annuals, seed being sown in early spring in a temperature of 18°C. (65°F.), the seedlings pricked out, hardened off and planted out in early summer. Plants average about 9 in (23 cm) in height and the sprays of small white, pink or crimson flowers are produced all summer and into the autumn until plants are killed by frost. Some varieties have bronze or purple leaves.

The large-flowered tuberous-rooted begonias in almost all colours except blue, are also used for summer bedding, especially in cool, partly shaded places, and the so-called multiflora begonias with smaller but more numerous flowers have the same origin and are grown in the same way, from seed or tubers. For cultivation see Greenhouse Plants.

Bellis (Daisy) The common daisy, which is such a troublesome weed of lawns, has produced numerous double-flowered varieties which are excellent garden plants, the smallest-flowered kinds for the rock garden, larger-flowered varieties for spring bedding displays. The largest flowered are usually listed in seed catalogues simply as Giant Red, Giant Pink or Giant White and are readily raised from seed sown outdoors in late spring. The plants are popular as a carpet for taller flowers such as tulips, and are usually thrown away after flowering, though they can be split up, replanted and kept for further use if desired.

Brachycome (Swan River daisy) This lovely South African annual (its full name is *Brachycome iberidifolia*) has dainty blue, pink or white daisy flowers produced all summer on a compact plant. It is not fully hardy, so seed should be sown in a warm greenhouse or frame in early spring, seedlings being pricked out and hardened off for planting outdoors in late spring or early summer. Alternatively, seed may be sown in late spring outdoors where the plants are to flower. In either case they should have a sunny place, preferably in rather light, well-drained soil.

Busy Lizzie, see Impatiens

Calceolaria The calceolaria with very large pouched flowers, often brilliantly spotted or blotched with one colour or another, is a greenhouse plant not suitable for growing outdoors, but it has a relative of a much stiffer, more shrubby habit of growth and with smaller yellow or chestnut-red flowers, which is almost hardy and an excellent summer bedding plant. Its name is *Calceolaria integrifolia*, though it is sometimes listed as *C. rugosa*, and it grows about 18 in (45 cm) high, flowers all the summer and does well in full sun or partial shade. It is raised from cuttings in late summer or early autumn, or by seed sown in a greenhouse in spring and should be kept in a frame or greenhouse in winter except in the mildest places.

Calendula (Pot marigold) This familiar orange daisy is often referred to simply as a marigold, but it is less confusing to use its proper name, calendula, to distinguish it from the African and French marigolds which are not only very different in appearance, but need different treatment in the garden. These are described under Marigold.

The calendula is one of the hardiest of annuals; a plant that, once admitted to the garden, is likely to reproduce itself year after year from its own self-sown seed. This will germinate equally well in spring or autumn, the only difference in results being that the autumn seedlings start to bloom earlier, but for best results self-sown seedlings should be discouraged as they usually deteriorate in quality. Instead, a fresh start should be made each year from good, purchased seed or seed carefully selected from flowers of good quality. There are yellow as well as orange varieties, and the best have fully double flowers with either broad and flat or quilled petals. Seedlings should be thinned to 9 in (23 cm) so that the plants have room to make a good display.

Californian poppy, see Eschscholzia

Calliopsis, see Coreopsis

Callistephus, see Aster

Canary creeper, see Tropaeolum

Candytuft There are perennial rock garden candytufts usually referred to by their botanical name, *Iberis*, as well as the annual kinds described here. The annuals have either flattish heads of white, pink or mauve flowers on 9-in (23-cm) stems in summer or, in the rocket candytuft, *I. amara*, broad foot-high spikes of white flowers in summer.

They are easily grown from seed sown in spring or early autumn where the plants are to flower and like a sunny place and almost any soil.

Canna Handsome plants with broad, tropical-looking leaves, often deep red in colour though some varieties are green leaved, and bearing, in summer, spikes of large, gaudy flowers in shades of red, yellow and orange, often with one colour splashed on another. They are more familiar in the elaborate bedding schemes seen in public parks than in private gardens, but there is no reason why they should not be more widely grown as they are not difficult to manage provided the fleshy roots can be started in a warm greenhouse each spring. At this stage they like a temperature of around 16°C. (60°F.) and plenty of water. They must be removed to a frame in late spring to become sufficiently hardened to be planted outdoors in a sunny place in early summer. Before frost occurs in autumn the plants must be lifted, brought back into the greenhouse and gradually dried off. Throughout the winter they can be kept in their pots without water and with no more heat than is needed to ensure complete protection against frost.

Division of the roots in spring is the easiest way to increase cannas, as seed needs a lot of heat for satisfactory germination.

Canterbury Bell This is a biennial campanula, properly known as *Campanula medium*, which must be renewed from seed annually. This is sown in late spring or early summer, preferably in a frame, though it can be sown outdoors. The seedlings should be pricked out a few inches apart into a nursery bed to grow on into sturdy plants to be placed in their flowering quarters in autumn. Space them at least 1 ft (30 cm) apart and give them rather good soil and a fully sunny or partially shaded position. They will flower early the following summer. They are usually about 3 ft (1 m) tall and the flowers are long bells with a handsome saucer-like appendage in the cup-and-saucer varieties. Colours are blue, mauve, pink and white and there are double forms. All come true from seed.

Carnation, Annual The so-called annual carnations are derived from the greenhouse perpetual-flowering carnations and are really short-lived perennials, but it is convenient to grow them from seed sown in a greenhouse in early spring, the seedlings then being pricked off into pots or boxes and transferred to a frame to be hardened off in time for planting outdoors in late spring or early summer.

They like a warm, sunny place and reasonably good soil, and are usually sold as Giant Chabaud carnations with an average height of 18 to 24 in (45 to 60 cm) in a mixture of colours including crimson, scarlet, rose, pink, salmon, yellow and white, but there are also dwarf varieties 9 to 12 in (23 to 30 cm) high.

Catchfly, see Silene

Celosia (Prince of Wales's feather) There are two very different forms of celosia, both varieties of *Celosia argentea*. One kind, known as the feathered form, and often sold as *C. plumosa*, has scarlet, crimson or yellow flowers in silken plumes; the other, known as cockscomb or crested type, and often sold as *C. cristata*, has its flowers

Cleome spinosa

tightly packed in curious sinuous clusters.

Both plants are half-hardy annuals, easily raised from seed if this can be given a minimum temperature of 18°C. (65°F.), in late winter. The seedlings are pricked off into small pots and are either removed to a frame in late spring to be planted outdoors in a warm, sunny place in early summer, or are moved into 4-in (10-cm) pots to be grown on in the greenhouse. The cockscomb type is usually only grown as a greenhouse pot plant and is more fully described on p. 118.

Centaurea, see Cornflower and Sweet Sultan

Cheiranthus, see Wallflower

Cherry pie, see Heliotrope

Chilean glory flower, see Eccremocarpus

Cineraria, see Senecio

Clarkia Hardy annuals which are readily raised from seed sown throughout the spring or in early autumn where the plants are to flower. The seedlings should be thinned to 9 to 12 in (23 to 30 cm) apart. The garden varieties of *Clarkia elegans* produce slender spikes of double flowers which may be pink, red or white. They vary in height from 1½ to 3 ft (45 cm to 1 m) and will grow in full sun or in partial shade, in practically any soil.

Clary, see *Salvia horminum*

Cleome (Spider flower) *Cleome spinosa* is an unusual and attractive half-hardy annual which is grown from seed sown in a warm greenhouse or frame in late winter or early spring. The seedlings are pricked off into boxes or small pots and are later placed in a frame so that they can be hardened off in

readiness for planting out in a sunny place in late spring or early summer. They should be placed about 18 in (45 cm) apart. The plants eventually grow about 3 ft (1 m) high, and produce big heads of pink (or occasionally white) flowers, notable for their narrow petals and long stamens which give them a curiously spidery appearance.

Cobaea (Cup and saucer vine) *Cobaea scandens* is a very quick-growing climbing plant with purple and green, or white flowers shaped rather like those of a Canterbury bell. Though a perennial, it is usually treated as an annual, seed being sown in a warm greenhouse in early spring and the seedlings potted singly and removed to a frame to be hardened off for planting outdoors in late spring.

Cobaea likes sun and warmth, but is not fussy about soil. In very mild districts or in a greenhouse it may survive for many years and grow into a large plant.

Collinsia A pretty hardy annual, 9 to 12 in (23 to 30 cm) high, with clusters of small purple and white flowers in summer. It is easily grown from seed sown throughout the spring or in early autumn where the plants are to flower. The seedlings should be thinned to 5 or 6 in (13 to 15 cm) apart. Collinsia likes a sunny place but is not fussy about soil.

Coneflower, see Rudbeckia

Convolvulus The annual convolvulus, often listed as *Convolvulus minor*, though its correct name is *C. tricolor*, is a sprawling plant with broadly funnel-shaped flowers which may be purple, blue, lavender, pink or cherry red. It is grown from seed sown in spring where the plants are to flower, the seedlings being thinned to about 9 in (23 cm) apart. It likes a sunny place and is not fussy about soil. Other plants sometimes known as convolvulus will be found under Morning Glory.

Coreopsis (Calliopsis) The annual coreopsis closely resembles some of the perennial kinds and produces a profusion of flowers which are usually deep yellow blotched with maroon, but in some varieties are all yellow and in some bronzy red or chestnut red throughout. They are carried in sprays on rather slender 2-ft (60-cm) stems all summer. Seed should be sown in spring or early autumn in ordinary soil and an open place where the plants are to flower. The seedlings are thinned to 9 in (23 cm).

In catalogues this plant is often listed as calliopsis, though *Coreopsis tinctoria* is the correct name.

Cornflower The common cornflower is botanically *Centaurea cyanus*, a hardy annual easily grown in any fairly open place from seed sown in spring or autumn where

the plants are to flower. All that is necessary afterwards is to thin the seedlings to about 1 ft (30 cm) apart and stick a few twiggy branches around them for support.

In addition to the familiar blue cornflower there are pink and white varieties. There are also dwarf varieties 9 to 12 in (23 to 30 cm) high which need no support and can be grown 6 in (15 cm) apart.

Cosmos Popular half-hardy annuals also known as cosmea. Varieties of *Cosmos bipinnatus* have fine, fern-like foliage and daisy flowers, in shades of pink, rose, purplish red and white. The plants grow 3 to 5 ft (1 to 1·5 m) tall and flower in late summer and autumn. They should be given a fully open and sunny position, as in shade they are apt to produce a great quantity of foliage and few flowers.

Varieties of *C. sulphureus* are stiffer in habit with yellow or orange flowers and are only 2½ ft (75 cm) high. Seed of both kinds is sown in a warm greenhouse in early spring and the seedlings are pricked off and later hardened off for planting out 1 ft (30 cm) apart in late spring in an open, preferably sunny place.

Cup and saucer vine, see Cobaea

Cypress, Summer, see Kochia

Dahlia Although dahlias are tender plants, likely to be damaged by the slightest frost, they can be grown quite satisfactorily without a greenhouse or frame because they have tuberous roots which can be stored dry throughout the winter. These roots are lifted in autumn when the foliage has been blackened by frost and, after the stems have been cut off a few inches above the tubers, they are placed in boxes or simply stacked on the floor in any dry, frostproof place. A spare room, cupboard, loft, shed or cellar will serve, but it must be frostproof. It is wise to sprinkle the tubers with flowers of sulphur as a protection against disease. The

Cosmos bipinnatus

Dimorphotheca hybrids

following year in mid- to late spring, the roots are planted outdoors in rather rich, well-cultivated soil and a sunny position. If desired, the roots can be carefully divided before being planted.

Alternatively, dahlias can be grown from cuttings. For this purpose the tubers are placed in a warm greenhouse in early spring and are just covered with soil. Shoots will soon appear and are severed when about 3 in (8 cm) long and inserted as cuttings in a close frame. When rooted they are potted singly in small pots, grown on in the greenhouse for a few weeks and then removed to a frame to be hardened off in time for planting outdoors in late spring or early summer.

Yet a third way to grow dahlias is from seed sown in a warm greenhouse in early spring, the seedlings being pricked out into boxes or potted singly and hardened off for planting out when there is no longer danger of frost. This method works especially well with the short bedding varieties.

There are a great many varieties of dahlia, differing in height, and in shape, size and colour of flower. These different types are distinguished by names such as decorative, cactus, pompon, collerette, bedding, etc. Some are only 18 in (45 cm) or so in height, but most are from 3 to 5 ft (1 to 1·5 m) high and must be well staked and tied to prevent breakage of the rather brittle stems.

To obtain the finest flowers, buds are restricted to one per stem, the end bud being retained and side buds removed, but when varieties with small or medium-sized flowers are grown solely for garden display this disbudding need not be carried out. It is important that faded flowers should be removed regularly, both for the sake of appearance and to keep the plants flowering.

Daisy, see Bellis

Dianthus, see Carnation, Pink, and Sweet William

Digitalis, see Foxglove

Dimorphotheca (Star of the veldt) These are amongst the most beautiful of daisy-flowered annuals. Plants are about 1 ft (30 cm) high and the quite large flowers can be had in all shades from pale beige or lemon, through apricot and salmon or orange.

For flowers in early summer, seed should be sown in a greenhouse in early spring, the seedlings being pricked off and later hardened off for planting out in late spring. Flowers from mid-summer onwards can be obtained by sowing directly outdoors in mid-spring, where the plants are to flower, and thinning seedlings to 9 in (23 cm). In either case a sunny position should be chosen, for preference in well-drained soil.

Dusty Miller, see Senecio

Eccremocarpus (Chilean glory flower) *Eccremocarpus scaber* is a beautiful and unusual climber which can be grown very easily from seed. Growth is slender and the leaves have an elegant, ferny appearance, but it is the tubular orange-scarlet flowers, produced in long sprays, that are really striking.

Seed should be sown in a warm greenhouse in spring and the seedlings potted singly and hardened off for planting out in late spring or early summer. The plants should be given a warm, sunny, sheltered place and some good support to climb on, such as a trellis against a south-facing wall. In such a place they will live for years and flower profusely every summer, though they may be killed right back to their fleshy roots each winter. Because it blooms so readily from seed and is not fully hardy, it is often treated as an annual and renewed from seed every year.

Echium In some very mild gardens giant echiums may be grown from seed. These carry tall stiff spikes of blue or pink flowers and are biennial species from the Canary Islands. They must be renewed annually from seed sown in a warm greenhouse and can only be overwintered in a greenhouse or in an almost frost-free place.

Far more useful for the ordinary garden are the varieties of *Echium plantagineum*, a bushy hardy annual about 1 ft (30 cm) high with clusters of blue, lavender, rose or white flowers all summer. It is easily grown from seed sown in spring where the plants are to bloom, seedlings being thinned to 6 or 8 in (15 to 20 cm). It is a plant that enjoys warm, sunny places and well-drained soil.

Eschscholzia (Californian poppy) Annuals of sprawling habit with grey-green, ferny leaves and poppy-like flowers produced in profusion throughout the summer. The commonest variety has orange flowers, but

Eschscholzia californica

Digitalis hybrid (Foxglove)

Gazania hybrid

there are others ranging from ivory white, through pink to crimson, double as well as single.

All can be raised from seed sown in spring or early autumn in sunny places outdoors where the plants are to flower. Thin the seedlings to at least 8 in (20 cm) apart. Self-sown seedlings usually appear freely, especially in warm, well-drained soils, but they usually revert fairly rapidly to the wild, orange-yellow single type.

Flax, Scarlet, see Linum

Forget-me-not In addition to the common forget-me-not, which is used for spring bedding or as a carpet plant beneath trees and shrubs, there are various other kinds, such as the alpine forget-me-not (*Myosotis alpestris*), which is more dwarf and compact, and the water forget-me-not (*M. palustris*), which is looser in habit and has a yellow eye to the small blue flowers. Both these are commonly grown as perennials and increased by division after flowering.

The common forget-me-not is usually grown as a biennial, seed being sown each year in early summer, and the seedlings planted out 4 to 6 in (10 to 15 cm) apart to grow on into sturdy plants which can be transferred to their flowering beds in autumn. This forget-me-not will grow in practically any soil and sunny or shady place and if some of the old plants are scattered over the ground when they have

finished flowering they will usually seed freely and produce an abundance of seedlings.

Foxglove These plants, derived from a native plant known botanically as *Digitalis purpurea*, are usually treated as biennials, seed being sown outdoors each spring to provide plants which will flower just over a year later. The seedlings are pricked off into a nursery bed, preferably in a shady place, and are transferred in autumn to their flowering quarters. Sometimes plants will continue for several years, but usually they die after flowering and producing seed. Once established they will often renew themselves by self-sown seed.

Foxgloves like cool, rather moist soils and partially shaded places, but will grow practically anywhere. The Excelsior varieties have large flowers standing out all round the stems instead of hanging down on one side to form the typical spike of the wild foxglove. Colours range from white and pale pink to crimson, often heavily netted or spotted with one shade on another. There is also a variety that will flower the same year if sown in a warm greenhouse in early spring.

Gaillardia One very popular kind of gaillardia is a hardy perennial but another, *Gaillardia pulchella*, often listed as *G. picta*, is a half-hardy annual with large single or double, daisy-type flowers, usually orange

red and yellow, but in some varieties entirely blood red or chestnut red.

Seed is sown in a greenhouse or frame in early spring, or outdoors in late spring. Gaillardias like sunny places and well-drained soils. Their average height is 15 in (38 cm) and their flowers are useful for cutting.

Gazania Very showy perennials which are not quite hardy enough to be grown outdoors reliably in winter and summer, though they do survive in many seaside gardens. They are trailing in habit and the daisy flowers are produced during most of the summer. They may be lemon, orange, bronze, rose or purple, often with a band of a darker, almost black colour.

They like light, well-drained soils and hot sunny places, and are ideal for planting on dry banks, terrace walls and rock gardens, or they may be used for carpeting formal beds. They can be raised from seed sown in spring or from cuttings of firm young shoots taken at almost any time from spring to autumn.

Geranium, see Pelargonium

Gloriosa daisy, see Rudbeckia

Godetia Hardy annuals easily grown in practically any soil and sunny or shady position. There are two main types, the tall godetias with spikes of flowers 2 to 3 ft (60 cm to 1 m) high, and the dwarf or azalea-flowered varieties which make bushier plants around 1 ft (30 cm) in height with the flowers in clusters. The colour range is from white to crimson with many lovely shades of pink.

All godetias are grown from seed sown in spring or early autumn where the plants are to flower. Seedlings should be thinned to 6 or 9 in (15 to 23 cm).

Gypsophila The annual gypsophila, *Gypsophila elegans*, has much larger flowers than the perennial gypsophila, but they are borne in loose sprays on equally slender stems and are as useful for mixing with other heavier flowers. It grows to a height of about 1 ft (30 cm) and typically has white flowers, but there are varieties with pink flowers.

All are grown from seed sown in spring or early autumn where the plants are to flower and it is desirable to make several sowings to ensure a succession of flowers. The seedlings are thinned to about 6 in (15 cm). The annual gypsophila likes sunny places and well-drained soils.

Helianthus, see Sunflower

Helichrysum There are several grey-leaved helichrysums which are shrubby plants, but the plant which most people know under this name is *Helichrysum bracteatum*, a showy, hardy annual with 'everlasting' flowers, that is, flowers which, being composed of rather chaffy petals, can be dried and used for winter decoration. For this purpose the flowers are cut just before they are fully open and are suspended head downward in a cool, airy shed or room for a few weeks to dry.

The annual helichrysum is grown from seed sown in a warm greenhouse in early spring, the seedlings being pricked out and later hardened off for planting out 9 in (23 cm) apart in late spring or early summer in a sunny place and well-drained soil. In warm places seed can also be sown outdoors in mid-spring where plants are to flower, seedlings being thinned to about 6 in (15 cm).

The varieties grown are all double flowered, 1½ to 2½ ft (45 to 75 cm) high and in a variety of colours including red, crimson, pink, yellow, orange and white.

Heliotrope (Cherry pie) A favourite plant used for summer bedding or as a greenhouse pot plant. It is famous for the perfume of its lavender-purple flowers, though some forms have less of this than others.

Heliotrope is a half-hardy perennial which can be grown from seed or cuttings. Seed is sown in a warm greenhouse in late winter or early spring, the seedlings being pricked off or potted singly and subsequently hardened off for planting outdoors in early summer. Cuttings are prepared from firm young shoots in spring or early summer, and are rooted in a propagating frame with bottom heat.

Heliotropes like a sunny place and a fairly good soil and at the end of the season plants can be overwintered in a greenhouse with a minimum temperature of 7°C. (45°F.), but when used for summer bedding they are usually discarded in the autumn, new stock being raised annually from seed.

Hollyhock The botanical name of the common hollyhock is *Althaea rosea*. Typically it grows 6 to 8 ft (2 to 2·5 m) high with spires of large showy flowers, single or double, in a good range of colours including yellow, orange, pink, rose, red, crimson and mauve. There are also short varieties only 2 ft (60 cm) high.

Though strictly a perennial, it is usually grown as a hardy biennial or as a half-hardy annual. If grown as a biennial, seed is sown outdoors or in a frame in late spring or early summer. Seedlings are pricked out 6 in (15 cm) apart in a nursery bed and later are removed to the places where they will flower the following year. If grown as a half-hardy annual, special strains, known as annual hollyhocks, must be used and seed sown in a warm greenhouse in late winter or early spring. Seedlings are pricked out or potted singly and hardened off for planting in their flowering positions in late spring or early summer.

Hollyhocks like warm sunny places and well-drained soils. Many strains are susceptible to a rust disease which disfigures their leaves but this can be controlled by occasional spraying with a fungicide such as benomyl or triforine.

Heliotrope

Iberis, see Candytuft

Impatiens (Balsam, busy Lizzie) The balsam is *Impatiens balsamina*, a half-hardy annual with spikes of flowers, always double in the cultivated varieties and anything from 9 to 18 in (23 to 45 cm) in height according to variety, with pink, salmon, scarlet, crimson, mauve or white flowers in summer. It can be planted outdoors in summer but is most popular as a pot plant for a sunny greenhouse.

The busy Lizzie is *I. walleriana* (in catalogues it usually gets called *I. holstii* or *I. sultani*) which is a half-hardy perennial, nowadays usually grown as a half-hardy annual. Like the balsam it makes an excellent pot plant for greenhouse or room but it is also a first-class summer bedding plant which will thrive in partially shady as well as sunny places. The colour range includes pink, scarlet, purple, orange and white. Heights vary from 4 to 18 in (10 to 45 cm) and in a warm greenhouse plants practically never stop flowering. Outdoors they can be expected to flower all summer.

Plants of both balsam and busy Lizzie are raised from seed sown in a warm greenhouse in spring, seedlings being pricked out and then either hardened off for planting outdoors in late spring or early summer, or potted singly and grown on in the greenhouse. Plants of busy Lizzie can also be grown from cuttings of young shoots rooted in a warm propagator in spring or summer and this is the only way of increasing varieties with variegated leaves (there is one with an excellent white variegation) as this is not transmitted by seed.

Outdoors, plants should be given reasonably good soil and should be well watered in dry weather.

Ipomoea, see Morning Glory

Joseph's coat, see Amaranthus

Kochia (Summer cypress) A half-hardy annual grown for its foliage and distinctive habit. It makes a neat, egg-shaped bush with narrow leaves which become crimson in the autumn.

Kochia is grown from seed sown in a warm greenhouse in spring, seedlings being pricked out and hardened off for planting out in late spring or early summer. They can be used as a little hedge or as dot plants to emphasize a pattern. The sunnier the position the better the autumn colour.

Larkspur The annual larkspurs are really delphiniums, derived from a species named *Delphinium ajacis*, but in gardens the name delphinium is almost invariably reserved for the perennial kinds.

The larkspurs are quite hardy and very easily grown in any reasonably good and well-drained soil. Seed can be sown where the plants are to flower, the seedlings being thinned to about 1 ft (30 cm) apart. If seed is sown in late summer or very early autumn, plants will start to flower late the following spring, whereas if seed is sown in spring, flowering will commence about mid-summer. The flower spikes are long and narrow, 1 to 3 ft (30 cm to 1 m) high, and colours range from white, pale blue and pink, to dark blue and scarlet.

Lathyrus, see Sweet Pea

Lavatera There is a shrubby lavatera, but the kind most commonly seen in gardens is an annual, *Lavatera trimestris*, which makes a bushy plant 2 to 3 ft (60 cm to 1 m) high, covered with large rose-pink flowers throughout the summer.

It is easily grown from seed sown outdoors in spring or early autumn where the plants are to flower. Seedlings should be thinned to 18 in (45 cm) and the plants will grow in almost any soil and an open, sunny place.

Limonium, see Statice

Linaria (Toadflax) There are perennial kinds of linaria, but one of the prettiest and most useful is a hardy annual. It is named *Linaria maroccana*, and it has slender 12-in (30-cm) spikes of flowers, rather like tiny antirrhinums, produced all summer in a great variety of colours.

It is grown from seed sown in spring where the plants are to flower; seedlings being thinned to about 6 to 8 in (15 to 20 cm). It likes sunny places and is not fussy about soil.

Linum (Flax) The annual or scarlet flax, *Linum grandiflorum*, is a rather fragile, foot-high plant with sprays of vivid scarlet flowers in summer. It likes sunny places and well-drained soils and is quite hardy, so it can be grown from seed sown outdoors in spring or early autumn where the plants are to flower. Seedlings should be thinned to about 6 in (15 cm) apart.

Livingstone daisy, see Mesembryanthemum

Lobelia Everyone knows the blue lobelia, *Lobelia erinus*, one of the most popular summer-flowering plants and a favourite for edging beds, either by itself or in company with white alyssum. There are light blue, dark blue, purple, rose and white varieties and also trailing kinds, often sold as *L. pendula*, which are excellent for window boxes and hanging baskets.

Though all are actually half-hardy perennials which can be overwintered in a frost-proof greenhouse, they are usually grown as half-hardy annuals from seed sown in a warm greenhouse in late winter or early spring, seedlings being pricked out and hardened off for planting out, or, in the case of the trailing lobelia, planting in hanging baskets and window boxes, in late spring. They will grow practically anywhere and should be spaced 6 in (15 cm) apart for a good display.

Love-in-a-mist, see Nigella

Love-lies-bleeding, see Amaranthus

Lunaria (Honesty) This is a hardy biennial grown both for its branching 3-ft (1-m) sprays of purple flowers in spring and early summer and for its curious seed vessels like oval parchment discs. These can be cut when ripe and dried for winter decoration. There is also a variety with white-variegated leaves which comes true from seed, a rather unusual thing with leaf variegation.

All kinds must be renewed annually from seed sown outdoors in spring or early summer to give flowering plants the following year. Once established, honesty will often seed itself about freely so that nothing further need be done except thin out or transplant the seedlings. They need 9 to 12 in (23 to 30 cm) each.

Lupin The most familiar lupin, and in many ways the best for the garden, is the herbaceous lupin (see page 65), but there are also annual kinds with shorter, less showy spikes of flowers in summer produced on plants which are rather too coarse and leafy. The average height is 3 ft (1 m), but there are dwarf varieties about 1 ft (30 cm)

high. Colours are shades of blue and rose as well as white.

Annual lupins are grown from seed sown outdoors in spring or early autumn where they are to flower, the seedlings being thinned to at least 1 ft (30 cm) apart. They flower in summer.

Malcomia, see Stock, Virginian

Malope *Malope trifida* is a hardy annual, not unlike lavatera but with magenta flowers. It makes a big, leafy plant 3 ft (1 m) high and flowers all the summer.

Seed should be sown in spring or autumn where the plants are to flower, the seedlings being thinned to 15 in (38 cm). Malope likes a sunny place but will grow in practically any soil.

Marigold The two popular kinds of marigold are the French marigold, *Tagetes patula*, and the African marigold, *T. erecta*; the first with yellow and crimson or chestnut-red flowers, single or double; the second all orange or yellow and so double that they look rather like balls of foam rubber. However, the two types have been so interbred that it is impossible to distinguish clearly between them and choice will be determined largely by height and size of flower. The shortest may be no more than 6 in (15 cm) high with flowers to match; the tallest 3 ft (1 m), with blooms 4 or 5 in (10 to 13 cm) across.

There is also another species, *T. signata*, which is not known popularly as marigold and is always listed as tagetes. This is understandable since it is very different in appearance from the other two, making low mounds of finely divided leaves, covered in small, single, daisy-type flowers which may be lemon, yellow, orange or bronze red according to variety.

All are half-hardy annuals flowering in summer and are raised from seed sown in a greenhouse or frame in early spring. Seedlings are pricked out and hardened off for planting out in late spring or early summer. The French and African marigolds prefer rather rich soils and sunny places, and the dwarf *Tagetes signata* likes well-drained soils, but all will grow almost anywhere.

Marigold, Pot, see Calendula

Matthiola, see Stock

Mesembryanthemum Succulent plants which can be grown outdoors in winter only in the milder parts of the country, but are quite safe in the open during the summer, and are then most useful as display plants. They delight in sun and warmth, will thrive in the sandiest of soils, and have flowers which bear a superficial resemblance to those of daisies, though they are quite unrelated. Colours are varied and often extremely brilliant, as in *Mesembryanthemum roseum*,

A dwarf variety of nasturtium

which is a vivid rose pink, and *M. aurantiacum*, which is reddish orange.

Most kinds are perennials and can be increased by cuttings in summer or early autumn, but there are also a few annuals of which the most popular is the Livingstone daisy, *M. criniflorum*, a prostrate plant with flowers in a variety of colours including apricot, pink, carmine, purple and red. Seed of this is sown in a greenhouse or heated frame in spring, and the seedlings are pricked out into boxes and hardened off in time for planting outdoors in late spring or early summer in a warm, sunny place. It makes a brilliant bed on its own but its colours do not associate too well with those of most other plants.

Mignonette This highly fragrant, though not very showy, flower is a hardy annual grown from seed sown in spring where the plants are to flower. Seedlings should be thinned to 6 in (15 cm) or thereabouts.

Mignonette likes a sunny place and will grow in practically any soil with a preference for those containing lime or chalk. Its botanical name is *Reseda odorata*.

Morning Glory These vigorous twining plants, botanically rather confused, are usually listed as varieties of ipomoea. Some are perennial in places where there is no frost but one of the best, *Ipomoea purpurea*, is a half-hardy annual. This has a particularly lovely variety named Heavenly Blue, with broadly funnel-shaped, sky-blue flowers, produced from mid-summer onwards. Flying Saucers is similar but blue and white, and Scarlet O'Hara is rosy crimson.

They can be grown as greenhouse pot plants trained around three or four slender bamboo canes, or can be planted outdoors in early summer in a warm, sunny spot. In either case they are grown from seed sown in a warm greenhouse in late winter or early spring, the seeds being sown two in a pot, and grown in this until planting-out time.

Myosotis, see Forget-me-not

Nasturtium The common nasturtium is botanically named *Tropaeolum majus*, and is one of the most easily grown annuals, thriving in any fairly open place, however poor the soil. There are climbing and dwarf forms and some with semi-double flowers, all in bright shades of yellow, orange, pink and red.

Seed should be sown thinly ½ in (1 cm) deep in spring where the plants are required to flower.

Nemesia Pretty half-hardy annuals up to 12 in (30 cm) in height, producing flowers in many colours throughout the summer. The range is from white, pale yellow and mauve, to orange, blue and red.

Seed should be sown in a warm greenhouse in spring, the seedlings being pricked out and hardened off for planting outdoors, 6 in (15 cm) apart, in late spring or early summer, preferably in a sunny place and a rather rich soil with plenty of moisture in summer.

Nemophila (Baby blue eyes) A charming hardy annual, 6 in (15 cm) high with small sky-blue flowers freely produced in summer. Seed should be sown in spring in a sunny place where plants are to flower and seedlings thinned to 6 in (15 cm).

Nicotiana (Tobacco) The smoker's tobacco is not an ornamental plant, but the white-flowered, sweet-scented or jasmine tobacco, *Nicotiana affinis*, (*N. alata*) is a popular summer-flowering annual which grows well in shady as well as in sunny places. The red-flowered tobacco, *N. sanderae*, is a similar plant with carmine flowers and there are numerous garden varieties from 1 to 3 ft (60 cm to 1 m) high with white, lime green, pink, carmine or crimson flowers.

All are raised from seed sown in a warm greenhouse in early spring, the seedlings being pricked out into boxes and later hardened off for planting out in late spring or early summer. All will grow in any reasonable soil in sun or partial shade. By nature they close their flowers by day and open them in the evening but garden varieties have been produced which remain open during the daytime.

Nigella (Love-in-a-mist) Pretty hardy annuals with fine, ferny foliage and blue, mauve, purple, rose, pink or white flowers a little like cornflowers but surrounded by lacy bracts. All are raised from seed sown outdoors in spring or early autumn where the plants are to flower, preferably in a well-drained soil and a sunny position. Seedlings should be thinned to at least 9 in (23 cm) apart.

Pansy Pansies belong to the viola family and are perennial plants, but they are commonly treated as annuals or biennials and raised anew each year from seed. This can be sown in a frame or greenhouse in early spring. Seedlings are then pricked out and hardened off to be planted out as soon as they are large enough, and will flower from late spring onwards. Better plants can be obtained by sowing the seeds in a frame or greenhouse in early summer, pricking them out into boxes or a frame and then planting them outdoors in early autumn to flower the following spring and summer. So-called winter-flowering varieties are available which, treated in this way, even if they do not produce many flowers actually in winter, will certainly start to make a display very early the following spring. Alternatively, cuttings of pansies can be rooted in a frame in early autumn and over-wintered in the frame until the spring.

The colour range is very wide including lavender, blue, purple, orange, yellow, primrose and white, sometimes with dark, almost black markings.

All pansies like good rich soil and sunny places and should be watered freely in dry weather.

Papaver, see Poppy

Nicotiana affinis Lime Green

Pelargonium (Geranium) These plants are commonly, though erroneously, called geraniums. Some are purely greenhouse plants but some are much used for summer display in beds and borders. There are two principal groups for this purpose: the zonal-leaved pelargoniums, bushy plants with scarlet, carmine, pink or white flowers and popular both for summer bedding and as pot plants, and the ivy-leaved pelargoniums which are sprawling in habit, usually pink flowered though there are red, purple and blue varieties, and useful in hanging baskets, window boxes, tubs, or trained as climbers.

All like sun and warmth and need complete protection from frost. They are easily raised from cuttings of firm young shoots taken in spring or late summer. They are not fussy about soil but flower best in warm, sunny places. There are varieties of the zonal-leaved type with elaborately variegated leaves in which yellow, green, red and silver may appear in varying combinations. These also make good bedding plants.

Because of their susceptibility to frost, pelargoniums should not be planted outdoors until late spring or early summer and should be returned to the greenhouse to overwinter before frost threatens in the autumn. Some varieties can also be raised from seed sown in a warm greenhouse in late winter or early spring and later potted individually and hardened off for planting out in early summer, but seedlings are sometimes slow in coming into flower. Varieties have been bred to overcome this difficulty.

Penstemon, see p. 67. (Hardy Perennials)

Petunia Half-hardy annuals with very showy flowers produced all the summer. Petunias like sun and warmth and do particularly well in light, well-drained soils. They are raised from seed sown in a warm greenhouse in late winter or early spring, seedlings being pricked out and hardened off for planting out in late spring or early summer.

There are a great many varieties which fall into two main groups; one known as grandiflora, with very large flowers, the other, known as multiflora, with smaller flowers more freely produced. The colour range includes practically everything except deep yellow and orange and some varieties have two sharply contrasted colours such as purple or carmine and white. There are also double-flowered varieties but these are, on the whole, most suitable as pot plants for greenhouses or in window boxes and on balconies.

All kinds flower throughout the summer, and though the flowers of many are readily damaged by rain, some varieties recover quickly.

Phacelia Pretty hardy annuals of which the best is *Phacelia campanularia*, a low-growing plant with intensely blue flowers rather like those of a campanula. It likes sun and a well-drained soil and is grown from seed sown in spring where the plants are to flower in summer. Seedlings should be thinned to about 6 in (15 cm).

Phlox In addition to the herbaceous phlox (see p. 67), and the moss pink (see p. 81), there is an annual phlox, known as *Phlox drummondii*, a sprawling plant with a long flowering season in summer and a colour range from white, pale pink and lavender to scarlet, crimson, violet and purple. Heights range from 6 to 15 in (15 to 38 cm).

The annual phlox is half hardy and so is grown from seed sown in a warm greenhouse in spring, the seedlings being pricked out into boxes and hardened off for planting out in late spring or early summer in a sunny place and any reasonable soil.

Pink In addition to the perennial pinks, (see p. 60) there are the so-called Chinese or Indian pinks, varieties of *Dianthus chinensis* and a form of this known as *heddewigii*. All are showy plants with fine single or double flowers, usually with red, crimson or maroon blotches on a white background, though there are also all-red, all-white, pink and salmon varieties.

All are best grown as half-hardy annuals to be raised from seed sown in a greenhouse or frame in early spring or outdoors in late spring. Seedlings raised under glass are hardened off for planting out in late spring or early summer. These annual pinks like sunny places and well-drained soils.

Polyanthus The polyanthus is a particular kind of primrose which carries its flowers in clusters on fairly stout stems. It has been wonderfully developed to give a vast colour range from white, pink and pale blue, to scarlet, crimson and violet, and including many unusual coppery shades. It is a hardy perennial which will live for years in good rich soil and partly shaded places, but it is fairly easily raised from seed and is usually treated as a biennial, especially some modern large-flowered strains which appear to be less winter hardy than the old polyanthus.

Seed is sown in spring or early summer in a frame, the seedlings are pricked out into boxes or a frame, and planted out in early autumn where they are to flower the following spring.

They make fine beds on their own or may be used as a groundwork for spring-flowering bulbs, or be grown in groups in shrubberies or herbaceous borders. If plants are kept from year to year it is wise to lift and divide them after flowering every second year.

Poppy (Papaver) In addition to the herbaceous perennial poppies, there are annual poppies and poppies which are usually treated as biennials. All like sunny places and fairly well-drained soils.

The most popular annual poppies are the Shirley poppy, *Papaver rhoeas*, and the peony-flowered poppy, *P. somniferum*. The first is a rather slender plant with a wonderfully delicate colour range, the second is more robust, grey leaved, with big flowers often very double and in a wider range of often rather rich colours. Both are readily grown from seed sown outdoors in spring or early autumn where the plants are to flower, the seedlings being thinned to at least 9 in (23 cm). The average height of Shirley poppies is 2 ft (60 cm), peony-flowered poppies, 3 ft (1 m). Both kinds are liable to reproduce themselves freely by self-sown seedlings, but as a rule the range of colours and quality of bloom quickly diminishes.

The lovely Iceland poppy, *P. nudicaule*, is really a perennial, but is short lived and is usually grown either as an annual or biennial. In the first case, seed is sown in early spring in a greenhouse with a temperature of about 13°C. (55°F.) and the seedlings are planted out in late spring to flower in late summer. If the plant is to be treated as a biennial, seed is sown in a frame in early summer, the seedlings being planted out in late summer to flower early the following summer. The colour range is mainly in yellow and orange, but with some pink and white as well. Average height is 2 to 3 ft (60 cm to 1 m).

Portulaca Half-hardy annuals with succulent leaves and very showy single or double flowers in a wide range of colours including scarlet, carmine, purple, pink, orange and yellow. They delight in sun and warmth and look well on top of a terrace wall or raised bed in reasonably good but very porous soil.

Seed should be sown in early spring in a warm greenhouse and seedlings pricked out and hardened off for planting out in late spring and early summer when there is no further danger of frost.

Pot marigold, see Calendula

Primrose The common yellow primrose is usually only planted in woodland and wild gardens but the cultivated varieties, which are available in a good range of colours including pink, red, crimson, lavender and blue, are first-rate spring bedding plants grown in exactly the same way as the polyanthus.

Prince of Wales's feather, see Celosia

Prince's feather, see Amaranthus

Reseda, see Mignonette

Rocket candytuft, see Candytuft

Salpiglossis sinuata

Rudbeckia (Cone flower, gloriosa daisy) In addition to the cone flowers which are grown as hardy perennials, (see page 68) there are other kinds mainly derived from *Rudbeckia hirta* which, though perennial, are either not fully hardy or are naturally short lived and so are usually grown as annuals or biennials. The daisy-type flowers are yellow or chestnut red or a combination of these colours. The plants are rather coarse leaved, 1 to 3 ft (30 cm to 1 m) high and they flower all summer.

Seed can either be sown in a greenhouse or frame in spring; seedlings being pricked out, hardened off and planted out in late spring or early summer, or seed can be sown outdoors in early summer and plants transferred to flowering quarters in early autumn to bloom the following year.

They like sunny places and will grow in practically any well-drained soil.

Salpiglossis Half-hardy annuals with trumpet-shaped flowers in a wide range of colours, often with veinings of gold on a purple, rose or scarlet base. The flowers are carried in loose sprays on 3-ft (1-m) stems and are excellent for cutting.

Seed should be sown in a warm greenhouse in early spring, the seedlings being pricked out and eventually hardened off for planting out in late spring or early summer in good soil and a sunny, sheltered position. The plants should be spaced at least 9 in (23 cm) apart. Alternatively, salpiglossis can be grown as a pot plant for the cool greenhouse in summer, in which case the young plants should be potted singly in 5- or 6-in (13- to 15-cm) pots instead of being planted outdoors.

Salvia Some salvias are herbaceous perennials, (see page 68) and one is the sage, a popular herb, but here we are concerned with two very different plants, one, *Salvia splendens*, a half-hardy perennial, and the other, *S. horminum*, a hardy annual. Both are grown for their great flower displays in summer.

Though perennial, *S. splendens* and its varieties are nearly always grown as half-hardy annuals, seed being sown in a greenhouse with a temperature 16 to 18°C (60 to 65°F) in late winter or early spring, and the seedlings potted singly in small pots and eventually hardened off for planting out in early summer after all danger of frost is past. This salvia likes sun and warmth but is not fussy about soil. It makes bushy plants 9 to 18 in (23 to 45 cm) high, according to variety, and its spikes of vivid scarlet, pink or purple flowers are produced non-stop

Senecio cineraria **White Diamond**

from mid-summer to the first frost of autumn.

Salvia horminum is popularly known as clary. Its flowers are also borne in spikes about 18 in (45 cm) high but it is not the flowers themselves but the leaf-like bracts surrounding them that make the display. They may be blue, purple, pink, rose or white according to variety and they last a long time. Clary is grown from seed sown outdoors in spring or early autumn where the plants are to flower, seedlings being thinned to about 9 in (23 cm).

Saponaria (Soapwort) The annual soapwort, *Saponaria vaccaria*, is a graceful plant with loose sprays of pink or white flowers in summer. It is quite hardy and is grown from seed sown in spring where the plants are to flower, seedlings being thinned to 6 in (15 cm). A sunny place is desirable but it will grow in almost any soil.

Scabiosa (Scabious, pincushion flower) In addition to the hardy perennial scabious described on page 69, there is a useful hardy annual kind, *Scabiosa atropurpurea*, 1½ to 3 ft (45 cm to 1 m) high with sweetly scented, pincushion-shaped flowers in a variety of colours including lavender, blue, pink, red, crimson, purple and white.

Seed can be sown outdoors in spring or early autumn where plants are to flower, seedlings being thinned to at least 9 in (23 cm). Alternatively, seed can be sown a little earlier in a frame or greenhouse, seedlings being pricked out and hardened off for planting out in late spring.

It is a plant which enjoys sunny places and reasonably well-drained soil and its flowers are excellent for cutting.

Senecio (Dusty miller) *Senecio cineraria*, a plant sometimes called *Cineraria maritima*, is grown for its deeply divided silvery-

grey leaves. In time it will make quite a big bushy plant, 3 or 4 ft (1 to 1·25 m) high, but it is smaller, younger plants that are most useful as a foil to the stronger colours of such plants as salvias and geraniums.

Plants can be grown from cuttings rooted in a frame or greenhouse at practically any time in spring or summer, or from seed sown in a greenhouse in spring. *S. cineraria* is not fully hardy, though it will overwinter safely in mild winters. Usually it must be removed to a frost-proof greenhouse or frame in autumn or be renewed annually from seed or cuttings. It likes light soils and warm, sunny places.

Silene (Catchfly) There is one excellent annual catchfly, *Silene pendula*, a slender plant with sprays of single or double flowers in summer in shades of pink, salmon, scarlet, lilac and white. It is hardy and is grown from seed sown in spring where the plants are to flower, the seedlings being thinned to about 6 in (15 cm). It likes sun but is not fussy about soil.

Snapdragon, see Antirrhinum

Soapwort, see Saponaria

Spider flower, see Cleome

Star of the veldt, see Dimorphotheca

Statice There are both hardy perennial and half-hardy annual statices, but all have sprays of small flowers prized because they can be dried for winter decoration. The perennials are described on page 65.

The flowers of the annual statice, *Limonium sinuatum*, and the yellow statice, *L. bonduellii*, are larger than those of the perennials and together give a range of blue, pink, white and yellow.

Seed should be sown in a warm greenhouse in early spring, the seedlings being pricked out and hardened off for planting out in late spring or early summer at least 9 in (23 cm) apart in 18-in (45-cm) rows in good soil and a sunny place. The flowers should be cut with long stems just before they are fully open and suspended head downwards in a cool, airy shed or room to dry.

The candelabra statice, *L. suworowii*, is a more tender annual with narrow pink spikes in a candelabra-like formation. It is usually grown as a cool greenhouse pot plant from seed treated as for the other annual kinds.

Stock *Matthiola incana* is the botanical name of the plant that has produced the most popular races of spring- and summer-flowering stocks.

Ten-week stocks are half-hardy annuals from 1 to 3 ft (30 cm to 1 m) high, grown from seed sown in a moderately heated greenhouse in spring. Seedlings are pricked out and grown on with plenty of light and ventilation for eventual hardening off and planting out in late spring or early summer. There are many colours, from white, cream and palest mauve and pink to deep crimson and purple; all are fragrant.

Since it is the double-flowered plants that make the finest display, considerable ingenuity has been displayed by breeders in either increasing the number of doubles produced from seed, or by making it possible to differentiate between doubles and singles at an early age so that the singles can be discarded. In some strains the double-flowered plants have yellowish-green leaves in the seedling stage, the singles being a deeper green. This difference can be accentuated, making it easier to pick out the doubles, if the seed is germinated at about 15°C. (60°F.), but the temperature is dropped for a week to 10°C. (50°F.) directly the first pair of true leaves have been developed.

Brompton stocks are 2 to 3 ft (60 cm to 1 m) high with a less extensive colour range, and they are grown very much like wallflowers as biennials, seed being sown outdoors or in a frame about mid-summer to produce plants which can be placed in their final beds in autumn or early spring to flower in late spring or early summer. They need a sunny, sheltered place in well-drained soil.

East Lothian stocks are intermediate between the other two types. Sown in a greenhouse in late winter, they will flower in late summer; sown in late summer and over-wintered in a frame, they can be planted out in spring to flower in summer.

The night-scented stock, *M. bicornis*, is a very different plant; a hardy annual 1 ft (30 cm) high with dingy purple flowers that are intensely fragrant at night. Seed can be sown thinly any time in spring where the plants are to bloom and little or no thinning is necessary.

Stock, Virginian This pretty and easily grown annual has a totally different parentage to the ordinary stocks described above and is botanically *Malcomia maritima*. It is a plant 6 in (15 cm) high, producing small pink, lilac or white flowers throughout the summer. All that is necessary is to sprinkle seed very thinly in spring or early autumn where the plants are to flower. No thinning of seedlings is necessary.

Summer cypress, see Kochia

Sunflower There are both annual and perennial sunflowers. Most spectacular of the annuals is the giant sunflower, *Helianthus annuus*, with 7- or 8-ft (2·25- to 2·5-m) stems carrying huge flowers largely composed of a central, pad-like, brownish-purple disk which later produces a crop of large seeds, often used for poultry feeding. The disk is surrounded by a fringe of yellow petals.

The seeds should be sown in pairs a foot or so apart in spring where plants are to flower and later the seedlings should be thinned to one at each station. There are also smaller annual sunflowers from 3 to 4 ft (1 to 1·25 m) in height, with flowers from pale to deep yellow, and bronze and crimson which can be grown in the same way. All like reasonably good, well-drained soil and warm, sunny places.

Swan River daisy, see Brachycome

Sweet Pea These popular annuals can be treated in several different ways. To obtain the finest flowers, seed is sown in early autumn in small pots in a frame, the seedlings being kept in this until the following spring, when they are planted out in deeply worked, well-manured ground and an open, sunny place. They are spaced 1 ft (30 cm) apart, usually in a double row 1 ft (30 cm) wide, with a 4- or 5 ft (1·25- to 1·5-m) alleyway between this and the next double row. Each plant is given a tall bamboo cane and is restricted to one stem only, which is regularly tied to the cane. All side growths and tendrils are removed. When the plant reaches the top of the cane it is untied, lowered, laid along the rows for several feet and then tied to the bottom of another cane which it can continue to ascend. This is known as the cordon system.

The natural system is to allow the plants to grow unchecked and climb into bushy hazel branches stuck into the ground as for staking culinary peas. The seed can be sown in pots or boxes in a frame or greenhouse in late winter or directly into the open ground in spring; in the former case the seedlings are planted out about 6 in (15 cm) apart in mid or late spring. In the latter, the seeds are spaced 2 or 3 in (5 to 8 cm) apart and there is little or no subsequent thinning of seedlings.

Another way to grow sweet peas is to sow in small groups and place a few canes wigwam fashion or some bushy hazel branches to each group, so making columns or cones which can be very decorative.

There are a great many varieties and new ones are added to the list every year. There are dwarf varieties growing only about 1 ft (30 cm) high and needing little or no support, and other varieties only a few feet high.

Sweet Sultan This pretty hardy annual, with bright yellow, mauve or purple flowers rather like those of a cornflower in shape, is related to the cornflower and is botanically *Centaurea moschata*. The plants grow about 18 in (45 cm) high, flower in summer and like sunny places and well-drained soils.

Seed may be sown in spring or early autumn, seedlings being thinned to about 9 in (23 cm). All varieties are excellent for cutting.

Sweet William These charming plants, with their big, flattish heads of flowers in early summer, belong to the pink family and their botanical name is *Dianthus barbatus*. They are usually grown as biennials, though in favourable positions and well-drained soils they will often continue for a number of years. But the usual practice is to sow seed outdoors in late spring, prick out the seedlings 6 in (15 cm) apart in a nursery bed of good soil in a sunny position and grow on until autumn, when they are transferred to their flowering quarters. After flowering the plants are destroyed.

Sweet Williams will grow in practically any soil, though they prefer those that are reasonably well drained. There are numerous varieties, differing in height from about 9 in to 2 ft (23 to 60 cm), and in colour from white and pink to crimson. The auricula-eyed sweet William has rings of colour on a white base.

There are also annual strains of sweet William which can be sown in a greenhouse in early spring, hardened off and planted out in late spring to flower the same summer.

Tagetes The plant listed in catalogues as *Tagetes signata* is a dwarf marigold with single yellow or orange flowers. See Marigold.

Tassel flower, see Amaranthus

Toadflax, see Linaria

Tobacco, see Nicotiana

Tropaeolum (Canary creeper) This is the proper name of the showy annuals which every gardener calls nasturtium and which are described under that name on p. 99. There is also a climbing kind which is never called nasturtium but appears in catalogues as *Tropaeolum peregrinum* or *T. canariense*. This is the Canary creeper, a slender annual climbing plant with fringed, curiously shaped canary-yellow flowers all the summer. It is a hardy annual to be grown from seed sown in spring where it is to flower, seedlings being thinned to about 1 ft (30 cm). It likes a warm, sunny place and well-drained soil and should have some brushy branches pushed into the soil around it or be provided with some support.

Ursinia Brilliant half-hardy annuals, with orange daisy flowers, often with a central zone of crimson, maroon or black and produced throughout the summer.

Ursinias are raised from seed sown in a warm greenhouse in spring, the seedlings being pricked out and hardened off for planting out in well-drained soil and a warm sunny place, in late spring. They should be spaced about 1 ft (30 cm) apart and will reach a height of 12 to 18 in (30 to 45 cm).

Venidium Showy half-hardy annuals with large orange and black daisy flowers in summer.

Seed should be sown in spring in a frame

Helianthus annuus (Sunflower)

or greenhouse, the seedlings being pricked out and hardened off for planting out in late spring in a sunny place and well-drained soil. Heights vary from 2 to 3 ft (60 cm to 1 m).

Some remarkable hybrids, known as *Venidio-arctotis*, have been raised from a cross between these plants and *Arctotis*, with flowers in a range of pink, orange, copper and wine red. They are sterile and so cannot be raised from seed. Instead they are increased by cuttings in spring or summer but these cuttings must pass the winter in a frame or greenhouse as they are not hardy.

Verbena Some verbenas are hardy perennials and these are described on page 70. Others are more tender and, though also perennial, are usually grown as half-hardy annuals and raised anew each year from seed sown in a warm greenhouse in late winter or early spring. Seedlings are pricked out and hardened off for planting out in late spring in a sunny place. Some selected varieties, such as the scarlet Lawrence Johnston, are raised from cuttings taken in late summer or early autumn and rooted and overwintered in a frame or greenhouse.

All are rather sprawling plants with flattish heads of flowers which make a great display all summer. Colours available include many shades of pink to scarlet and crimson, also pale blue, lavender and deep blue.

Viola These low-growing spring- and summer-flowering perennials are very like pansies to which they are so closely allied and with which they have been so interbred that it is impossible to draw a firm distinction between them. Colours range from white, pale lemon and mauve to deep yellow, purple and violet. All make good bedding or edging plants, as they flower for a long time.

Violas are quite hardy and will grow in any reasonable soil. They appreciate a little shade, but will also grow well in full sun. All can be increased by cuttings in early autumn or by division in spring, but they are also readily raised from seed which is treated exactly like that of pansies (see p. 99).

Wallflower All wallflowers are perennials, but the familiar varieties of *Cheiranthus cheiri* used for spring bedding are usually treated as biennials.

Seed is sown each year in late spring, the seedlings are pricked out in a sunny nursery bed for the summer, are planted in early autumn where they are to flower and, after flowering, are pulled out and thrown away. This is because they tend to get straggly with age and are then frequently killed by wet and cold in winter. There are numerous colours, including ivory white, primrose, yellow, orange, orange scarlet, carmine, blood red, coppery red, purple, rose and rosy chamois and heights vary from 9 to 18 in (23 to 45 cm).

All thrive in sunny places and well-drained soils particularly on chalk.

The Siberian wallflower, *Cheiranthus allionii*, flowers a little later and goes on flowering for a longer time than the common wallflower. Another notable point of difference is that its vivid orange flowers are scarcely scented. It is grown in exactly the same way as the common wallflower.

Zinnia Half-hardy annuals with brilliantly coloured daisy-type flowers in summer. The colour range is from lemon and pink to orange and crimson and the flowers are very variable in size and form. Most are fully double, though some single or semi-doubles are likely to be produced. There are dwarf varieties only 6 in (15 cm) high with flowers to scale, as well as taller varieties up to 3 ft (1 m) high, some with quilled or shaggy petals more like chrysanthemums.

Seed may be sown in a frame or greenhouse in spring, the seedlings being pricked off and finally planted out in late spring in fairly rich soil and a sunny position. The plants should be spaced at least 1 ft (30 cm) apart. Alternatively, seed can be sown in late spring outdoors where the plants are to flower. Thin seedlings to 1 ft (30 cm).

Bulbs, Corms and Tubers

Bulbs, corms and tubers are really quite different things but since they can almost all be handled dry (lifted and left out of the ground for a while without any soil) they tend to be sold by firms who specialize in such things.

These firms are known as bulb merchants or bulb growers and they issue catalogues which list bulbs, corms and tubers more or less indiscriminately.

It is not essential for the gardener to understand the differences between a bulb, a corm and a tuber, but for those who are interested this is what they are.

A bulb is a kind of enlarged bud and, like a bud, is composed of layers of protective scales, which may be quite loose and clearly defined, as in some lily bulbs, or very closely packed together, as in a tulip or hyacinth bulb. In the centre of the bulb is an embryo shoot, and sometimes a flower as well, which explains why it is possible to grow some bulbs right to flowering stage with no more assistance than warmth and moisture.

A corm is solid flesh throughout, except that it may have a membraneous protective wrapping on the outside. It is, in fact, a swollen stem and it bears buds, some of which may contain embryo flowers.

A tuber is also solid flesh throughout and it may be either a thickened stem, in which case it will contain growth buds or eyes as in the potato, or a thickened root, in which case it will not have eyes and the new growth will come from a crown or upper part attached to it (really the base of a stem or stems) as in the dahlia.

What all these structures have in common is that they are storage organs. They contain considerable quantities of plant food and they enable the plant to survive for quite long periods on its own stored resources.

It is not surprising to find that a good many plants of this nature grow wild in places where there are long periods of drought during which the plant becomes more or less dormant. Then, when rain comes again, the plant starts rapidly into growth, making full use of the food it has stored within its bulbs, corms or tubers.

A plant will usually go on behaving more or less in the way nature intended even when it is grown under different conditions and so tulips, hyacinths and daffodils all die down a month or so after flowering even though there is enough moisture in the soil to keep them growing. It is at this period that they can be lifted and prepared for sale as dry bulbs.

Simulating Conditions of Nature Sometimes the gardener must try to simulate the conditions of nature. When tuberous-rooted begonias are grown in the greenhouse, they are given decreasing quantities of water in early autumn to encourage them to die down and go to rest for the winter. Similar treatment is given to greenhouse cyclamen, except that in their case the reduction in water supply comes in late spring as these plants rest in summer, whereas tuberous-rooted begonias rest in winter.

Transplanting Although all bulbs, corms and tubers can be transplanted while they are at rest, it is not always the best time to transplant them. Snowdrops, for example, seem to suffer least check to growth when transplanted just before they come into flower but this is usually inconvenient as it means that the flower display for that year is lost. They can still be moved quite well immediately after flowering and this is what many gardeners do.

Bulbs in Pots and Bowls Some spring-flowering bulbs, and particularly daffodils and hyacinths, succeed well in pots and bowls and can be used for room or greenhouse decoration. If the receptacles have

When potting hyacinth bulbs leave the noses just sticking out of the compost

drainage holes, ordinary potting compost can be used, but for undrained bowls special bulb fibre containing charcoal must be used. The bulb fibre should be well moistened and the bulbs need be barely covered with it.

For the first eight or ten weeks they must be kept cool and dark. They can be placed in a cupboard or plunged outdoors under 3 or 4 in (8 to 10 cm) of sand, peat or weathered ashes. When they have rooted well they can be brought inside and grown in a light, moderately warm place.

Recommended Bulbs, Corms and Tubers

Plants with bulbs, corms and tubers are of many categories. Some are hardy herbaceous plants to be grown outdoors winter and summer; some are half-hardy, which means that they can be grown outdoors in summer but need protection from frost in winter, and some are so tender that they are only grown in greenhouses. Obviously the treatment of so diverse a group of plants will differ considerably from one to another and few generalizations are of much help. Culture is dealt with individually under the name and description of each plant described in the list which follows.

Acidanthera The only kind grown in gardens is *Acidanthera bicolor murielae*. It has white and maroon, scented flowers, rather like those of a gladiolus, borne in late summer on 3-ft (1-m) stems.

It is not very hardy and needs a warm, sheltered place in well-drained soil, or alternatively the corms can be lifted in autumn, stored in a frost-proof place and be replanted in the spring.

African corn lily, see Ixia

African harlequin flower, see Sparaxis

Allium (Onion) Though the kitchen-garden onion has little decorative value, there are numerous ornamental onions, including *Allium moly* with roundish heads of buttercup-yellow flowers on 1-ft (30-cm) stems, and *A. rosenbachianum* which has much larger, globular heads of purplish flowers carried on 4-ft (1·25-m) stems, both in late spring. Both are perfectly hardy and are easily grown; in fact *A. moly* often makes itself so much at home that self-sown seedlings soon appear all over the place.

Other decorative kinds are *A. caeruleum*, blue; *A. neapolitanum*, white; *A. ostrowskyanum*, large heads of pinkish flowers on short stems, and *A. sphaerocephalum*, egg-shaped maroon flowers.

Most kinds like sun, but *A. moly* will put up with a good deal of shade. Seed and division provide ready means of increase. All ornamental onions retain some measure of the characteristic smell of the family; a few positively stink.

Amaryllis (Belladonna lily) Although not a true lily, the pink and white flowers of *Amaryllis belladonna* are trumpet shaped, like those of many lilies, and the plant makes large bulbs. These should be given a warm position near the foot of a sunny wall and should be covered with 5 in (13 cm) of soil for protection except in very mild places where they need be only just covered. The belladonna lily likes well-drained but fairly rich soil and should be disturbed as little as possible. The very fragrant flowers are produced in early autumn before the leaves.

Anemone Most important of the tuberous-rooted anemones are the poppy anemones, varieties of *Anemone coronaria*. These have showy flowers borne singly on stems 9 to 12 in (23 to 30 cm) high in winter, spring or early summer. There are various strains such as St Brigid, with double flowers and fringed petals, and De Caen with single flowers and plain petals, but all are brightly coloured in shades of pink, scarlet, blue and purple.

The small tubers are planted 2 in (5 cm) deep in early autumn or early spring according to the time at which flowers are required. Except in very mild places autumn plantings are usually in frames but spring plantings can be outdoors in a sunny place. These anemones like fairly rich, firm soil.

Autumn crocus, see Colchicum

Belladonna lily, see Amaryllis

Bluebell, see Scilla

Camassia Plants with narrow leaves and spikes of blue flowers in late spring or early summer. *Camassia cusickii* and *C. leichtlinii* are both 3 ft (1 m) high; the former grey blue, the latter white or blue. *C. esculenta* is 2 ft (60 cm) and deep blue. All will grow in sun or partial shade in any reasonably good soil.

Chincherinchee, see Ornithogalum

Chionodoxa (Glory of the snow) Delightful bulbous-rooted plants only a few inches in height and producing loose sprays of bright blue or blue and white flowers in early spring. They are excellent for the rock garden, border or shrubbery and will succeed in full sun or partial shade.

The small bulbs should be planted 3 in (8 cm) deep in early autumn. They are readily increased by lifting and dividing the clusters of bulbs at planting time.

Clivia, see p. 119 (Greenhouse Plants)

Colchicum (Autumn crocus) Despite the extraordinary superficial resemblance of its flowers to those of a crocus, this plant is not a crocus nor is it related to the crocus. Colchicums make very big bulbs which

should be planted in late summer and be covered with 2 in (5 cm) of soil. The lilac, pink or white flowers appear in early autumn before the large leaves.

Colchicums can be naturalized in grass, but are really happiest in rock gardens or at the front of shrubberies and herbaceous borders, in good, rich, loamy soil in a sunny or partially shady place. They can be increased by dividing the bulb clusters at planting time, but it is unnecessary to lift and replant the bulbs annually. In the right place they will continue for years, each cluster increasing in size all the time.

Corn lily, African, see Ixia

Crinum Showy plants with large, trumpet-shaped, lily-like flowers in late summer. Most kinds are too tender to be grown outdoors safely except in nearly frost-free places, but a hybrid, *Crinum powellii*, with pink (or occasionally white) flowers will stand more cold and is often planted in warm, sunny, sheltered gardens.

The very large bulbs should be planted in spring with their tips just appearing through the soil. They can be left undisturbed for many years and are increased by division in spring.

Crocosmia One fine kind is grown, *Crocosmia masonorum*, a plant rather like a montbretia but with larger, upfacing orange-red flowers in summer.

It needs a warm, sunny place in reasonably good, well-drained soil and is grown from corms which should be planted 2 to 3 in (5 to 8 cm) deep in spring. Increase is by division in spring.

Crocus In addition to the well-known garden or Dutch crocuses with flowers in various shades of mauve, purple, yellow and white, there are a number of wild crocuses well worth planting, especially in the rock garden. Their flowers are, in general, more fragile than those of the garden crocuses and, as some flower very early, they may need the protection of a pane of glass against heavy rain. Typical of these wildings are *Crocus speciosus*, which produces its mauve, blue or white flowers in autumn; *C. imperati*, buff outside, violet within and in bloom by mid-winter; *C. sieberi* and *C. tomasinianus*, both with pale mauve flowers in early spring; *C. chrysanthus*, yellow, orange, blue, purple and white, sometimes feathered with one colour on another or with bronze on the outside of the petals, and the cloth-of-gold crocus, *C. susianus*, with golden-yellow flowers in early spring.

All crocuses like sun, though most will also grow in light shade. The wild kinds like rather gritty, well-drained soils, but the garden varieties will grow in almost any soil. All should be planted in autumn except the autumn-flowering kinds,

Erythronium dens-canis

Fritillaria meleagris

which should be put in from mid- to late summer. They are increased by separating the clusters of corms.

Crocus, Autumn, see Colchicum

Crown imperial, see Fritillaria

Cyclamen Some cyclamen are grown primarily as rock garden or woodland plants and are described on p. 77, and some are grown as greenhouse or house plants and are described on p. 120.

Daffodil, see Narcissus

Dog's-tooth violet, see Erythronium

Endymion, see Scilla

Eranthis (Winter aconite) Early-flowering plants with yellow, buttercup-like flowers each surrounded by a little ruff of green leaf-like bracts.

Eranthis hyemalis, the kind most frequently grown, flowers in late winter and early spring and is 3 in (8 cm) high. It thrives in shady places and any soil and should be planted 2 in (5 cm) deep.

Eremurus (Fox-tail lily) Remarkable hardy herbaceous plants with long, stiff spikes of flowers in summer. The tallest, *Eremurus robustus*, may reach 10 ft (3 m) and is pale pink, but more useful for general garden use are *E. himalaicus*, 3 ft (1 m) and white, and the hybrid varieties which grow 4 or 5 ft (1·25 to 1·5 m) high and have flowers in various shades of pink, maize, apricot and soft orange. All have fleshy roots, radiating like the spokes of a wheel from a central crown, and need to be very carefully planted in good well-drained soil and a sunny place. The roots should have no more

than 4 in (10 cm) of soil over them and transplanting is best done in early or mid-autumn. Once established they should be left alone as long as possible.

Seed sown in early autumn in a frame is the best method of increase but they may be slow to flower for several years. In cold places, it is wise to cover the plants with sand, straw or bracken in winter.

Erythronium (Dog's-tooth violet) Attractive spring-flowering plants for a shady rock garden or border. The commonest kind, *Erythronium dens-canis*, has nodding pink or purple flowers on 4-in (10-cm) stems, only very slightly resembling violets, and attractive marbled leaves, but there are other, taller kinds, some with yellow, some with white flowers.

All like cool, partly shaded places and soil containing plenty of leafmould or peat. The tubers should be planted 2 in (5 cm) deep.

Fox-tail lily, see Eremurus

Freesia, see p. 120 (Greenhouse Plants)

Fritillaria (Crown imperial, fritillary) *Fritillaria imperialis*, the crown imperial, is a striking hardy plant with broad, strap-shaped leaves and stiff, 3-ft (1-m) flower spikes terminated by tufts of small leaves and showy hanging clusters of yellow or orange-red flowers with a rather unpleasant foxy smell. It is grown from large bulbs which should be planted in autumn in fairly rich soil and an open, sunny place.

Very different in appearance is the snake's head or chequered fritillary, *F. meleagris*, a distinctive and elegant plant with slender 1-ft (30-cm) stems terminated in April or May by quite large, pendent purple and white or purple and mauve flowers. It is grown from small bulbs, which should be

planted in autumn, 2 or 3 in (5 or 8 cm) deep, in soil which is fairly moist and rich. The bulbs need not be lifted annually and can often be naturalized in grass that is not mown before mid-summer.

Galanthus (Snowdrop) These lovely early-spring-flowering plants are grown from bulbs which can either be planted as dry bulbs in early autumn, 4 in (10 cm) deep, or as growing plants in early spring. They will grow in almost any soil and situation, though the common kind prefers cool, partially shaded positions and is ideal for planting around shrubs or trees. It can also be naturalized in grass, provided the grass is not cut until the snowdrop leaves have died down in early summer.

There is no kind more beautiful than this common snowdrop, *Galanthus nivalis*, but its double-flowered variety makes a better display in the mass, and there are several other kinds such as S. Arnott, Colesborne, *atkinsii* and Merlin, which have flowers of superior size. *G. elwesii* is a different species with much broader leaves and another vigorous kind well worth planting is *G. byzantinus*, both of which prefer sunny to shady places. All are white with green markings.

Galtonia This handsome plant is sometimes called the summer hyacinth but its tall spikes of nodding white flowers only bear a superficial resemblance to those of the true hyacinths. It flowers from mid- to late summer, is quite hardy, and will thrive in most reasonably good soils and open places. It makes large bulbs which should be planted 3 in (8 cm) deep in autumn.

Increase is by division of bulb clusters in autumn or by seed sown in a frame or greenhouse in spring, but seedlings take several years to reach flowering size.

Annuals make a colourful summer display

Gladiolus These brilliant summer-flowering plants are grown from corms, almost all of which must be planted in spring. They like a sunny, open situation and rather rich, well-drained soil. Corms should be spaced at least 6 in (15 cm) apart and be covered with 3 in (8 cm) of soil. The heavy flower spikes of some of the bigger varieties may require individual staking. About six weeks after flowering the plants should be lifted, the tops cut off about 1 in (2·5 cm) above the new corms, and the old withered corms removed from beneath the new ones. Then the new corms are stored away for the winter in a cool, dry, frost-proof place. A number of small cormlets may be found around the main corms. If desired these can also be stored and replanted the following spring, but they may take a year or so to attain flowering size.

There are a great many varieties differing in size, form and colour of bloom. The miniatures and the Primulinus varieties have smaller flowers but do not differ in their cultural requirements. The early-flowering gladiolus, which is sometimes called *Gladiolus nanus* and sometimes *G. colvillei*, is too tender to be grown outdoors except in very mild districts, and varieties of it are usually grown as pot plants in a slightly heated greenhouse. Potted in autumn and grown on in a temperature around 10°C. (50°F.), they will flower the following spring or early summer. After flowering the corms are treated like those of outdoor gladioli. *G. byzantinus*, with magenta flowers in early summer, is the hardiest of all and can be left outdoors throughout the year, except in very cold places.

Glory of the snow, see Chionodoxa

Grape hyacinth, see Muscari

Harlequin flower, African, see Sparaxis

Hippeastrum, see p. 121 (Greenhouse Plants)

Hyacinth, see Hyacinthus

Hyacinthus (Hyacinth) These popular spring-flowering bulbs are usually seen in pots or bowls indoors or under glass, but they can also be grown in beds outdoors. Bulbs should be obtained in late summer or early autumn for pot or bowl culture, mid- or late autumn for planting outdoors. If in drained pots, ordinary John Innes or soilless compost may be used; if in bowls without drainage holes, special bulb fibre containing charcoal and crushed oyster shell should be used. In either case the bulbs may be almost shoulder to shoulder and should be almost, but not quite, covered. Pots and bowls are best placed in a cool place to make roots. After this they may be brought into a living room or greenhouse either with or without artificial heat accord-

Summer bedding in a portable planter

Galanthus nivalis S. Arnott

ing to the time at which flowers are required. After flowering, bulbs can be planted outdoors.

Outdoor bulbs should be spaced 8 in (20 cm) apart and be covered with 2 in (5 cm) of soil. They like a fairly rich but porous soil and a sunny place. After flowering leave the foliage to die down, then lift and store in a dry, cool place until planting time.

Iris In addition to the irises grown as hardy herbaceous perennials, (see page 64) there are a number of delightful bulbous-rooted kinds. Most popular of these are the Spanish, English and Dutch irises, all similar in appearance and producing showy blue, purple, yellow, bronzy, or white flowers on 2-ft (60-cm) stems in late spring and early summer. They make excellent cut flowers as well as being highly decorative in the garden. They are easily grown in most soils and open places and should be planted about 3 in (8 cm) deep and 6 to 8 in (15 to 20 cm) apart in autumn.

A little more difficult are the winter or early-spring-flowering species such as *Iris histrioides*, blue, 4 in (10 cm); *I. reticulata*, deep violet purple, 6 in (15 cm); *I. danfordiae*, yellow, 4 in (10 cm). All these like well-drained but fairly rich soil and sunny places and look well in rock gardens or raised beds. They should be planted in early autumn, 2 in (5 cm) deep.

Ixia (African corn lily) Elegant plants with narrow, grassy leaves and slender arching spikes of starry flowers in spring. Colours include white, yellow, orange, pink, carmine and crimson. They are grown from corms which should be planted in autumn 3 in (8 cm) deep in light, porous soil and the sunniest, warmest place available as they are not very hardy.

Alternatively they can be grown in a frost-proof greenhouse, five or six corms in each 4-in (10-cm) pot, watered sparingly at first, then freely as growth starts, but being gradually dried off after flowering and stored dry for a couple of months before repotting in early autumn.

Hyacinth Pink Pearl

Lilium regale

Leucojum (Snowflake) Bulbous plants which look rather like large snowdrops but have more bell-shaped flowers. The three kinds commonly grown are the spring snowflake, *Leucojum vernum*, with white, green-tipped flowers on 6-in (15-cm) stems in early spring; the summer snowflake, *L. aestivum*, with similarly coloured flowers on 18-in (45-cm) stems in late spring, and the autumn snowflake, *L. autumnale*, with small, white, pink-tinted flowers on 6-in (15-cm) stems in autumn.

All like rather rich, moist soil and semi-shady places and the spring and summer snowflakes should be planted, like snowdrops, in autumn. The autumn snowflake should be planted in the latter half of summer.

Propagation is by division of the bulb clusters at planting time, but the less frequently the bulbs are disturbed the better.

Lilium (Lily) A great many plants which are popularly called lilies, for example African lily, arum lily, belladonna lily, are not really lilies at all, but there are, in addition, so many true liles that it is difficult to give anything but a very brief account of them. All have bulbous roots and all can be planted in autumn, though they do not like being out of the ground for long, for which reason some experts prefer to treat them like herbaceous plants, moving them in early spring when they are already growing. Imported bulbs often do not arrive until mid-winter and then they may either be started in pots, from which they will be planted out when they are growing, or they may be kept until early spring and planted where they are to flower.

From the cultural standpoint lilies may be divided into hardy and slightly tender varieties. The hardy lilies can all be grown outdoors, but the slightly tender varieties are better treated as cool greenhouse plants except in the mildest parts of the country. The most important of these greenhouse kinds is the Easter lily, *Lilium longiflorum*, with long, white trumpet flowers in spring. The bulbs should be planted low down in 9- or 10-in (23- or 25-cm) pots, one in a pot, and should be repotted each year in October. Only frost protection is essential but a temperature of 16°C. (60°F.) will produce earlier flowers.

The hardy lilies should almost all be planted so that the bulbs are covered with about twice their own depth of soil, for example, a 2-in- (5-cm-) deep bulb will need a 6-in- (15-cm-) deep hole. One notable exception to this is the popular white Madonna lily, *L. candidum*, which should be barely covered with soil, and will, after a while, work itself out so that the top of the bulb is exposed. This lily is also exceptional in that it is best planted in late summer. The nankeen lily, *L. testaceum*, also likes shallow planting.

Many lilies like to have their flowers and leaves in the sun but their roots in the shade. This can be arranged by planting them among low-growing shrubs or leafy plants such as evergreen azaleas or peonies. The majority of lilies like deep soils containing plenty of leafmould or peat and few like really chalky soils, but there are exceptions to this, notably the Turkscap lilies, *L. chalcedonicum* and *L. martagon*.

One of the easiest of all lilies to grow is the regal lily, *L. regale*, with broad white trumpets on 4-ft (1·25-cm) stems in summer. Others that can be grown in most gardens are the orange lilies, usually listed as *L. umbellatum*, but correctly known as *L. hollandicum*, and the Mid-Century Hybrids in a variety of shades from pale yellow to crimson, all with clusters of large, upward-pointing orange or yellow flowers on 2- to 3-ft (60- to 1-m) stems in early summer. The tiger lily, *L. tigrinum*, has hanging clusters of orange, maroon-spotted flowers on 5-ft (1·5-m) stems in late summer; *L. henryi*, similar in habit but taller and with orange flowers, and the martagon or Turkscap lily, *L. martagon*, which bears 20 to 30 dull purple or waxy white flowers on 5- to 6-ft (1·5- to 2-m) stems. The golden-rayed lily of Japan, *L. auratum*, is a giant of 6 to 8 ft (2 to 2·5 m), with wide, white trumpets, spotted with gold and sometimes flushed with pink. It needs a peaty soil and is not one of the easiest to keep going for many years. The very graceful lily with white, crimson-spotted, hanging flowers in early autumn, which is a favourite in florists' shops, is *L. speciosum*. It can be grown outdoors in a sheltered place, but is often grown as a greenhouse plant, like the Easter lily.

All lilies can be increased by division of the bulb clusters at planting time. A few, and notably the regal lily, can be raised easily from seed sown in a frame or cool greenhouse in spring. Some lilies, such as the tiger lily and *L. henryi*, make tiny bulbs up the flowering stems where the leaves join them and these bulbils can be detached in late summer and planted separately, preferably in boxes or a frame until they get larger. Some lilies can also be increased by detaching individual bulb scales in autumn and placing these in boxes filled with sand and peat.

Lily, see Lilium

Lily, Belladonna, see Amaryllis

Lily, Fox-tail, see Eremurus

Lily, Wood, see Trillium

Montbretia Very easily grown hardy perennials which make rapidly spreading clusters of small corms. By separating these and planting them singly about 2 in (5 cm) deep in spring, they can be increased very rapidly. The orange-yellow or coppery-red flowers are produced in slender 3-ft (1-m) spikes in late summer and early autumn.

Montbretias like sun and warmth and will thrive in the poorest of soils, though to see some of the newer large-flowered varieties at their best they should be given a reasonably good, well-drained soil and be removed to the safety of a frame during the winter as they are less hardy than the common kind.

Muscari (Grape hyacinth) Spring-flowering bulbs with 6-in (15-cm) spikes of blue flowers, like miniature hyacinths. They are easily grown in almost any soil and fairly open position. Bulbs should be planted 2 to 3 in (5 to 8 cm) deep in autumn, and need only be lifted again when the clusters are so overcrowded that flowering begins to suffer.

Narcissus bulbocodium

One of the finest varieties is Heavenly Blue. There is also a beautiful kind with much larger but almost prostrate spikes which have a plumed appearance, for which reason it has been called the feather hyacinth, *Muscari comosum plumosum*. All can be increased by separating the bulb clusters in late summer.

Narcissus (Daffodil) Though daffodil is the popular name of all kinds of narcissus it is usually applied to the trumpet-flowered varieties, the smaller-cupped kinds being known as narcissi. These smaller-cupped (or crowned) varieties are available in many different combinations of white, cream, yellow, orange and red; and pink and green are now making their appearance. The colour range of the trumpet-flowered daffodils has also been extended to include all-white and pink and white as well as the older all-yellow and yellow and white combinations. Heights vary from miniatures such as the cyclamen-flowered narcissus, *N. cyclamineus*, and the hoop-petticoat daffodil, *N. bulbocodium*, both about 6 in (15 cm) high, to the tall hybrids such as Unsurpassable, King Alfred and Carlton, which are 2½ ft (75 cm) or more.

All narcissi like fairly rich, loamy soils, though they will grow tolerably well in almost any soil. They like sun but do not object to shade provided it is not too dense. Bulbs should be planted in late summer or early autumn and should be covered with their own depth of soil. They can be lifted and the bulb clusters divided in summer when the leaves turn yellow and die down, but it is not desirable to lift them every year as they make a better display when well established. They do well planted in grass, provided this is not cut until the narcissus leaves have died down in summer, or at least until six weeks after the flowers have faded.

Nerine In addition to the tender nerines (see p. 122), which are grown in pots in the greenhouse, there is one beautiful kind which is sufficiently hardy to be grown outside in warm, sheltered places. Its name is *Nerine bowdenii* and it has heads of rose-pink flowers in early autumn, before the leaves.

The bulbs should be planted in autumn, immediately after flowering. They like good, well-drained soil and a sunny, sheltered place such as the foot of a wall or fence facing south. The bulbs should only be just covered with soil and should be left undisturbed for several years until they become overcrowded, when they can be lifted after flowering, and the clusters of bulbs separated out.

Onion, Ornamental, see Allium

Ornithogalum (Star of Bethlehem, chincherinchee) Bulbous-rooted plants with loose sprays of white flowers in early summer. The true star of Bethlehem, *Ornithogalum umbellatum*, is about 1 ft (30 cm) high and perfectly hardy; a useful plant as it will grow practically anywhere.

More exacting is the chincherinchee, *O. thyrsoides*, with spikes of papery-white, 'everlasting' flowers. This should be grown like a gladiolus, bulbs being planted in fairly rich soil in spring, watered freely in summer and lifted in autumn for dry storage in a frost-proof place until planting time. All can be increased by division of the bulb clusters in autumn or by growing on tiny bulbs.

Ranunculus The most popular kind is the turban ranunculus, *R. asiaticus*, a remarkable plant with flowers so double that they are almost globular. They are highly coloured, in a variety of shades of yellow and red, and are carried on 9-in (23-cm) stems in late spring and early summer. The plant makes small, clawed tubers which can be planted 2 in (5 cm) deep, claw sides downwards, in autumn or early spring, the latter being preferable on all heavy soils.

The turban ranunculus likes sun, warmth and good drainage. The tubers should be lifted each summer and stored in a dry, cool place until planting time. Increase is by division of the clusters of tubers.

Scilla (Squill, bluebell) The common bluebell, still usually known in gardens as *Scilla non-scripta*, though its present botanical name is *Endymion non-scriptus*, is a lovely spring-flowering bulb but it grows so freely wild that it is not often planted in gardens. The Spanish bluebell, *S. hispanica* or *Endymion hispanicus*, is not a native plant and, as it produces a stiffer and more substantial flower spike than the common bluebell, it is frequently planted. There are pink- and white-flowered forms as well as blue. *S. sibirica* is a much smaller plant with 3- to 4-in (8- to 10-cm) spikes of rich blue flowers in early spring. *S. tubergeniana* has larger spikes of pale blue flowers and is even earlier in bloom. *S. peruviana* has a very broad, conical spike of blue or white flowers.

All these scillas will grow in almost any soil. The common and Spanish bluebells do not mind shade; the other two prefer sun. Bulbs should be planted in autumn 2 to 3 in (5 to 8 cm) deep for most kinds but 6 in (15 cm) for the common and Spanish bluebells. All can be increased by division of the bulb clusters in late summer.

Snowdrop, see Galanthus

Snowflake, see Leucojum

Sparaxis (African harlequin flower) These resemble ixias in many respects and require identical treatment, but the sprays of brightly coloured flowers branch and there are often two strongly contrasted colours in the same flower, hence the popular name of harlequin flower; there are also softer colours including cream. All delight in sun, warmth and good drainage and should be planted 3 in (8 cm) deep in autumn.

Squill, see Scilla

Star of Bethlehem, see Ornithogalum

Tiger flower, see Tigridia

Tigridia (Tiger flower) *Tigridia pavonia* is a bulbous-rooted plant for well-drained soils and sunny, sheltered places outdoors, or for growing as a pot plant in cool greenhouses. The flowers, rather like wide open tulips

Narcissus cyclamineus

Nerine bowdenii

Trillium grandiflorum

and in various bright shades of pink and yellow, often spotted or blotched, are produced on 18-in (45-cm) stems in late summer.

The bulbs should be planted or potted in spring and should be lifted in autumn for storing dry in a frost-proof place, except in mild or sheltered places where they can be left in the ground for several years.

Trillium (Wood lily) Hardy herbaceous plants with fleshy roots, trilliums prefer shady places and leafy or peaty soils. They grow 12 to 18 in (30 to 45 cm) high and have three-petalled flowers which may be pure white or rose, as in *Trillium grandiflorum*, or deep maroon as in *T. erectum*. All flower in late spring and can be increased by careful division in early spring.

Tulip These popular spring-flowering bulbs thrive in rather light but rich soils and sunny, open places. The bulbs should be planted 4 or 5 in (10 to 13 cm) deep in autumn, and can, with advantage, be lifted in summer when all foliage has died down, and be stored in a dry, cool place until planting time.

There are a great many different kinds and varieties, some such as the water-lily tulip, *Tulipa kaufmanniana*, and the early double tulips, being less than 1 ft (30 cm) high, others such as the Darwin, cottage and lily-flowered tulips, 2 to 2½ ft (60 to 75 cm) tall. The Duc van Thol varieties are the earliest to flower, but need glasshouse protection. If potted in early autumn, plunged outdoors under 2 in (5 cm) of ashes for eight weeks, and then brought into a warm greenhouse, they will bloom by mid-winter. The early tulips and Kaufmanniana and Greigii hybrids are in bloom outdoors in early spring, the Mendel and triumph tulips follow them, and are followed in their turn by the Fosteriana and Darwin hybrids, the Darwin tulips themselves and the cottage (or May-flowering), parrot, lily-flowered, Rembrandt and peony-flowered tulips in late spring. All are increased by division of the bulb clusters when lifted.

Buying and Equipping a Greenhouse

In a greenhouse the gardener can create his own climate to suit the needs of almost any plant. He can heat the air when it is too cold and add moisture to it when it is too dry. He can provide varying degrees of shade or exposure to sunshine and he can even provide extra 'sunshine' where it is required in the form of artificial light. The water supply can be adjusted to meet the needs of every individual plant throughout its changing periods of growth. It is not surprising that the possession of a greenhouse enormously increases the range of plants that can be grown. It can be used as a place in which to raise seedlings or strike cuttings and so feed the outdoor garden with new plants; it can be a permanent home for plants which could not thrive in the normal climate of an unaccustomed country; or it can be used for the cultivation of special or out-of-season food crops. These uses are not mutually exclusive but the greater the variety of uses the more ingenuity must be exercised to provide, within the same structure, for the differing needs of various types of plants. For this reason it is wise to commence with a limited range of plants with similar requirements, and to diversify as experience is gained.

Types of Greenhouse and their Fitments

There are many different types of greenhouse and much has been written about ideal shapes and materials. Yet, in practice, gardeners have proved conservative and since the demand is mainly for a few conventional types, these are the ones made by most manufacturers and most readily obtained.

These types are the span-roof and the lean-to and they may be glazed to ground level or to within about 2½ ft (75 cm) of the ground with solid walls of wood, brick or concrete from the glass to ground level.

The span-roof greenhouse is intended to stand in the open with light reaching it from every side, whereas the lean-to greenhouse must stand against a wall or other solid background which deprives it of light from that side. A development of this is the kind of structure often referred to as a home-extension, sun room or loggia which is intended to be built on to the house to give extra living space as well as to provide a place in which to grow plants.

The advantage of the span-roof house is that a wider variety of climatic conditions can be provided within it. The lean-to scores, first in cost, and also probably in running costs as it may require less artificial heat to maintain the required temperature. Sometimes it is possible to heat the lean-to, and even more the house extension, from the normal heating system of the dwelling house, and this can effect further economies in cost.

Full or Partial Glazing Something rather similar applies to glazing to ground level as compared with the house that stands on low solid walls. The fully glazed house provides better lighting but may be more difficult to heat. Aesthetics play a part here too, for though a fully glazed house can look attractive from outside if plants are growing from ground level, it is less attractive if the plants within are on staging with empty space or storage beneath.

Wood or Metal Frames? Much has been written about the rival merits of wood and metal frames. Wood is, in general, cheaper and it is easy to fix fitments, such as shelves or blinds, to wood-framed houses. Deal needs fairly frequent painting if it is to be maintained in good condition, but western red cedar resists decay and can be used without painting or other treatment.

Metal is durable, and since metal glazing bars are usually narrower than wooden ones, they cut off rather less light, though this seldom appears to be a critical factor. Iron and steel rust so readily that they require a considerable amount of maintenance. This does not apply to aluminium alloys but these are comparatively expensive. However, they may be regarded as the ideal materials for greenhouse framing.

Ventilation Ventilation is exceedingly important, not so much because plants require fresh air as because it is only by changing the air in a house rapidly that its temperature can be kept down in sunny weather. It should be possible to get 30 complete atmospheric changes per hour in a greenhouse even though this may only be required on a few days each year.

There are two principal ways of ventilating small greenhouses: one by hinged ventilators, the other by extractor fans. The most important ventilators are those at the apex of the house, usually hinged close to the ridge bar, because hot air rises and so escapes most readily at the top of the house. Usually there are also some hinged ventilators in the sides to allow cool air to enter but these need not be so large, or so numerous as those at the top of the house. Hinged ventilators can be automatically operated by a simple piston and lever device which obtains its power from a heat-

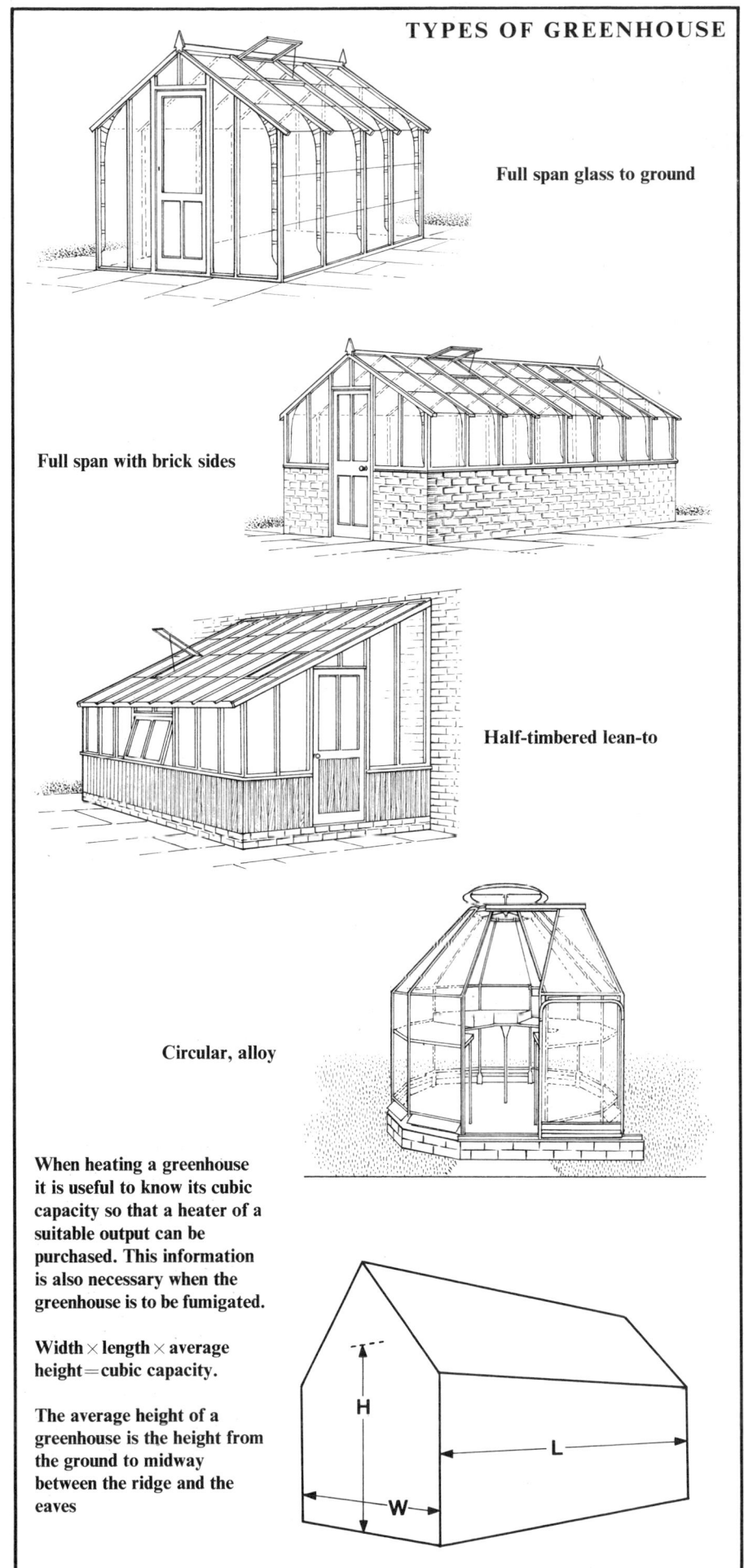

TYPES OF GREENHOUSE

Full span glass to ground

Full span with brick sides

Half-timbered lean-to

Circular, alloy

When heating a greenhouse it is useful to know its cubic capacity so that a heater of a suitable output can be purchased. This information is also necessary when the greenhouse is to be fumigated.

Width × length × average height = cubic capacity.

The average height of a greenhouse is the height from the ground to midway between the ridge and the eaves

A piston-operated ventilator (here used in conjunction with roller blinds) is one way of automating ventilation

sensitive liquid inside a sealed cylinder.

In a small greenhouse, fan extractors are usually fitted in the end panels, as high up as convenient for the same reason that this is where the hottest air will be. It takes quite a powerful fan to give an equivalent rate of atmospheric change to hinged ventilators of good size. As a rule, electric fans are operated by a thermostat which automatically switches them on and off at a predetermined temperature.

Artificial Heating Artificial heating greatly increases the utility of a greenhouse, provided that sufficient heat is available to exclude frost at all times. The method by which the heat is applied is not of prime importance so long as no harmful fumes get into the greenhouse.

Broadly, the possibilities are paraffin, solid fuel, electricity and gas, and many different types of apparatus are manufactured to consume each. In some, the air is heated direct, in others via pipes circulating hot water from a boiler. Water systems tend to be more costly to install and may require more maintenance, but good installations of this type give an excellent distribution of heat, a quality most appreciated in greenhouses of fair size. In small houses there is much to be said for the cheapness and simplicity of direct air heating provided that it can be done without the introduction of harmful fumes.

Some forms of heating, notably electricity and gas, lend themselves to thermostatic control, by which the heat is automatically turned off or on as the temperature of the air in the greenhouse rises above or falls below a predetermined level. This greatly increases the accuracy of control which the gardener has over his artificially imposed climate and also usually results in a considerable fuel economy. But thermostats should be carefully sited in the greenhouse, screened from direct sunlight, which may falsify the true air temperature, and placed where the mean rather than the extreme temperatures of the house are registered.

Siting the Greenhouse

Unless there is some overriding reason to the contrary, such as that a greenhouse is to be used exclusively for the cultivation of shade-loving plants, it should be sited in the open where it gets the benefit of sunshine for as many hours of the day as possible. It is easy enough to provide shade when and where it is needed; not so easy to provide extra light when it is lacking.

Fuel and Water Supplies If the greenhouse is to be heated by electricity or mains gas it will be wise to bear in mind the distance these supplies must be brought. If they are coming from the domestic supply it may be a good reason for siting the greenhouse near the dwelling house even though this involves some loss of light.

Water will be needed and it is convenient, though not essential, to have it laid on in the house. If it is so connected it will be possible to use it for automatic systems of watering such as capillary bench watering and mist propagation but these are labour-saving refinements, not essentials to good cultivation.

Pots and Composts

For convenience most greenhouse plants are grown in pots, though some large plants are grown directly in beds of soil on the floor of the house and this method is also commonly used for tomatoes.

Pots may be of earthenware (clay pots) or of plastic. Clay pots, being a little porous, tend to dry out more rapidly than plastic pots and this involves a different frequency in the watering of plants grown in them. If pots of both types are used for the same kinds of plant in the same house it can be confusing and it is really better to determine to use either all clay pots or all plastic pots. Plastic pots are more easily cleaned than clay pots and they are much less likely to break, but they do not 'breathe' like clay pots and some gardeners regard this as a disadvantage.

Pots are made in different sizes and are usually referred to according to their diameter at the top. Thus a 3-in (8-cm) pot is one that measures 3 in (8 cm) across at the top and a 6-in (15-cm) pot one that measures 6 in (15 cm) across.

Plants usually do best when their roots occupy all or most of the soil in the pots. Overpotting means putting a plant into a pot much larger than is needed to accommodate its roots and is usually to be avoided. As plants grow they are potted on, that is, moved to pots of larger size, and generally it is wise to adopt a steady progression, potting from 3-in (8-cm) into 4-in (10-cm) or $4\frac{1}{2}$-in (12-cm) pots, then on into 6-in (15-cm) pots, then perhaps to 8-in (20-cm) or 9-in (23-cm) pots.

The Basic Ingredients of Compost It is rarely that ordinary garden soil without additions can be used satisfactorily for pot plants. Usually the soil, whether from the garden or fresh soil brought in from a meadow – in which case it will probably be described as virgin soil or loam – is mixed with other ingredients such as peat, leafmould and sand. The resulting mixture is referred to as a compost, which can be confusing as compost is also the name given to rotted vegetable refuse, a very different material.

Potting and Seed Composts Composts for use in the greenhouse fall broadly into two groups; potting composts and seed composts. The former are intended for mature or semi-mature plants, the latter for the germination of seeds and the cultivation of young seedlings. Potting composts are usually richer and more complex than seed composts.

The John Innes Mixtures. The name John Innes Compost is given to a range of potting and seed composts developed at the John Innes Horticultural Institution. This research station first produced these composts for its own use, but published the formulae, so making them available to anyone else who cared to make them. Many horticultural suppliers do this and sell their products as John Innes Compost, but this does not mean that they have been approved by the John Innes Horticultural Institution, nor is it a guarantee of quality. That will depend upon how carefully the manufacturer has chosen the ingredients and how well they have been prepared and mixed.

Basically the John Innes Potting Composts are composed of 7 parts, by bulk, loam, 3 parts peat and 2 parts sand. It is recommended that the loam should be fertile, neither light nor heavy, but slightly greasy when smeared without being sticky. The peat should be fibrous or granulated, grading up to $\frac{3}{8}$ in (0·75 cm) particle size with a preponderance of $\frac{1}{8}$-in (0·25-cm) particles and pH between 4·0 and 5·0. The sand must not be too fine and should be clean and reasonably lime free.

The loam is to be steam sterilized before use but not the other ingredients. When the mixture is prepared, a base fertilizer is added and this is prepared by mixing 2 parts, by weight, of hoof and horn meal ($\frac{1}{8}$ in, 0·25 cm, grist), 2 parts superphosphate of lime and 1 part sulphate of potash. For ordinary purposes 4 oz (110 g) of this mixture is added to each bushel of the compost and this is referred to as John Innes Potting Compost No. 1, or J.I.P.1 for short, to distinguish it from John Innes Potting Compost No. 2 and John Innes Potting Compost No. 3, which contain respectively 8 oz (225 g) and 12 oz (340 g) of base fertilizer per bushel of compost. These richer composts are used for strong-growing plants or plants that have reached the larger sizes of pot – say 5 in (13 cm) and over.

One further addition has to be made before the compost is complete, of chalk or limestone or of flowers of sulphur. For ordinary plants $\frac{3}{8}$ oz (21 g) of either finely ground chalk or limestone is added to each bushel of compost. For plants such as heathers and rhododendrons, which dislike lime, $\frac{3}{4}$ oz (21 g) of flowers of sulphur per bushel is used instead of chalk or limestone. These quantities are doubled for John Innes Compost No. 2 and trebled for John Innes Compost No. 3.

The John Innes Seed Compost is simpler, consisting of 2 parts by bulk of loam, 1 part peat and 1 part sand, the specifications for each ingredient being the same as before. The loam is steam sterilized. No base fertilizer is added but 1½ oz (40 g) of superphosphate of lime per bushel are added, and also $\frac{3}{4}$ oz (21 g) of chalk, limestone or flowers of sulphur, exactly as directed for J.I.P.1.

In these John Innes composts, practically every known kind of plant can be grown successfully. They represent an enormous advance on the haphazard and miscellaneous mixtures formerly used but, largely because of the variability of loam, even when it seems to conform to the standard laid down, gardeners have continued to search for composts with an even greater uniformity.

Soilless Composts As a result of this search for more uniform composts, a number of so-called soilless composts have been put on the market. These are mostly mixtures of peat and sand, or peat and vermiculite, or simply carefully chosen peat, with added fertilizers.

Soilless composts usually become exhausted more rapidly than loam composts and so established plants require more frequent feeding.

Traditionally it was the practice to place broken pieces of pot, known as crocks, or a perforated zinc disc in the bottom of each pot to prevent the drainage hole becoming blocked with soil. For some plants, such as cacti and succulents, which appreciate quick drainage, this may still be desirable but with the highly porous John Innes and soilless composts now used, crocking is becoming a thing of the past. Few commercial growers of pot plants use drainage materials and amateur gardeners appear to be gradually dispensing with them, too. In any case most plastic pots have several holes per pot instead of the single hole usual with clay pots, so that if one should become accidentally blocked there is still ample outlet for the excess water through the others.

Potting on:
Knock the plant out of its original pot and remove any crocks from the soil ball

Sit the plant at the correct depth in its new pot and firm the soil well around it using a rammer if necessary

Technique of Potting

Potting a plant is very similar to planting it. A little soil is placed in the bottom of the pot, the plant is held in position in the centre of the pot and prepared compost is run in all around it. Then, when the pot is nearly full, the compost is pressed in around the sides with the fingers and the pot is given a sharp rap on something firm (it is convenient to have a substantial wooden potting bench) which settles the plant firmly in the pot and distributes any remaining loose soil evenly over the surface. When finished, the level of the soil in the pot should be just a little below the rim of the pot so that, when it is watered, the water will not run off the surface but will be retained and soak down to the roots. These should all be covered by the compost but the uppermost roots need be only just beneath the surface.

Potting Large Plants Most potting can be done in this simple way, with the fingers only, but when it comes to big plants going into pots 8 in (20 cm) or more in diameter in soil compost, it may not be quite enough to get the soil evenly firm all round the plant. Then a rammer is used which may be any piece of wood about 1 ft (30 cm) long and 1 in (2.5 cm) in diameter. A short length of old broom handle, rounded off at one end, does well. This is used to ram the soil in round the edge of the pot before it is given its final rap to settle everything down.

Degrees of Compost Firmness The terms 'light potting' and 'firm potting' are sometimes used to distinguish between soil that is left rather loose and that which is made fairly hard. Some plants seem to have a preference for one, some for the other, but these are refinements which can only be learned by experience and about which there is, in any case, considerable disagreement.

Peat composts are never made very firm but are simply pressed in lightly with the fingertips and then settled in by two or three sharp raps on the potting bench.

Aspects of Watering

Watering By Hand Watering can be done by hand or can be made automatic. The

On this capillary bench the bottle contains water which moistens the sand; from this the plants take up what they need

object in either case is to keep the roots adequately supplied with water according to the changing needs of the season. Too little water will result in wilting of leaves and a check to growth. Too much water will drive out air from the soil and literally drown the roots, for roots as well as leaves need air for their survival.

When watering with a watering-can each plant can be considered individually. An inspection of the soil may indicate at once whether it is dry but may not be so sure a guide as to whether it is sufficiently wet. Soil in a pot has a deceptive habit of looking damp on top after it has become dry below. One can feel the soil with the finger or lift the pot and judge its weight, for wet soil weighs much more than dry soil. When in doubt, a plant can be carefully tapped out of its pot and examined. All one need do is to turn the plant upside down, place one hand beneath it for support and give the rim of the pot a sharp rap on something firm like the edge of the staging. If it has been well potted in a clean pot it should come out quite cleanly. I do not recommend this as regular practice but it is a useful method of gaining experience. After a while it will be possible to water most of the time by eye alone.

When water is needed, give sufficient to soak the soil right through. If in doubt, wait a few moments after applying the water,

then lift the pot and see if water is trickling out of the drainage hole in the bottom. It should be.

Do not splash water on leaves or on the crowns of plants. Some do not mind but some emphatically do and it is wise to get into the habit of watering carefully. Do not use a rose on the can, except for small, newly potted plants, but water direct from the spout. Hold this close to the rim of the pot and use the forefinger to deflect the water if necessary.

Automatic Watering The simplest method of automatic watering is that which uses a capillary bench. This means standing the pots on a bed of wet sand, or a mixture of sand and pea gravel, from which the soil inside the pots sucks up water. The sand can be kept wet in many ways: by allowing water to trickle very slowly over it; by inverting a large water-filled jar at one end with its aperture in a shallow water container about 1 in (2·5 cm) below the level of the sand; or by using special feed cups, themselves supplied with water from a tank fitted with a ball valve controlling a mains supply, which means that it can be left for weeks at a time with little or no attention.

Whatever the method of wetting the sand, it is essential that the compost in the pot comes directly in contact with it. There must be no drainage material in the bottom of the pot to break the rise of water. Thick clay pots may need a wick of glass wool through the drainage hole to carry the water up, but with thin plastic pots this should not be required.

Another essential with capillary bench watering is that the compost in the pots should be very porous. If the compost is too close, the soil draws up too much water and there is little or no air left around the roots.

Not all plants thrive on this capillary watering but a great many do, and it is certainly worth trying if it is impossible to give the plants daily attention.

There are other more sophisticated methods of watering automatically and perhaps the best of all consists of very small bore plastic pipes attached to a larger supply pipe. One or more of the small pipes is placed in each pot so that water drips in slowly and the water supply is either turned on by hand or is controlled by a time switch and solenoid valve.

Atmospheric Moisture Moisture in the air is as important as moisture in the soil. A few plants, notably cacti and other succulents, like a dry atmosphere, but most plants need a fairly moist atmosphere while they are growing and some tropical plants like the air to be saturated with moisture, especially in summer.

Automatic apparatus, known as humidifiers, for maintaining moisture in the air are much used in hospitals and other buildings but have only just begun to be used in greenhouses. The usual way of controlling

atmospheric moisture in these is by wetting paths, stages, and even the leaves of the plants themselves if more moisture is required, or by using a little artificial heat and opening the top ventilators a little if the air needs to be dried. This is perhaps the most difficult aspect of greenhouse management to teach. The experienced gardener can tell by the feel of the air on his skin whether it is damp or dry. He is guided, also, by the look of leaves – a slight tendency to lose colour and even to scorch if the air is too dry, a readiness to suffer from moulds and decays if it is too wet. None of this helps the beginner very much but simple meters, knowns as hygrometers, can be purchased to measure atmospheric moisture and one of these hung in the house will at least show what the humidity is at any moment.

What the plants actually need is determined by their state of growth but if instructions are to keep the air 'moist', a relative humidity of 90 per cent or more is desirable, if it is to be 'buoyant' (a popular expression with gardeners) it should be around 70 per cent and if 'dry', 50 per cent or less.

Spraying water on the floor or stages to increase atmospheric humidity is known as damping down. In summer it may be necessary to do this two or three times a day to maintain ideal conditions, once early in the morning, again at mid-day and in the late afternoon. Obviously this is impossible for many amateurs who have to be away from home by day. They may try alternatives such as shallow trays of water placed on the floor of the house or a slow trickle of water down the path from a tap. One of the side benefits of capillary bench watering is that the bed of wet sand does help to keep the air moist.

Temperature Categories
Ventilation is primarily a method of controlling the temperature of the house. The ventilators are increasingly opened or the extractor fan is used more frequently as the temperature rises above the most favourable point. This will differ at different times of the year and according to the kind of plant being grown. To simplify description, gardeners usually distinguish four main temperature ranges for the greenhouse and refer to them as cold, cool, intermediate and warm.

The Cold Greenhouse A cold greenhouse is one that has no method of artificial heating. In winter the temperature will sometimes fall well below freezing point and so, at that season, no really tender plants can be grown in it.

On bright days in summer the temperature might run up to 38°C. (100°F.) without ventilation, but would quickly fall at night, which would be bad for most plants. So the best average temperature for a cold house in spring would be about 13°C.

(55°F.) rising to 16 or 18°C. (60 or 65°F.) in summer, but it may fall as low as 4°C. (40°F.) at night.

The Cool Greenhouse In the cool house there must be enough artificial heat to exclude frost in winter and generally a minimum of 7°C (45°F) is recommended. In spring and summer optimum temperatures similar to those for the cold house will be aimed at but with less fluctuation – no more than 5°C. (10°F.) below the optimum – at night.

The Intermediate Greenhouse In an intermediate house a winter minimum of 13°C. (55°F.) is maintained with an average from autumn to spring of 13 to 16°C. (55 to 60°F.) and never falls below about 7°C. (45°F.). In summer the optimum will be 16 to 21°C. (60 to 70°F.), maintained even at night at about 13°C. (55°F.). For a warm greenhouse a further 3 to 5°C (5 to 10°F.) must be added to all these temperatures.

Cost of Heating Increasing the temperatures at which a greenhouse is to be operated considerably increases the cost of heating it. A rise of 5°C. (10°F.) in the average temperature of a greenhouse from autumn to spring can easily double the fuel bill.

On the other side of the reckoning must be taken into account the fact that a well-heated greenhouse is easier to manage than an under-heated greenhouse. Plants are more likely to grow well and losses from disease will be reduced. All the same, the cool or intermediate range of temperatures are usually the best with which to start one's greenhouse experience.

Shading

There remains the question of shading. In winter most greenhouse plants can do with all the light they can get but in summer it is very different. Cacti and other succulents may take all the sunshine that is going and so may some bulbs that are resting and ripening at that time. But most plants that are in active growth will need some protection from direct sunshine.

There are many ways of shading a greenhouse, one of the simplest being to spray or paint limewash on the glass. This is effective but it cannot be adjusted to suit changing conditions. As a rule the limewash is applied in late spring and washed off in early autumn and the plants have to make the best of it in between. In practice it works quite well.

Another way is to pin butter muslin to the rafters inside the greenhouse. This cannot be removed very quickly but it is easier to get rid of than limewash.

A further refinement is to have blinds, either inside or outside the house, which can be raised or lowered at will. The blinds may be of plastic or thin material if inside, or of hessian, wood laths or split bamboo canes if outside. Whatever kind of blind is used, it will be possible to adjust the shading whenever the gardener can attend to it.

Recommended Greenhouse Plants

Acacia (Mimosa) These Australian shrubs, commonly known as mimosa, are nearly all too tender to be grown outdoors except in the mildest parts, but several, including *Acacia drummondii* with the typical, fluffy yellow flowers clustered in catkin-like trails, and *A. armata*, with tiny pompon flowers all along the stems, make good pot plants for the greenhouse and need no more than frost protection in winter. They can be grown in 7- to 9-in (18- to 23-cm-) pots in J.I.P.2 or soilless composts and can be repotted when necessary in spring after flowering. In summer they can be stood outdoors if more room is needed in the greenhouse. Water fairly freely in spring and summer, rather sparingly in autumn and winter. If plants get too large, stems can be shortened or removed after flowering.

They can all be raised from seed sown in spring in a warm greenhouse and cuttings can also be rooted in summer in a frame inside the greenhouse.

Achimenes (Hot water plant) This plant gets its popular name because some people think it likes to be watered with hot water. In fact, it will thrive with the ordinary treatment given to rather tender greenhouse plants, that is, a temperature of at least 16°C. (60°F.) while it is growing and fairly frequent watering with tepid water.

Achimenes makes small tuberous roots which can be stored dry in a frost-proof place in winter and can be repotted in J.I.P.1 or soilless compost and started into growth in successive batches during the winter and spring. The stems are rather weak and the flowers, which are produced continuously for several months, are brightly coloured in shades of purple, crimson and rose. These plants are often grown in hanging baskets, but are equally happy in pots. They are easily increased by separating the tubers in autumn or winter.

African lily, see Agapanthus

African violet, see Saintpaulia

Agapanthus (African lily) This is the blue-clustered lily (it is not really a lily at all) that is so frequently grown in tubs or large ornamental vases for summer decoration in the garden. It can equally well be grown as a greenhouse pot plant in ordinary potting compost and can be repotted, when necessary, in J.I.P.2 in spring. It likes sun and needs no shading.

It can be increased very readily by dividing the roots in spring or from seeds sown in spring, though it will be several years before seedlings make really good plants.

Arum lily, see Zantedeschia

Azalea The greenhouse azaleas are compact evergreen shrubs with large double flowers. They make fine pot plants and are sold in great quantities by florists throughout the winter. They need complete frost protection in winter but in summer can be placed outdoors, during which period they must be freely watered and frequently syringed. They can be repotted, when necessary, immediately after flowering and need fairly large pots, 7 to 9 in (18 to 23 cm) in diameter, and a very peaty, lime-free compost.

They can be raised from cuttings of firm young shoots in a frame in mid-summer, but are usually purchased as mature plants just coming into flower.

Barbados lily, see Hippeastrum

Barberton daisy, see Gerbera

Begonia There are a great many different kinds of begonia and no one system of cultivation can be applied to all, but all are tender plants requiring greenhouse protection for at least part of the year – some kinds for the whole year round.

Most popular are the summer-flowering, tuberous-rooted begonias, usually with large double flowers, though there are single-flowered forms as well. The tubers can be stored dry in a frost-proof place from autumn until late winter or early spring. Then, in successive batches according to the time at which they are required to flower, they are put into seed boxes filled with damp peat and are placed in a greenhouse with a temperature of 16°C. (60°F.). When leaves appear the tubers are potted singly in J.I.P.2 or soilless compost in 5- or 6-in (13- or 15-cm) pots and placed in a shaded, well-ventilated greenhouse. The tubers should be kept almost on the surface of the compost. They are watered freely in spring and summer but the water supply is gradually reduced in autumn until the leaves die down and the tubers can be shaken out and stored dry for use another year.

The tuberous-rooted, pendulous begonias are grown in just the same way except that, once started, they are placed in hanging baskets, or in pots stood on inverted pots or pedestals so that the flowers can hang down.

Winter-flowering, fibrous-rooted begonias have sprays of much smaller, pink, salmon or red flowers and like a really warm greenhouse. They must not be dried off completely at any time but are watered rather sparingly for a few weeks after flowering and are then cut back and re-started with increasing supplies of water. They do well in J.I.P.1 compost. They are usually raised from cuttings taken after flowering.

Rex begonias are grown for their very large handsomely marked leaves. They need

Bougainvillea Killie Campbell

an intermediate greenhouse and should be kept growing in winter and summer. They are so tolerant of shade that they can be grown satisfactorily under the greenhouse staging. They are increased by dividing the fibrous roots in early spring, or by leaf cuttings taken in spring or summer.

Beloperone (Shrimp plant) The popular name refers to the shrimp-like appearance of the curling white flower spikes sheathed in pinkish bracts. There is also a lime-green variety. *Beloperone guttata* will flower all the year round in a moderately heated greenhouse and can be grown in a cool house – minimum temperature 7°C. (45°F.) – but will then stop flowering in winter. It should be grown in pots in J.I.P.1 or soilless compost and should be watered fairly freely in spring and summer, moderately in autumn and winter. Repot when overcrowded in spring.

Bird of paradise flower, see Strelitzia

Bougainvillea One of the most brilliant of tender climbing plants, the bougainvillea is familiar to all visitors to the Mediterranean coasts where, in summer, it covers walls and buildings with its vivid magenta blooms. It must be given greenhouse protection in this country, but does not need a lot of heat, a winter minimum of 7°C. (45°F.) sufficing. It can be trained to wires against a wall or beneath the greenhouse roof, can be cut back quite a lot each year in late winter if space is limited, and is not at all fussy about

soil. It should be well watered in summer, moderately at other times.

Cuttings of firm young shoots in spring will root readily enough in a propagating frame provided they can be given a temperature of around 21°C. (70°F.). In addition to the common magenta variety there are others with pink or orange flowers.

Calceolaria The curiously pouched and often rather luridly coloured flowers of these plants never fail to attract attention. The greenhouse varieties are treated as annuals and are raised from seed each year. This is sown in early summer, the seedlings are pricked off into boxes and later potted singly, first into small pots and J.I.P.1, but finally, early in spring, into 5-in (13-cm) (or bigger) pots and J.I.P.2 in which they will flower in later spring.

Throughout they need cool greenhouse treatment, plenty of ventilation, except in cold weather, a minimum temperature of 7°C. (45°F.) and careful watering. Particular care should be taken to prevent water lodging at the base of the large leaves where it may cause decay.

Camellia These evergreen shrubs grow well in a frost-proof greenhouse and some of the large-flowered varieties are only seen to perfection when protected in this way. However, they do make large bushes in time and must be grown in tubs or really big pots in a mixture of 4 parts lime-free loam, 2 parts peat, one part coarse sand plus 4 oz (110 g) of John Innes base fertilizer per bushel of this mixture.

From late spring until mid-autumn the plants can stand outdoors since they are hardy and it is only the flower buds and flowers, appearing as they do from autumn to spring according to variety, that require protection. Water freely in spring and summer, moderately in autumn and winter. Shade from strong sunshine in summer but grow in a light place as this helps flower buds to form freely.

If plants grow too large, some flowering stems can be shortened or removed when in flower (they are excellent for floral arrangements) or as soon as the flowers fade, but excessive pruning will restrict flowering the following year.

Carnation There are two principal classes of carnation, the perpetual-flowering carnation which is purely a greenhouse plant and the hardy border carnation which is primarily an outdoor plant, though it is sometimes grown in unheated greenhouses for the purpose of producing its beautifully formed flowers to perfection. There are great differences both in the cultivation and the appearance of the two classes of carnation.

The perpetual-flowering carnations are rather tall plants, and their flowers, always very double, lack the perfection of form which characterizes the best border carna-

tions. They can be made to flower continuously throughout the year and are grown from cuttings of young side shoots taken in winter or early spring. These cuttings are rooted in sand in a propagating frame within the greenhouse and in a temperature around 16°C. (60°F.). When rooted, the cuttings are potted singly in J.I.P.1 in small pots and are moved on gradually into 6- or 7-in (15- or 18-cm) pots and J.I.P.2 in which they will flower.

The tops of the shoots are broken out twice, first when the young plants have seven pairs of leaves and a second time when the side shoots resulting from the first stopping have made about seven pairs of leaves each; the aim being to encourage the plants to branch more freely. When flower buds appear, the small side buds are removed and only the terminal bud on each shoot is permitted to develop into a flower.

An average temperature of around 13°C. (55°F.) is required in autumn and winter, and as much ventilation as possible should be given consistent with this. It is best to discard the plants after their second year, or at latest when they have completed their third year.

Border carnations are much shorter and more spreading in habit and need no stopping of shoots to make them branch. They are grown from layers made from non-flowering shoots pegged to the soil in summer and lifted for planting or potting in autumn. They only flower in summer and require no artificial heat, even in winter.

Celosia (Cockscomb) The plumed form of *Celosia argentea*, described on p. 93 as a bedding plant, also makes an excellent greenhouse pot plant. In addition there is a curious form of it, *C. argenta cristata*, which is known as cockscomb because the small flowers are crowded together into a wavy ridge like a fowl's comb. There are various colours, including crimson, yellow, orange and pink.

Celosia is raised from seed sown in early spring in a temperature of 16 to 18°C. (60 to 65°F.), the seedlings being potted singly in J.I.P.1 and flowered in the greenhouse in summer, after which the plants are discarded. They will need no artificial heat from late spring onwards and like plenty of light.

Chrysanthemum All varieties of chrysanthemum that flower before mid-autumn can normally be grown outdoors, though it may be necessary to lift some plants after flowering and place them in a frame or greenhouse during the winter. This is more a protection against damp and slugs than against cold. The autumn- and winter-flowering chrysanthemums require greenhouse protection from the time that frost first threatens in autumn to prevent the flowers or flower buds being damaged. Enough artificial heat will be required to keep out frost, and if cuttings are being rooted, to maintain a temperature in the region of 10 to 13°C. (50 to 55°F.).

Most chrysanthemums are increased by cuttings of young shoots (preferably from shoots growing directly from the roots) taken as they become available in winter and spring. The cuttings are rooted in sandy soil in a frame or greenhouse. (Some kinds, notably the Charm and Cascade varieties with masses of small single flowers, are commonly grown from seed sown in a temperature of 15°C. (60°F.) in spring.) Rooted cuttings or seedlings are potted singly in J.I.P.1 or soilless compost. The outdoor varieties are planted in their flowering beds in spring, but the greenhouse varieties are usually grown on in richer compost and pots up to 10in (25cm) diameter and J.I.P.3 by late spring. From then until autumn the pots are usually stood outdoors in a sheltered but sunny position. Some gardeners prefer to plant out in good soil and then to lift the plants carefully in autumn and transplant them to a sunny border within the greenhouse. For ease in transplanting they are often grown in wire baskets.

All chrysanthemums like rather rich but reasonably well-drained soil. They should be given as much sun and light as possible and plenty of water in summer.

If large flowers are required the number of stems per plant is restricted, occasionally to one, though more usually from three to twelve stems are retained. In addition, only one flower bud per stem is permitted to remain, all other buds being removed at the earliest possible date. The alternative is to allow all buds to develop in sprays of smaller flowers.

Chrysanthemums are divided into a number of groups according to their flower size and shape and their time of flowering. Thus there are incurved chrysanthemums with ball-like flowers, reflexed varieties with petals curling outwards, singles, anemone-centred varieties and pompons with button-like flowers. The divisions according to flowering time are: early-flowering, August and September; mid-season, October, and late, from November.

Cineraria Very showy plants with coloured daisy-flowers in winter or spring. They make good pot plants for the slightly heated greenhouse. The plants have big, rather coarse leaves and large, loose sprays of flowers in a wide range of colours, including many shades of blue, purple, pink and crimson, often with bands of white for contrast. There are large-flowered and small-flowered races.

All are treated as annuals, seed being sown in a temperature of 13 to 15°C. (55 to 60°F.) some time between mid-spring and mid-summer according to the time that flowers are required – in mid-winter from the earliest sowings, in late spring from the latest. Seedlings are potted singly in J.I.P.1 or soilless compost and moved on into 5-

Annuals such as celosias provide colour in the greenhouse

or 6-in (13- to 15-cm) pots as necessary. They need rather careful watering, and during summer are really happier in a frame than in a greenhouse, for they are nearly hardy. Even in mid-winter they need only enough heat to keep out frost.

Clerodendrum The scarlet clerodendrum, *Clerodendrum fallax*, is a plant for the warm greenhouse and one that is usually renewed from seed every year, though it is a perennial and can be cut back after flowering and kept through the winter. The vivid scarlet flowers are borne in fine, showy heads; in autumn if seed is sown in late winter, or in summer if seed is sown in late summer the year before. The plants like plenty of warmth; certainly the house should never fall below 10°C. (50°F.), and 13°C. (55°F.) is better. They do well in J.I.P.1.

The climbing clerodendrum, *C. thomsonae*, is a very showy perennial plant with loose sprays of crimson and white flowers in summer. Once it was very common in greenhouses, either trained beneath the rafters or over large, crinoline-like frames of wire, but, like the scarlet clerodendrum, it needs plenty of warmth and so is less seen nowadays. It can be grown in large pots or tubs filled with J.I.P.1 but is happier planted in a bed of good loamy soil made

within the greenhouse. Side shoots can be cut back quite severely after flowering.

Clivia (Kaffir lily) Showy and easily grown fleshy-rooted plants for the slightly heated greenhouse, clivias have trumpet-shaped flowers in clusters on stiff stems and are at their best in spring. The commonest variety is scarlet and yellow, but there are variations in yellow and orange.

Bulbs should be potted in late winter in J.I.P.2 and the plants grown in a cool or intermediate greenhouse, minimum temperature, 7°C. (45°F.), throughout the spring; being removed to an unheated frame (or left in the greenhouse without heat) for the summer. During late autumn and early winter they should be returned to the greenhouse and will need little or no water, but at other times they should be watered fairly freely. They can be increased by division at potting time.

Cockscomb, see Celosia

Coleus A popular greenhouse foliage plant with nettle-shaped leaves, very handsomely marked and coloured, green or yellowish with splashes or bands of crimson or maroon or sometimes bronze or crimson throughout. The coleus is a soft-stemmed, bushy plant which grows well in pots. It needs a frost-proof greenhouse and responds quickly to warmth. It should be grown in J.I.P.1 and be well watered in spring and summer, moderately at other times. It is easily raised from seed sown in a temperature of 15°C. (60°F.) in spring, but seedlings are likely to vary in the colourings of their leaves, so especially desirable forms should be increased by cuttings of firm young growth rooted in a propagator in spring or summer.

The winter-flowering coleus, of which there are two kinds, *C. frederici* and *C. thyrsoideus*, have long spikes of purplish-blue flowers in mid-winter. Cultivation is similar, but a winter temperature of 13°C. (55 °F.) or more should be maintained.

Cyclamen The greenhouse cyclamen, *C. persicum*, is grown from seed sown in early spring or late summer in an unheated greenhouse. The seedlings are pricked out and later potted singly in J.I.P.1 in small pots. They are then repotted at intervals until, by the following summer, they reach the 5- or 6-in (13- to 15-cm) pots and J.I.P.2 in which they will flower. They should bloom during autumn and winter.

For the first 18 months the cyclamen should remain in a greenhouse, though artificial heat will be needed only in winter to maintain a minimum temperature of 7°C. (45°F.). In late spring, after flowering, plants can go to a frame without heat and remain until late summer, when they should be repotted and returned to the greenhouse. At all times the corms should be kept sitting almost on top of the soil. Water should be applied moderately in autumn and winter, more freely in spring and summer to young plants, but hardly at all in early summer to plants that have flowered and are resting; these are best kept almost dry for a few weeks before being repotted.

Cymbidium One of the most popular and easily grown groups of orchids, cymbidiums produce their flowers in graceful, arching spikes, mainly in late winter and spring. They last a long time either on the plant or when cut. The plants make bulbous-like growths above ground and are increased by careful division of the clusters of bulbs (they are rightly called pseudo-bulbs) in spring, after flowering, when cymbidiums are repotted. They may be grown in a mixture of two parts peat and one part polystyrene granules which can be purchased from orchid nurseries. Pots must be very well provided with crocks for drainage and the pseudo-bulbs are kept sitting on top of the compost.

Cymbidiums need a temperature around 10°C. (50°F.) in winter and in summer will need no artificial heat, being permanently shaded and syringed frequently with clear water to maintain a cool, moist atmosphere. They should be watered freely in spring and summer; moderately in autumn and winter. There are a great many garden varieties differing in colour.

Cypripedium (Lady's slipper) Another of the fairly easily grown orchids with which to start orchid growing. Each flower has a large pouch and, behind this, a broad, upstanding sepal flanked by two petals.

Cypripediums grow in a compost of 2 parts good loam, 1 part chopped sphagnum moss and 1 part osmunda fibre, or in a peat and polystyrene granule compost similar to that recommended for cymbidiums. Plants should be potted just like any other greenhouse subject and grown in a cool greenhouse with a temperature around 7 to 10 °C. (45 to 50°F.) in winter, with no artificial heat in summer, at which season they should be shaded from hot sunshine. They should be watered freely in summer, moderately at other times.

In addition to *Cypripedium insigne*, one of the easiest and best species, there are many garden varieties and hybrids, some very magnificent and expensive, but many obtainable at quite modest prices. All kinds can be increased by careful division at potting time. The correct name for these greenhouse cypripediums is now paphiopedilum.

Euphorbia (Poinsettia, crown of thorns) There are three euphorbias that are showy greenhouse plants, *Euphorbia pulcherrima*, more familiar as the poinsettia, *E. fulgens* and *E. splendens*. They are very different in appearance and require different methods of cultivation.

The poinsettia is grown for its rosettes of large coloured bracts produced in winter and is very popular for Christmas decorations. The common colour is scarlet, but there are also pink varieties and some, known as the Mikkelsen varieties, are shorter and so make better plants for use indoors. All need intermediate house conditions, minimum temperature 13°C. (55°F.) It is best to raise new plants from cuttings each year as old plants are apt to get too big and straggly, but they are perennial and can be kept for years if desired. Cuttings of young shoots about 3 in (8 cm) long are rooted in spring in a propagator, preferably with bottom heat. When well rooted they are potted singly in 4-in (10-cm) pots in J.I.P.2 or peat potting compost. Water moderately and grow in summer in a lightly shaded greenhouse but give full light from September onwards. From June to September feed every ten days or so with weak liquid fertilizer. Pot on into larger size pots if the first pots become overcrowded with roots. After flowering reduce the water supply considerably for a few weeks and then cut all stems back to 9 or 10 in (23 to 25 cm). This will help to keep the plants more compact and will also encourage production of plenty of strong new shoots for use as cuttings if desired.

Euphorbia fulgens also flowers in winter but its flowers are small, vivid orange scarlet and produced freely along arching stems.

It is a popular flower for cutting. It is a little more tender than the poinsettia and prefers a winter temperature around 15°C. (59–60°F.). In summer it will grow without artificial heat, but should have all the light available. Grow in J.I.P.1 or peat potting compost and water fairly freely from spring to autumn, but rather sparingly in winter. Either cut the flower stems for use in floral arrangements or as soon as the flowers fade. Repot each year, moving on to a larger size pot as necessary to accommodate the roots.

Euphorbia splendens is a semi-succulent and adapted to grow in hot dry places. It is a very spiny, angularly branched plant, often known as crown of thorns, and it has orange-red flowers in summer. It is hardier than either of the others and will survive in a cool greenhouse, minimum temperature 7°C. (45°F.), though the higher temperatures of the intermediate house will suit it better. Grow it in J.I.P.1 with a little extra sand or grit, water moderately from spring to autumn but keep nearly dry in winter. Do not shade at any time of the year. This is a plant which often succeeds well in a sunny window as it is able to withstand quite a dry atmosphere.

Freesia These lovely winter flowers, notable for their fragrance, can be grown from seed or from corms. Seed is sown in a temperature of 15 to 18°C. (60 to 65°F.) in late winter or spring, the seedlings being grown six or seven together in a 5-in (13-cm) pot filled with J.I.P.1 or soilless compost. These seedlings are grown on in a frame or unheated greenhouse during the summer, after which they may be given just a little warmth to bring them into flower during the winter. After flowering the plants are gradually allowed to die down until by early summer they will require no watering. A few weeks later the corms are shaken out and repotted in similar soil and the same number to the pot as the seedlings. These corms will give flowers a little later than the seedlings, continuing into the spring. It is also possible to buy specially prepared corms which can be planted outdoors in spring to flower in the same position in summer.

The colour range is from white, palest lavender and soft lemon, to deeper shades of blue and yellow and cerise red. All grow about 18 in (45 cm) tall and carry their clusters of flowers on slender stems which need some support, such as a few thin sticks with soft string looped round them.

Fuchsia These make excellent pot plants for the slightly heated greenhouse and they can be grown in a number of ways: as bushy plants; as tall pyramids; trained to the greenhouse rafters, or in baskets suspended from the rafters. No artificial heat is required in summer and only sufficient in winter to exclude frost.

Fuchsias are raised from cuttings of

young growth which root readily in spring or summer. When rooted, they are potted in small pots in J.I.P.1 and are moved on to larger sizes and J.I.P.2 as the smaller pots become filled with roots. Good flowering plants can be produced in 5-in (13-cm) pots but really big plants may reach 8- or 9-in (20- to 23-cm) pots. Water freely in spring and summer and give light shade from strong direct sunshine. In autumn and winter water rather sparingly, give full light and enough heat to exclude frost at all times. If there is not room for all plants in the greenhouse, the surplus can be planted or stood outdoors in summer.

Gardenia This delightfully fragrant evergreen shrub requires a warm greenhouse, in which it may either be planted directly in a bed of fairly rich soil or be grown in large pots or tubs in J.I.P.2. During the winter the plants can be grown in a temperature of 7 to 13°C. (45 to 55°F.), but for early flowers, plants should be given 5 to 10°C. (10 to 18°F.) more from mid-winter onwards. In summer plants must be freely watered and frequently syringed with clean water and should be shaded from strong sunshine. The large white flowers are produced mainly in spring and early summer but odd flowers may appear at any time.

Genista The fragrant genista, which is sold in tens of thousands as a pot plant each spring, is really a broom and its proper name is *Cytisus spachianus*. It is on the borderline of hardiness and can be grown outdoors in mild places, but if grown in a 6- or 7-in (15- or 17-cm) pot, it will make a neat plant 2 ft (60 cm) high, smothered in small, sweetly-scented, yellow flowers in spring or early summer.

It will thrive in J.I.P.2, should be watered fairly freely in spring and summer, sparingly in autumn and winter, and given full light at all times. In summer, plants can be stood outdoors so long as they are properly watered. Prune lightly after flowering.

Geranium, see Pelargonium

Gerbera (Barberton daisy) These graceful plants, with narrow-petalled, daisy-like flowers, are a little too tender to be grown outdoors, except in mild places. They like a gritty, well-drained soil and make good pot plants for the slightly heated greenhouse.

Plants can be raised from seed sown in a cool greenhouse in spring. Later, seedlings should be potted singly in J.I.P.1 with $\frac{1}{6}$ its bulk extra sand. Plants must be watered freely in summer, very sparingly in winter. They like sun, air, and just enough artificial heat to exclude frost.

The Barberton daisy produces its flowers in summer on 18-in (45-cm) stems. The colour range is from pink to flame, with many lovely intermediate shades of apricot and orange.

Gerbera jamesonii

Gloxinia Immensely showy plants with velvet-green leaves and large funnel-shaped flowers in rich or brilliant shades of purple, violet, pink and red, sometimes spotted or veined on a white ground.

Gloxinias have tuberous roots which can be stored dry during the winter in a minimum temperature of 10°C. (50°F.). Start the tubers into growth in late winter or spring by placing them almost shoulder to shoulder in seed boxes filled with peat or sand, placed in a temperature of 18°C. (65°F.), and pot them singly in J.I.P.1 or soilless compost in 3-in (8-cm) pots as soon as they start to make leaves. Thereafter grow on in a similar temperature and move on into 5- or 6-in (13- to 15-cm) pots and J.I.P.2 or soilless compost for flowering in summer.

They must be watered freely and be shaded from strong sunshine. In autumn, they are gradually dried off and may be tapped out of their pots, but are best not shaken clear of soil till they are restarted into growth.

Guernsey lily, see Nerine

Hibiscus (Rose mallow) Some kinds of hibiscus are hardy but the most beautiful of all, *Hibiscus rosa-sinensis*, is a tender shrub for a moderately heated greenhouse. It has flamboyant scarlet, pink, yellow or buff flowers in summer and at this season it can be grown without artificial heat, but in winter the temperature should not fall below 10°C. (50°F.).

Grow in J.I.P.2 or soilless compost, water freely and maintain a fairly moist atmosphere in spring and summer but water only moderately in autumn and winter. If desired, plants can be pruned quite severely each spring.

Hippeastrum (Barbados lily) These showy bulbous-rooted plants are sometimes known as *Amaryllis*, a name that really belongs to the belladonna lily. The Barbados lily, *Hippeastrum equestre*, has clusters of large, funnel-shaped flowers, usually crimson or scarlet, though there are also pink and white varieties. The flowers are carried on stout stems, 2 ft (60 cm) high, in spring and early summer, and the strap-shaped leaves appear after the flowers.

Plants must be grown in a greenhouse throughout. In winter they are rested and need little water and a temperature around

Hibiscus rosa-sinensis

7 to 10°C. (45 to 50°F.). During late winter and early spring plants are started into growth in batches, by being given more water and a temperature of 16 to 18°C. (60 to 65°F.). After flowering the plants should have all the sun possible to ripen the bulbs.

Specially prepared bulbs can also be obtained in late summer or early autumn for winter flowering and, if potted as described and kept in a warm greenhouse or room, will quickly come into bloom.

Hot water plant, see Achimenes

Hoya (Wax plant) Lovely and rather uncommon climbing and trailing plants for a moderately heated greenhouse. *Hoya carnosa* climbs by twining, has rather fleshy leaves and in summer flat circular clusters of fragrant pale pink flowers that have a waxen appearance. This plant can be grown in a large pot, but is really better in a border of fairly rich peaty soil. It needs a minimum winter temperature of 7°C. (45°F.), rising to 16°C. (60°F.) or more in summer, with plenty of water while in growth and very little in winter. Stems should be thinned a little in late winter to prevent overcrowding.

Hoya bella is a smaller trailing plant suitable for hanging baskets but otherwise requiring similar treatment to *H. carnosa*. The flowers are similar in form and equally sweetly scented but they have more colour. Both kinds can be increased by cuttings in spring, or by layering in spring or summer.

Hydrangea These shrubs make excellent pot or tub plants. They are grown from cuttings of young growth taken in spring or summer and spring-struck cuttings will make good flowering plants in 5- or 6-in (13- to 15-cm) pots by the following year and can be potted on annually if there is room for larger specimens or can be discarded after a further batch of cuttings has been taken. They thrive in J.I.P.1 or soilless compost and must be watered freely in spring and summer, rather sparingly in autumn and winter. They require no more than sufficient heat to exclude frost in winter but a little more heat, applied in spring, will give earlier flowers, in spring rather than in summer. The plants can be stood outdoors in summer.

There are a number of varieties, some with white, some with blue, purple, carmine or pink flowers, but the colour of all except the white kinds can be influenced by the acidity of the soil. The more acid it is, the bluer the colour. Alkalinity can be easily achieved by mixing a little ground chalk or limestone with the soil. Acidity may be produced by using acid loam and peat and also by using aluminium sulphate or one of the special blueing compounds sold for the purpose. Proprietary blueing compounds must be used in accordance with the manufacturer's instructions. Aluminium sulphate is used at $\frac{1}{4}$ oz (7 g) per gallon, applied several times in winter and early spring in place of ordinary water.

Kaffir lily, see Clivia

Lady's slipper, see Cypripedium

Leadwort, Climbing, see Plumbago

Lily, African, see Agapanthus

Lily, Barbados, see Hippeastrum

Lily, Guernsey, see Nerine

Lily, Kaffir, see Clivia

Lily, Scarborough, see Vallota

Mimosa, see Acacia

Nerine (Guernsey lily) Bulbous-rooted plants for the slightly heated greenhouse. All produce their flowers in rounded clusters on bare 12- to 18-in (30- to 45-cm) stems in early autumn, the leaves appearing later. The colour range is from white and pink to scarlet, with some curious shades of puce as well in the many garden varieties and hybrids that have been raised, mainly from *Nerine sarniensis*.

Bulbs should be potted in late summer in J.I.P.1, watered fairly freely from then until late spring, but kept almost dry during the first two months of summer, during which time they may, with advantage, be placed on a shelf near the greenhouse glass or be kept in a sunny frame. They require only enough artificial heat to keep out frost.

Passiflora (Passion flower) Several highly distinctive climbers with flowers of curious formation and said to represent, in their floral parts, the instruments of the crucifixion.

Passiflora caerulea, with blue and white flowers, can be grown against a south wall in mild places and will flower in late summer, but it is also an excellent climber for a fairly large greenhouse or conservatory with just enough artificial heat to exclude frost in winter. Occasionally orange fruit pods may be produced, about 1 in (2·5 cm) long. It is best planted direct in a bed of good soil within the greenhouse. There is a pure white variety named Constance Elliott.

Other passion flowers such as *P. allardii*, purplish, blue, pink and white; *P. quadrangularis*, with large flowers fringed with hanging filaments, and *P. antioquiensis*, rose red, should be grown in a similar manner but require a minimum of 10°C. (50°F.) in winter.

Passion flower, see Passiflora

Pelargonium (Geranium) There are a lot of different pelargoniums and two groups, the zonal pelargoniums and the ivy-leaved pelargoniums, are the plants that most people call geraniums. They flower all the summer and as they are sufficiently hardy to be grown outdoors at that season, they are very popular for bedding. They also make excellent greenhouse plants, the zonal varieties grown in pots, the ivy-leaved varieties in baskets, over the sides of which they can cascade. The cultivation of these plants for bedding is described on p. 100 and the only difference, if they are to be grown in greenhouses throughout the year, is that they must be kept well watered in their pots during the summer and be fed from time to time with liquid fertilizer.

Two other important classes of pelargonium, the regal pelargoniums and the scented-leaved pelargoniums, are only grown as greenhouse pot plants. The regal varieties have large, showy flowers in spring and early summer. Cuttings are taken in the latter half of summer and, when rooted, are potted singly in 3-in (8-cm) pots in J.I.P.1 and overwintered in a minimum temperature of 7 to 13°C. (45 to 55°F.). They are potted on as necessary in J.I.P.2 and will flower the first spring in 5- or 6-in (13- to 15-cm) pots. They are watered moderately in winter, freely in spring and early summer, but as flowering ceases watering is reduced and plants are cut back fairly severely. As young growth starts, more water is given again and a week or so later cuttings can be taken to repeat the process. The old plants can also be repotted and grown on in 6-, 7- or 8-in (15- 18- or 20-cm) pots for another year.

The scented-leaved varieties are grown for the aromatic fragrance of their leaves, their flowers being comparatively insignificant. Culture is as for zonal varieties under glass.

Plumbago (Leadwort) The climbing leadwort, *Plumbago capensis*, is a slightly tender plant and needs the protection of a frost-proof greenhouse, though it can be grown without artificial heat for most of the year. It is a vigorous plant producing its large clusters of light blue flowers during the summer.

It can be grown in large pots or tubs in J.I.P.2 but is really happier planted in a bed of good soil in the greenhouse and trained up wires fixed to the rafters. Where space is restricted the long stems can be cut back quite drastically early each spring. It can be increased by cuttings taken in mid-spring.

Poinsettia, see Euphorbia

Polianthes (Tuberose) This tender tuberous-rooted plant is grown for its 2- to 3-ft (60-cm to 1-m) spikes of very fragrant, funnel-shaped white flowers, which can be obtained at almost any time of year under glass, provided sufficient warmth is available. This, however, requires some skill and experience, and the simplest method of

Solanum capsicastrum

growing the tuberose is to purchase the imported tubers in spring, pot them at once in J.I.P.1 or soilless compost either singly in 4-in (10-cm) pots, or two or three in a 5- or 6-in (13- to 15-cm) pot, and place them in a greenhouse in a temperature of 18 to 21°C. (65 to 70°F.). This high temperature will be needed for only a few weeks until growth begins, after which a temperature of 13 to 16°C. (55 to 60°F.) will suffice. A propagating frame inside the greenhouse can be used to obtain the high starting temperature. Throughout their growth the plants will need plenty of water and light. Treated in this way they will flower in late summer. It is seldom worth trying to keep the tubers for a second year.

There are double-flowered varieties as well as the single type, and both are popular as cut flowers for corsages and button-holes.

Primula There are three popular races of winter-flowering greenhouse primroses, the Chinese primrose, *Primula sinensis*, with showy clusters of pink, salmon, orange, crimson or blue flowers; the rather similar but taller *P. obconica*, and the fairy primrose, *P. malacoides*, which bears its smaller mauve, pink or carmine flowers in fine sprays.

All are grown from seed sown under glass in a temperature of 16°C. (60°F.), in spring for *P. sinensis* and *P. obconica*, in early summer for *P. malacoides*. Seedlings are pricked off and later potted singly into small pots in J.I.P.1 or soilless compost. They are moved in early autumn to the 5-in (13-cm) pots and J.I.P.2 in which they will flower during winter and early spring. They need a light, airy greenhouse and a temperature between 7 and 13°C. (45 and 55°F.). Water fairly

Strelitzia reginae

freely in summer, moderately in winter, taking care then not to wet the leaves unduly. They are not worth keeping after flowering as better plants are obtained from seed.

Rose mallow, see Hibiscus

Saintpaulia (African violet) *Saintpaulia ionantha* is a small and very-free-flowering plant for warm greenhouses and rooms. The leaves are deep green and velvety, the flowers, clustered on 6-in (15-cm) stems, are violet-purple in the common form, but there are many variations in the colour of the flowers, which range from pale blue to pink, rose and pure white. Some have double flowers.

All are grown in a peaty compost such as J.I.P.1 with $\frac{1}{4}$ its bulk extra peat, in high humidity and with plenty of warmth – certainly a minimum of 13°C. (55°F.), even in the coldest weather, and an average of around 18°C. (65°F.). They will need shade in summer but in winter should receive all the light possible. Under good conditions they will flower throughout the year.

Propagation is usually by leaf cuttings taken in summer but plants can also be raised from seed or increased by careful division in spring.

Scarborough lily, see Vallota

Shrimp plant, see Beloperone

Solanum (Winter cherry) *Solanum capsicastrum* is a small shrubby plant which produces abundant crops of cherry-like orange-red fruits in winter and is popular for indoor decoration.

It is raised from seed sown in a temperature of 18°C. (65°F.) in late winter or early spring, seedlings being potted singly in J.I.P.1, first in 3-in (8-cm) pots, later in the 5- or 6-in (13- or 15-cm) pots in which they will fruit. During summer they may be placed outdoors or in a frame without lights, but should be returned to a moderately heated greenhouse before frost threatens. Water fairly freely throughout,

Streptocarpus **Constant Nymph**

and when in flower in summer syringe frequently with clear water to assist the flowers to set and produce fruits.

Strelitzia (Bird of paradise flower) A remarkable greenhouse plant with large leaves and stiff 3-ft (1-m) stems terminated by purple, blue and orange flowers shaped rather like the head of a crested bird.

It is not a difficult plant to grow in large pots in J.I.P.2, provided it can be given a winter temperature of around 13°C. (55°F.), rising towards flowering time, in late spring or early summer, to 18°C. (64°F.) or more. It should be watered and syringed generously with clear water during spring and summer, but only moderately watered and not syringed at all in winter. Increase is by division in early spring, the best potting time.

Streptocarpus Greenhouse plants with trumpet-shaped blue (or occasionally pink and white) flowers carried in loose sprays on 12- to 18-in (30- to 45-cm) stems in summer or early autumn. For early flowering, seed is sown in a greenhouse in mid-summer and the seedlings are potted singly in J.I.P.1, first into 3-in (8-cm) later into 4- or 5-in (10- to 13-cm) pots. In winter they are

kept in a temperature around 13°C. (55°F.) and are watered sparingly, but in spring the temperature can rise to 16 to 18°C. (60 to 65°F.) and water can be given fairly freely, also daily syringing. For late flowering the same general procedure is followed, but seed is sown in late winter in a temperature of 18°C. (65°F.). Sometimes plants are grown from leaf cuttings taken in spring or summer.

Tuberose, see Polianthes

Vallota (Scarborough lily) *Vallota purpurea* is not a true lily but a tender bulb with lily-like flowers which makes a fine decorative plant for the greenhouse. The trumpet-shaped, scarlet flowers are produced in a cluster on top of an 18-in (45-cm) stem in late summer or early autumn.

The bulbs should be potted in J.I.P.1 in early spring in 6-in (15-cm) pots and may either be repotted annually into larger pots or the bulb clusters can be divided so that they can remain in 6-in (15-cm) pots. Very little heat will be needed at any time, just sufficient to exclude frost. They need less water in summer when they are resting than during the rest of the year when they are growing and they need maximum light.

The Scarborough lily can be increased by division of the bulb clusters when repotting or by seed sown in a warm greenhouse in spring.

Wax plant, see Hoya

Winter cherry, see Solanum

Zantedeschia (Arum lily) This is the correct name of these popular plants which are also sometimes sold as richardia, a former botanical name. They all have handsome spear-shaped leaves and flowers which consist of a single 'petal' (it is correctly known as a spathe) folded around a narrow, column-shaped spadix. This spathe is white in the common arum lily, white and green, pink or yellow in some other kinds.

All are grown from fleshy roots which are potted singly in late summer in J.I.P.1 and are grown in a frost-proof greenhouse, preferably one with a minimum temperature of 13°C. (55°F.) for the coloured varieties. Higher temperatures can be used to obtain earlier flowers. Water moderately at first, freely as growth appears, but reduce the water supply for a few weeks in summer before repotting. Increase by division at potting time.

Home-grown Vegetables

Vegetables can be just as interesting to grow as flowers and a well-kept vegetable garden can be as attractive, to the eye of the gardener, as any flower border. This attractiveness can be increased by adopting the old-fashioned practice of laying out the vegetable garden as a pattern formed by geometrically shaped and arranged beds, each clearly defined by an edging of bricks, clipped box, thyme or something of the kind. This is a style frequently used for herb gardens with excellent results and is equally applicable to more varied plantations including fruit as well as vegetables.

Even in a small garden it may be worth while to devote some space to vegetables,

particularly to those that are required frequently in small quantities, such as parsley and mint, or vegetables such as celeriac and asparagus peas, which cannot readily be purchased at the greengrocers'.

Soil Preparation

All vegetables need clean, well-cultivated soil and almost all need feeding, though what they are fed with and when it is used will depend on the kind of vegetable.

Thorough digging in autumn or winter with spade or fork is the best soil preparation for vegetables. The earlier this can be done the better so that the rough-turned soil

can have all the weathering possible before crops are sown or planted in the spring.

Lime is a more generally useful soil-dressing in the vegetable garden than it is in the flower garden and hydrated lime at 4 to 6oz (110 to 170g) per square yard (per square metre) can usually be given with advantage at least once in three years. It can be scattered over the surface as soon as digging has been completed and left to be washed in by rain and further mixed with the soil when seed and planting beds are prepared. Only on naturally chalky or limy soils is lime unlikely to be required at some time.

Animal manure is also very valuable,

An attractive arrangement of succulents

though it will not be required where root crops such as carrots and parsnips are to be grown. Decayed garden refuse may be used instead of manure, or granulated peat, but the last is best used as a surface dressing raked or lightly forked in, whereas animal manure and vegetable compost are best dug in as the work of soil preparation proceeds.

There are exceptions, but most vegetables are either sown or planted in spring and the object is to get the ground quite clear of weeds and broken down to a fine, crumbly, level surface by that time. Winter frost will help to break up the lumps of soil but the work must be completed by the gardener with fork and rake or with a rotary motor cultivator. Whatever tool is used for the work, the vital thing is to do it when the soil is in the right condition, neither too wet nor too dry. One can work on light sandy soils when they are wet without doing them too much harm, but heavy clay soils become so pasty that it is difficult to get any kind of fine crumbly surface (the gardener calls it a tilth) in which to sow or plant. Soil that is too dry can be equally difficult to work, as many of the lumps may have become hard and will refuse to break down.

Usually as winter draws to a close, or very early in the spring, there are a few windy or sunny days when the surface of the soil begins to dry out and as soon as it is possible to walk on it without getting a lot of soil stuck to one's boots it is time to get busy and break down the clods of soil to a crumbly condition.

The Four Cultural Groups

From the point of view of cultivation, vegetables fall into four groups:

[1] those that are raised from seed sown directly where the crop is to mature

[2] those raised from seed sown in a seed bed from which they are planted out where they are to mature

[3] those planted annually from bulbs or tubers

[4] those grown more or less permanently in the same place.

Group 1 This includes peas and beans, carrots, parsnips, turnips, beetroots, spinach, radishes, and parsley. Lettuces may be grown in this way or they may be sown in one place and transplanted to another. Sweet corn is sown where it is to mature except in cold places, where it can be sown in small peat, sawdust or paper pots and transplanted in these to the place in which it is to mature. Onions may be grown from seed where they are to mature, or be planted as young seedlings raised in frame or greenhouse, or as small bulbs, known as sets.

Group 2 This includes all the brassicas, a term which embraces cabbage, cauliflower, brussels sprout, broccoli and kale, all of which are closely related. All these, as

well as leeks, are usually sown in a seed bed in the open ground, but tomatoes, vegetable marrows, squashes and pumpkins, all of which come into Group 2, being more or less tender, are usually raised in a greenhouse or frame and only planted out when danger of frost is past, and celery, though considerably hardier, is treated in the same way.

Group 3 The most important crop in Group 3 is the potato, but it also contains the Jerusalem artichoke, the shallot, garlic, and the onion when grown from sets instead of from seed.

Group 4 More or less permanent crops which occupy the same ground for years include rhubarb, asparagus, mint, sage, thyme and other herbs and the globe artichoke.

Raising Plants in Group 1

Seed crops need a fine, crumbly soil and a level surface so that seeds can be sown at an even depth. Final preparation of seed beds should be with a rake used both to level and further break up the soil and at the same time the seed bed can be trodden to make it evenly firm all over. Loose soil dries out too rapidly and may settle unevenly.

It is most convenient to sow seed crops in straight rows as then it is easy to cultivate between the rows to keep down weeds. The rows should usually be at least 1 ft (30 cm) apart and, for tall crops, such as broad beans and many varieties of pea, it is better for them to be 2 or even 3 ft (60 cm to 1 m) apart.

Drill Preparation and Seed Sowing The rows are made by stretching a line across the vegetable garden and then scratching out a little furrow (known as a drill) against this with the corner of a hoe or a pointed stick. For most small seeds the drills should be about ½ in (1 cm) deep but for big seeds, such as those of peas and beans, they may be 1 to 2 in (2·5 to 5 cm) deep. If seeds are sown too deeply they may be slow to germinate or not germinate at all. If they are not covered sufficiently rain may expose them to birds. When a drill has been made the seeds are sprinkled thinly along it and then the displaced soil is drawn back over it.

Weed Suppression and Seedling Thinning Nothing further is needed until two or three weeks later, on the appearance of the seedlings, when a Dutch hoe can be run between the rows to cut off weed seedlings without injuring the crop seedlings. Weeds that actually come up in the rows will have to be pulled out by hand and at the same time the number of crop seedlings can be reduced to a reasonable spacing, which will vary from about 3 to 9 in (8 to 23 cm) from plant to plant according to the nature of the crop. This is known as thinning, and may not be required for crops such as radish, small carrots and spinach if they have been sown thinly.

Sowing vegetables:
Take out drills using a draw hoe and line

Sow the seed along the rows taking care not to sow too thickly

Cover the seed lightly, drawing the soil over carefully with a rake

Providing Support Very shortly after this, some of the taller crops, especially peas and runner beans, will want support. For peas, bushy hazel branches are often used, stuck firmly into the soil on either side. Alternatives are string or wire netting stretched between stakes driven into the ground.

Raising Plants in Group 2

Very much the same methods as those described above may be used for sowing crops that are to be transplanted but, since they will not remain in the seed bed for long, the rows may be closer together, even as close as 6 in (15 cm) for some small crops such as lettuces. If room is scarce these crops may even be sown broadcast, which means that the seed is distributed evenly all over an area of soil instead of being confined to a row. The drills for this are made by drawing a rake across the surface in one direction, so leaving a lot of tiny furrows close together. When the seed has been scattered, the rake is drawn across the surface at right angles to the first raking, so filling up the furrows and mixing the seed with the soil.

Transplanting When the seedlings are large enough to handle conveniently, which may vary between 1 in (2·5 cm) high for lettuces, to 4 or 5 in (10 to 13 cm) for cabbages, brussels sprouts and cauliflowers, they are carefully lifted with a handfork, separated out into single seedlings and re-planted, with as little delay as possible, where they are to mature. They are usually planted in straight rows, marked out with the garden line, because this makes subsequent cultivation easier. They can be planted with a stout, pointed stick, known as a dibber, or with a trowel. The soil should be made firm around the roots and it is usually necessary to water them in to give them a good start and prevent leaves flagging unduly; it will also settle the soil around the roots.

Frost-tender Plants A variation on this method is required for crops such as tomatoes, vegetable marrows and cucumbers, which can stand little or no frost. Seed of these is sown in a greenhouse or frame and the seedlings are grown on in pots, gradually being given increasing ventilation and lower temperature until danger of frost outdoors is past and they can be planted out with safety.

Raising Plants in Groups 3 and 4

Crops that are planted from sets, tubers, etc., are also grown in straight rows. Some, such as potatoes and Jerusalem artichokes, need to be covered with 3 or 4 in (8 to 10 cm) of soil and as the tubers are themselves 2 in (5 cm) or more in diameter, this means that furrows 5 or 6 in (13 to 15 cm) deep must be made for them. There are two ways of doing this, one to dig the furrows with a spade, the other to drag out the soil with a draw hoe. In either case, when the tubers have been spaced in the furrow, the displaced soil is drawn back with a hoe or rake to cover them.

However, not all planted crops need covering like this. Some, such as shallots, onions from sets (which are really very small onions) and garlic, are planted simply by pressing them firmly into the soil. They do not even have to be completely out of sight.

The more permanent crops, such as rhubarb, globe artichokes and asparagus, often have such large roots that a spade is the most convenient tool with which to plant them, but the small kinds can be planted with a trowel.

Seedlings can be thinned as soon as they are large enough to handle

Maintaining a Succession

Some crops can be used a little at a time as required, but few will remain in good condition for more than a few weeks. After that they become tough, or run to seed, or in some other way become useless as food. One of the major problems of the small garden is organizing crops so that there is never an unusable surplus and yet never a serious gap between successive crops. Root crops, such as beetroots, carrots and parsnips, can be lifted and stored when they reach the best stage for eating. So can tubers, such as potatoes, and bulbs, such as onions, shallots and garlic. But leaf crops, including spinach, lettuce and all the cabbage tribe, must be used as they become ready and this is also true of peas and beans, though they may be deep frozen or otherwise preserved.

Alternative Methods One way of ensuring a succession of any one crop is to make several sowings at intervals of two to three weeks. Another is to grow early, mid-season and late varieties. These are varieties of some vegetables which have different rates of growth so that, even if they are sown or planted at the same time, they will mature at different times, thus ensuring a continuous supply.

With the exception of the permanent crops, most vegetables are cleared away once the edible portion has been harvested.

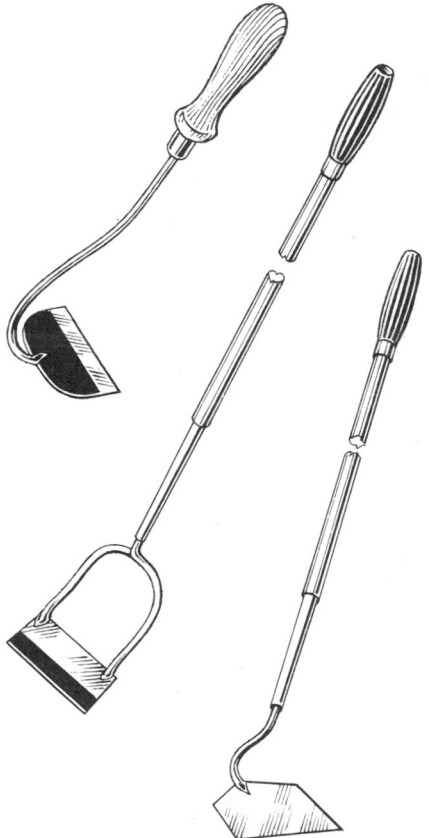

Types of hoe
Top: Onion hoe – thinning vegetable crops
Centre: Dutch hoe – general weed control
Bottom: Draw hoe – drawing drills, earthing up

The sooner this can be done the better because the ageing plants are likely to attract pests and diseases and are unsightly. As soon as a strip or plot has been cleared in this way it can be dug or forked and, if the season is not too advanced, it may be used again.

Blanching

Some crops are only edible when they have been blanched, that is, prevented from producing any green or other colouring in their leaves or stems. This is done by excluding light and one of the simplest ways of doing this is by drawing soil around that part of the plant that is to be blanched; a process known as earthing up. This is how leeks and celery are blanched:

Leeks Leek seedlings, raised in a seed bed, are lifted and replanted in holes about 8 in (20 cm) deep made with a dibber. This blanches the lower part of the stem. To get a longer blanched area the soil is pulled towards the plants from either side of the row when the plants are well grown, so forming a ridge out of the top of which the green leaves emerge.

Celery Celery seedlings are planted in trenches about 6 in (15 cm) deep. When the plants are well grown at the end of the summer the trenches are filled in, so blanching the lower parts of the stems, and then more soil is banked up around the plants, just as with leeks.

Potatoes If potato tubers are exposed to light they become green and bitter. To prevent this, soil is drawn from between the rows towards the plants in late spring and early summer, so forming ridges in which the tubers are well covered. The young shoots of potatoes are tender and so, if they appear above soil while there is still risk of frost, it is a good plan to draw soil over them at once as a protection.

Storage Methods

Storage methods for vegetables vary according to the crop. Potatoes can be stored in sacks or brown paper bags in a shed, provided it is frost proof, but if the tubers get frozen they will become sweet or go soft and rotten.

Carrots are much hardier and can be stored in boxes filled with dry sand. This method also suits beetroots which can survive some freezing but will not put up with very low temperatures. Parsnips, turnips and swedes are sufficiently hardy to be left in the ground and used as required.

Recommended Vegetables

Artichoke, Globe Grown for the flower heads which are gathered before they open; these are enclosed in thick green bracts, like scales, and it is the fleshy base of each scale that is the most succulent edible portion.

Artichokes are grown from rooted suckers or off-shoots of the main plant. They should be planted in spring, 3 ft (1 m) apart, in rich, well-drained soil and a sunny, sheltered place. Plants will continue to bear for several years but should be replaced with young plants every third or fourth year as old plants get progressively less productive.

Artichoke, Jerusalem This plant, which is a species of sunflower, is grown for its tubers produced in the soil like those of the potato. These tubers are planted in late winter or early spring, 6 in (15 cm) deep and 15 in (38 cm) apart in rows at least 2½ ft (75 cm) apart. The plants are very hardy and can be lifted as required in autumn and winter so that the tubers can be collected and used.

Asparagus This is a permanent crop which may occupy the ground for many years. It needs good, rich, well-drained soil. It can be raised from seed but this is slow and it is better to start with two-year-old male roots, that is, plants which produce only male

One of the most satisfactory ways of growing runner beans is on tripods

flowers and so can never bear the red asparagus berries as fruits.

Roots are planted in spring 3 in (8 cm) deep and 18 in (45 cm) apart. No shoots should be cut for the first year. After this the shoots are cut well below soil level when they are from 1 to 4 in (2·5 to 10 cm) above soil level. No cutting should be done after mid-summer. In autumn all top growth is removed just above soil level. Manure or compost should be spread over the bed each spring.

Asparagus Pea A plant grown for its pods, which are cooked and eaten when they are about 2 in (5 cm) long. It is raised from seed sown under glass in early spring, the seedlings being hardened off for planting out in late spring when danger of frost is past. Space them 1 ft (30 cm) apart in rows 2 ft (60 cm) apart in good soil and a sunny place.

Aubergine Sow seed in late winter or early spring in a temperature of 18°C. (65°F.). Pot seedlings singly in 2½-in (6·5-cm) pots and later move on into 6- or 7-in (15- to 18-cm) pots and fairly rich compost. Grow throughout in a sunny, frost-proof greenhouse. Water fairly freely and feed when fruits are formed. Pinch out the tip of each plant when about 6 in (15cm) high to make it branch, and train later stems to a cane or wire. Restrict fruits to a maximum of six per plant and gather as soon as ripe.

Beans, Broad In mild districts and on well-drained soil, sow in mid-autumn; elsewhere, sow in early spring. Space seeds 6 in (15cm) apart in drills 2 in (5cm) deep and 2 ft (60cm) apart. Pinch out tops of plants when two or three clusters of pods are forming on each plant. Gather frequently as beans in pods reach usable size.

Beans, French Sow seed in mid- to late spring, spacing 6 in (15cm) apart in drills 2 in (5cm) deep and 18 in (45cm) apart. Gather beans frequently as the pods reach usable size.

Beans, Runner Sow in late spring, spacing seeds 8 in (20cm) apart in a drill 2 in (5cm) deep. Make two such drills, 10 in (25cm) apart to form one row of beans. If a second double row is required, space it at least 8 ft (2·5m) from the first. Other small crops such as lettuce, radish, carrot and turnip, can be grown between.

Alternatively, beans may be sown in a single drill 1 ft (30cm) from the base of a wall or fence which the plants will clothe.

Calabrese (see Broccoli)

Strings or wires can be attached to the fence to support the beans. In the open they need stakes or netting, extending to at least 7 ft (2·25m) above soil level. Water freely in dry weather. Gather frequently as pods attain usable size.

Beetroot Sow in mid- to late spring, two or three seeds together, in groups spaced 6 in (15cm) apart in drills 1 in (2·5cm) deep and rows 15 in (38cm) apart. Thin seedlings to one at each cluster. Pull roots as they attain usable size and in early autumn lift all remaining and store in sand or dry soil in a shed or sheltered place.

There are three principal types: globe, with globular roots; long, with tapering roots, and tankard with cylindrical roots.

The first and last are most suitable for small gardens.

Broccoli, Sprouting This is closely related to cauliflower but produces numerous small heads on quite long stalks, instead of forming one large head. There are purple and white sprouting varieties differing in the colour of their heads, and also a green sprouting kind, also known as calabrese, which is the vegetable usually served as broccoli in restaurants. Purple and white sprouting broccoli are at their best in the spring, whereas calabrese matures more rapidly and is ready in summer. Seed is sown and plants treated as for cauliflower.

Brussels Sprouts Seed should be sown in a frame or seed bed in early spring and seedlings planted out in late spring at least 2½ ft (75cm) apart on good soil. There are early, mid-season and late varieties which extend the sprout picking season from early autumn to late winter. After the sprouts have been picked the heads can be cut as greens.

Cabbage For summer, autumn and winter use, seed is sown in a seed bed in spring, seedlings being planted out in late spring or early summer, 18 in (45cm) apart in good rich soil. Early, mid-season and late varieties are available which, between them, spread the cutting season from about mid-summer to mid-winter. Special spring varieties are also available for sowing in a seed bed, mid- to late summer, planting out 1 to 1½ ft (30 to 45cm) apart in early autumn and cutting the following late spring or early summer. These varieties need fairly rich, well-drained soil.

Savoy cabbages have wrinkled leaves and, being very hardy, are useful for cutting in winter. Seed is sown in a seed bed in late spring, seedlings being planted out mid- to late summer at 18 in (45cm) apart in good rich soil.

Carrot Sow seed thinly from early spring

Self-blanching celery

to mid-summer in drills ½ in (1 cm) deep and 12 in (30 cm) apart, in good soil where the crop is to mature. Thin seedlings to 5 in (13 cm) apart for large roots, but if carrots are to be pulled young no thinning should be required, provided sowing has been carefully done.

Both early and main-crop varieties are available, the latter giving larger roots which take longer to mature. Young carrots can be pulled all summer as required. In early autumn any remaining roots should be lifted and stored in sand or peat in a shed or sheltered place.

Cauliflower Seed is sown in a frame or seed bed in spring and the seedlings are planted out in late spring or early summer, 2 ft (60 cm) apart, in good soil and an open but not too exposed position. As the white curd begins to form, some of the inner leaves are broken down over them as protection.

Varieties are available for cutting from summer until the following spring but it is the summer and early autumn varieties that are easiest to grow and most useful in gardens.

Celeriac This is sometimes known as turnip-rooted celery because it makes a large, turnip-like root which has the flavour of celery. It can be chopped or ground and used for cooking.

Seed is sown as for celery, the seedlings being planted out in late spring or early summer in good rich soil, 12 in (30 cm) apart in rows 18 in (45 cm) apart.

Celery Sow in a greenhouse or frame in late winter or early spring, prick off seedlings into boxes and harden off for planting out in late spring or early summer. Plant in trenches 6 in (15 cm) deep and 1 ft (30 cm) wide, made by digging out the soil to a depth of about 18 in (45 cm) and then returning about half of it mixed with a generous quantity of decayed manure or vegetable refuse. The remaining displaced soil should be left in two low ridges on each side of the trench. The plants are spaced 9 in (23 cm) apart in a single row down the middle of the trench and are watered freely. In late summer the remaining displaced soil is returned around the plants and then, a little at a time, more soil is thrown up round them to form a ridge which will blanch the stems. These, when well blanched, may be dug as required in autumn and winter.

White, pink and red varieties are available and the coloured varieties are hardier than the white which, for that reason, should be used first.

For summer use a different kind of celery should be grown, known as self-blanching. Seedlings of this are raised in the same way but are not planted in trenches. Instead, they are planted in good rich soil, 9 in (23 cm) apart each way in several rows so

Endive (curled type)

that the leaves form a dense cover and exclude light from the stems. Later, boards on edge can be placed around the block of plants to exclude light further, but no earthing up is required.

Chicory Sow outdoors in mid- to late spring in rows 15 in (38 cm) apart and later thin seedlings to 9 in (23 cm). In autumn and winter lift plants a few at a time and pack quite closely in large pots or deep boxes with moist soil or peat around them. Place in a warm dark place and cut young blanched shoots at root level when 6 to 9 in (15 to 23 cm) high for use as salad.

Chives Plant tufts obtained by splitting up old plants in spring. Space 6 in (15 cm) apart and leave to grow more or less permanently. Chives are quite decorative and can be used as an edging to beds. Cut stems at ground level as required for use as flavouring but only take a few at a time from any one plant leaving others to maintain growth.

Cress Sow rather thickly at about weekly intervals during spring and summer in boxes filled with fine soil, place in a greenhouse, frame or sunny window, and cover with brown paper. In about seven to ten days seedlings should appear and the paper should be removed. Two or three days later, the cress should be ready for cutting.

Cucumber Two kinds of cucumber are available: the frame cucumber for cultivation in greenhouses or frames, and the ridge cucumber for cultivation outdoors.

Seed of both can be raised under glass, the seeds sown two or three together in a 3-in (8-cm) pot of good seed compost and thinned to one per pot later. For planting in heated greenhouses, sow in late winter; for unheated greenhouses or frames, in early spring; for planting outdoors, in late spring. A temperature of about 18°C. (65°F.) is required for germination. Alternatively, seed of ridge cucumbers can be sown outdoors in late spring where the plants are to mature.

Cucumbers need very rich soil with plenty of rotten manure or garden compost. They are planted, 3 ft (1 m) apart, on small mounds or ridges and are watered freely. Under glass they need permanent light shading in summer. When stems are 1 ft (30 cm) long, the tips are pinched out to make the plants branch. Flowers and fruits should appear on these side shoots. Under glass more elaborate training to wires may be undertaken. Cucumbers should be cut as soon as they attain usable size to keep the plants cropping.

Endive Used like lettuce and particularly useful in autumn. Sow seed in good soil in drills ½ in (1 cm) deep and 12 to 15 in (30 to 38 cm) apart. Thin the seedlings to 9 in (23 cm). If desired the thinnings can be replanted elsewhere, 9 in (23 cm) by 12 in (30 cm) apart.

When plants are well grown, place a small piece of board or an inverted saucer over each plant to exclude light and blanch the

Kohlrabi

leaves. Plants from the later sowings may be transplanted to a frame in early autumn and be blanched by shading the frame.

Garlic The bulb of garlic consists of several sections, known as cloves, and it is grown by planting these cloves separately, 9 in (23 cm) apart in rows 15 in (38 cm) apart, in winter or early spring in good, rich, well-drained soil and a sheltered, sunny place. The bulbs are lifted in late summer and stored in any dry place.

Kohlrabi This turnip-like vegetable is grown from seed sown in spring in drills ½ in (1 cm) deep and 15 in (38 cm) apart in good soil where it is to mature. Seedlings are thinned to 9 in (23 cm) and the swollen stems are pulled for use when they are about the size of an orange.

Leek Seed is sown thinly in early or mid-spring in drills ½ in (1 cm) deep and 9 in (23 cm) apart in good soil. The seedlings are carefully lifted in early summer and are replanted in deep holes, made with a dibber. These holes should be 6 to 8 in (15 to 20 cm) deep and 12 in (30 cm) apart in rows 18 in (45 cm) apart. Later some soil can be drawn up around the stems to blanch them still further. Dig as required for use in autumn and winter.

Lettuce Seed should be sown every second or third week throughout spring and early summer. Sow in drills ½ in (1 cm) deep and 12 to 15 in (30 to 38 cm) apart and thin seedlings to 9 in (23 cm) apart. If desired the thinnings can be replanted elsewhere 9 in (23 cm) apart in rows 12 in (30 cm) apart.

Lettuce needs good rich soil and should be well watered in dry weather.

There are three distinct types of lettuce: the cabbage lettuce, with rounded heart; the cos lettuce, with elongated oval heart, and the loose-leaf lettuce, with no heart at all. There are numerous varieties of both the cabbage and the cos types and the cabbage varieties are further sub-divided into butterheads, with soft, tender leaves, and the crispheads, with crisp leaves.

Mint Plant roots in spring by spreading them out thinly and covering with 1 in (2·5 cm) of soil. Subsequently do not disturb even by hoeing, but remove weeds by hand. A mint bed can remain in the same place for years and if roots stray too far they can be chopped back with a spade or trowel at any time. Gather leaves as required.

Some roots can be lifted each autumn, placed in boxes of old potting soil and stood in a frame or greenhouse for early supplies.

Mustard This is grown in exactly the same way as cress, but since it germinates and grows more rapidly, it should be sown three days later than cress if it is to be cut at the same time.

Onions There are two ways of growing onions; from seed and from sets (small bulbs). Seed is cheaper, but on some soils, particularly those that are heavy, it is difficult to get good germination. Sets rarely fail and can be grown on any reasonably good soil.

Seed is sown in spring, in drills ½ in (1 cm) deep and 12 in (30 cm) apart, in rich, well-dug soil. Seedlings are thinned to 6 in (15 cm) apart. Bulbs are lifted in late summer or

early autumn when the tops begin to turn yellow, are laid out to dry in a shed or frame for a few days and are then stored in a dry, airy store shed in shallow trays or in strings made by plaiting the dry tops together.

For early use seed can be sown in late summer in drills 6 in (15 cm) apart in a frame or sheltered place outdoors, the seedlings being transplanted the following spring, 6 in (15 cm) apart in rows 12 in (30 cm) apart, in rich soil. Bulbs can be used in summer as they attain size.

Salad onions are grown from seed sown in spring and late summer as described for bulbing onions, but there is no thinning out, the seedlings being pulled for use as they attain sufficient size.

There are a great many varieties but not all are suitable for late summer sowing. Catalogues usually indicate these and also those which are good for salading.

Onion sets are planted in spring, 6 in (15 cm) apart in rows 12 in (30 cm) apart. A trowel can be used to make a little hole for each set, but it should be barely covered with soil. The bulbs are lifted and stored in late summer as for onions grown from seed.

Parsley Sow seed in spring and early summer in drills ½ in (1 cm) deep and thin seedlings to 6 in (15 cm) apart. Seed often takes three or four weeks to germinate.

Parsnips Sow seeds in good, well-dug soil, in spring in drills 1 in (2·5 cm) deep and 18 in (45 cm) apart. Space seeds thinly and thin seedlings to 8 in (20 cm) apart. Roots can be left in the ground in autumn and winter, being dug as required.

Peas Sow during spring and early summer in good rich soil, in drills 2 in (5 cm) deep or in very shallow flat trenches about 2 in (5 cm) deep scooped out with a spade. Scatter the seeds thinly about 2 in (5 cm) apart. There are many varieties ranging in height from 1½ to 5 ft (45 cm to 1·5 m). Even the short varieties are better for some support and the taller varieties must be supported, either with bushy sticks, such as hazel branches, pushed firmly into the soil, or with string or wire netting. Protection from birds may be needed as the pods swell. The pods should be picked as soon as they are reasonably well filled and before the peas begin to get hard.

Potato Grown from small potatoes, known as sets or seed potatoes. It is an advantage if these can be sprouted by standing them, eyed ends upwards, in shallow trays in a light but frost-proof place in late winter.

The sets, sprouted or unsprouted, should be planted in spring, 5 or 6 in (13 to 15 cm) deep and 12 to 15 in (30 to 38 cm) apart in rows 2½ ft (75 cm) apart. Soil should be well cultivated and enriched with animal manure or compost as well as a compound fertilizer

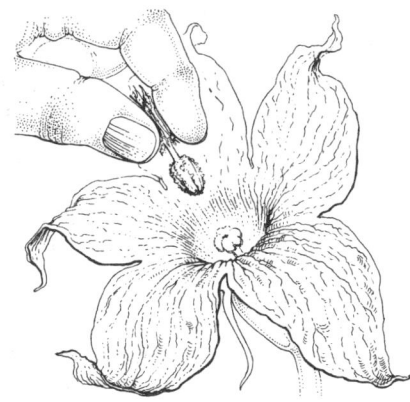

To set fruit, marrows must be pollinated by hand. A male flower is removed and pushed into the centre of the female flower

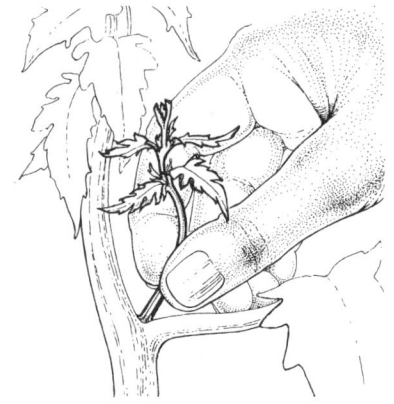

With the exception of bush varieties, all sideshoots are removed from tomato plants and the fruits limited to four or five trusses

prior to planting. When shoots appear, the soil is drawn over them from between the rows and this process of earthing up is continued in early summer until the soil is ridged to a height of 8 or 9 in (20 to 23 cm) along the rows.

There are early, second-early, maincrop and late varieties which differ in the time they take to reach maturity. Digging of earlies can commence 10 to 12 weeks after planting, second-earlies 12 to 16 weeks. Early varieties are generally used as they are dug and so are second-earlies, but maincrop and late varieties are usually lifted, when mature, for storing.

Stored potatoes must be kept in darkness and free from frost. They can be in sacks in frost-proof sheds or outhouses or may be clamped outdoors. This is done by placing a thick layer of clean straw on the ground, piling the potatoes on this in a cone or ridge, putting more straw over them to a thickness of at least 9 in (23 cm) and then throwing a layer of soil about 9 in (23 cm) thick over the straw and beating it down with the back of a spade.

Radishes Sow seed every fortnight in spring and the first half of summer in drills ½ in (1 cm) deep and 9 in (23 cm) apart, or scatter the seed broadcast all over the prepared soil and rake it in. Start pulling radishes as soon as they are large enough to use. They do best in rather rich soil.

Rhubarb Plant roots in spring 3 ft (1 m) apart in good rich soil. The crowns (tops of the roots) should just appear on the surface after planting. Without any special treatment, sticks can be pulled in late spring and summer, but not in the first year of planting.

For earlier supplies, strong roots are covered in winter with barrels, boxes, large flower pots, large drain pipes with a slate or tile on top, or special forcing pots. If possible heap straw, bracken or dry leaves over these, the object being to exclude light and keep the plants as warm as possible. Even earlier supplies are obtained by lifting roots

in autumn or winter and bringing them into a heated greenhouse or shed. They are replanted in soil, kept moist, and light is excluded. In a greenhouse this can often be done conveniently by planting under the staging and hanging sacks in front. Roots that have been forced in this way can be replanted outdoors afterwards but should not be forced again for at least two years.

Sage Purchase young plants in spring or raise from seeds or cuttings. Seed is sown in spring in a frame or outdoors or cuttings can be rooted in a frame in late summer. Whichever method is used the plants should eventually be placed in good, well-drained soil in a warm sunny position. Sage makes a small bush 12 to 18 in (30 to 45 cm) high and one or two plants are usually sufficient to meet the needs of a household. Plants will live undisturbed for years. Gather leaves as required and in summer cut some shoots, tie them in small bunches and hang in a dry, airy place to dry for storing.

Shallots Grown from small bulbs which are planted in late winter or early spring 9 in (23 cm) apart in rows 12 in (30 cm) apart. Planting is done by pressing the bulbs firmly into the loose soil so that they are almost buried.

About mid-summer, or soon after, growth will die down and the clusters of bulbs can be lifted and placed in a dry, sunny place for a few days, after which they are stored in boxes or trays in any cool, dry, airy place.

Spinach Seed is sown every three or four weeks in spring and summer in drills 1 in (2·5 cm) deep and 12 in (30 cm) apart. Seedlings are thinned to 3 in (8 cm) apart and picking of the leaves begins as soon as these are large enough to use.

One of the several varieties of summer, or round-seeded, spinach should be used for all except the last sowing, towards the end of summer, when the hardy winter, or prickly seeded, spinach should be used.

Swede Seed is sown in late spring or early summer in drills ½ in (1 cm) deep and 18 in (45 cm) apart and seedlings are thinned to 9 in (23 cm). Roots can be lifted as required in autumn and winter.

Sweet Corn Seed can be sown in mid-spring in small paper or peat pots in a frost-proof greenhouse or frame. Place two seeds in each pot, reduce to one seedling per pot and harden off for planting out in a warm, sheltered place in late spring or early summer, spacing the plants 2 ft (60 cm) apart each way. Alternatively, sow in late spring in the open ground where plants are to mature, putting three seeds into each hole 1 in (2·5 cm) deep and spacing these seed groups 2 ft (60 cm) apart. Later, seedlings will be thinned to one at each point. It is better to grow sweet corn in blocks rather than in single rows as the female flowers are then more likely to be fully fertilized.

The cobs are ready to gather as soon as the tassel at the end of a cob withers. Another test is to open the sheath-like covering of the cob and test a corn with the thumb nail. It should be firm but not hard.

Thyme This is grown in the same way as sage and again one or two plants may suffice for all ordinary needs. Thyme also likes warm sunny places and does particularly well on limestone or chalk soil.

Tomato These can be grown under glass or outdoors but for the latter purpose only quick-maturing varieties should be used. Seed for greenhouse cultivation is sown in late winter or early spring in a temperature of 18°C. (65°F.). Seedlings are pricked out and later potted singly in 3-in (8-cm) pots in John Innes or soilless compost. When well grown in these pots they are transferred to larger pots, 8 to 10 in (20 to 25 cm) in diameter, or boxes filled with J.I.P.3 compost, or they are planted directly in a bed of good soil in the greenhouse, spaced 18 in (45 cm) apart in rows at least 2 ft (60 cm) apart.

An alternative method is to plant in bottomless rings about 10 in (25 cm) wide and nearly as deep filled with J.I.P.3 and stood on a 6-in (15-cm) -thick bed of well-weathered boiler ashes or pea-size gravel. One tomato plant is put in each ring and well watered in, but subsequently water is applied only to the ashes or gravel, into which the plants will root. Spacing of the rings should be as for plants growing in soil beds.

Yet another way to grow tomatoes is in bags of specially prepared peat. These bags can be purchased ready for use. Lay flat on the ground, end to end, split open the upper side of each bag and fold the flaps of plastic under to form a kind of rim to the exposed peat, and plant three or four tomato plants in each bag. When using this

Vegetables all the year round

A chart showing sowing, planting and transplanting times, and availability from open ground or store

CROP	DEPTH TO SOW	DISTANCE BETWEEN ROWS	DISTANCE BETWEEN PLANTS	DISTANCE TO SOW OR THIN	JAN.	FEB.	MAR.	APR.	MAY	JUNE	JULY	AUG.	SEPT.	OCT.	NOV.	DEC.
ARTICHOKE																
Globe		4ft	3ft					▲				□	□	□		
Jerusalem	6in	2½ft	15in		□	▲□	□								□	□
Asparagus	2–3in	15in	18in					▲	□	□						
BEANS																
Broad	2in	2ft		6in	▨	▨	◉▨	◉▨	▨	□	□	□	▨	▨	◉▨	▨
French	1in	18in		6in	▨	▨	▨	◉▨	◉▨	▨	□	□	□	▨		▨
Haricot	1in	18in		8in	▨	▨	▨	◉▨	◉▨	▨	▨	□				
Runner	2in	8ft		8in	▨	▨	▨	▨	▨	◉▨	◉▨	□	□	□	▨	▨
Beet	1in	12–15in		6–8in	▨	▨	▨	◉▨	◉		□	□	□		▨	▨
Beet, Seakale	1in	18in		9in	□	□	◉□	□	□				◉□	▨	□	□
Borecole (Kale)	½in	2½ft	18in		□	□	□	◉	◉□		△	△			□	□
Broccoli	½in	2½ft	2ft		□	□	◉□	◉□	◉△□	△□				□	□	
Brussels Sprouts	½in	2½ft	2½ft		□	□	◉	◉	△	△			□	□	□	
CABBAGE																
Summer	½in	2ft	2ft					◉	△			□	□	□	□	
Autumn	½in	2ft	2ft					◉	△							
Winter	½in	2ft	2ft		□	□		◉	◉	△	△					□
Spring	½in	18in	1ft				△□	□	□	□	◉	◉	△	△		
Carrots	½in	8–15in		2–4in	▨	▨	◉▨	◉▨	◉▨	◉□	□	□	□	□	▨	▨
Cauliflower	½in	2½ft	2ft			◉	◉		△	△	□	□	□	□		
Celery	¼in	3ft	9in		□	◉□	◉□			△	△		□	□	□	
Cucumber, Ridge	1in	4ft	3ft					◉	◉	△	□	□				
Endive	½in	1ft		9in	□	□	□	◉	◉	◉	◉	◉□	□	□		□
Kohlrabi	½in	15in		9in				◉	◉	◉	◉□	◉□	□			
Leek	¼in	18in	1ft		□	□	◉□	□		△	△					
Lettuce	½in	9–12in		6–9in			◉	◉	◉	◉□	◉□	◉□	□	□		
Onion	½in	1ft		6in	▨	▨	◉▨				□	□	□	□◉	▨	▨
Onion Sets	½ covered	1ft	6in		▨		▲				□	□	▨	▨	▨	▨
Parsley	½in	9in		5in			◉	◉	◉	◉□	◉□	◉□	□			
Parsnip	1in	18in		8in	□	◉□	◉□	▨	▨	▨					□	□
Peas	2in	2–5ft		3in	▨	▨	◉▨	◉▨	◉▨	◉□	□	□		□		
POTATOES																
Early	4–5in	2½ft	1ft					▲			□	□				
Mid-season	4–5in	3ft	15in					▲				□	□	▨	▨	▨
Late	4–5in	3ft	15in		▨	▨	▨	▲▨	▨	▨	▨		▨	▨	▨	▨
Radish	½in	9in						◉	◉□	◉□	◉□	◉□	◉□	□		
Rhubarb		3ft	3ft				▲□	□	□	□	□					
Savoy	½in	2ft	18in		□	□	□	◉	◉	△	△	△		□	□	□
Shallots	½ covered	1ft	9in		▨	▲▨	▲▨				▨	▨	▨	▨	▨	▨
SPINACH																
Summer	1in	1ft		3in				◉	◉	◉□	◉□	◉□	□	□		
Winter	1in	1ft		6in	□	□	□					◉		□	□	□
Beet	1in	18in		9in	□	□	◉□	◉□		◉□	◉□	□	□			
Swede	½in	18in		8in	▨	▨	▨		◉	◉	◉			▨	▨	▨
Tomato	¼in	2ft	18in			⊞	⊞			△		□	□	□		
Turnip	½in	12–15in		4–8in	▨	▨	◉▨	◉▨	◉	◉	◉□			□	▨	
Vegetable Marrow	1in	4ft	3ft		▨	▨	▨	◉	◉	△		□	□	□	▨	▨

◉ *Sow* ⊞ *Sow under glass* ▲ *Plant* △ *Transplant* □ *Fresh from garden* ▨ *Available from store*

IMPERIAL	METRIC
$\frac{1}{4}$ in	0·5 cm
$\frac{1}{2}$	1
1	2·5
2	5
3	8
4	10
5	13
6	15
7	18
8	20
9	23
10	25
11	28
12 (1 ft)	30
15	38
18	45
2 ft	60
2$\frac{1}{2}$ ft	75
3 ft	1 m
4 ft	1·25 m
5 ft	1·5 m
6 ft	2 m

method be especially careful to water well so that the peat never gets really dry.

Whichever method is used, plants are trained up canes, strings or wires to which they must be tied frequently, or they can be wound around string. All side shoots are removed, each plant being restricted to a single stem. When this reaches the roof of the house, its growing tip is also broken out to prevent further growth.

As soon as the first fruits begin to form, plants are fed once a week with liquid fertilizer containing a fairly high percentage of potash. When plants are grown in rings, feeding is into the soil in these, not into the ashes or gravel.

For outdoor growing, seed is sown in early to mid-spring in a greenhouse or frame in a temperature of 18°C. (65°F.). The seedlings are treated in the same way up to the 3-in (8-cm) pot size, when they are hardened off for planting out in early summer in a warm, sunny, sheltered place. Space as for greenhouse plants, restrict each plant to a single stem and tie this to a cane firmly embedded in the soil. Pinch out the top of each plant as soon as it has produced four trusses of flowers. In autumn, when frost threatens, pick all remaining fruit, even if green, place in boxes and keep indoors to ripen, or green fruits can be used

to make chutney. Bush varieties are often favoured out of doors and require no staking or removal of side shoots or stopping. Plant 2 ft (60 cm) apart, and place straw or polythene under the plants in summer to keep the fruits clean.

Turnip Sow seed in spring and early summer in good soil in drills $\frac{1}{2}$ in (1 cm) deep and 12 in (30 cm) apart. Thin seedlings to 4 or 5 in (10 to 13 cm) and start pulling roots as soon as the most forward are fit for use. In autumn, lift remaining roots and store in sand in a sheltered shed or outhouse.

Vegetable Marrow Sow the seeds in pairs in 3-in (8-cm) pots in mid-spring and germinate in a greenhouse or frame in a temperature of 18°C. (65°F.). Thin the seedlings to one per pot and harden off for planting outdoors in late spring or early summer. Plant 3 ft (1 m) apart in very rich soil and keep well watered. Alternatively, sow seeds, two or three together, in clusters 3 ft (1 m) apart in late spring where they are to grow, covering with $\frac{1}{2}$ in (1 cm) of soil and thinning seedlings to one at each cluster.

Marrows should be cut when large enough for use. Any remaining in autumn when frost threatens may be cut and stored in a dry, airy, frost-proof place.

Home-grown Fruit

The range of possible fruits for the garden is great, from the strawberry, a herbaceous plant occupying only a square foot or so of ground, to the apple, pear, plum or cherry, any one of which can produce a large tree 20 ft (6 m) high and as much in diameter. Between these extremes are cane fruits, such as the raspberry, loganberry and blackberry, which can be trained to wires or against fences, and bush fruits, such as the gooseberry and currant, which are shrubby in habit and occupy as much space as a moderate-sized shrub.

There is nothing particularly ornamental about a strawberry, raspberry, gooseberry

or black currant, but red and white currants can be quite attractive when in fruit and well-grown apples and pears really add something to the appearance of the garden, both when in flower and in fruit.

Another point that must be considered is that fruit often requires rather special attention. It is not always easy to fit in fruit with other plants and the idea that a few fruit trees can be planted in the middle of the vegetable garden is likely to result in poor fruit as well as inferior vegetables.

The ideal thing is to keep fruit in a section to itself, but, where space forbids this, fruit should at least be kept sufficiently

separate to enable it to be sprayed, thinned, pruned, fed and picked without interference with other plants nearby.

Propagation and Training

Gooseberries and currants are produced from cuttings which are grown on for two or three years by nurserymen and sold as young bushes of an age for fruiting. Raspberries are grown from suckers produced quite naturally by the plants and these start fruiting in their second year. Strawberries are produced from little plantlets on runners which grow naturally from the

Apples grown as cordons produce plenty of fruit in a relatively small space

Fruit tree forms, clockwise from top: espalier, cordon, fan, pyramid

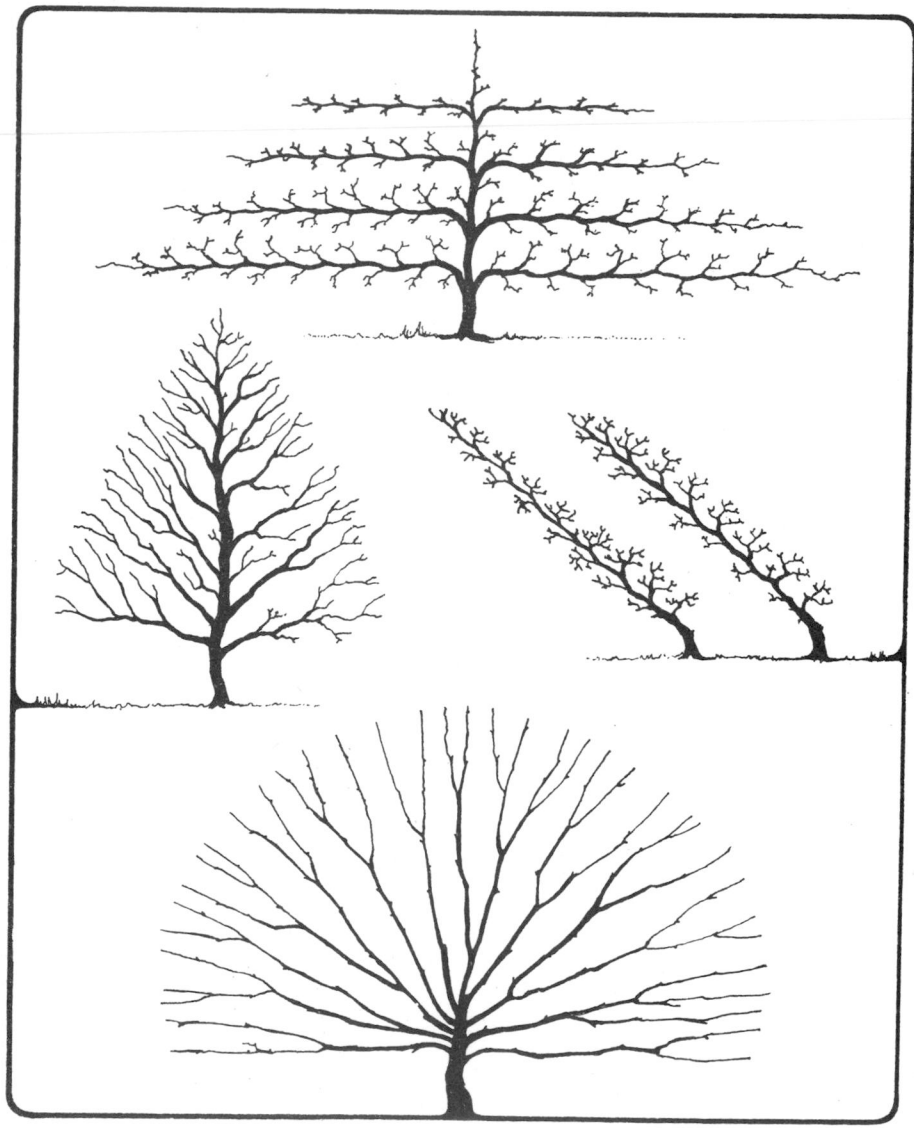

mature plants, and will fruit in the summer following planting, but more freely the second year.

All these plants are said to be grown on their own roots. This means that the plant or bush is of the same kind throughout, its roots having been produced by natural processes from its above-ground parts.

Grafted Tree Fruits This is not so with the tree fruits; apples, pears, plums, cherries, etc. Only very rarely are these on their own roots, and never when purchased in the normal way from nurserymen. This is for two reasons; one is that they are difficult to increase by cuttings or layering, the other is that by grafting them on to a different rootstock very substantial advantages can be gained.

Grafting is an operation whereby a shoot or growth-bud of one plant is joined to the roots of another, which is subsequently prevented from producing any more top growth of its own. A grafted plant is therefore a union of two different, and even dissimilar, plants, one of which, known as the scion, provides all the branches, and the other, known as the stock, provides all the roots.

The two parts, though completely and permanently joined together, continue to preserve their own individuality, the scion producing the stems, leaves, flowers and fruit characteristic of it, and the stock its own particular kind of root system. But though the two parts do not intermingle, they do exert an effect upon one another. A given variety of apple, for example, may grow more rapidly and make a bigger tree on one rootstock than upon another, or it may start to fruit at a younger age.

Dwarfing and Vigorous Stocks A great many rootstocks have been tested and classified for just these kinds of effect. Those that restrict the growth of trees are known as dwarfing stocks and those that encourage growth are known as vigorous stocks. Invariably the dwarfing stocks encourage early fruiting and as a rule the more vigorous the stock the slower is the tree grafted on it to come into bearing.

All this is obviously of the greatest possible interest to the owner of a small- to medium-sized garden. Fruit trees of restricted size that start to fruit almost at once are likely to be much more suitable than very large fruit trees that may not bear much for eight or ten years.

The Malling Apple Stocks There are so many stocks available for apples that they have been given numbers preceded by a letter; M for Malling, indicating that the stock was selected at the East Malling Research Station, and MM for Malling-Merton, indicating that it was produced jointly by this station and the John Innes Horticultural Institution. Thus M 2, M 7, M 9, M 16, M 25 and M 26 are all useful apple stocks in the Malling range and MM 106 and MM 111 are two good apple

136

An exceptionally well grown fan-trained pear taken up the side of a cottage

stocks in the Malling-Merton range. M 9 gives the smallest tree and the earliest fruit but on poor soil or with varieties of naturally weak growth it can be too dwarfing. M 7, M 26, and MM 106 are not quite so restrictive and are probably the three best apple stocks for most gardens. M 2 and MM 111 are fairly vigorous and suitable where sturdy bushes are required. M 25 is the most vigorous of all and very suitable for standard apple trees.

Pear Stocks With pears there is not such a wide selection. Quince stocks are commonly used and are fairly dwarfing, that known as Quince C being more dwarfing than Quince B, which in turn is more dwarfing than Quince A. Seedling pear stock grows a much larger tree.

The Single Stem Cordon It is not necessary for the amateur gardener to become an expert on fruit stocks, for the nurseryman from whom he buys his trees should be able to provide them on stocks suitable for the purpose for which they are required, but the gardener should know that different stocks exist and he should have a general idea of what influence they have on his trees.

By using a dwarfing stock it is possible to restrict a fruit tree to a single stem, no more than 7 or 8 ft (2·25 to 2·5 m) in length, and still pick worthwhile crops from it. Such trees are known as single stem cordons and they are very useful in the small garden. They can be planted in rows, the cordons

as close as 2 ft (60 cm) apart with 5 or 6 ft (1·5 to 2 m) between the rows. A single row of apple or pear cordons can make a most attractive screen between one section of the garden and another, may be grown against a fence or may border a path.

Espalier Another way of training fruit trees is the espalier. This is a French name for a post and wire fence but it is also used for fruit trees trained to grow against such a fence. Each espalier or horizontal-trained tree has a stout central stem from which grow horizontal arms in one plane only. The arms are spaced about 15 in (38 cm) apart and there may be three, four or five tiers of these arms, giving a tree from 4 to 7 ft (1·25 to 2·25 m) in height. Espaliers are usually spaced about 8 ft (2·5 m) apart so that, after a few years, their horizontal arms meet and they make a continuous fence or screen. They can be highly decorative but need a little more management than cordons. Espaliers need not be trained against wire fences; they are equally suitable for training against walls.

The Fan A third form of trained tree, particularly suitable for walls and fences, is the fan. In this the main branches radiate from one place like the ribs of a fan. It is a form of training that suits plums, cherries, peaches and nectarines better than either the cordon or the espalier form as it allows for a lighter system of pruning, to which these trees respond.

Soil Preparation and Planting

The details of soil preparation and of planting are exactly the same for fruit trees and plants as they are for ornamental trees, shrubs and herbaceous plants. Like them they will occupy the ground for a considerable time, during which it will not be possible to dig or fork the soil deeply, so the initial cultivation should be thorough and the ground clear of weeds at the time of planting.

All the large fruits need secure staking or, if they are grown against walls or fences, secure tying. Autumn and winter are the best times for planting everything except strawberries, which are best planted in late summer but, failing this, they can be planted in early autumn or spring.

Pruning

It is the pruning of fruit trees that seems most puzzling to the inexperienced and this is not surprising for even the experts differ in the methods they advise. However, it is possible to reduce pruning to quite simple rule-of-thumb methods which will give good results.

Cane Fruits Taking the simplest first of all; the cane fruits, a term which includes raspberries, loganberries and blackberries, bear their fruit on one-year-old stems or canes. These canes are produced during the

late spring and summer and one lot of young canes will be growing up while the previous lot is fruiting. As soon as the fruit has been gathered, the old canes that have borne the crop are cut right out and the young canes take over. If there are too many of them – and from five to seven per root is usually enough – the excess can be cut out at the same time. The ones to retain are the strongest and most conveniently placed for training.

Exception to this general rule must be made for autumn-fruiting raspberries which crop on the current year's growth. All canes are cut practically to ground level in late winter and the best of the new canes are retained for fruiting, others that would cause overcrowding being cut out at an early stage.

Black Currant The pruning of black currant is not dissimilar to that of cane fruits for this also bears its fruit best on year-old stems. As soon as the fruit has been picked, or at any time during the autumn or winter, as many as possible of the stems that have borne fruit are cut out, but all the strong young stems are retained. It may not be possible to cut out all the old stems, because some good young stems may be growing from them. The new growth does not all come from the base or from the roots, as it does with raspberries, loganberries and blackberries, so a little common sense is required. The rule should be to get rid of as much as possible of the old without wasting anything good of the new.

Peaches, Nectarines and Morello Cherries Again there is a similarity between pruning black currants and the pruning of peaches, nectarines and morello cherries. All fruit on year-old stems and the aim is to get rid of the old fruiting stems and replace them with the profitable young ones. Sometimes the trees need a little assistance to make enough young growth to replace the old. This is done, in late spring and early summer, by thinning out the young shoots a little at a time until there are only about three to each fruiting stem; one somewhere near its base, one about half way up, the third at

Summer-fruiting raspberries are pruned by removing the fruiting stems as soon as the crop has been picked

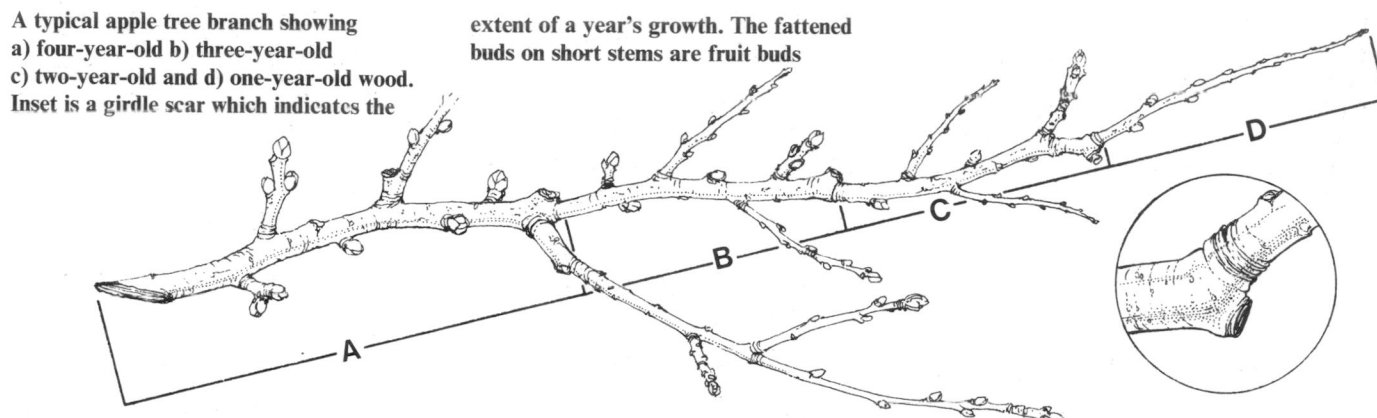

A typical apple tree branch showing a) four-year-old b) three-year-old c) two-year-old and d) one-year-old wood. Inset is a girdle scar which indicates the extent of a year's growth. The fattened buds on short stems are fruit buds

the tip. The last two are left to draw sap up through the stem and help to swell the fruit. It is the shoot near the base that will be retained at pruning time, after fruit has been gathered or in the autumn or winter. The rest of the fruiting stem is then cut out and the young basal shoot trained in its place.

Apples, Pears and Red and White Currants
When we come to look at apples, pears and red and white currants we find a quite different system of bearing fruit. It is not carried on the year-old stems but on older branches and in particular on short side growths from them that are composed almost entirely of fruit buds. They are quite unlike any other shoots, indeed they are not shoots at all in the popular sense but little congested clusters of fat buds. They are called 'spurs' and they are very important as the whole object of pruning is to encourage their formation.

A tree left to its own devices will produce spurs freely along the length of stems two years and more old. But a completely un-pruned tree soon becomes such a tangle of growth that it is difficult to do anything with it, even to pick the fruit, and this may be produced in such quantity that indi-vidually the fruits tend to be small.

The easiest way to prune apples and pears is simply, in autumn or winter, to thin out the older branches so that the tree does not get overcrowded. Particular attention should be paid to the centre of the tree which should be kept fairly open so that light and air can penetrate and the fruit grower can get in to pick the fruit. If two branches cross and cut off the light one from another, one should be removed. If the trees get too big some of the branches can be cut back. Where possible the cut should be made at a fork so that another smaller branch continues to draw sap up through the stump. This is known as de-horning and may only be necessary every eight or ten years – perhaps not at all if the trees were grafted on fairly dwarfing stocks. It is trees on vigorous stocks that tend to get out of hand and grow so tall that it is very difficult to gather fruit from the topmost branches.

This kind of common-sense thinning, and occasional de-horning, is known as regulated pruning. It is suitable for trees grown in

more or less natural shapes, as bushes with a head of branches on a short leg or main trunk, or as standards with a head of branches on a taller trunk. It is not suitable for trained trees, such as cordons or espaliers, which must be restricted to a much more formal plan imposed upon them by the gardener.

For these pruning must be done in sum-mer, as this has the effect of depriving the trees of a lot of leaves and so restricting their growth. The work is usually done a little after mid-summer but it is the state of growth rather than the calendar date that really matters. By late spring fruit trees are usually growing fast and they continue to do so for several summer weeks. Then they slow down and the young shoots begin to change colour and texture, becoming browner and harder, particularly near the base. This is the signal to start summer pruning.

The operation itself is quite simple. All the young stems, except those extending the ends of branches, are shortened to a few inches. At the base of each young shoot there is a little cluster of very small leaves; ignore these. Above this basal rosette are the properly developed leaves. The shoot should be cut off just above the fourth or fifth of these leaves. In autumn or winter these summer-pruned shoots should be further shortened to 1 or 2 in (2·5 to 5 cm).

The only other pruning that trained apples and pears need is a shortening of the leading stems, that is, those that are extend-ing the ends of the branches. In a cordon tree only one such leader is needed at the summit of the tree. It is left unpruned until the cordon reaches the maximum desired height, after which it is cut out. In an espalier there will be one leader at the summit and one at the end of each hori-zontal branch or arm. Each should be shortened to about 15 in (38 cm). Only one new shoot will be required the following spring at the end of each horizontal arm to extend it still further, but three shoots can be retained at the top of the tree; one to go straight upwards and so increase its height and two to be trained to right and left as a further tier of horizontal arms. When all available space is filled, or the espaliers have reached the maximum desired height,

all further extension shoots are removed.

Sweet Cherries Sweet cherries are pruned in a similar way, except that when the shape of large trees is regulated the work is done in late summer or early autumn. This is to lessen danger of infection by a disease known as bacterial canker which is liable to enter through wounds in late autumn or winter.

Plums Bush and standard plum trees are usually regulated, the work being done as soon as the crop has been gathered. When plums are trained, the fan form is usually adopted and summer pruning is applied, but rather earlier than for apples and pears. About mid-summer, or even a week or so before, each young shoot is shortened by a few inches. Plums do not submit so well to really severe pruning and so are seldom grown either as single stem cordons or as espaliers.

Pruning After Planting

The first pruning after transplanting should usually be rather more severe than that which follows. This is essential with all cane fruits which should be cut to within 4 in (10 cm) of ground level, and usually also with blackcurrants which should be cut back to about 6 in (15 cm). Weak gooseberry and red currant bushes may be similarly hard pruned but strong bushes can be treated more lightly and permitted to carry some fruit the first year.

Thinning

Left to their own devices some fruit trees produce more fruit than they can mature to a satisfactory size and therefore the young fruits need to be thinned. This is most likely to occur with cooking apples, which need to be individually large. The thinning is commenced when the fruits are no larger than marbles but it should not be completed until after mid-summer as quite often there is a considerable natural drop of fruit about then. Peaches may also need thinning if they are carrying a big crop and this, too, is done in stages, completion being left until the stones have formed within the fruits, a condition that can be ascertained by cutting a fruit in half.

Failure to Fruit

One of the biggest problems for inexperienced fruit growers is the tree that fails to fruit. When this happens occasionally, it can usually be attributed to bad weather at blossom time. In order to set fruit, blossom must be fertilized and with some fruits the pollen, to effect fertilization, must be brought from other neighbouring trees. This is largely the work of bees, though other insects and wind assist. If weather is wet or cold when blossom is open there may be too few bees about to effect pollination or the pollen may be too damp to be readily blown about by wind.

Frost Damage Another possibility is that the blossom itself has been damaged by frost. The trees themselves may be perfectly hardy but fruit blossom is not. Even a few degrees of frost, continued for an hour or so, is sufficient to damage it so badly that it cannot be fertilized, and this is quite likely to happen in spring in low-lying places where cold air can collect.

There is not much that can be done about weather damage to fruit blossom except to avoid planting fruit in cold hollows. Sometimes it is possible to protect small bushes or wall trees with netting or old curtains, and strawberry flowers may be protected by placing cloches over the plants.

Other Reasons for Failure Quite often failure to fruit can be traced to a quite different cause – failure to flower. If there are no flowers there cannot be any fruits, and lack of flowers may be due to incorrect pruning, the use of an unsuitable rootstock, bad feeding, or it may simply indicate that the tree is too young.

Some fruit trees only bear if they are fertilized with pollen from another fruit tree of the same kind but of a different variety. Commercial apple growers always plant two varieties together for this reason; for example, apple Cox's Orange Pippin with apple Worcester Pearmain. The lone fruit tree is often barren because it lacks a mate or, if it has one, the mate flowers at a slightly different time or produces pollen which is incompatible. All good fruit nurseries can give advice as to which varieties pollinate each other most effectively.

Spraying

Most plants are subject to a variety of pests and diseases and some require routine spraying to keep them clean and in good health. However, at least one of the worst diseases of apples and pears, scab, is far less likely to prove troublesome in gardens situated in areas where there is considerable smoke since the sulphur left in the air acts as a kind of permanent mild fumigation, killing the spores of the scab disease before they have time to do much harm.

Three-Period Programme Broadly speaking the spray programme for fruit trees and bushes divides into three periods. In winter, when there are no leaves on the trees, winter washes such as tar-oil or DNOC are applied to clean the bark and to kill the eggs of insects. Then, in the spring, fungicides are applied to kill the spores of various diseases and sometimes insecticides are added to these to kill any early caterpillars that have escaped the winter spray. Finally, in summer, insecticides are applied several times to deal with particular pests which appear at specific times, and further periodic spraying with fungicides may be necessary to control diseases such as scab and mildew.

Picking

It is quite obvious when to pick a strawberry, a raspberry or a currant. The fruit turns colour and becomes pleasant to eat, and since it will not continue in this condition for more than a few days, it must be picked and used.

There is a little more latitude with gooseberries as they can be used unripe for cooking or ripe for dessert. As a rule, picking begins directly the fruits are large enough to be serviceable for cooking but at this stage it is a thinning, rather than a clearing operation. Quite a lot of fruits are left to get larger and to be further thinned until finally some reach full size and ripeness.

Plums, cherries, peaches and nectarines are fruits in which ripeness, readiness for use and picking time all coincide. With apples and pears this is only true of the early varieties, those that are ready to eat in the late summer or early autumn.

A Simple Test Mid-season and late varieties of apple and pear are picked before they are fully ripe, or perhaps it would be more correct to say that they have two periods of ripeness, one when they are ready to part from the tree, the other when they have acquired their full flavour and correct texture and are ready to be eaten. Most of these later apples are picked in mid-autumn but there is a simple test for readiness for harvesting. A fruit is grasped gently and lifted with the thumb pressing downwards on the stalk. If it parts readily and cleanly from the tree it is ready to pick and it is probable that most of the other fruits on that tree are also ready.

Some operations, notably the application of chemicals to control pests and diseases, must be timed by the state of growth. Important stages in apple tree development are: a) Breaking; the bud scales loosening and opening b) Bud burst; tips of leaves showing c) Mouse ear; individual leaves more clearly visible d) Green cluster; flower buds visible in tight clusters but still entirely green e) Pink bud; flowers still closed but looser and showing petal colours f) Petal fall g) Fruitlet; the fruits clearly visible and pea sized

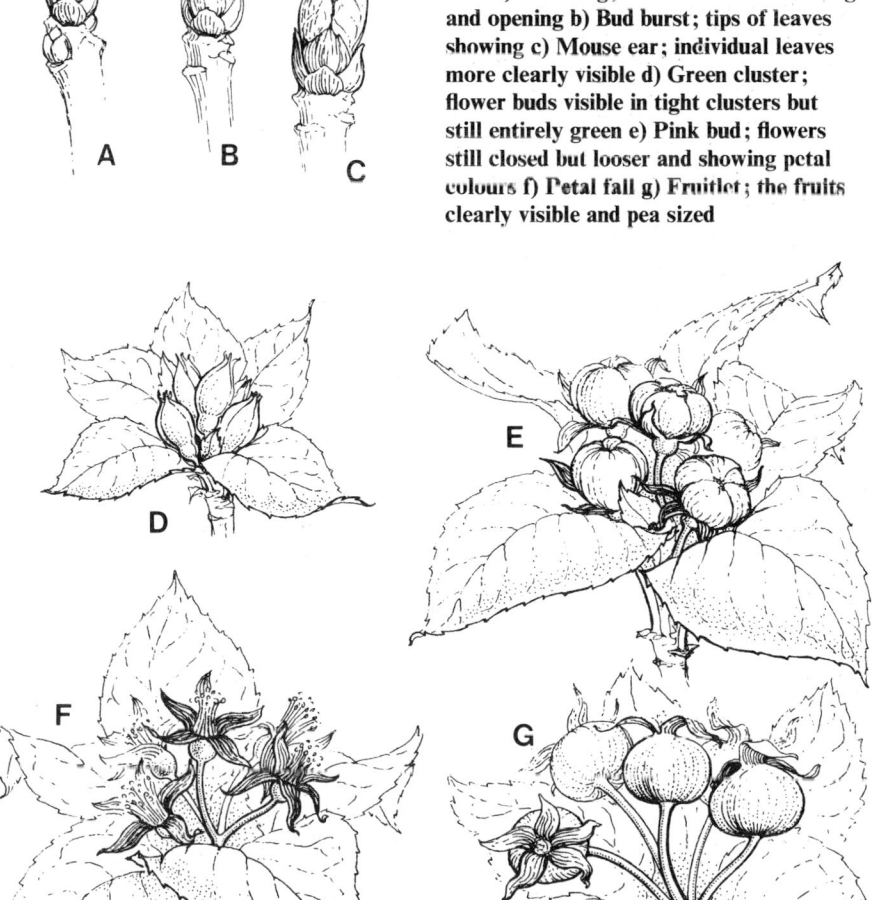

As soon as apples are ripe they will part from the tree if gently twisted

Planting and Cultural Advice

Apples These can be obtained as single stem cordons, espaliers, bushes, pyramids, half-standards and standards. They will grow well in any reasonably good and properly drained soil and like an open, sunny situation with free circulation of air. A few varieties, notably Bramley's Seedling, Blenheim Orange and Ribston Pippin, are self-sterile, which means that their flowers will only set fruit if fertilized with pollen from a different variety of apple. Such varieties are unsuitable for planting alone. Other varieties will fruit even in complete isolation from other varieties but all fruit more freely if other varieties, flowering at approximately the same time, are growing nearby.

Apples are nearly always grafted or budded on to a stock and, for garden planting, stocks that encourage early fruitfulness and only a moderate amount of growth are best, such as M 7, M 9, and MM 106.

Some apples ripen on the tree in late summer or early autumn. These are known as early varieties. Others are not fully ripe at the time they are about to fall and must therefore be stored for a while, those that ripen quickly in store being known as mid-season varieties and those that are not ready until mid-winter or later as late varieties.

Apples are picked when they part readily from the tree. They store best in a cool, rather moist atmosphere such as a shed with an earthen floor. In warm dry rooms they are apt to shrivel.

In gardens, scab is the commonest disease. It produces black blotches on the leaves and dark scabs, sometimes developing into cracks, on the fruits. It is controlled by spraying with captan or lime sulphur in spring and summer. Greenfly may attack the leaves and young shoots in spring and summer. They can be killed by spraying with malathion, lindane or derris as soon as seen.

Caterpillars may eat the young leaves. They can be killed by spraying with lindane or diazinon as soon as seen.

Maggoty apples are due to attacks by the grubs of the apply sawfly in early summer or the caterpillars of the codling moth a few weeks later. These can be controlled by protective spraying in late spring or early summer with lindane or derris.

Apples should be fed annually in late winter with a compound fertilizer supplying nitrogen and potash. Special fruit fertilizers are prepared by most fertilizer manufacturers, or a general fertilizer such as National Growmore can be used.

Trained apples are usually pruned in summer and autumn or winter. Large bush, half-standard and standard apples are usually pruned lightly in autumn or winter.

Some varieties of apple are only suitable for cooking, some only for dessert, while a few, known as dual-purpose apples, can be used either for cooking or for dessert.

RECOMMENDED VARIETIES

FOR COOKING	FOR USE
Arthur Turner	mid-season
Bramley's Seedling	mid to late
Early Victoria	early
Edward VII	late
Grenadier	early to mid
Lane's Prince Albert	late

FOR DESSERT	
Beauty of Bath	early
Cox's Orange Pippin	late
Egremont Russet	mid-season
Ellison's Orange	mid-season
Epicure	early
Fortune	mid-season
James Grieve	early
Lord Lambourne	mid-season
Sunset	mid-season
Tydeman's Late Orange	late

Blackberries There are excellent cultivated varieties of blackberry, such as Parsley-leaved, John Innes and Merton Thornless, which are well worth growing in the garden trained on fences or against wires strained between posts. They will thrive in any reasonable soil and sunny place, are not much attacked by pests or diseases and are pruned after the crop has been gathered in summer, when all canes that have fruited are cut out and the best of the young are tied in their place.

Cherry The sweet or dessert cherries are all vigorous and as no really dwarfing stocks are available for them, they are not very suitable for small gardens. Moreover, they are all self-sterile, which means that each variety is unable to set fruit when pollinated with its own pollen. Not only must it have pollen from another cherry but it must be a cherry of a particular group, so two sweet cherries are the minimum for a garden unless a neighbour will co-operate and grow one that is a suitable pollinator. Each tree will reach a height and spread of 20ft (6m), perhaps more, but it will pay for its space by carrying a splendid crop of white blossom each spring, followed by white, black or red fruits.

By contrast the best of the sour or cooking cherries, the morello, makes a quite low, rather spreading tree and does not at all mind being trained in the form of a fan against a wall or fence. Moreover, it is fully self-fertile and so one morello cherry can be planted with every prospect of a good crop of its handsome black fruits every year. The method of pruning these fan-trained trees is as for fan-trained peaches.

All cherries like light, well-drained soils and do well on chalk add limestone. Sweet cherries should be pruned lightly after the crop has been gathered, all that is necessary being to remove badly placed or over-crowded branches.

The principal disease is bacterial canker which often attacks trees at the crotch or point of branching. The bark is killed and gum may exude in quantity. Round holes appear in the leaves and whole branches wither and die. Such branches should be cut off and trees may be sprayed with a copper fungicide such as Bordeaux mixture in late summer or early autumn but this is a difficult disease to control. Fortunately it rarely attacks the morello cherry.

Suitable varieties of sweet cherry to plant, any one of which will pollinate any other, are Bigarreau Napoleon, yellow to red, late; Governor Wood, yellow to red, mid-season; Kent Bigarreau, yellow to red, mid-season; Merton Bigarreau, black, late, and Early Rivers, black fruits, mid-season.

Currant, Black Usually grown as bushes but if these are planted about 3ft (1m) apart they will soon meet and can be used as a screen or division between one part of the garden and another. Black currants like rich, rather moist soil and will grow in full sun or partial shade. They may be pruned either immediately after fruiting or in autumn or winter, and as many as possible of the old stems are cut out but all the strong young stems are retained.

The principal pest is the big bud mite, which infests the buds and causes them to swell up in winter. Such buds should be picked off and burned and the bushes sprayed with lime sulphur in spring when the trusses of unopened flowers hang like tiny bunches of green grapes.

The principal disease is reversion, caused by a virus which may be spread from bush to bush by the big bud mite. The leaves become smaller, bunched at the tips of the shoots and with fewer and less well-defined lobes. There is no cure and affected bushes should be dug up and burned.

Recommended varieties are Boskoop Giant and Mendip Cross, early; Wellington XXX, mid-season, and Amos Black and Baldwin, late.

Currant, Red and White The red and white currants are simply colour variations of the same fruit. They grow and fruit in exactly the same way and require similar soil and treatment. But they are quite distinct from the black currant, have a different origin and require different treatment.

The red and white currants like ordinary soil which is reasonably well drained and moderately rich. They stand pruning well and can be grown as cordons with one, two or three main stems, as well as in the more ordinary form of bushes which will attain a height of 4 or 5 ft (1·25 to 1·5 m) and similar spread but can be kept smaller by pruning.

Red and white currants bear their fruit on the older branches. Pruning is usually done in autumn when all side shoots are cut back to within about an inch of the main branches, which themselves can be allowed to extend until available space is filled. When trained as cordons, sideshoots can be shortened in summer exactly as with apples and pears.

These currants do not suffer greatly from pests or diseases, though greenfly sometimes attacks them. If it does, spray at once with malathion or derris.

Good varieties are Laxtons No. 1 and Red Lake, red, and White Dutch and White Versailles, white.

Gooseberry These grow well in most soils and are not at all difficult to manage. Usually they are grown as bushes, the branches of which are simply thinned each autumn to prevent them becoming overcrowded. When thinning, it is the oldest stems that should be removed and the sturdiest of the younger stems (which can be distinguished by their smoother, lighter coloured bark) retained. But where space is limited, gooseberries can be trained as cordons with one, two or three main stems, in which case all side shoots are cut back to about an inch each autumn or they can be summer and autumn pruned like apples and pears.

Gooseberries should be fed each year in late winter with a compound fertilizer rich in potash. They are occasionally severely attacked by caterpillars, when they should be sprayed at once with derris or lindane. The most troublesome disease is American gooseberry mildew, which produces a dense, felt-like mould on fruits and leaves. If this disease proves troublesome gooseberries should be sprayed in late spring and early summer just before the flowers open, at fruit set, and fruit swelling, 14–21 days later, with dinocap. There are green, yellow and red and white varieties. Good examples of each are Keepsake, green; Leveller, yellow; Whinham's Industry, red, and Careless, white.

Gooseberry pruning involves the removal of old stems and a light tipping back of the younger growths

Peach and Nectarine These fruits, though superficially different, are actually closely connected, the nectarine simply being a smooth-skinned version of the peach. It follows that their cultivation is identical. Since both flower very early in the spring and their blossom is easily destroyed by frost, they are more suitable for warm and sheltered than for cold and exposed places. They thrive in good, well-drained soils and may readily be trained in fan formation against a wall or fence. A sunny situation suits them best.

They bear their fruit on year-old stems and the object in pruning is to ensure a sufficiency of these (see p. 137).

The fruits themselves should be thinned, a little at a time, starting when they are the size of cobnuts and finishing when the stones have formed in them. One fruit to every square foot (30 cm square) is a fair average.

Late-ripening varieties are only suitable for greenhouse cultivation, except in very mild places. Good early or mid-season varieties of peach are Duke of York and Peregrine, and of nectarine Early Rivers and Lord Napier.

The most troublesome disease is leaf curl which causes a thickening, reddening and curling of the leaves. It can be checked by spraying in late winter or spring with a copper fungicide such as Bordeaux mixture.

Pears These like good, well-drained soils and warm, sunny positions. They make excellent trained trees in single stem cordon or espalier (horizontal) form but for this purpose they must be grafted on the quince stock, which is moderately dwarfing.

Nurserymen sometimes use seedling pear as a stock and this makes a much larger tree not really suitable for gardens.

As with apples, there are a few varieties of pears which are completely self-sterile; this means that they cannot produce a crop unless pollinated by a different variety of pear. Jargonelle, Pitmaston Duchess, Vicar of Winkfield and Marguerite Marillat are of this kind. Most varieties will produce some fruit if the blossom is self-pollinated but all bear much better crops if fertilized with pollen from other varieties. It is, therefore, unwise to plant pears in isolation.

Pears are pruned just like apples, the trained trees in summer, with a little further tidying up in autumn or winter, bush and standard trees in autumn or winter mainly by thinning out overcrowded branches and shortening any that are getting too long for convenience.

Pears that ripen at the end of summer or early autumn are eaten as soon as they part readily from the tree. Later pears may be picked in mid-autumn and stored until they are ripe but it is sometimes rather difficult to tell when this is. The ripening process with pears is more sudden than it is with apples and they must be watched more closely. Ripening fruits feel softer, particularly around the stalk, and develop a characteristic smell, but often the only reliable test is to cut a sample fruit in half. Pears must be stored in a drier, warmer atmosphere than apples. A room or airy cupboard suits them well or a shed with a wooden floor.

Strawberries can be propagated by pegging their runners into pots sunk in the ground and severing them when established

Some varieties suffer badly from scab disease and these should be avoided in gardens. Aphids may attack the leaves and young shoots but can be controlled by spraying with malathion, lindane or derris as soon as these pests are seen.

Reliable varieties for the garden are Jargonelle, early; Beurré Hardy, Conference and Beurré Superfin, all mid-season, and Josephine de Malines, late. Near large towns or in fairly dry areas, where scab disease is not troublesome, Williams' Bon Chrétien, early, and Doyenné du Comice, mid-season to late, can also be planted.

Plums The principal difficulty about plums in the garden is that they tend to make big trees and do not take kindly to hard pruning, but some varieties are fully self-fertile and one such tree on its own can be expected to produce good crops. If there is room for one fairly large standard tree it might well be an easily grown plum, such as Victoria, Pershore Egg or Warwickshire Drooper. But these are not fruits of the highest quality and the delicious gage plums, such as the Old Greengage, Laxton's Early Gage and Dennistons Superb, are more difficult to grow. Fortunately they are also less vigorous and if grafted on the Mussel or Brompton stock make good fan-trained trees for sunny walls and fences.

All plums like good, well-drained but not dry soils. Bushes and standard trees only need light pruning, mainly the thinning of overcrowded branches and shortening of any that grow too long, and this is best done in late summer as soon as the crop has been gathered.

Trained trees are summer pruned, badly placed shoots being rubbed out early and the tips of others pinched out when they are 5 or 6 in (13 to 15 cm) long. By this means the whole available wall or fence space can be covered without overcrowding.

The worst disease of plums is silver leaf, caused by a fungus which gets right into the branches. The leaves develop a very distinctive silvery sheen in summer, not to be confused with mildew which causes a powdery white outgrowth on the surface of the leaf. Branches showing leaf silvering should be cut off and burned at once and wounds painted with Stockholm tar, warm grafting wax or a tree wound dressing.

A particular blue-grey aphis attacks plums causing the leaves to crinkle and become sticky. It can be controlled by spraying as soon as it is seen with malathion, lindane or derris.

Raspberry The fruits of summer-ripening varieties are borne on year-old canes produced directly from the roots and after fruiting their place is taken by a new growth of canes. Autumn-ripening varieties bear on the current year's growth. The soil in which raspberries are planted must be sufficiently rich to support this annual cane growth and at the same time nourish the ripening crop of fruit. For this reason, and also because they do not like being dried out in summer, raspberries benefit from an annual dressing of well-rotted manure or garden refuse spread an inch or two thick for a width of 2 or 3 ft (60 cm to 1 m) on either side of each row every spring.

Young canes are planted in autumn or winter, 18 in (45 cm) apart in rows 6 ft (2 m) apart and are immediately cut back to within 4 in (10 cm) of ground level. No fruit will be produced the first summer, except perhaps in autumn varieties, but each root should produce several new canes which are tied to wires stretched between strong posts driven firmly into the ground and extending at least 5½ ft (1·75 m) above the ground. Two wires, one at 3 ft (1 m), the other at 5½ ft (1·75 m), are usually sufficient.

These canes will fruit the following summer and as soon as the crop has been gathered are cut out. Young canes are trained in their place but not more than about seven per root. If more grow, the weakest, or those furthest from the row, are cut out. Autumn varieties are pruned in a different way, the previous year's canes being cut almost to soil level in late winter.

Three of the most reliable varieties are Malling Exploit, Malling Promise and Norfolk Giant. Lloyd George is superior in flavour and gives some autumn fruits as well

as a summer crop, but it is susceptible to virus disease. September is a good autumn-ripening variety.

Virus is the commonest disease of raspberries. It stunts growth, reduces the crop and causes a mottled yellowing of the leaves. There is no cure and affected plants should be destroyed.

Strawberry There are three main classes of strawberry; the summer-fruiting varieties, which have large fruits ripening early in mid-summer; the perpetual or remontant varieties, which produce smaller fruits more or less continuously from mid-summer to autumn, and alpine strawberries which are also small fruited and continuous cropping but which produce no runners and so must be raised from seed sown in a frame or sheltered place in spring.

All strawberries like good, well-cultivated soil, neither very dry nor waterlogged. They deteriorate quickly and plantations should be remade at least every three years.

Most strawberries produce runners in summer and along the length of these are small plantlets which root themselves into the soil. These runners must be removed except when required for producing new stock. Even then only about four per plant should be retained, from healthy plants only, and only one plantlet, that nearest to the parent plant, should be retained on each runner. This plantlet is pegged with a piece of wire, bent like a hairpin, into a 3-in (8-cm) flower pot filled with good soil and sunk into the ground conveniently close to the parent plant. If this is done about mid-summer the plantlets will be rooted into the pots by late summer, the runners attaching them to the parent plant can be severed and a week or so later the pots can be lifted, the plants carefully tapped out and planted to form a new bed.

Nurserymen raise thousands of such plants annually and it is better to purchase new plants than to raise them at home because of the difficulty of excluding disease.

Late summer to early autumn is the best planting period, though strawberries can also be planted in spring. They are spaced 2 ft (60 cm) apart with the topmost roots just covered with soil.

In late spring the strawberry bed is covered with clean straw, special mats or black polythene film to keep the fruits clean and as these commence to ripen they are protected from bird attack with nets. After all the crop has been gathered, the remaining leaves are cut off and the straw is burned where it lies, so cleaning the plants of pests and diseases. New growth will appear in a week or so as the fast-burning straw does not kill the plants.

Good summer-fruiting varieties are Cambridge Favourite, Red Gauntlet, Grandee and Royal Sovereign, but the last is very subject to virus disease and it is essential to

A cool greenhouse display

obtain virus-free plants. Good perpetual-fruiting varieties are Hampshire Maid, Gento and Sans Rivale. A good alpine strawberry is Baron Solemacher.

Strawberries suffer from numerous virus diseases which do not kill them but weaken them and reduce cropping. These viruses cause patchy yellowing of the leaves, leaf crinkling, dwarfing of plants and other symptoms. There is no remedy, but if virus-free plants are obtained every second or third year and all old plants are destroyed virus diseases should not prove a serious problem. Likely to be more troublesome is grey mould disease which attacks the fruits causing them to rot. It is most prevalent in wet seasons and on heavy soils. Spray in late spring and early summer with captan.

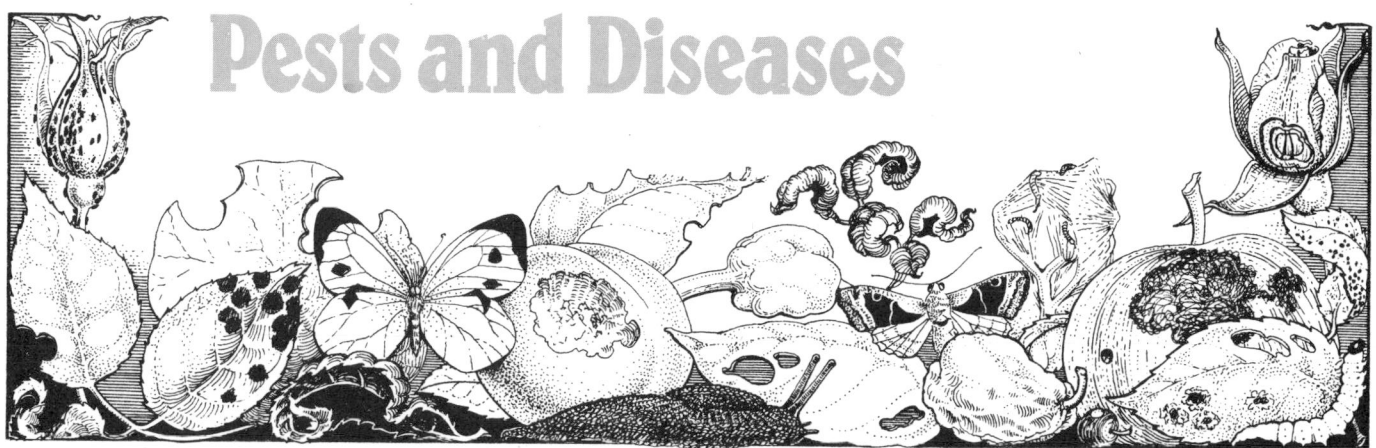

Pests and Diseases

Plants are attacked by various diseases, and various small creatures, including a number of insects, feed on them. It is scarcely possible, and certainly not necessary, to have a garden from which pests and diseases are completely excluded, but it is essential to keep them within reasonable bounds. To do this successfully it is not necessary to have a detailed knowledge of pests and diseases but it is necessary to have a general idea of the main groups into which they fall, especially from the standpoint of treatment.

Insect Pests

Consider the insect pests first. The two most familiar are the greenfly and the caterpillar. There are, in fact, a great many different kinds of greenflies and of caterpillars, which will be found described in detail in books devoted to garden pests, but since the methods of control are very similar for most kinds, the gardener can usually get along with no more knowledge than that which enables him to distinguish a greenfly from a caterpillar.

Greenflies Greenflies are often referred to as plant lice and it is a good description. They are small and soft skinned and they breed rapidly so that, given favourable conditions, in a few days the young shoots and leaves of plants may become covered with them. They suck the sap, greatly weakening the plant in so doing, and often causing leaves to curl and become sticky. Moreover they act as carriers of disease, principally of virus diseases, and so it is very necessary to keep greenflies under control. They are most likely to be troublesome in spring and early summer, for it is the young shoots and leaves of plants that they like.

Greenflies are generally controlled by spraying and there are a number of good insecticides available for this purpose. Some of them, such as menazon, formothion and dimethoate, are absorbed by the plant and are carried about inside it in the sap. This type of insecticide is known as systemic, and it is very useful because it cannot be washed off by rain nor is it likely to do a great deal of harm to those insects that do not damage plants.

The drawback to the systemic type of fungicide is that, if it is used on a food plant, a lettuce for example, or an apple, it cannot be removed by wiping or washing. Most systemic insecticides sold for garden use break down fairly quickly in the plant and food crops can be used safely a few weeks after application. However, some gardeners may prefer to reserve this kind of insecticide for the ornamental garden and use non-systemic insecticides for vegetables and fruit.

There are plenty of these capable of killing greenflies, including lindane, malathion, derris and pyrethrum. The last two are relatively harmless to all warm-blooded creatures which, of course, include human beings.

All greenflies are species of aphis and there are other aphis species which are not green but are similar in other respects and can be killed in the same way. Some are grey or blue-grey, some black, and these last are usually called blackflies.

Caterpillars Caterpillars are the grubs or larvae of moths and butterflies. Most people have a general idea of what a caterpillar looks like but they sometimes confuse them with large fly larvae, such as leatherjackets, the larvae of the daddy-long-legs. Obvious points of difference are that every caterpillar has short legs and a distinguishable head, whereas the fly larva has not. Derris is a good caterpillar killer and various other chemicals are available including malathion, lindane, carbaryl and trichlorphon.

Caterpillars do not suck sap but bite holes in leaves, fruits and even in stems and branches. So do the many weevils that attack plants and the damage they do may often be mistaken for the work of caterpillars. Weevils look like little beetles and they are so active that it is usually difficult to find them, particularly as most of them feed at night. However, the chemicals recommended for use against caterpillars are also poisonous to most weevils, so if you are doubtful whether it is caterpillars or weevils that are eating holes in the leaves of plants use a spray containing one or other of these chemicals.

Beetles As a class these are friends rather than foes but two exceptions are the flea beetle and the raspberry beetle. The former attacks the first young leaves of turnips, cabbages, brussels sprouts and other allied crops, filling them with tiny circular holes. It is very small, lively and black and it is easily killed by dusting or spraying with lindane or carbaryl. The raspberry beetle feeds on the flowers of the raspberry, but it is its little creamy-white grubs that are most troublesome for they eat right into the raspberry fruits. Derris is the best chemical to kill them with and it must be applied at just the right time – as the first fruits turn pink.

Cabbage Root, Onion and Other Flies Fly larvae often attack at or just below soil

Red Spider Mites A rather similar grey or yellowish mottling is caused by red spider mites. These are not spiders and they are rust coloured rather than red. They are so tiny that a hand lens is required to see them clearly and they live on the underside of leaves, sucking the sap from them. They thrive in hot, dry weather and hate damp and cold, so that one way to keep them down is to spray frequently with water. Even more effective is derris.

Thrips Thrips also cause mottling but of a more streaky kind, usually with a good deal of brown marking. They are very small, long in proportion to their breadth, and they run fast when disturbed. They often attack rose flowers, causing them to become deformed and develop dark markings. If such a bloom is tapped smartly over a piece of white paper the thrips will fall on to it and will be seen running away. They attack a great many other plants and the best way to deal with them is to spray with lindane or malathion.

Slugs and Snails Slugs and snails can be very troublesome, particularly in wet mild weather. They feed largely at night, eating leaves and young stems, and there are few plants they will not attack. Since they hide by day their presence is not always suspected.

They cannot be killed with any of the insecticides mentioned, since they are not insects. They are very fond of bran and so one way to kill them is to mix a slug poison, such as metaldehyde, with bran and place it near plants that are being attacked. Ready prepared bait is sold by all dealers in horticultural sundries. Another method is to use a liquid slug killer containing metaldehyde, distributing this from a watering-can fitted with a rose and applying it freely to creeping plants under which slugs and snails may be hiding, or to dead leaves, rubbish and stones. Metaldehyde is most effective in fairly dry conditions. If it is wet, methiocarb is better. It is prepared ready for use to be sprinkled around plants likely to be attacked. But whatever is done, slugs and snails are likely to return and so treatment must be repeated fairly frequently.

Greenflies on apple can be controlled by spraying with a suitable insecticide

level. If young cabbage or brussels sprout plants start to flag and, when pulled up, it can be seen that the roots have been gnawed, it is very likely that the cabbage root fly is responsible. Another fly attacks young onions and a third attacks the young roots of carrots. Lindane or trichlorphon can be used to kill them with no trouble.

The grubs of some flies tunnel into leaves and are called leaf-miners. Most insecticides do not get at them because they are protected within the leaf, but again, trichlorphon and lindane will kill them.

Sawflies Sawflies are not true flies and they produce larvae which look very much like the caterpillars of moths, having legs and a distinct head. Some eat into fruits, for example the apple sawfly, whose white grubs cause the maggoty apples one finds in the early summer. Some eat the surface

of leaves, leaving a transparent skeleton, and some cause leaves to roll up. All can be destroyed by spraying with lindane, trichlorphon or derris.

Capsid Bugs Capsid bugs bring us back to the suckers as distinct from biters. They feed like the greenfly but they are larger and usually far less numerous. They do a quite disproportionate amount of damage, causing leaves to pucker and become stunted and flowers to be deformed. Since they are active and hide quickly when disturbed, it is often difficult to find them but the damage they do is very distinctive. Lindane and malathion are effective in killing them.

Leaf Hoppers There are also leaf hoppers, little bug-like creatures which live on the undersides of leaves, sucking the sap and making the leaves become mottled and weak. They change their skins from time to time and the empty white skin-cases remain attached to the lower side of the leaf, providing a ready means of identification. Once again, lindane and malathion are effective.

Diseases

The common diseases can also be grouped according to their symptoms and treatment, so that the interested gardener can soon acquire a working knowledge of them.

Powdery Mildew All the powdery mildews make plants look as if they had been dusted with flour. Roses can suffer very badly, especially in dry summers, and so can Michaelmas daisies. There are mildews which attack peas, apples, vines, gooseberries and a great many other plants. All can be tackled with dinocap, but it is necessary to get the treatment started early as it is a means of prevention rather than of cure. Some of the systemic fungicides, such

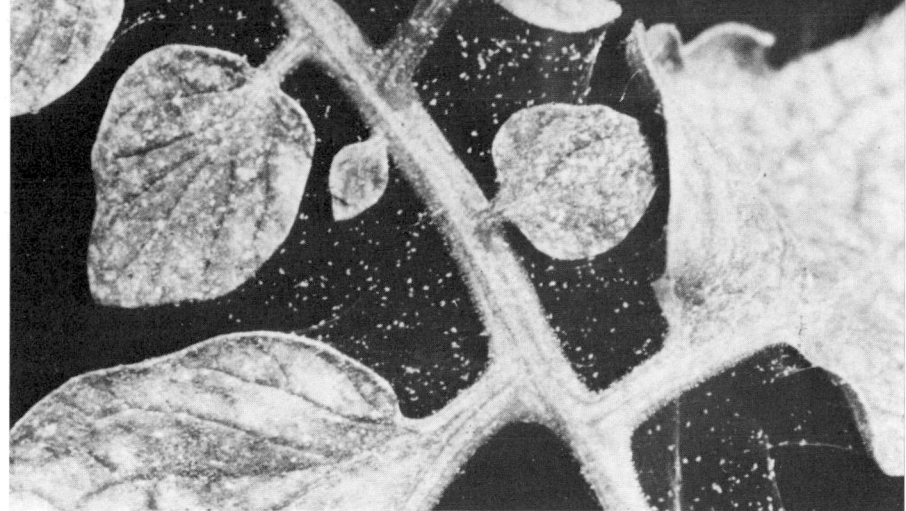

A particularly advanced attack of red spider mite showing webs over the leaves

as benomyl and triforine, will actually kill mildew in the plant but in general these treatments are more expensive.

Rusts Then there are the equally numerous rusts, so called because they produce rust-coloured spots on the leaves, and sometimes the stems, of plants attacked. There is a very troublesome rust disease of hollyhocks and another of antirrhinums. These and most other rusts can be prevented by occasional spraying in summer with thiram, or triforine may even kill rust after infection has occurred.

Spot Diseases There are a great many spot diseases and they are rather diverse in their origin. One of the worst is black spot of roses, which produces roundish black spots on the leaves which fall prematurely. The remedy is either to spray frequently with captan or maneb, starting in spring and continuing every 7 to 10 days all summer, or rather less frequently with a systemic fungicide such as benomyl or triforine.

Captan is also a good means of preventing scab disease of apples and pears which also starts by producing black spots or patches on leaves and fruits.

The very widespread disease of potatoes known as blight is another that starts by producing dark spots or patches on the leaves. These spread rapidly, so that all growth above ground withers and dies. By this time the disease has spread to the potatoes themselves, which develop brown patches of decay. The same disease attacks tomatoes and makes the fruits rot. The best preventive is a copper fungicide such as Bordeaux mixture, but it must be sprayed over all the leaves and stems before infection occurs.

Grey Mould One of the most widespread of diseases is grey mould, also known as botrytis. It attacks all manner of plants, causing a soft, dark decay and a characteristic is the fluffy white outgrowth which quickly follows this decay. It is a disease that is very prevalent in damp, cool weather and it is very difficult to control. Thiram and captan are the most useful chemicals to check it.

Damping Off Seedlings in the greenhouse

will often collapse in hundreds, stricken by fungi in the soil which kill their roots or attack their stems near soil level. This is known as damping off and it is most likely to occur when seedlings are overcrowded or when they are kept too wet and insufficiently ventilated. Sterilized soil helps to prevent this disease. Seed can also be dusted before it is sown with captan or thiram as a preventive.

Viruses Lastly there is a whole class of diseases caused by various kinds of virus. These produce many different symptoms and are amongst the most difficult of plant diseases to diagnose with accuracy. Leaves may be mottled with yellow in a quite attractive way, or they may be deformed and become twisted or very narrow. Growth may be stunted or dry brown spots and streaks may appear on stems and leaves.

There is no cure for virus diseases that can be applied in the garden and all infected plants must be destroyed, but before doing so it is wise to get the advice of an expert for sometimes symptoms very similar to those of virus disease may be caused by bad cultivation or by the careless use of a selective weedkiller.

Trade Names

The names of chemicals given in this chapter are those commonly used to distinguish them and they should appear somewhere on the market pack though usually in small type and not prominently displayed. This is because several manufacturers or distributors may be marketing the same chemical and so they prefer to use their own trade names which are then widely publicized and displayed. Even the assistants in garden shops and centres can find this confusing and some keep check lists of the chemicals with the various trade names under which they may appear on their shelves. Unfortunately it would be of little use to print such a check list here since there are so many brands and some of the brand names may change, drop out, or the list may be added to.

The white growths of powdery mildew are most evident on the growing tips of plants

How Plants Feed

The bulk of every green plant comes from water and air. The air supplies mainly carbon; the water, oxygen and hydrogen. The green colouring matter in the leaf (it may be masked by other colourants but this does not matter) is able to synthesize these, using sunlight for energy, into complex substances which become sugars, starches and proteins. But to perform these marvels the plant also needs very small quantities of a whole range of chemicals.

Soil Enrichment

There are a number of ways in which the gardener can enrich the soil. Dead plants still contain most of the chemicals they have taken from the soil and as they decay these chemicals will be made available once again. At the same time, the decaying vegetable refuse will improve the texture of the soil and enable it to hold more moisture.

Animal manure behaves in the same way. As it decays chemicals are liberated from it and the texture of the soil is improved.

If the animal manure is already well decomposed when it is applied, the chemicals will be more immediately available. Precisely the same applies to vegetable refuse, which is one reason for building it up into heaps, known as compost heaps (see p. 149), and leaving it for a few months to rot before it is used, either as a surface mulch or dug in.

Animal droppings and vegetable refuse are known as bulky manures because they contain comparatively small quantities of chemicals and so should be applied in considerable quantity. A hundredweight of stable or farmyard manure or of well-made garden compost will be adequate for 5 sq. yd (5 sq. m) of land, though as a rule gardeners cannot afford to be so generous and must be content to spread it over 10 or 12 sq. yd (10 or 12 sq. m).

So far as the chemicals in the manure are concerned, a similar effect might be produced by spreading one pound of well-chosen concentrated fertilizer, but this would be unlikely to have any beneficial effect on the texture of the soil, that is, its ability to hold plenty of water and still retain enough air to keep itself and the roots growing in it in good health.

The aim in manuring the soil is, therefore, twofold: to improve texture and to improve chemical content. As a rule this can be done most efficiently by using chemical fertilizers in conjunction with bulky manures or composts, or with peat, which is a kind of natural compost which has the merit of being readily available at reasonable prices and in well-defined grades.

Fertilizers

The Most Important Chemicals Plants need a considerable number of different chemicals but only a few are likely to be deficient in most soils. The most important of these are nitrogen, phosphorus and potassium, followed by magnesium, iron and manganese.

There are a great many ready-mixed fertilizers available, often referred to as compound fertilizers, and these usually provide nitrogen, phosphorus and potash. The makers are obliged by law to state how much of each of these elements their fertilizers contain, the figures being quoted as percentages of nitrogen, phosphoric acid and potash. When a fertilizer contains approximately the same amount of these three items, it is referred to as well balanced. The National Growmore fertilizer is of this character, its formula being 7 per cent nitrogen, 7 per cent phosphoric acid and 7 per cent potash. Often these figures are quoted without the percentage sign, so that National Growmore may be referred to as a 7:7:7 fertilizer. Such a quotation is always in the order nitrogen, phosphoric acid and potash.

Action of Specific Chemicals Well-balanced fertilizers are excellent for maintaining the general fertility of the soil, but for special purposes one may require a fertilizer that is richer in one chemical than in another. Nitrogen tends to promote growth, so that for a leaf crop such as lettuce, cabbage or grass it may be desirable to use a fertilizer that has a lot of nitrogen in proportion to phosphoric acid and potash. Phosphorus is particularly necessary in the early stages of growth when seedlings or young plants are making a lot of roots, so fertilizers for seedlings and root crops usually have a high phosphoric acid ratio. Potash has a marked bearing on fruitfulness and ripening, so potash tends to be the highest percentage in fertilizer specially prepared for fruit trees or for tomatoes, once they have started to crop.

Ingredients Most Commonly Used This kind of analysis shows quite accurately the kind of fertilizer one is buying but it tells us nothing about its ingredients. National Growmore, for example, might be prepared in several different ways provided these gave the desired 7:7:7 percentage of nitrogen, phosphoric acid and potash.

The three ingredients most commonly used are: sulphate of ammonia for nitrogen, superphosphate of lime for phosphorus, and sulphate of potash for potassium. These are good ingredients and they can be mixed together without troublesome chemical interactions.

Other popular sources of nitrogen are dried blood and hoof and horn meal. As they are animal residues they are much more complex than the fairly simple chemicals just named. Plants cannot make use of these complex chemicals, which must first be broken down into simple chemicals by normal processes of decomposition in the soil. This takes time and so such organic fertilizers have a longer life in the soil than some readily available inorganic chemicals. They are sometimes referred to as slow acting, though this is a purely relative term. Certainly both dried blood and finely ground hoof and horn meals can have an effect on growth within a week or so in warm damp weather, but their effect will be slower in cold, dry conditions because these slow down the rate of decay. Very coarse hoof and horn meal also takes longer to decay and liberate its chemical plant food than fine hoof and horn meal.

Bonemeal Bonemeal is an animal source of phosphorus and exactly the same applies to it as to hoof and horn meal. Its availability is directly related to the fineness of grinding, for bone flour will decompose quickly in the soil whereas coarsely crushed bones may take years to decay.

Wood Ashes Wood ashes are a natural source of potash and seven pounds of fresh wood ash may contain as much potash as one pound of sulphate of potash. It is always worth while to preserve wood ashes in a dry place and to scatter them over the soil as a fertilizer where potash is required.

Mixed Fertilizers Occasionally the gardener may need to use single chemicals but as a rule mixtures will suit his purpose better and there are plenty of these available for almost every conceivable purpose – general fertilizers, rose fertilizers, chrysanthemum fertilizers, vegetable fertilizers, fruit fertilizers, tomato fertilizers, lawn fertilizers and so on. The important thing with all these is to use them at the right rate and at the right time. As a rule, manufacturers give full instructions, but failing this some general observations may be useful.

The greater part of these fertilizers is usually readily soluble, which is a good thing since plants can only take in chemicals from the soil in solution. But it does also mean that, if they are applied a long time before the plants need them, they may be largely washed out of the soil uselessly. They are, therefore, primarily for spring and summer use.

Most are highly concentrated and so 4oz (110g) per sq. yd, or sq. metre, of a compound fertilizer such as National Growmore is usually the maximum safe application at any one time, and something like 8oz (225g) per sq. yd, or metre, the maximum safe application throughout any one year. A normal treatment for vegetables, for example, would be to give the soil 4oz (110g) per sq. yd, or metre, of a well-balanced compound fertilizer in early spring and then two more applications, each of 2oz (55g) per sq. yd, or metre, one in late spring, the other in mid-summer. To give too much at any one time would be to risk scorching roots and leaves by raising to too high a level the concentration of chemicals in the soil water. If by some mischance too much is given, the best way to get rid of it is to soak the soil heavily with water and so wash the chemicals out.

Since they are soluble and easily washed into the soil by rain, these fertilizers may be scattered over the surface of the soil and either be left there or be raked or watered in. Bulky manures and composts, by contrast, are more effective if mixed with the soil when digging or forking, though they can also be spread on the surface, a process known as mulching.

Counteracting Soil Deficiencies One of the side benefits obtained from using bulky manures and composts is that they provide a great variety of plant foods, not just the three major chemicals nitrogen, phosphorus and potassium. It is true that the other chemicals are usually present in sufficient quantity but this is not always so. When they are deficient there can be some spectacular results. Shortage of iron

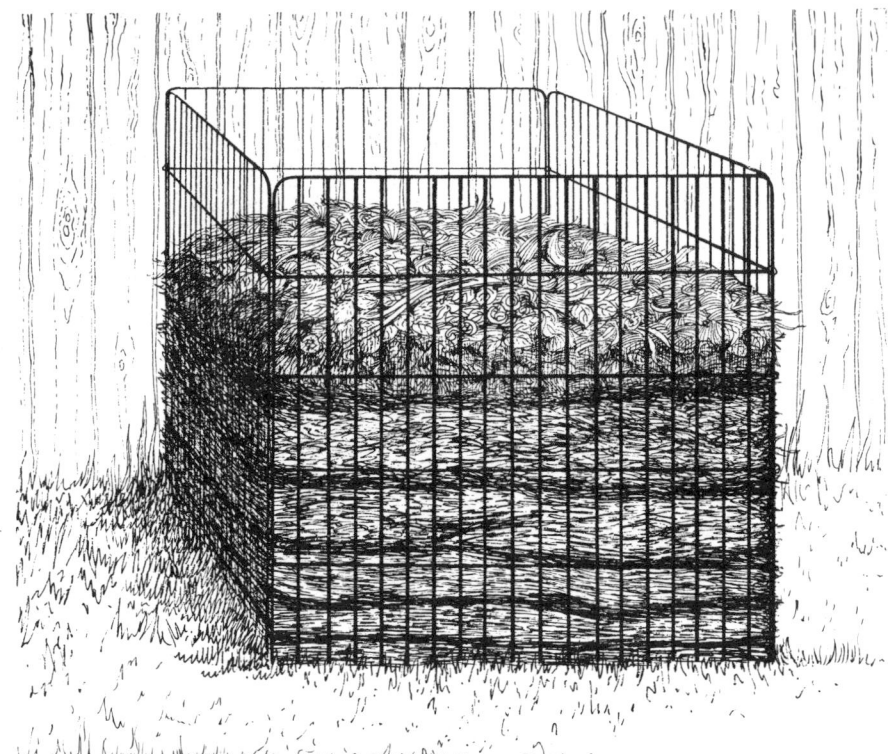

Valuable manure can be made in the garden by rotting down all vegetable waste into compost. Each 6-in (15-cm) layer of vegetable waste can be covered with a fine layer of compost accelerator to speed up the rotting process. The heap should be turned, outside to inside, once a month and watered in dry weather. A wire cage is an effective means of containing the heap

may cause leaves to go bright yellow; lack of magnesium or manganese can have a similar effect or magnesium deficiency may produce brown patches between the veins of the leaves. These particular shortages are most likely to occur when the soil contains a lot of chalk or lime and are due to chemical reactions in the soil which do not remove the iron or magnesium but make them insoluble so that plants cannot use them. If sulphate of iron or sulphate of magnesium (Epsom salts) is applied there may be an immediate improvement but the treatment may have to be repeated over and over again since the fresh supplies also get locked up through chemical interaction in the soil.

To overcome this difficulty, special forms of iron manganese and magnesium have been prepared, known as sequestrols. They are of varying efficiency and are fairly expensive, so if such deficiencies are suspected it is best to get expert advice on the spot before doing anything about it. Regular use of good animal manure or vegetable compost will help to prevent these difficulties both by returning such elements to the soil and by using up surplus lime or chalk and so preventing the conditions in which these deficiencies are most likely to occur.

The Compost Heap Animal and vegetable refuse of any kind can simply be dug into the soil and left to rot but it is often more convenient to rot it down first in a compost heap. This has the additional merit that by the time the compost is ready for use many of the desirable chemicals will have already been liberated and be available to plants, and also that the compost itself will have been reduced to a crumbly brown material easily spread and not at all unsightly. Well-made compost, spread as a mulch on top of the soil, can look very nice.

Soft refuse will decay much more readily than woody refuse and so it is usually best to separate the latter and burn it. The soft refuse is then built into a heap not more than 3ft (1m) wide or high – so that air can penetrate it – but of any length. If the refuse is dry it is wise to soak it with water as the heap is built. Decay will be more rapid and a richer compost will result if the refuse is lightly sprinkled with one of the chemical accelerators sold for this purpose, or simply with Nitro-chalk.

After a month or so the whole heap should be turned with a fork, the outer portions of the old heap being transferred to the middle of the new heap and vice versa, and any dry portions wetted. Two or three months later the compost should be ready for use, but the real test is that it should be of a more or less even texture and colour throughout, all the ingredients having decayed so much that they have lost their individual appearance. Decay is more rapid in summer than in winter.

Dealing with Weeds

'If weeds won't grow nothing else will.' Experienced gardeners are fond of saying this and they are quite right. Fortunately the problem of keeping down weeds has been greatly simplified by the introduction of safe and efficient weedkillers.

But there are some places in which weedkillers cannot be used satisfactorily. This is particularly true of any bed that is densely covered with plants so that it would be impossible to apply weedkiller to weeds without also treating at least some of the plants. Rock gardens are seldom suitable for chemical weed-killing, nor are beds devoted to annuals and bedding plants.

In all places such as those just described, weeds must be removed by hoeing or by hand. Various patterns of hoe are available: Dutch hoes that permit the user to walk backwards, leaving the hoed soil untrodden; draw hoes that are used with a chopping motion and are useful on hard soil or for tough weeds; small onion hoes that are operated with one hand; all kinds of patented hoes each with its own particular advantages. (See page 128.) But with all the aim is similar – to stir the soil very lightly, certainly not more than 2 in (5 cm) deep, and to sever weeds rather than to drag them out. To do this effectively hoe blades must be sharp and it is worth while touching them up occasionally with an old file.

Hand weeding is necessary where plants are so close together that it would be impossible to hoe between them without risk of damaging them. Weeds may be pulled out with the fingers or levered out with a trowel or a small tool known as a Widger. Many new gardeners think of hand weeding as a boring, laborious task but to the keen gardener it offers opportunity for a close inspection of plants which is full of interest. The weeds removed can be placed on the compost heap to rot into useful soil dressing.

Weedkillers

Weedkillers (or more accurately herbicides, since no chemical can distinguish between a cultivated plant and a weed which is simply a plant in the wrong place) are useful on paths and in courtyards, for lawns and in shrub borders and rose beds where it is possible to apply a chemical direct to the soil or weeds without getting it on the plants.

Three types of weedkiller are useful in the garden and they are known respectively as contact, selective and residual.

Contact Weedkillers Contact herbicides kill plants to which they are applied. Usually they kill practically everything, garden plants as well as weeds, and some enter by the roots just as easily as by the leaves or stems, so that soil to which they are applied may remain poisonous to plants of all kinds for weeks or months. Sodium chlorate is of this kind. It can be applied as a dry powder or dissolved in water and it has its uses where a clean sweep of all vegetation is required. But it is readily washed about in the soil, may get into places it was not intended to reach, and suffers the further drawback of being highly inflammable.

More generally useful for the gardener is

A sprinkle bar attached to a watering can gives a relatively even application of herbicide over a large area

paraquat, a chemical which enters plants through their leaves or young stems, but is inactivated by the soil. Paraquat in solution can be applied directly to weeds in paths, courtyards, etc., or growing beneath shrubs, roses, fruit trees or bushes without risk of injury to anything but the weeds. The best way to do this is by means of a short sprinkle bar attached to a watering-can as this will deliver the liquid low down without risk of drift. One application of paraquat is unlikely to kill docks, dandelions and some other deep-rooted weeds which may require repeated treatment.

Selective Weedkillers Selective herbicides kill some types of plant but not others. Most useful in the garden are those that kill many lawn weeds but not the grass itself. Three in common use are 2,4-D, MCPA and mecoprop. There is not much to choose between the first two, both of which are effective against most of the commoner lawn weeds but not against clover, for which mecoprop should be chosen. Some manufacturers produce mixtures of either 2,4-D or MCPA with mecoprop to give as wide a band of effectiveness as possible or use other chemicals with similar properties.

The method of application is similar to that for paraquat, except that on lawns a wide sprinkle bar can be used to put the diluted weedkiller rapidly on to the turf without risk of drift on to neighbouring plants, most of which it would kill just as effectively as the lawn weeds. Selective lawn weedkillers can be used at any time but are most effective in spring when growth is young and tender. It also helps to apply a lawn fertilizer a few days before the weedkiller is applied as this both makes the weeds more susceptible and enables the grass to recover more rapidly from the slight check to growth imposed by the weedkiller.

Residual Weedkillers Residual herbicides are so called because they remain as a residue near the surface of the soil and kill seedling weeds as they emerge. Two of the best for the garden are simazine and dichlobenil. The first is primarily intended for use on paths, courtyards, etc., but it can also be applied carefully at half strength to clean ground beneath shrubs, roses, fruit trees and bushes to prevent further seedling weed growth for several weeks or even months. Again the watering-can with sprinkle bar provides an easy and safe means of application. Dichlobenil is marketed as fine granules prepacked in a pepper-pot-style canister so that it can be sprinkled very thinly and evenly on the soil or on the leaves of the weeds which are to be killed off.

Pre-emergent Weedkilling This is a method greatly used by market gardeners but not, as yet, widely adopted in private gardens. It is based on the fact that many weed seeds germinate more rapidly than seeds of garden crops. The garden seeds are sown and a calculation made as to when they will germinate and push their first seed leaves through the soil. Two or three days before this date a contact weedkiller, which will have no residual effect and will not damage seeds in the soil, is applied all over the surface to kill all weeds that have already appeared. Many chemicals are used by commercial growers because they are chosen for specific crops, but in private gardens paraquat is the most useful weedkiller for this type of application.

Trade Names
Similar remarks apply to the trade names of herbicides as to those of insecticides and fungicides (see page 147). Here I have given the common names as denominators. The brand names under which they are sold are likely to be quite different but somewhere on each pack the correct name should appear.

How Plants Are Increased

Plants are increased in many ways but all can be grouped under one or other of two main headings, one known as sexual propagation, which means increase by seeds, and the other known as asexual or vegetative propagation, which means increase by some part of the plant other than a seed.

Plants from Seed
A plant that is raised from seed is a new individual in a sense that is not true of a plant raised vegetatively. It is the result of the union of a male and a female cell, each contributing its own set of the genes which control inheritance. If these sets of genes are markedly different, as they well may be in plants of hybrid origin, the seedlings resulting from the union will be different from their parent or parents (for in plants the male and female elements may be supplied by one plant or by two plants). By contrast, a plant increased by vegetative means is not the result of the union of male and female cells and its genetical make-up, except in rare cases, is exactly the same as that of the plant from which it came. It will, therefore, resemble this plant in every detail, whereas a seedling usually varies in some way, even if only minutely. Often the variation is great and the plant may be a distinct improvement on its parent.

Because a seedling is a new individual, it has its own lease of life. It usually, though not invariably, starts life unburdened by the diseases that have attacked its parents and it often shows a vigour which old plants have begun to lose.

The vegetatively increased plant cannot be guaranteed these advantages. It may or may not be free of inherited diseases and though it may sometimes show at least a period of greater vigour this, too, may tend to decline if the process of vegetative increase is continued from generation to generation.

Seed or Vegetative Increase? So we see that seed gives the possibility of variation, which may be useful and represent progress, and that it maintains vigour. Vegetative increase is desirable where it is important to preserve every detail of the parent plant unchanged.

For details of the methods of raising plants from seed, see page 20.

Vegetative Increase

The principal methods of vegetative increase are by division, cuttings, layers and grafting.

Division Division is the simplest of all. It simply means that the plant is lifted and split up into several pieces, each of which can, if desired, be replanted to form a new plant. Many herbaceous plants can be split up very easily with the fingers but some make such thick, tough clumps of roots and shoots that some extra leverage must be applied. One way of doing this is to push two hand forks or small border forks back to back through the middle of the clump and then pull their handles outwards, in opposite directions. With really big, old clumps this can be repeated several times with successive pieces until they are reduced to a size that can be tackled by hand.

Some plants make solid fleshy crowns which cannot be broken easily and are better cut through with a knife, but take care that the roots are not also severed in the process.

It is nearly always the younger outside portions of the plant that will grow into the best new plants. The centre of an old clump

Leaf cuttings:
A leaf of *Begonia rex* can be slit at the veins and pegged down on moist sand

is often starved and half dead and is best discarded. The best time to divide plants is generally just as they start to grow, usually in the spring but clusters of bulbs can be split up into separate bulbs when they are dormant, which is often in summer.

CUTTINGS

Cuttings may be prepared from stems, leaves or roots and each type has its uses. Whereas the division starts life with shoots and roots, the cutting has either a shoot or leaf without roots or a root without shoots. It must be induced to produce the missing part.

Stem cuttings (See also page 91.) Stem cuttings may be prepared from young growth, when they are often referred to as soft cuttings; from older growth that is beginning to get firm, when they are called half-ripe cuttings; or from stems at the end of a season of growth, when they are called ripe or hardwood cuttings. At whatever stage they are taken the method of preparation is similar but the methods of making the cutting produce roots are different.

A stem cutting may be anything from 1 in to 1 ft (2·5 to 30cm) in length according to the kind of plant from which it is taken. It usually has several leaves or leaf buds and it is often cut off just below one of the leaves or buds. This may be referred to as a joint or node and such a cutting may be called a nodal cutting. Occasionally cuttings are severed half way between leaves or nodes and such cuttings are called internodal. Quite often cuttings are pulled off the parent plant where the shoot joins a main stem. Such cuttings are often called slips or, since they come away with a small piece, or heel, of the older stem attached, are called heel

cuttings. Before insertion the heel is trimmed with a sharp knife or razor blade.

The problem with cuttings is to keep them alive while they are making roots. Soft cuttings die very quickly but they also tend to make roots quickly. Cuttings of firm growth take longer to die but are usually slower in forming roots. Hardwood cuttings die most slowly but also root most slowly. With all kinds rooting can be speeded if the base of the cutting is dipped in special hormone rooting powder. Different strengths can be obtained to suit soft, half-ripe and hardwood cuttings.

Cuttings are inserted in sandy soil, pure sand, peat, vermiculite, perlite and various other materials; some gardeners favouring one, some another. Soft and half-ripe cuttings are often placed in a small frame, a box covered with glass or in a pot in a polythene bag, the object being to cut down loss of water and keep the cutting fresh while it is rooting. A little artificial heat, especially from below (known as bottom heat), will also speed rooting. Ripe or hardwood cuttings are often inserted outdoors, and since they do not lose moisture so readily, are not so much in need of covering.

Leaf Cuttings These are mainly used for a few greenhouse plants, such as African violets (saintpaulias) and rex begonias. Well-grown leaves are carefully removed and either inserted like cuttings, stalk first, into the soil, sand or peat, or placed flat on the surface and held there by hairpins or little stones. When this latter method is used, cuts are usually made in the main

The young plants which sprout from the cuts can be removed and potted up when large enough to handle

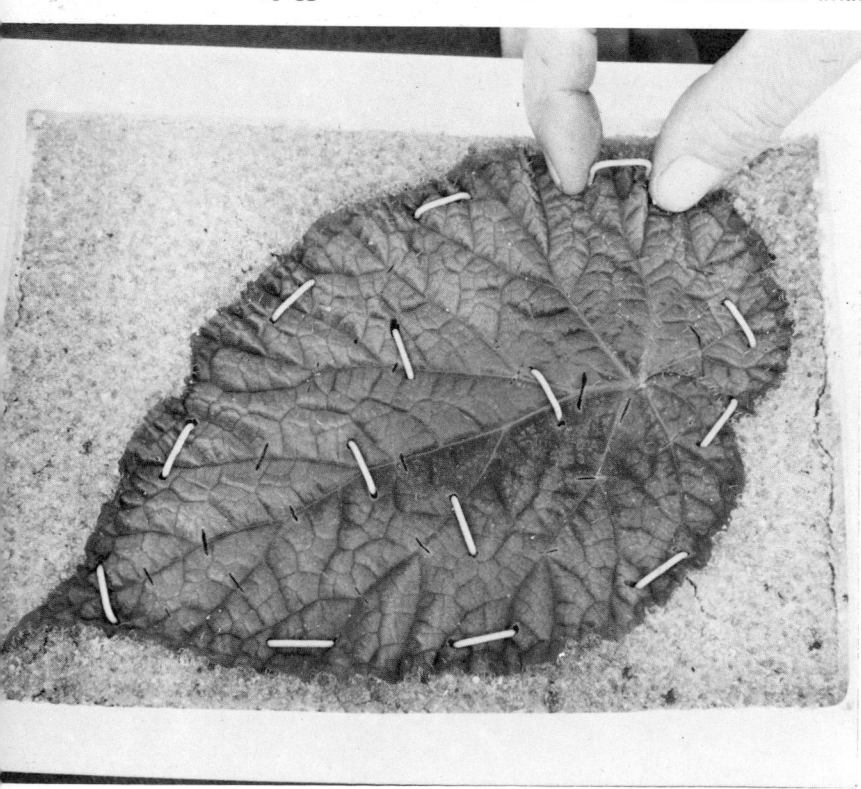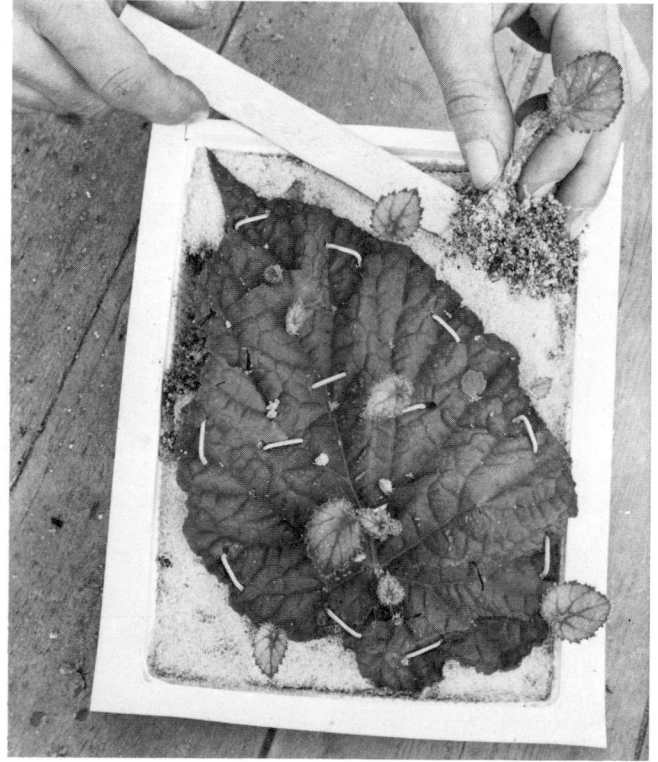

When preparing root cuttings ensure that they are inserted the correct way up. If inserted upside down they will not grow

veins of the leaf to encourage rooting. Almost always some bottom heat is advantageous. Leaf cuttings are usually taken in summer.

Root Cuttings These are used for a few plants, mostly with rather thick roots, such as anchusa, verbascum, hollyhock, limonium and romneya, but phlox and gaillardia which have relatively thin roots can be propagated in the same way. The roots are cut up into pieces an inch or so in length and are either laid horizontally or inserted right way up in sandy soil, usually in a frame or greenhouse. This is usually done in winter or spring.

LAYERING

The object of layering is to induce stems to form roots before they are severed from the parent plant, which sustains them with sap during the period of rooting. Some plants adopt this as a natural method of increase. Both the strawberry and the violet throw out long runners in summer along which are little clusters of leaves and shoots – incipient plants. Where these touch the soil they form roots and actually grow into new plants. With plants such as this the gardener merely assists nature by holding the runner firmly to the soil with a piece of bent wire or a stone and by limiting the number of runners and the number of plantlets on each so that the plant is not overstrained.

Layering Plants Without Runners There are many other plants which do not produce runners and yet can be layered. It may be possible to bend down pliable stems to soil level and cover them with a little soil, holding them in place with bent wire, a forked stick or a stone. Rooting is likely to be made more certain if the stem, where it is to be buried, is first wounded and the wound dusted with hormone rooting powder. A slit may be made through a joint or an encircling cut made in the bark just below a joint, or the shoot may simply be twisted or bent sharply so that some of the tissues are bruised and the sap flow restricted. It is from the callus which forms to heal such wounds that roots are most readily formed.

Air-layering If no stem can be bent to ground level a system known as air-layering may be used. It is mainly applied to shrubs and young stems are most suitable. The chosen stem is wounded in one or other of the ways just described and the wound is dusted with hormone rooting powder. Then damp sphagnum moss is wrapped quite thickly around the wound and a sleeve of polythene film pulled over it and tied on each side so that the damp moss is completely enclosed. In time roots will grow into the moss and when there are plenty of these the layer can be severed and potted or planted to grow into a new plant.

Air Layering
c) A cut is made in the stem and the slit held open and surrounded with sphagnum moss and polythene film. The stem is removed when it has rooted

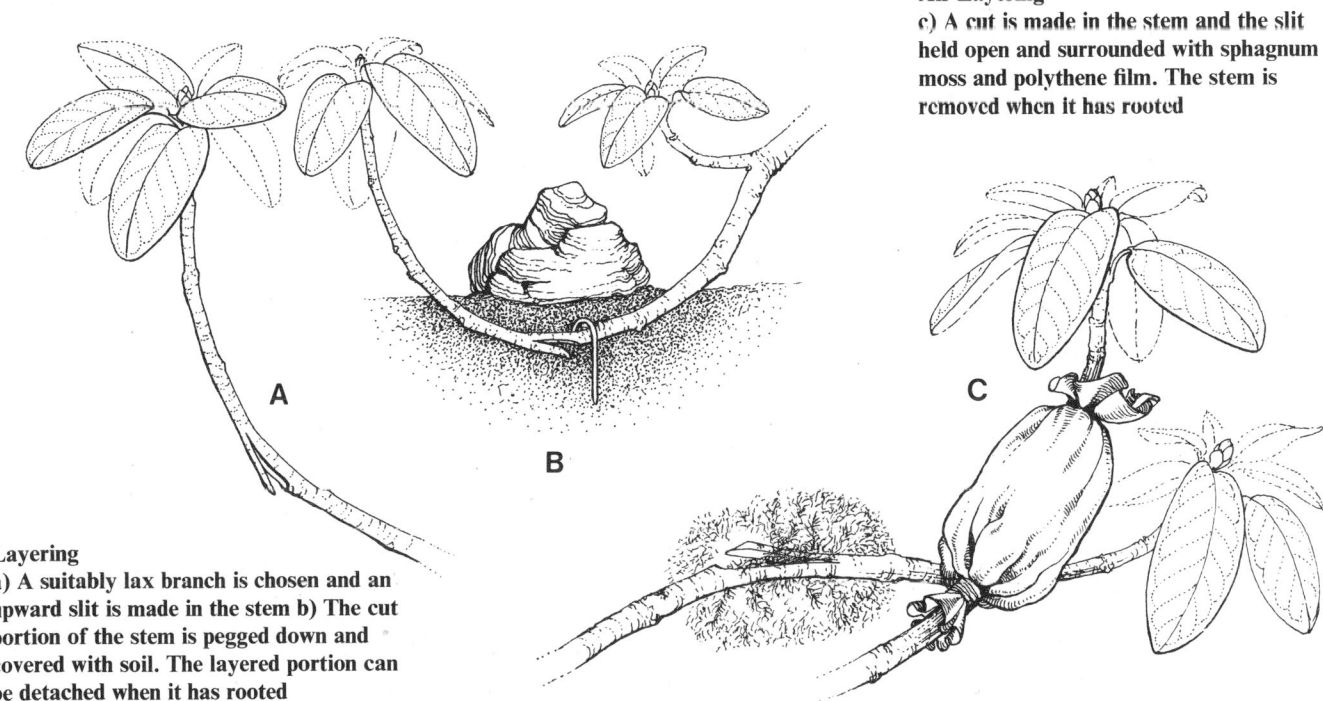

Layering
a) A suitably lax branch is chosen and an upward slit is made in the stem b) The cut portion of the stem is pegged down and covered with soil. The layered portion can be detached when it has rooted

A

B

C

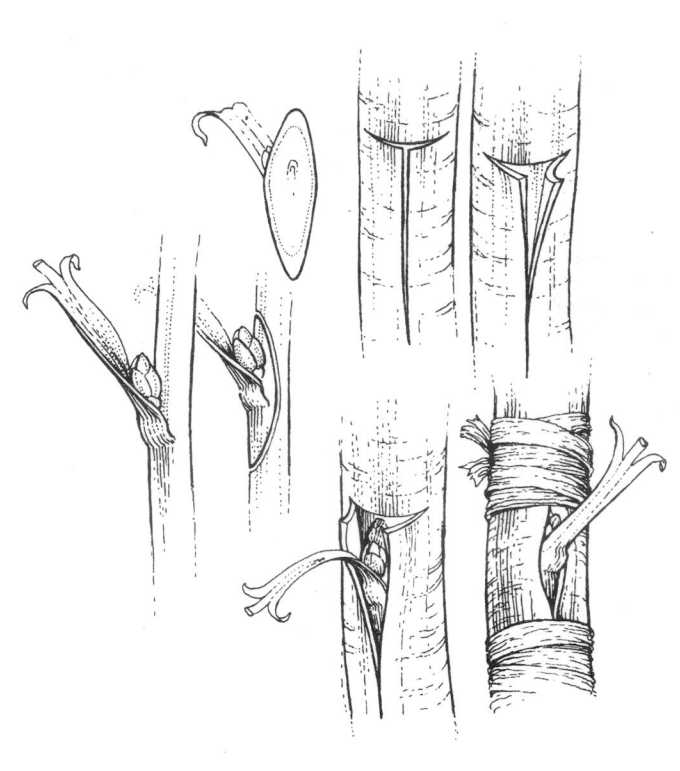

Budding (Left)
Growth buds are cut from young stems as described on p. 155 and the small piece of wood at the back of each bud is removed. A 'T'-shaped incision is made in the bark of the stock, the incision prised open and the bud inserted. The bud is then bound firmly in place with budding tape. Bush roses are budded just below soil level, standard roses about 3 ft 6 in (1·10 m) above soil level on the base of the young sideshoots, except on *R. rugosa* stocks which are budded direct on to the main stem

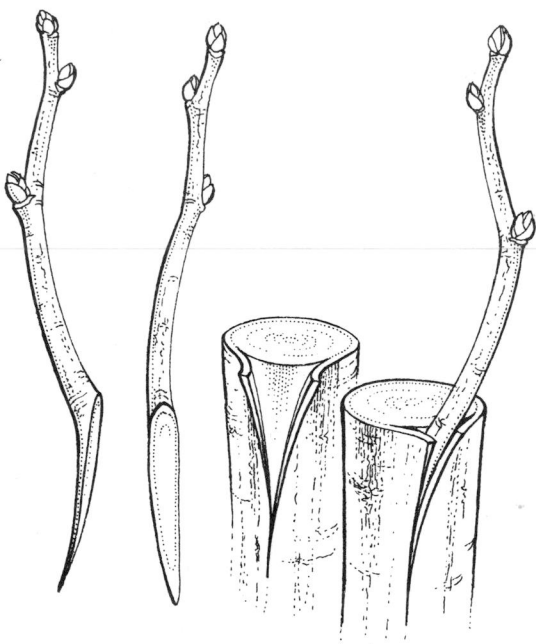

Rind Graft (Right)
The scion is cut, prepared and inserted as shown. The graft is then bound with string and sealed with wax

Whip and Tongue Graft (Left)
This graft can be used either when the stock and scion are of a similar thickness or when the stock is the thicker of the two. Like the rind graft, the point of union is bound and sealed with wax

When to Layer Layering can be done at any time of the year but for shrubs is usually most successful in spring or early summer. Border carnations are layered soon after mid-summer.

GRAFTING

This is a surgical operation whereby a shoot or bud, known as the scion, of one plant is joined to the root system of another plant, known as the stock. It is used to increase many plants which cannot readily be increased by cuttings. Commercially produced roses are nearly always raised by budding, a form of grafting, and apples, pears, plums and cherries are also increased by some form of grafting.

Budding Budding is in many ways the simplest both to describe and carry out. It is usually done in summer when plants are in full growth. The buds, which are dormant growth buds, not flower buds, are cut from firm young stems. They are usually cut out with a shield-shaped slip of bark and wood $1\frac{1}{2}$ to 2 in (4 to 5 cm) in length and usually the sliver of wood cut with this bark is removed. The stock is prepared by making a T-shaped incision in the bark of a young stem and prising this open so that the prepared bud can be slipped under the flaps of bark. It is then bound in place with raffia, soft string or special budding strips. In a few weeks the bud should have united with the stock and the following winter the stock is cut off immediately above the bud which thereafter channels all further growth above ground. The growth will partake of the character of the bud and not of the stock, though the latter may influence rate of growth, ultimate size and anchorage in the soil.

Rind Grafting A simple form of grafting, which is not unlike budding, is known as rind grafting. The stock needs to be fairly stout and the top is cut cleanly across. A downward incision, about 2 in (5 cm) in length, is made in the bark from this point of severance. A firm young stem is cut from the plant to be increased and a long, sloping, wedge-shaped cut is made at the lower end. The shoot is then pressed gently beneath the bark of the stock with its cut face against the wood of the stock. It is bound in place with soft string and the wounded area is completely covered with grafting wax.

Whip and Tongue Grafting Slightly more complicated is the whip and tongue graft. This is most suitable when scion and stock are similar in thickness. The scion is prepared much as for rind grafting except that a second cut is made in the opposite direction to form a thin tongue on the cut face. The stock is prepared with two similar cuts in reverse, so that the two tongues can be fitted together and will hold the two cut surfaces in exact register. The scion is then firmly bound to the stock and the whole wounded area covered with grafting wax.

When to Graft Grafting is usually done in late winter or early spring and growth from the scion should start within a few weeks. Once a good union has been made, the stock must not be permitted to make any growth of its own, a stipulation which applies to all forms of grafting.

Index

Abbreviations: d=line drawing p=photograph or illustration